A New Philosophy of Modernity and Sovereignty

A New Philosophy of Modernity and Sovereignty

Towards Radical Historicization

Przemysław Tacik

BLOOMSBURY ACADEMIC
LONDON • NEW YORK • OXFORD • NEW DELHI • SYDNEY

BLOOMSBURY ACADEMIC
Bloomsbury Publishing Plc
50 Bedford Square, London, WC1B 3DP, UK
1385 Broadway, New York, NY 10018, USA
29 Earlsfort Terrace, Dublin 2, Ireland

BLOOMSBURY, BLOOMSBURY ACADEMIC and the Diana logo are trademarks of
Bloomsbury Publishing Plc

First published in Great Britain 2021
This paperback edition published 2023

Copyright © Przemysław Tacik, 2021

Przemysław Tacik has asserted his right under the Copyright, Designs and Patents Act,
1988, to be identified as Author of this work.

For legal purposes the Acknowledgments on p. vi constitute an extension
of this copyright page.

Cover design: Charlotte Daniels
Cover image © Baivector / Shutterstock

All rights reserved. No part of this publication may be reproduced or transmitted
in any form or by any means, electronic or mechanical, including photocopying,
recording, or any information storage or retrieval system, without prior
permission in writing from the publishers.

Bloomsbury Publishing Plc does not have any control over, or responsibility for, any
third-party websites referred to or in this book. All internet addresses given in
this book were correct at the time of going to press. The author and publisher
regret any inconvenience caused if addresses have changed or sites have
ceased to exist, but can accept no responsibility for any such changes.

A catalogue record for this book is available from the British Library.

A catalog record for this book is available from the Library of Congress.

ISBN: HB: 9781-3502-0126-2
PB: 9781-3502-0130-9
ePDF: 9781-3502-0127-9
eBook: 9781-3502-0128-6

Typeset by RefineCatch Limited, Bungay, Suffolk

To find out more about our authors and books visit www.bloomsbury.com
and sign up for our newsletters.

Contents

Acknowledgments		vi
	Introduction	1
1	The Mirror Star	9
2	For a Derridean-Copernican Revolution: Modernity Before History	69
3	Modernity as a Construct of Sovereignty	81
4	The Unfinished Time of Modernity	99
5	Sovereign Suspension and Provisionality	115
6	The Big Bang of Modernity	131
	Conclusion	151
Notes		161
Bibliography		203
Index		217

Acknowledgments

Books like this one are wrenched from life rather than written. Their creation sucks everything around into their maelstrom, which is why apologies are owed as much as thanks. Apart from those whom I would be able to mention, they must go to every *Tsaddik Nistar* who lent me a hand on the way.

I would like to express my deepest gratitude to those who helped me with their advice and support. My thanks go to Dr. Cosmin Cercel, whose ingenuity and friendship were invaluable on my way. I would also like to thank Professor Agata Bielik-Robson, Professor Jan Hartman, and Dr. Gian-Giacomo Fusco for all of their help. Without the indispensable support of my editor, Jade Grogan, the book would never have taken this final form. My thanks also go to the institutions which allowed me to spend time reading, thinking, and writing: Universität Heidelberg and Bibliothèque Nationale de France, and the French government which funded the stipend.

This book has its own Bright Star, the one who always believed in it, even among the ocean of darkness. תברוך כוכבי

Voilà ce que j'appris par le récit de ceux qui m'avaient relevé et qui me soutenaient encore lorsque je revins à moi. L'état auquel je me trouvai dans cet instant est trop singulier pour n'en pas faire ici la description.

    La nuit s'avançait. J'aperçus le ciel, quelques étoiles, et un peu de verdure. Cette première sensation fut un moment délicieux. Je ne me sentais encore que par là. Ja naissais dans cet instant à la vie, et il me semblait que je remplissais de ma légère existence tous les objets que j'apercevais. Tout entier au moment présent je ne me souvenais de rien; je n'avais nulle notion distincte de mon individu, pas la moindre idée de ce qui venait de m'arriver; je ne savais ni qui j'étais ni où j'étais; je ne sentais ni mal ni crainte ni inquiétude. Je voyais couler mon sang comme j'aurais vu couler un ruisseau, sans songer seulement que ce sang m'appartînt en aucune sorte.

Jean-Jacques Rousseau, *Les rêveries du promeneur solitaire*.[1]

Und ich glaube auch, daß Gedenkengänge wie diese nicht nur meine eigenen Bemühungen begleiten, sondern auch diejenigen anderer Lyriker der jüngeren Generation. Es sind die Bemühungen dessen, der, überflogen von Sternen, die Menschenwerk sind, der, zeltlos auch in diesem bisher ungeahnten Sinne und damit auf das unheimlichste im Freien, mit seinem Dasein zur Sprache geht, wirklichkeitswund und Wirklichkeit suchend.

Paul Celan, *Ansprache anlässlich der Entgegennahme
des Literaturpreises der freien Hansestadt Bremen*.[2]

Introduction

Modernity is a time shrouded in confusion. We know a lot about it, but the more we know, the more bedazzled we are. It is just as if all the knowledge we have on it melted into an ocean of uncertainty that we now wade in. There is a fundamental contradiction between what we know—we know a lot, basically everything—and the satisfaction we have with this knowledge. It seems as if, on the one hand, we fathomed out the greatest depths of modernity, circumscribed its boundaries and almost agreed upon its characteristics, but, on the other hand, we remain painfully insatiate in our quests for modernity's beginnings, specificity, and presumed end.

Why is modernity so paradoxical? Why so often do we feel that nearly no step has been taken to overcome the modern predicament, whereas inenarrable effort has been spent to confront it? Why do we still await the final answer, if almost everything has already been said? Why does each new hope wears off so quickly and mires in dull lasting that seems a *basso continuo* of modernity? Politically speaking, why does the left think that despite having precious volumes, an impressive history of socialist or communist organizations, and a good few major revolutionary attempts, it still needs to try again, just as if nothing were done properly or even, worse enough, nothing really happened?[1] Finally, why has our knowledge evaporated and become an object of unceasing study that never brings about an informed action?[2] Clearly, our knowledge of modernity is ravaged by some structural entanglement which offers knowledge at the price of deactivating it. It quenches our thirst like demineralized water, rinsing out remainders of premodern knowledge and making us drink more and more insatiably.

As if to take one more sip, this book aims to address a few qualities of modernity. A presumptuous task, given that they were, in one way or another, outlined almost at the very beginning of the modern era; a daunting task, if everything would have to be finally said adequately. It is, however, more about arranging the already existing pieces of the riddle into a different constellation rather than building an entirely new theory. We do not need new theories of modernity; what we lack is their radical critique that will elucidate the conditions of possibility which ground them.

The concept which is a common thread for the book, the Mirror Star, is drawn from a reinterpretation of one of the forgotten passages by Hegel. This short, unfinished text, originally the last part of his inaugural address at the University of Berlin (1818) and never, in this form, pronounced publicly, is a hidden treasure of modern thinking. It sparks off a lightning that pierces the dark realm of modernity, revealing contours of things which once seemed so familiar but now glow with black light. The concept of the Mirror Star, drawn from it, aims to catch this universe at the precise moment when it is ripped up by the enlightening thunder.

This reading of Hegel, a starting point for this book, is deeply indebted to the whole context of reinterpretations that for at least three decades transformed the way in which we perceive the event of the so-called "German Idealism." Thanks to thinkers such as Jacques Lacan, Slavoj Žižek, Judith Butler, Catherine Malabou, Alain Badiou, and Alenka Zupančič, it is no longer just a stupefyingly inventive period of modern philosophy, or, for some, a spell of intellectual insanity, but a field of most profound reconfigurations which still determine our thinking. The work of retracing, coextensive with relooking into the dark well discovered very early in the history of modern philosophizing, remains unfinished. It is perhaps a characteristically modern trait that vital events of thinking, once arrived, keep happening still, linger in their sometimes obsessive recurrences, echo in more and more references, as if burning into their ungraspable core. This book attempts to strike, once again, the chords that resonate surprisingly well with the nature of the modern universe. In order to do that, it calls for a radical temporal circumscription, a kind of historical modern *epoche*, in which modernity is seen not as part of history, but as a universe in itself.

The imagery around which this book revolves—sidereal metaphors, symbols and allegories—has uncannily often been used as a language for describing modernity. The image of the star that modern thinking grasps two crucial characteristics of its time: unsettlingly dynamic ubiquity and dependence on a tiny, hidden condition. In their far-off perfection—to say after Mallarmé: "froide d'oubli et de désuétude"[3]—stars symbolize an unshatterable guiding point, a foothold, both distant enough not to be mired in our world and to be a working force within it. They embody both humankind's estrangement from nature[4] and the promise of salvation. Thanks to these qualities, stars return in pivotal moments of history of modern Western thinking. With Kant, they constitute an element of one of the most popular portrayals of the human condition ("the starry heavens above me and the moral law within me"). In Hegel's Inaugural Address, they build a parable that offers an unsettling insight into the very construction of the modern era. Later on, they return occasionally, in Nietzsche, Rosenzweig, Heidegger, and Celan—and many others—each time summoned when an acute need of orienting oneself in time is experienced. Through some oblique historical irony, Copernicus' term for rotation of heavenly spheres, *revolutio*, became a seal of modern political upheavals. Stars are taken for emblems of political movements, especially those which unleash revolutionary and messianic power. Sidereal imagery appears at historical crossings, when time is ripe enough to break into a new form and we feel stranded on the immense and empty plateau of modernity.

This book is by no means a treaty on how stars were metaphorically exploited in philosophy. It rather inscribes itself into a long tradition of sidereal thinking in order to look at modernity as a specific universe of murky origins and even more doubtful end. In this regard, it pays little attention to the already hollow novelty of "postmodernity," which, at best, remains just a name for one of many phases of the modern time.[5] Modernity, as described in this book, is here to stay unless some meta-messianic moment makes it disappear without a proper end.

The book is not a comprehensive treaty on modernity either (if such could ever be written). Rather, it tries to give thinking a new orientation at a peculiar moment of modern era, in which new paths seem already open, although at the price of general exhaustion. Orientation, groping for what is close and outlining the distant, has always been a primary gesture of the practice of deconstruction: it is now needed more than ever. The almost non-Copernican revolution which shattered thinking in the second part of the twentieth century—with late Heidegger, poststructuralism, and deconstruction—put us in a unique position: perhaps never before did we have so much accumulated knowledge, such honed techniques of reading, and such subtlety of musing on the past; and yet, we are paralyzed with knowledge, just as if it all were a kind of a momentary discharge, possible thanks to a historical respite. This book, clearly opposed to obliterating the grandiosity of twentieth-century thinking,[6] wants to reconsider it again at the moment when the wave of history already begins to retreat.

If, as Giorgio Agamben once suggested, being contemporary means to face the obscurity of one's time and to dip one's pen in it,[7] this book hopelessly strives to confront its own times. In order to do so, it approaches the present from the point of view of the entire epoch. All puzzles are in front of us, even if we cannot see most of them. Perhaps it is now that we are summoned to the greatest perspicacity in recollecting traces of what happened within the last few decades. If we do that, we will be able to recognize the ubiquity and profundity of the modern cut, the indelible mark of the modern universe that makes historical continuity a necessary perhaps, but still a delusion.

Moreover, the time is ripe enough to undertake a systematic confrontation with the question of sovereignty, already prepared by late works of Jacques Derrida and Agamben (not to mention, as a study example, Heidegger). Derrida's last leap into a new philosophical territory concerned precisely the question of sovereignty in its complex manifestations, particularly in relation to animals and the living:[8] as in so many other fields, Derrida's opening demands to be further explored. In this book, sovereignty is an emblematically modern phenomenon, undetachably embedded in the very construction of modernity. It is theorized far beyond its ordinary political or subjective meanings and, in this new role, attempts to describe the curvature of the tissue of the modern universe. Sovereignty is the most emblematic and ubiquitous feature of this time; it constitutes the organizing principle of its discourses, histories, and power relations. As it will be argued, it has the role which in the premodern era was played by transcendence. Therefore, no in-depth study of modernity can abstract from sovereignty: here, the two will be grasped in their mutual entanglement.

In this regard, the book is particularly indebted to Agamben's immense work. Still, in all its indispensability, his thinking is perhaps just the beginning of the tremendous task that needs to be continued. Sovereignty must be recognized as not just a phenomenon of power or law, but the constitutive framework of modernity. Archaeology of this concept, much as it is useful, should be reconsidered within a different approach to historicity; the modern times must be the focus of this study. Sovereignty remains the final frontier of modern thinking, a loophole in explicit Marxism and a trap for all who live within the modern universe. As I will argue, modernity might be seen as a zone organized by it. Especially today, when its political form is once again, unsurprisingly, gaining in power, it must be thoroughly reconsidered and, as far as it is at all possible, provisionally defused. With necessary emphasis, it must be stated that this book is not by any means an exhaustive treatise on forms or historical manifestations of sovereignty: rather, it aims to remold the concept itself, leaving the immense historiographical work for future efforts.

Finally, there is one crucial aspect that inextricably joins modernity and sovereignty: historicity. As it will be argued, modernity inaugurates history proper. When analyzing this question, thinking can never be too radical, especially given that Heidegger, Derrida, and Agamben did not yet push the relationship between modernity and historicity to its very end. This book, by virtue of a thought experiment, does not attempt to lose its breath in looking for the abyssal ground in which historicity melts with ontology of the modern universe. Modernity will be treated here not just as an epoch, not even as a special one, but as the overarching framework of the very possibility of history as such. In this sense, the path of this book could be described as powering through towards radical deconstruction of modernity. Nonetheless, it drags deconstruction itself into the maelstrom and reveals it as a properly modern and non-universalizable practice, against the grain of Derrida's work. The book strives to push forward the revolution of twentieth-century thinking in order to circumscribe modernity as the grounding philosophical problem, whose recognition might put us on, or rather within, the map. For too long, we were caught up in endless debates about what modernity is, when it began, or ended. The field marked by such questions is clearly aporetic and, as such, demands deconstruction, even if at the price of elevating modernity to the rank of differentiation itself and dismantling deconstruction with its own push. We need the latter move more than ever: deconstruction, exactly in all its intellectual splendour, must be rethought as an impoverished and problematic practice,[9] which gives us freedom, deferral, and perspicacity at the price of serving the framework of sovereignty. And perhaps it is now that we need to perform, once again, the properly Marxian gesture of overbidding and use this late flower of sovereignty for the critique of the soil it rose from. It is in this point that deconstruction can one more time jump over itself and, in a late swansong, reveal its deepest conditions of possibility.

In all the three above mentioned aspects—modernity, sovereignty, and historicity—this book attempts to break through a new entrance. By no means should it be taken for a complete work: it is much rather a preliminary conceptual blow that will require continuation in further enquiry.

A few words need to be said about the discourse of the book. Despite the general aura of exhaustion that shrouds philosophy—especially that which draws from most vivid currents of twentieth-century thinking—this book still pleads loyalty to the philosophical. Over the uneasy and discontinuous relationship with philosophical discourse, it still recognizes itself as a late part of it. Philosophy is not dead;[10] as it will be argued, it lives its afterlife. And just as spectres might know—and support—more than the living, so might philosophy in its afterlife still find answers to a few questions about the structure of modernity. Stock-still in its prolonged crepuscule, it seizes things, in Agamben's words, as "fixed forever in the impossibility to end their being seen."[11]

Even so, we are not exempted from confronting some uneasy dilemmas, which now more than ever shatter the easiness of philosophical reflection. What is the future of philosophy? Can the discourse of philosophy support the complexity of thinking? Do we have adequate words for it? Do we understand its coherence? Do we demand coherence and *can* we demand it?

The revolution of the late twentieth century—particularly with late Heidegger's, Derrida's, and Lacan's œuvres—leads us to a brave new land of thinking, which perhaps begins to resemble science in Lacan's portrayal.[12] Its true core is impossible to understand in symbolic terms; it can only be written down, and it is writing that supports the weight of philosophical discoveries. Nonetheless, this writing is excessive, overdetermined, necessarily inconsistent. There has been a world-shattering event for the philosophical discourse and the latter can no longer claim that it is transparent and able to express thinking losslessly. For the first time, philosophy should openly acknowledge its core internal unintelligibility and confront it. It is perhaps why Heidegger wanted to leave philosophy as a hopelessly metaphysical discourse, one that should be overcome with "thinking." For the very same reason, he wrote some of his texts not in the framework of delivering a message for the addressee, but in preparation of a locus of thought.[13] Consequently, if we stay attached to the very word "philosophy," it must be at the price of radical disillusionment, displacement, and destabilization that remolds the relationship between what can be thought and what writes itself.

Consequently, philosophy must let itself be guided by writing.[14] It must expect its happening in writing, must await an event which will continue it, retrospectively, through writing. In a sense, and just in a sense, it is still deconstruction, but this time, taken courageously and, against its original spirit, played much more seriously. To let writing finally think: this would be the task philosophy might find itself burdened with in order to survive. Against this background, this book takes its shot and lets writing think about modernity.

How could it be done? First of all, it needs to be acknowledged that thinking both produces and requires a *permanent structural excess*. Thinking about modernity—especially nowadays—is inherently excessive. It must support the burden of innumerable contradictions, the entanglement of infinite paths, the confusion of unceasing beginnings, and the vertigo of recurrent abyssal crossings. For this reason, what we knew as philosophy is no longer possible, worse even: it lives its afterlife since its death a long time ago, when it crumbled under the catastrophe it had intended to take on its shoulders. But if philosophy in its traditional sense is barred, writing can take its role for one principal reason: it supports contradictions. It records them, pushes on through each new world that dawns in thinking, it lives after the death of philosophy. Writing is then the only possible space for excess. Philosophy returns to it in its lucid intervals only to be eclipsed a while after and be carried over the abyss by its indefatigable companion.

Writing can think more than philosophy will ever dare and manage to do. Therefore, the struggle of the self-proclaimed, lucid consciousness to get hold of writing is not only compromised (especially after deconstruction), but disastrously counter-productive. True miracles happen when philosophy openly embraces writing not as a process of expressing a ready-made thought, but as thinking itself. Deconstruction developed the category of *écriture* as a non-concept: but it needs to become a carrier of philosophy.

Accordingly, this book pushes forward with the stream of writing, each time clinging to its carrier, through cracks, rifts, and abysses, without stitches or sealants, with internal excess that cannot be ultimately subordinated to an overarching framework. In this manner, philosophy reveals its paradoxical and truly impossible position. It abstains from filling out the cracks with commentaries as deconstruction was wont to do, and leads writing through accumulating excess. In such a practice, concepts begin to melt into each other, revealing their mutual dependence, hitherto veiled under ritual conceptual schemes and intellectual joints. Perhaps then only philosophy as marching-through is a faithful companion to writing. In the incomprehensible continuity that characterizes them both, concepts begin to interact beyond their ossified connections. Thinking goes deeper and deeper into the level on which concepts themselves are born from the maelstrom of differentiation. Despite taking the depth metaphors with due irony, this book attempts to bring to the surface a few of its underwater findings in order to displace the manner in which we so far linked concepts into chains. In other words, it aims to write-through modernity.

The book consists of six chapters. The first one is focused on Hegel's parable and elaborates the concept of the Mirror Star which derives from it. It aims to grasp modernity as an impoverished universe, in which sovereignty takes the place formerly occupied by transcendence. The second chapter grounds the proper path to deconstructing modernity and history. It zeroes in on finding the "navel"—to use Freud's old enigmatic metaphor[15]—that contains the conditions of possibility of the modern universe. On the basis of this work, the third chapter investigates modernity as a universe based on sovereignty. This line of thought culminates in the fourth chapter, that ventures to outline the nature and specificity of modern temporality.

The fifth chapter returns to the concept of sovereignty in order to portray modernity as a realm of ineradicable provisionality, one of the sources of our modern misery. It argues that provisionality is a mode of government arising under modern sovereignty. Finally, the sixth chapter addresses modernity as the expanding universe which remains *properly inenarrable* in its entirety and accessible only through parables on its nature. Against the somewhat carefree universalizing spirit of Agamben's breakthrough research in the *Homo sacer* series,[16] the chapter develops the concept of bare life as pertaining strictly to the modern universe.[17] The sixth chapter paves the way for an ethical critique of modernity, developed in the Conclusion. Apart from chapters, the book is divided into paragraphs and sub-paragraphs that intersect with each other.

Finally, what demands confessing is the fact that this book has its tacit mentor, the hidden master of thinking, whose teachings we still decipher on the walls of our modern reality: Isaac Luria. His Kabbalistic vision of *shevirat ha-kelim*, "breaking of the vessels"—a powerful event that marked our time and built a unique universe, in which negativity, not to say primordial emptiness, gains a foundational character—is, to all intents and purposes, an unsurpassed account of modernity.[18] Indissociably, messianism—or rather messianicity, as Derrida proposed[19]—becomes part and parcel of the modern universe, for thick and (all-too-often) thin. In this role, Luria's searing conception, apart from its actual historical influences, is a guiding star for all secular or post-secular messianisms of the modern times, including the most significant one which originates in Marx's thinking. If I ventured to reveal cards right away, in a kind of a cryptic addendum to the book that is just beginning, I would call it a contribution to *(post-deconstructionist) Marxism-Lurianism*.

Hegel was cruelly right when he claimed that the owl of Minerva sets out at dusk. He might well have meant a dusk that falls repeatedly after each day. But quite probably, it is just one dusk that long ago seized the Earth and will not let go of it soon. It is for this reason that Hegel—when read properly—constitutes *nec plus ultra* of modern thinking: his owl, long time overdue, has always just arrived. From such a perspective, this book will be nothing but its knock on the window when the evening comes. What it means to be is perhaps not a *tikkun*, an act of rectifying the world—that would be preposterous—but a passing glance at the conditions of the possibility of *tikkuns*.

1

The Mirror Star

1.0 Modernity, like no other era, has a paradoxical status. On the one hand, there seems to be some working consensuses on when modernity began: the most serious candidate would be eighteenth century, with the Enlightenment, the Industrial Revolution,[1] the French Revolution, the birth of modern subjectivity (Jean-Jacques Rousseau), individualism and human rights, secularization, nation-state and Immanuel Kant's "Copernican Revolution."[2] On the other hand, such an easy list of historical breakthroughs does not seem to exhaust the specificity of modernity. Perhaps even it only whets our appetite. Modernity appears as an enigma, a yawning gap in the continuity of history, something which transcends all particular events we would like to link it with. Debates on the beginning and nature of modernity never end.

It seems, therefore, that there might be a structural mechanism which is responsible for modernity's irremovable elusiveness. It can be found already in the beginnings of modern philosophy—in the miraculous epoch opened by Rousseau and Sade and closed by Hegel—namely, at the time in which its possibilities and blockades were being determined.

Kant: Stars, the law, and the remainder

1.1 History of modernity is sprinkled with philosophical dicta—well known, but even more misunderstood—whose almost ahistorical tranquillity contrasts sharply with stark brutality of events that they presage. One of these dicta was authored by Immanuel Kant just a year before the outbreak of the French Revolution. His *Critique of Practical Reason*, published in 1788, concludes with this famous passage, so mercilessly exploited by commentators:

> Two things fill the mind with ever new and increasing admiration and awe, the oftener and the more steadily we reflect on them: the starry heavens above and the moral law within. I have not to search for them and conjecture them as though they were veiled in darkness or were in the transcendent region beyond my horizon; I see them before me and connect them directly with the consciousness of my existence. The former begins from the place I occupy in the external world of sense, and enlarges *my connection therein to an unbounded extent with worlds upon worlds and systems of systems* [emphasis added], and moreover into limitless

times of their periodic motion, its beginning and continuance. The second begins from my invisible self, my personality, and exhibits me in a world which has true infinity, but which is traceable only by the understanding, and with which I discern that I am not in a merely contingent but in a universal and necessary connection, as I am also thereby with all those visible worlds.[3]

Against all pseudo-philosophical daydreaming about the beauty and sublimity of the Kantian world, this piece grasps the new, *modern terror* and crystallizes it into the furthest and the most material of all metaphors, a metaphor of astronomical relation.

1.2 In this fragment, Kant portrays the universe as split into two seemingly irreconcilable sides. The first one (let us call it *the outside*) is constituted by "the starry heavens," "der bestirnte Himmel." These heavens are, in fact, "worlds upon worlds," that is, boundless spaces of emptiness which always empty into an even greater void. The moment we think about it, we are lost, dwarfed by the incessant motion of spheres, whose terrifying magnitude once made Pascal tremble and Blanqui believe in sidereal eternity.[4] But this picture is even more horrifying than the famous Pascalian "silence éternel de ces espaces infinis,"[5] "the eternal silence of infinite spaces." Pascal's infinite spaces seemed to neighbor each other, being of the same level. Here, however, one infinite void is just *a unit of a higher one*. Infinities are built one upon another. As a result, the progression of empty, abstract, and lifeless spaces reaches a new dimension.

If physical metaphors are justified in this context, we could speak of a three-dimensional horror of mutually embedded voids. Pascal might have feared the infinity which opened up above his skull, but it was a mere infinity of his world, the world which still constituted a whole. Contrariwise, Kantian thought seems to open the third dimension, in which just one infinity is not enough. In Kant, there are innumerable infinities and even if we managed to cross the one we live in, we would only shift the level and perceive *the infinite chain of infinities* in which we are trapped. Thus, the heavenly emptiness we dread cannot be neatly opposed to our solid, earthly life. The infinity of infinities already took it all from within: we are always within it. Our world is no longer a tiny, but steady, island in the ocean of nothingness. On the contrary, it belongs to a complex system of mutually embedded infinities and, as such, offers no shelter.

Kant openly admits that we are always-already enmeshed in this terrifying chain of infinities: the outside "begins from the place I occupy in the external world of sense, and enlarges my connection therein to an unbounded extent with worlds upon worlds and systems of systems." In other words, where I stand, the universe begins. Or rather, to put it more explicitly, I stand where the universe had already begun, ages ago, and thus deprived me of any solid ground. *Thus, the outside has hollowed me out, I belong to it, I am out.*

When did that happen? Has it always been like that and I have been just mistaken, lured by an illusion of unknown origin? Or was there perhaps a precise moment in which my solid ground has been undermined? Where does the Kantian "awe" stem from, if not from the discovery that I belong fully to the outside? Or maybe this awe is nothing but a tribute that the outside pays to itself, with me watching the scene with a paralyzed gaze? But if so, who am I? And what is my gaze, the only point which pierces the otherwise continuous tissue of the outside? All these questions resound with the echo of spectral figures of thought, desperately conceived to grasp perhaps nothing more than the experience of fundamental modern destitution: from Descartes' *malin génie*, through Marx's mole of history, up to Heidegger's *Geworfenheit*.

1.3 Yet, the outside is just one part of this universe: the other part is law. In Kantian thought, law acts as the inexplicable cut in the causal chain which imposes upon the natural stream of causes and effects a new beginning, an act based only on loyalty to duty. Law perforates the outside and renders it inoperative. Freedom, based on the sovereign act, in which law self-imposes itself, carves us out of the common causality. The outside cannot operate on me if I exert my freedom through the act of self-legislation.

In the first part of the above cited paragraph, the outside appeared to take our ground, or even worse: to have taken our ground in advance. But then Kant's argumentation prepares a sudden miracle: law saves us. Contrary to all anthropocentric imagery, which stifles Kant's notions like cotton wool of self-assuring pathos, this passage does not restore the dignity of human beings denigrated by the immensity of the universe. Law makes an incision in the continuity of the outside, just in the place in which we seem to find ourselves. Through this incision, law opens the abyss of human self-constituting—the abyss, in which we expect to find the grounds for validity of law, for spontaneity of action, for development of human history, but, in truth, in which we grope our way through the dark incomprehensibility of happening, through macabre ages of terror, utter subjugation, and cruel irrationality that constitute our real history. What Kant seizes as the phenomenon of law is, in fact, a much broader and ambiguous area of modern sovereignty.

If we wanted to run away from the overwhelming pressure of the outside, we would find ourselves in a different, yet symmetrical emptiness. The abyss of the universe was constituted by the infinite chain of infinities. However, the second one, the abyss of law, is structured analogically. Every act of self-legislation opens up an infinity of potential applications of thus constituted law; law cannot be exhausted in a singular act of applying it. Application of law always repeats itself, because its iteration is inscribed into its construction. Therefore, the dimension of law also constitutes an infinity (of acts of legislation) of infinities (of applications of each laws). Both abysses, in and above us, are thus infinities of infinities.

1.4 Both Kantian abysses seem mutually exclusive: once we focus upon one of them, it takes the whole ground except for a tiny remainder of the second one. The outside excludes law and vice versa. Consequently, both of them cannot be conceived of in the same dimension. The outside, if taken autonomously, absorbs all that exists—including us—except for the small domain of law, which rescues us from the voracious totality. Analogously, law—taken in itself—throws us into a dark space of self-constitution, in which the actual continuity of the outside loses all its power but does not disappear: it collapses into an inert residue of materiality. With the outside thus rendered inoperative, we would be totally overwhelmed by law if it were not for the tiny grain of matter which stays put. As a consequence, the outside and law never meet in their full forms. Whenever one triumphs, the other one must always collapse into a remainder, thereby giving way for the dimension of totality and simultaneously constituting its last obstacle.

Thus, Kant was one of the first to discover the incessant, terrifying throb which punctuates the history and thought of modernity, the "epoch" whose inner rhythm oscillates between the non-Whole and its tiny remainder.

1.5 The tension between the outside and law paved the way for future struggles of German Idealism. But if we look at his discovery with a clear eye—and some clarity might be reached when history holds its breath for a moment—we will see that it shifts the basic lines of previous, premodern ontology. Kant's thought—despite his docile habitus—marks the irretrievable switch of paradigms from which a new, modern "ontology" arises.[6]

What are its traits? First, the universe becomes excessive. Nothing has its predetermined, tranquil place. All is in relation, in a restless grid of relations, constantly switching perspectives and attempting to gain the whole ground against the resistance of the remainder. In this sense, the universe becomes determined, at its base, by a political grid of forces. The political seems the utter, though essentially senseless ground for all sense. Just like space gives anchor to objects and allows to describe them in the most "neutral" way, so does the political become the ultimate common ground for things. As such, it is the basic fluctuating constellation of bare relations on the level in which all explanations lose their push.

Second, we are being thrown into a play of powerful forces which know us inside out. Nothing can separate us from them; it might be only one force turned against the other that gives a temporary shelter. It seems as if, deep inside, we have always already belonged to them—even if this primordial dependence is nothing more than a result of an act of destitution, whose construction makes us indebted to some vague, past era and thus creates the modern sense of historicity. If there is any "us", it is a contingent intersection of the outside and law, nothing more than *a place*, which is repeatedly swept away by the tide of new forces gaining the upper hand. In "us," being made up from two adjacent lacks—the lack in the outside created by law and the lack in law pierced by the resistance of materiality—the two infinities of infinities switch places.

Third, the world becomes utterly estranged from us, with infinity of infinities taking the place of celestial spheres and natural law. Moreover, the modern struggle cuts through us and we are at least as much estranged as the world itself. If the world is estranged and we are estranged, there is almost no barrier between us and the world, except for the tiny remainder which is the thing we are actually estranged from and which keeps us differentiated from the world. If so, we are, in fact, always at home, and only the most intimate part of ourselves, the one thing we truly are and fear to lose, *only the deepest "us"*, is what remains the strangest. No matter which side we start from, do not we merely switch constellations of the remainder? Is not it miraculous that we can complete our journey from total destitution to total restitution in a twinkling of an eye? Such miracles did not happen before modernity and their common existence among us proves the extent of inaugural historical catastrophe whose traces we still attempt to recollect.

1.6 Let us look, once again, at the above cited passage from *The Critique of Practical Reason*:

I have not to search for them [starry heavens] and conjecture them as though they were veiled in darkness or were in the transcendent region beyond my horizon; I see them before me and connect them directly with the consciousness of my existence. The former begins from the place I occupy in the external world of sense, and enlarges *my connection therein to an unbounded extent with worlds upon worlds and systems of systems* [emphasis added], and moreover into limitless times of their periodic motion, its beginning and continuance.

This fragment brings the imagery of stars, heavens, and skies back to philosophical life. In Aristotelian thinking, stars were simply out there, revolving endlessly in their orbits as perfect beings.[7] But, in Kant, after the modern break in the structure of knowledge, they suddenly stop being indifferent and transcendent.[8] They are seen directly before us and make us conscious about our existence. Between "us" and the starry heavens there is a kind of mysterious connection. Stars are somehow *present* before us, and in this presence they draw us into "the unbounded extent with worlds upon worlds." All of a sudden, stars are part of the strange link between "us" and the universe: the link which is in constant tension and motion.

In other words, Kant's starry heavens have a double effect. First, they wake us up to the consciousness of "our" existence. Second, they pull this freshly emerged "us" into a dynamic relation with the universe. All of that is simultaneously possible only at the intersection with the dimension of law, that cuts "us" from the outside. But why *on Earth* should stars wake up our existence? Why should they create something like "us"? And for which reason does the sidereal imagery unanticipatedly crawl into the heart of philosophical thinking at the outbreak of modernity? As we will see, it is not just Kant's idiosyncrasy. Wherever the deepest mechanisms of modernity are explored, stars unmistakeably accompany our thinking.

We will now take a longer detour to find in Hegel the most accurate linking between modernity and the language of astronomy.

Modernity's greatest apocrypha: Hegel's Berlin address

2.1 No later than thirty years after the publication of Kant's *The Critique of Pure Reason*, Hegel took up his professorship at the University of Berlin.[9] The world was completely different; since 1788, it had revolved around itself. In the meantime, it went through the outbreak of the French Revolution, the unprecedented rise of masses, and short, but obsessively remembered days of terror, culminating in the politically and philosophically hottest summer of 1794. Then the Napoleonic Wars swept through the Europe of *anciens régimes* and undermined the legitimacy of former institutions and rulers. Millions of human beings were left to hunger, terror, and doubt. And, last but not least, thinking was molded anew by the philosophical ferment of German Idealism, which seemed as if some potential that had been accumulating for ages suddenly discharged and shortened the usual time for development of thought to meteoric creation.[10] But all the forces which had been released seemed to collapse under their own impact and finally faded.[11]

Thus, 1818 was the year in which tensions of the past three decades could be finally cast in restored molds of the old world. Appointing Hegel to a professorship in the capital of a new, stabilized nation-state serves as an all too obvious symbol of solidification of powers of negativity. But this parallel is much more pertinent than it might initially appear. Hegel as state professor was equally absurd as the modern state itself. Just as the unleashed power of thinking, which learns to treat all obstacles as already created and surmountable, and then itself casts its forms only to claim that they are its results, so does the negative power of modern sovereignty let itself be channelled into the nation-state. Hegel-professor embodies the spirit of these times and their "morning after" atmosphere. The world had been rebuilt, but its inner devastation was palpable under new, reconstructed forms. At that moment, Hegel was an accomplished philosopher who had left the existential turmoil of his earlier days far beyond himself. His system ossified, his pace slowed down. He finally found himself at the right time. Having accepted the appointment in Berlin—a formerly provincial city with little history of its own, but furiously ravaged by pan-European storms of history—he left Heidelberg, the reverent and conservatively mediocre stronghold of the German academic past.[12]

2.2 On 22 October 1818, Hegel gave his inaugural address at the University of Berlin.[13] Perhaps, some day, this date will be celebrated as the first cryptic, yet profound recognition of modernity's nature. The speech Hegel actually delivered—basing heavily on his previous address from Heidelberg (1816)[14]—survived in full to our times,[15] but what is much more interesting is the draft that preceded it. Whereas the small pronounced part was published already in 1830, the rest was either unfinished or incomplete and survived only in manuscript.[16]

Essentially, it is a short introduction to his philosophy, interspersed—as usual, in the case of Hegel—with his remarks on the historical condition of philosophy. At the end of the draft, however, the speech begins to shine with a quasi-poetical light of sober wandering through the desert. The tone changes; the otherwise quite sober speech suddenly turns into a poignant narrative of the fall and recovery of thinking:

The decision to philosophise throws itself purely into thinking (– thinking is lonely with itself),—it throws itself as if into a boundless ocean; all the miscellaneous colors, all footholds have disappeared, all other friendly lights have extinguished. Only the one star, the inner star of the spirit shines; it is the Polar Star. But it is natural that the spirit in its solitude with itself is seized with horror; one does not know yet where it's going, where one is heading. Among what has disappeared is much of what one would not give up at any price, and in this loneliness it has not yet restored, and one is uncertain whether it will find itself again or will be given back.

Der Entschluß zu philosophieren wirft sich rein in Denken (– das Denken ist einsam bei sich selbst),—er wirft sich wie in einen uferlosen Ozean; alle die bunten Farben, alle Stützpunkte sind verschwunden, alle sonstigen freundlichen Lichter sind ausgelöscht. Nur der eine Stern, der innere Stern des Geistes leuchtet; er ist der Polarstern. Aber es ist natürlich, daß den Geist in seinem Alleinsein mit sich gleichsam ein Grauen befällt; man weiß noch nicht, wo es hinauswolle, wohin man hinkomme.

Unter dem, was verschwunden ist, befindet sich vieles, was man um allen Preis der Welt nicht aufgeben wollte, und in dieser Einsamkeit aber hat es sich noch nicht wiederhergestellt, und man ist ungewiß, ob es sich wiederfinde, wiedergeben werde.[17]

This pivotal, forgotten passage deserves as close attention as only modernity itself might attract. The cut with the previous part of the address is clearly noticeable. A new spirit is breathed into Hegel's discourse, which makes this fragment a surprisingly enlightening parable on modernity. It might, and should, be read as a tale about what modernity is and how it started. Let us then reread it as carefully as possible.

2.3 What Hegel describes is nothing less than modern Genesis. He outlines a history of thinking, but, in fact, it is the history of the whole modern spirit. In this narrative, true thinking begins with a decision. But whose decision? Here comes the first rift that severs modernity from any imaginable past: Hegel does not refer to any figure of a thinker. In fact, the decision to philosophize is not taken by any philosopher. Under close scrutiny, two acting subjects appear in the first sentence of the above cited paragraph. The first one is the one which takes this decision, the second one is the decision itself which throws itself into thinking. The first one remains unknown; it is only lured by the image of philosophizing which it wants to undertake. Once the decision is taken, this subject is definitively erased and is no longer known. Only the syntax of the sentence preserves its spectral (ab/pre)sence. What remains is solitary thinking, pure, refined to its core.

Therefore, Hegel describes the process of radical refinement, in which first a vague, unstable, but supposedly rich subject collapses into its own decision. Then, *this decision itself takes the ground and continuously falls into the loneliness of thinking*. Instead of focusing on which subject turns into which, Hegel highlights the irreparable process of total impoverishment which acts as a meta-trap for everything that comes into its orbit. In fact, no one took this decision: it seems to have happened, it might be reconstructed, imitated, iterated, attributed, but it has always been already there. There is no longer a Big Other, or a subject, that would be involved. The decision takes the lead and collapses into itself in a process as "objective" as a landslide.

2.4 This decision entails a catastrophe of immense proportions. The catastrophe pierces through all layers of reality, conditions them, but remains unconditioned by what it affects. It knows nothing of the distinction between subjectivity and objectivity. It concerns neither the inner world of a philosopher nor "the outside world"—it simply renders this distinction inoperative, making it a trace on sand subject to erosion by history. The impersonal decision "turns all the worldly lights off," presumably leaving all the devices of the world still in existence, but in the state of inoperativeness.[18] Here, we encounter the purely modern power of cut, which acts like an intervention from another dimension, conserving and deactivating the whole world, whose colors fade, supports disappear, and all friendly glimmers are subdued.

2.5 It was a recurring intuition of Hegel that the modern cut makes matter emerge. The cut sips all sense from the universe, leaving it bleak and meaningless. And where sense is no longer felt, matter arises. For instance, in his *Lectures on the History of Philosophy* Hegel describes the Reformation as nothing less than the creation of matter from the previously existing realm of (religious) meaning:

> Two stages have here been given, the first of which is the stage of devotion, of worship, such as that reached in partaking of the Communion. That is the perception of the divine Spirit in the community in which the present, indwelling, living Christ as self-consciousness has attained to actuality. The second stage is that of developed consciousness, when the content becomes the object; here this present, indwelling Christ retreats two thousand years to a small corner of Palestine, and is an individual historically manifested far away at Nazareth or Jerusalem. It is the same thing in the Greek Religion where the god present in devotion changes into prosaic statues and marble; or in painting, where this externality is likewise arrived at, when the god becomes mere canvas or wood. The Supper is, according to the Lutheran conception, of Faith alone; it is a divine satisfaction, and it is not adored as if it were the Host. Thus, a sacred image is no more to us than is a stone or thing.[19]

A sacred image is now nothing more than a stone: the realm of matter becomes homogenous because there is no precedence between things as far as materiality is concerned. This unexpected emergence of matter—in a place previously occupied by a meaningful reference to transcendence—seems to be an emancipation of thingness from the harness of the symbolical. Now, deserted by meanings, matter starts to appear in all its muteness, numbness, and ultimate equality.

Therefore, the catastrophe that Hegel describes reduces the whole world to a senseless and colorless mass of unfamiliar things which are hardly distinguishable. In this strangeness, we can discern the birth of modern materiality, construed no longer as simple matter, but as things infected with the dimension of the Real, the *unheimlich*. There seems to have been a sort of fundamental displacement. It is neither epistemological, although it might appear that only our perception of the world changed, nor purely ontological. *All previous differences seem to have nothing in common with the new one, introduced by this uncanny catastrophe*. Reality gains a new dimension: a dimension to which everything that had existed lays open for dissection, preserved, inert, and deactivated.

2.6 "The decision to philosophise," says Hegel, "throws itself purely into thinking (thinking is lonely [*einsam*] with itself)." German *einsam* means "lonely," as well as "unique," or "unmanned." The decision, once executed, unleashes powers which lead to its self-destitution and estrangement. These powers tend to produce something singular, unique, something that merely exists, not through its actions, attributes, or inner richness, but through the very position of standing out against the background. The landscape introduced by Hegel's thinking is extremely somber, governed by its black-and-white goal. It is un(wo)manned, as there is nothing human in it. Human beings, like all the other "positive material" (to use this Hegelian term[20]), are irrelevant in this picture. Reduced to the basic difference between solitary existence and its outside, this universe is the ultimate result of the self-propelled tendency to find itself. But "itself" is no more than pure difference without any positive content. This unfinished process of continuous impoverishment, with the most basic difference as a goal whose complete form thinking might only conjure up, has the structure of sovereignty.

Let us summarize this reading of Hegel's: through some vague decision, which cascaded into itself, new powers of radical destitution have been unleashed. As a result, the whole universe has been reduced to a senseless mass. What remains is just the pure thinking, utterly refined, thrown into some boundless, all-encompassing ocean. The metaphor of the ocean connotes nothing but an immense mass of undifferentiated substance. The decision, whose initial move made the universe collapse, is thrown into this ocean. There seems to be nothing except thinking and senseless mass of matter, equally dangerous, strange, and inhumane. All feelings of certainty disappear. Pure thinking against pure, undifferentiated universe is what remains.

2.7 Before we move on, two questions need to be addressed. First, why is this catastrophe, which we painstakingly attempt to grasp, dependent on a decision? If it is impersonal, as we have just seen, does it contain any element of personal agency? And, second, what does this "thinking" (*Denken*), the propulsion of the developing catastrophe, stand for?

Let us begin with the first question. The existence of decision presumes both will and a set of choices. Responsibility and guilt are not far away either. Assuming that the universe is dependent on a decision has a few intuitive consequences: the universe might have been shaped differently, there were other options, there were reasons for selecting only one of them and, finally and perhaps most importantly, something or someone may bear the guilt for the choice.

Naturally, the dependence of the universe on a decision is not particularly stunning in philosophy, given that ages of ontotheology linked the existence of the universe with a divine decision. But Hegel's intuition steers towards a decision which is not only independent from its "subject," but which also eclipses it. Every decision consists in the collapse of the preexisting array of choices and switching between two different states.[21] But here the decision becomes a *continuous process of self-development, in which the incessant act of deciding consumes the universe and takes its place*. It is a totally new dimension of deciding, in which Hegel uses the long (post-)nominalist tradition of philosophy—from Ockham through Descartes up to Schelling—as the final nail to the coffin of comprehensible continuity.

Every decision entails some kind of break, a passage from an array of options to a state based on only one option.[22] Intuitively, the decision is what links (and simultaneously separates) two incomparable worlds: pre- and post-decision. The former seems to have the latter as one of its options, but, in fact, collapses into it irretrievably. But Hegel's *Entschluß* is even more powerful: although, as a pure act of choosing, it is contentless, it dwarfs both the world it originated in and the world it leads to. It is not determined by the initial set of choices: it had only one imaginary option, thinking, but it collapsed into a process that this option merely masked. In fact, the choice chose itself. Through this back door, the standard framework of deciding (a set of options, a chosen option) has been displaced. *The decision turned into a pure contentless process whose impact destroys the worlds that it pierces through.*

Now it becomes clear why Hegel refers to a decision whose development conditioned the universe. It is not a hackneyed theological move of reducing the universe to a decision of a stable divine subject.[23] On the contrary, Hegel releases the incomprehensible power of negativity that resides in the pure act of choosing. This power transcends all its particular constellations in each and every world it passes through. It simplifies, purifies, and hollows them out. As a decision, it is always perspectival, biased, and essentially different from any content it might concern. It introduces a new dimension into the universe: particularity at the heart of universality.

Decision connotes responsibility and guilt. But Hegel's *Entschluß* has no subject, or rather it is its own subject. It spirals into itself, pulling the universe in. As a consequence, nothing and no one can stand out as a unique subject of guilt. The decision conditions everything that happens and exists in its happening. Thus, it opens up the distinctively subjectless modern universe entirely permeated with guilt, whose description cost and will cost more lives than just Kafka's.

2.8 But why should thinking make the universe collapse? And what is that thinking? Much as these questions reek of idealism, the above cited passage from Hegel's Inaugural Address does not posit thinking as primary in relation to the universe. In close reading, it turns out that thinking itself is a fundamentally impoverished practice/event which emerges after the catastrophe. The decision which sparked off these accidents was not a decision to think, but to philosophize, namely to undertake a legitimate activity within a given discourse. Yet, philosophizing could not be carried out; it swiftly evaporated as a fantasy and gave way to a tougher and teeth-gritting kind of activity: thinking. More than a century before Heidegger eulogized thinking as something that we still must learn after millennia of all-too-ontic philosophy[24]—and before Lacan's analogous gesture[25]—Hegel had pinpointed the unrelieved drabness of destitute thinking. It is a solitary activity, deprived of any external supports such as discourse marks, that painstakingly traces its own path. Thinking is—contrary to images of philosophizing—what has already lost everything. Its casual name has this truly egalitarian potential which buds only when all substantive differences are gone. "Thinking" becomes an all-encompassing term, so universal that it transcends its particular incarnations. This drab, but egalitarian activity has a distinctively modern flavor which was absent in premodern philosophizing.

The decision throws itself into thinking, but with this act thinking itself becomes "a boundless ocean" with no friendly lights. But was not it the universe itself that we described as "*uferloser Ozean*"? Now it turns out that thinking, equally contentless and senseless mass of matter, is like this ocean. *Thinking and the universe approach a point of indifferentiation in their impoverishment.* As a result of this pancatastrophe, in which all positive content vanished, thinking and the universe are separated only by a tiny formal difference.

Perhaps the true heritage of Hegel's idealism, if there ever was such a thing, consists in this radical thought: there has been a total catastrophe[26] which put the basic coordinates of reality out of joint and whose nature we still need to reconsider. In the post-apocalyptic landscape of reality, thinking and the universe became impoverished to the point of their indistinguishability, supported only by the basic formal difference. The difference between thinking and the universe turns out to be subsidiary to a much more powerful one, the only one that remained after the catastrophe and the one towards which the constant process of impoverishing steers. Let us call it, for lack of a better word, *basic difference*. It divides the non-Whole and the tiny remainder (the Lacanian *Yad'lun* and One it cannot capture[27]), although it might as well be dressed up, in one of its many incarnations, as the difference between thinking and the universe. In the universe after the catastrophe all substantial differences, as we already remarked, were rendered inoperative.

This is the power and the poverty of philosophy after Hegel: in its destitution, fully analogical to the destitution of modern universe, it holds a key to understanding the epoch, or at least imagines itself having it. But this understanding is as equally destitute as philosophy itself. As a consequence, impoverishment turns into the underlying topic and attracting power of modern thinking.

2.9 The impersonal decision deserted the universe and thinking, making both a "boundless ocean" with no friendly lights. It seems as if some basic link between words and thoughts (like the early Foucauldian *episteme*[28]) had been displaced, as a result of which, both thinking and the universe had been thrown into equally abject poverty. However, the universe had been represented in thinking, the catastrophe turned these representations into a shapeless mass of matter. Both thinking and the universe are now like a boundless ocean of darkness. Thinking does not represent the universe, the universe does not accept references from thinking. Both lie in contentless ruins, resembling each other through their own destitution, imagined with a purely material third object (*uferloser Ozean*). The inner richness of thinking fades, but thinking itself reveals itself as dependent on one particular foothold. The same applies to the universe. The solid and unique world which might be directly cognized is no longer available, but there is a point from which this mass of ruins is visible. Cognition might be only perspectival and must include in itself its own conditions of possibility. Knowledge becomes displaced at its core: since this catastrophe, it will always contain a dark side which will suspend all the positive content and confront it with its finitude.

Thus read, the Inaugural Address gives a body to the idea over which the twentieth century will obsessively ruminate under the name of "the crisis of representation."

2.10 The universe after the catastrophe is profoundly melancholic. It has this surprising richness which is typical for people consumed by long-lasting melancholia. It has everything within its borders, at its disposal, and this availability of all worldly matter builds up its self-confident position. But whatever has been thus preserved is always deactivated. The melancholic modern cut introduces a third dimension, in which things that seem to be within our reach are, in fact, light years apart. All positive material, though available, is nothing more than a piled-up infinity of spectral (pre/ab) sence. Bringing it back to life seems an unachievable work which would demand disproportionate efforts, because all activities undertaken within this universe can never effectuate a real change.

Such a universe has no place for hope. But the need for hope persists, since the universe is perceived as the most extreme destitution that might have ever happened. It preserves something from the previous world: if these are not memories, which had already withered, *it is an overwhelming feeling of inappropriateness*, verging on some primordial injustice for which this universe stands wholly as one telling sign. Its poor homogeneity, coupled with its clearly marked boundaries, seem to refer to something, something impossible, because this universe is what it is, without any outside. It may find itself in utter destitution, but its state cannot be deemed final. On the contrary, in its entirety, it calls for a radical transformation. Unsurprisingly, as in Kant's metaphor, the philosophical universe expands to a gigantic size, which only astronomical imagery might be potent enough to grasp.

The Polar Star of spirit: Faith and exception

2.11 And with astronomical imagery, Hegel breaks the bleak scenery of destitute universe. The second sentence of the above cited fragment of the Inaugural Address introduces a new player. "Nur der *eine* Stern, der *innere Stern* des Geistes leuchtet; er ist der *Polarstern*," says Hegel with cold self-confidence. Creation in the Torah began with a dark ocean and spirit hovering above it.[29] But here, on the contrary, some world *came to an end* in the gloom of undifferentiated mass. Above these ruins there is a star, one and lonely star, the Pole Star of the spirit. It does not operate upon the ocean and does not penetrate it like the biblical spirit seemed to do. The Pole Star shines over the impoverished universe, but, paradoxically, does not seem to belong to it. Thus, it embodies the third dimension that has been introduced into the universe in the aftermath of the catastrophe.

If we read jointly Kant's fragment from 1788 and Hegel's from 1818, we will recognize the full scope of the catastrophe. Hegel's Address refers to only one star instead of Kant's "starry heavens." Kant highlighted the tension between two dimensions: the outside, symbolized by astronomical terms, and law. Both intersected and were cogged precisely in the place occupied by the modern subject, evoked by hopeless pseudo-philosophical pawns like "me" or "us." But in Hegel's imagery, there is no "me," to say nothing of "us." There is no tension between the "starry" outside and law. All that is left is a bleak ocean—which is either the universe itself or the destitute thinking, or rather both, perhaps—and the lonely star above. Instead of recalling Kant's two, interrelated, but separate dimensions of tension, Hegel reduces the scenery to one basic tension between the Pole Star and the pan-ocean, whose protean nature stands both for thinking and the universe. This tension, in all its apparent simplicity, embodies, as we will see, the basic machinery of modernity.

2.12 This universe, as we already remarked, is deprived of hope. But it has a sense of hopeless desperation, a need to escape or to find the way out, which is incarnated in *der Polarstern des Geistes*, "the Pole Star of spirit." Seen from the ocean, the star appears not as a symbol of hope, but as an untouchable and invulnerable *place*. The scale of the impoverishment in the universe fully corresponds to the heights which this star occupies. Both are at the extreme: the bleaker the ocean, the clearer and brighter the star. *Der Polarstern*, even though it somehow belongs to the universe, seems to be totally external. As a consequence, it embodies craving for a different universe, a need for radical change. In this universe, small changes are meaningless, since all small things have been engulfed by the catastrophe. Either everything is changed or nothing is changed. The very existence of the Pole Star seems to prove that there is something outside of the bleak ocean of reality.

This outside, epitomized by the *Polarstern*, is the focal point of the universe which exerts some eerie kind of gravity upon everything. All the bleakness of the destitute universe is directed to this immutable point. The reality from Hegel's parable is always internally imbalanced, dependent on a particular zone which attracts it, but, simultaneously, cannot be approached. *The Pole Star reigns over the universe in the full position of sovereignty, both belonging and transcending its domain.* Thus, it occupies a paradoxical place, within and outside, neither within nor outside; it is a Derridean supplement[30] to the universe, always too much and too little. Its quasi-presence destabilizes the whole reality. With its advent, no element of the universe might exist in tranquillity. Everything is always almost-full, everything seems to demand one more crucial element for its completeness.

This element, however, is not an actually lost thing. What appears as particular lack is here nothing more than a structural effect of the entire universe, whose nature might be imagined as the curved space-time of Einsteinian physics. The structure of the Hegelian universe precedes particular features of beings. Therefore, it seems that the apparent lack in beings might not be removed through individual, local changes, but only through a total act of transformation of the entire universe. In the language of Jewish theology, which so closely, and surprisingly, adheres to descriptions of modernity, it might be said that it is not by individual *tikkuns*, but only through the universal redemption that this "lack" could be erased.

Hegelian universe, in all its radicalism, outlines the grounds of messianism of modernity, whose incessant impulses lead this epochs to most magnificent and most appalling mobilizations.

2.13 The position of the Pole Star in this narrative clearly refers to Aristotle's concept of god, which Hegel painstakingly attempted to reread throughout his later philosophy.[31] Aristotelian deity notoriously returns in many pivotal places in Hegel's texts, from *Lectures on the History of Philosophy*, where the chapter on Aristotle obsessively revolves around god, up to *Encyclopedia*, whose last fragment is entirely built on a quote from book Λ of *Metaphysics* that concerns deity.

What made Hegel so focused on Aristotle's concept of god is its purely structural character. God is not a *demiourgos*, it is not a person, less even—will; it is not a primordial being, but a necessary element of the universe.[32] Aristotle, attempting to link deity with pure act, notoriously posed thought as god. It is but a very particular thought: a thought which thinks itself (ἡ νόησις νοήσεως νόησις).[33] Aristotelian god is immaterial and purely actual. In its perfect circularity and autarchy, it eschews reference to anything else. This self-thinking thought is a model for Hegel's Absolute.

There is, however, one crucial difference between Aristotle's god and Hegel's Absolute.[34] The self-thinking theorized in *Metaphysics* is an empty, self-referential point, which exists separately from all other beings.[35] Even though it constitutes their moving force, its influence does not undermine their real and independent existence. For this reason, Aristotle can take god as *his unproblematic object of thinking*, one of many, even if the most perfect. All beings might participate in god's perfection through contemplation, but they exist separately and take god as their lodestar.

Hegel's pivotal idea is also a self-thinking thought,[36] but contrary to Aristotelian calm "unmoved mover," it cannot be autarchically self-referential, because since the "critical breakthrough" of Kant, cognition and its object are inseparably entangled. When Aristotle thinks about the self-thinking thought, he is uncritical in Kantian sense, because he does not problematize his own position as a subject reflecting on an object. Obviously, he depicts the role of god as a yardstick of contemplation for all beings, but does not conceive of the framework which allows him to think about the relation between god and beings. Hegel, however, who brought the "critical breakthrough" to its ultimate consequences, can no longer think, as a neutral, self-effaced subject, about the relation between the self-thinking thought and other beings. *His* thought, the very one about this relation, must be also part of this relation. If we want to think about the thought, we are part of the process.

As a consequence, the self-thinking thought in Hegel's philosophy cannot be a separate point of the universe. This thought engulfs everything. Therefore, it takes the form of the Absolute, which is *the whole reality thinking itself*. Everything thinks everything, as a whole: this is the shortest formula of the absolute knowledge. Hegel takes the pure form of Aristotle's god and fills it up with all material content of reality. Therefore, god becomes Absolute, the all-encompassing whole which refers only to itself not because it is secluded in its purity and perfection, but because it has no outside. The absolute knowledge, if taken literally, is a placid tautology: everything is everything; but the key to Hegelian thought is understanding both its radical finality (there is nothing outside of everything) and richness (all material content must be imagined within the absolute knowledge, otherwise it will be empty and formal).

Aristotle imagined reality as revolving around the pure, self-referential point of deity. His universe does not change its basic structure, even though nearly all beings evolve. Hegel, on the contrary, assumes that reality progresses to see itself in its entirety and, in this way,—coincides with god, since there is nothing outside of it. Hegel's philosophy cannot settle for constructing a pure, empty self-thinking thought, but must sweep through the whole reality, all its domains and disciplines, and absorb its content. Therefore, Hegelian thought is inextricably intertwined with material content, from which Aristotle could abstract. But, whether it can truly stop in consuming reality is another matter and one of the greatest challenges for this philosophy.

The problems with closure stem from the fact that in Hegel's world no thought can be isolated. Nothing that exists or can be conceived of can ultimately stand on its own. Whoever claims the contrary, uses *Verstand*, particular and half-blind understanding, not *Vernunft*, the true reason. In truth, all that has ever existed, even in the weakest sense, already belongs to the Absolute. Philosophy is thus built on either/or: either you remain in a confined, delusory world of understanding, or you see everything in everything, the thought absorbs all reality, and you find the true, complete philosophy which coincides with the Absolute.

This seemingly paranoiac path traces, as we will see, the *nec plus ultra* of modernity. This era is systematically colonized by the virus of "either/or." In Hegel's view, either we do not accept the self-thinking thought as the Absolute, thus sticking to partial and illusory knowledge, or we assume its demands and start the journey in which the thought must conquer all that exists. In this journey of the Absolute, the Pole Star of spirit plays the key role.

2.14 Let us now turn back to the "ocean narrative" to look at why the Polar Star of spirit is an antidote to the pan-catastrophe. Hegel's journey starts with the recognition that our knowledge is partial, not because it only progresses on its way to completion, but because it is irreparably corrupt by its confined framework which limits the scope of what can be known. Consequently, Hegel's philosophy opens with the stunning realization that our knowledge, although adequate and useful to a certain extent, *is flawed at its core*. Once we discern the scope of error, we have only two paths. The first one is denial: we proceed as we used to, we amass yet next pieces of objectified knowledge, stick to seemingly immutable oppositions, over which we endlessly and repetitively muse.[37] This is the path of understanding, *Verstand*, which deludes itself that the old good world of knowledge still exists. But its edifice is rotten; its oppositions and constructions do not match the world as it is, but are built on some artificial assumptions which it must ignore.

The other path is much more radical. Its construction seems theological—and not (only) because Hegel was deeply indebted to theological ways of thinking, but because *modernity, whose knowledge he depicts, brings theological structures and history to the point of indifferentiation*. This path, the one of *Vernunft*, starts with pre-emptive rejection of all knowledge that we possess. Hegel, following in Descartes' footsteps,[38] repeats one of the most tempting and indispensable devices of modernity: the gesture of total suspension of reality which opens a way to reconstruction. Yet, whereas Cartesian skepticism was dressed up as a technical philosophical trick, Hegel's narrative is a poignant description of *the objective struggle of thought which gropes its way through its utter destitution*. It seems as if the speculative exercise from Descartes' *Meditations* turned here into a real nightmare: skepticism is no longer a gesture, but a real and ongoing collapse of the universe. Reality itself has been suspended and if we do not want to remain in delusion, we must assume the full scope of the catastrophe. Descartes' doubt was undoubtedly staged, in which his Catholic background played a crucial role. Hegel, however, perceives the suspension with full tremor of Lutheran disillusionment which smashes the whole subjectivity.

So, just as Luther gave up the whole world whose corruption seemed irreparable, so does Hegel's thought forgo all previous knowledge. What remains is our well-known "boundless ocean" with no friendly lights. Among this disillusionment, there is, however, one point of salvation. Lutheranism, with its omnipresent suspicion, had one solid foothold: faith.[39] Hegel, obviously having Protestant references in mind,[40] also pictures a foothold for thought: *der Polarstern des Geistes*. Among the ocean of suspended reality and knowledge there is one, inviolable Pole Star of spirit. What is it then?

2.15 Hegel's Pole Star is what remains after everything has fallen apart. The entire universe and all thought have been lost, but in the infinite empty space, there is still something, a singularity contrasting with the shapeless mass of matter symbolized by the "boundless ocean." This singularity comes from the Pole Star, which subsists among the catastrophe that ruined our world and knowledge. Its persisting presence reminds us that even after the catastrophe, after we have given up all the illusory knowledge, the universe remains excessive, unable to coincide with itself.

Unlike the Aristotelian universe, this one always remains in tension. Natural separation of things—their direct, tranquil existence—has been inexplicably ruined. The Pole Star does not appear as a lonely god, whom we admire, but who remains always distinct from us. The *Polarstern* exerts its constant influence and makes the universe need to break out of itself. *Hegelian universe struggles to pull out of itself and approach the outside which is embodied by the Pole Star.* The Pole Star, although it appears as the only stable point in this bleak universe, is, in fact, a radical factor of destabilization. Or, rather, its apparent stability is just an illusion created by the parallax view[41] which attracts the utterly destabilzed universe.

But the very same curse which made our knowledge incomplete and pushed us to the path of *Vernunft* returns now. We set out on our journey because our knowledge was rife with stiff oppositions, which did not stem from the world, but from the inner organization of knowledge. We suspended them, but all we got is a mass of undifferentiated matter with one power of externality, epitomized by the Polar Star which hovers above contentless universe. The curse has not been overcome, but refined to a crystal-clear opposition between "uferloser Ozean" and "der Polarstern." Thus, the total suspension revealed the most basic grid of differentiation, which is apparently mutable and might swiftly transform itself from one constellation into another. Its influence made us believe that the gesture of total suspension will remove the flaws, but, in fact, it only pushed us to do its job. Through burning down our knowledge, we have accomplished the seemingly last path of the basic difference which has set itself against the whole universe that it had previously deserted. What we were trying to escape from and what apparently pushed us onwards coincide in the Pole Star. We helped it on its way towards impoverishment.

2.16 The universe of the "boundless ocean" seems profoundly inhuman. Everything that made the previous world friendly to sensitive beings is now deposited—as dead capital of differences—within the undifferentiated mass. We might ask, then: is there anything alive in this universe? And, even more importantly, where is the one that thinks about it?

To answer this question, one has to notice that Hegel accomplishes the Kantian anthropology of the split subject.[42] Kant's distinction between the outside and law (→ 1.2) already cut through premodern human being, severing the causal part from the one based upon freedom. Hegel, however, depicts reality with an image of the bleak ocean irreparably split from the Pole Star. In this universe of *tertium non datur*, there seems to be no place for subject, even constituted by an internal rift.

In the universe where the basic difference celebrates its triumph, there can be only one cut: *and this cut absorbs even the rift of the split subject.* The seemingly infinite distance between the universe and the Pole Star is thus structurally the same one that constituted Kant's subject, but now it has a more radical, refined meaning. The ocean (which corresponds to Kant's outside) encompasses all material differences of the world, including beliefs, emotions, knowledge, sense, hopes, and everything that makes the world worth continuation. In fact, the ocean engulfs almost everything from the former human being, who, as in Luther's apocalyptic vision, is nearly entirely ensnared in the realm of matter.[43] Hegel's ocean inherits Luther's view on the world as the domain of Satan; but this time there is no personal evil, only the inert mass of ruins. The subject belongs to it almost completely. The world lost its sense for the subject and the subject—for the world. But as long as the Pole Star of spirit rises over this drab universe, there is still a foothold in subject. It is, however, totally impersonal; it belongs to the subject as little as to all other former beings.

Therefore, the thinking subject fully coincides with the world it reflects upon. The difference which separates this world from the subject is as inconsequential as all inoperative differences piled up in the mass of the universe. The playground of thought has been utterly reduced. Only the universe and the Pole Star remain the elements in play, so if there is any exit, it is through their interaction, in which the fate of objects, subjects and everything that is between them, coincides.

For the universe, the Pole Star is the *place* of the outside. For the subject, and in the subject, it is the place of the only solid foothold which might save it from despair and doubt. What is then *der Polarstern*?

2.17 *The Pole Star is self-confidence of spirit which knows that it cannot be lost, whatever happens to everything outside of it.* When reality collapsed, this was the lowest possible point which the catastrophe might have reached, but which it could not overcome. It is the point which resists all doubts, the one which remains unassailable among the collapsing world.

The Pole Star is the core point of the spirit. It is the first manifestation of the spirit, the one whose emergence already brings the spirit into existence and makes it unassailable. Once it appears, it seems to have existed forever and will exist forever. This is a brief definition of spirit from *Phänomenologie des Geistes*, with a short supplement:

> Die Vernunft ist Geist, indem die Gewißheit, alle Realität zu sein, zur Wahrheit erhoben, und sie sich ihrer selbst als ihrer Welt und der Welt als ihrer selbst bewußt ist.
>
> ... Das *an-* und *fürsichseiende* Wesen aber, welches sich zugleich als Bewußtsein wirklich und sich sich selbst vorstellt, ist *der Geist*.[44]

> Reason is spirit, when its certainty of being all reality has been raised to the level of truth, and reason is consciously aware of itself as its own world, and of the world as itself.
>
> ... The *in-* and *for itself existing* essence, however, which at once presents itself as actual consciousness and presents itself to itself, is *the Spirit*.[45]

The spirit arises from reason as a result of an *event*. Contrary to what might appear at first glance, the spirit is not simply reason plus the certainty of its being the whole reality. The spirit appears only when this claim is elevated to the rank of truth—and this is an act. As soon as this thought is accepted as truth—just like the thought about the eternal recurrence in Nietzsche's narrative from *The Gay Science*,[46] Fichte's self-grounded decision to follow the path of freedom which builds the only certain knowledge[47] or Lacan's presumption that psychoanalysis does not look for, but finds its object in advance[48]—it transforms the very framework within which it was conceived. Such an acceptance is nothing less than decision, a traumatic volitional cut,[49] such as the "decision to philosophize" which we previously traced to the origins of catastrophe from Hegel's "ocean narrative."

Once again, this mysterious act of impersonal decision—so often referred to in modern philosophy—brings a radical and irrevocable transformation. The act turns reason into spirit—as soon as the certainty that it is the whole reality becomes a truth. This claim repeats the gesture of Aristotle's god: it grasps itself, yet this time, unlike in *Metaphysics*, god is not a perfect being separate from the world, but it grasps reality *as* itself. In Hegel's radically desecrated world, god is no being. If modern thought is allowed to speak about god—and not as a religious delusion—then *god can be nothing more than the self-referential loop entering the reality*.

In fact, this is the utter consequence of secularity: if there is no transcendence within reality, reality almost perfectly coincides with the divine. The "almost perfectly" stands for a little fold, which gets removed once reason finds its certainty and turns into reason. From that moment on, reality is reality: this utmost banality becomes coextensive with the deepest philosophical truth. Nothing is truly transcendent, nothing is ineffable or ungraspable; the reason can recognize itself in everything, because it has decided to.

The thought about radical secularity and the certainty that it brings provide a foothold to reconstruct the damaged reality. Self-confidence becomes the sweetest promise and the sweetest trap: all that is opposed to the spirit, in truth belongs to it. There is no fundamental strangeness which could not be overcome. The Pole Star appears over the bleakest ocean as soon as this certainty becomes truth.

Once the spirit grasps its coincidence with reality, this coincidence is already granted; it only takes time to fill out such coextensiveness with material content. But this apparent universal rule of reason, the conquest of the universe by the spirit, is not as universal as it might appear. At the origin of its power lays an event, an act, a decision, whose very possibility is incarnated in the Pole Star. How come that all universality rests upon a tautological contentless decision to be universal? Why is universality founded by a radical exception? Modern sovereignty, in which universality is always founded upon exception, is the answer: the Polar Star embodies nothing else.

Modern sovereignty

3. Hegel's "ocean narrative" captures the structure of modern sovereignty which by far exceeds any formal relations of power. Its natural link with state power only obfuscates the fact that sovereignty, conceived of as general structure and not as an attribute of a political entity, is virtually omnipresent. It founds modern knowledge and science, provides a propulsion for the dynamics of capitalism and, last but not least, constructs

modern subjectivity. In all these areas the same structure multiplies itself and embeds one of its forms in others. Modernity is *the* epoch of sovereignty, an era built upon interactions between its different incarnations.

It is therefore crucial not to read the ocean narrative as a singular invention of *a* philosopher: that is tantamount to the highest form of idealism. Hegel wants to reconstitute philosophy not after deleting it himself, as Rebecca Comay and Frank Ruda noticed,[50] but after completing the process of destruction that philosophy was objectively pulled into. In doing this, he impersonates sovereignty acting upon philosophy.

What then is the structure of sovereignty? Drawing upon Hegel's Inaugural Address, we can outline the first approach to its nature. *Modern sovereignty consists in relation between a non-Whole and a remainder.* The non-Whole is an entire universe, seemingly all-encompassing, but with one point of curiosity that spoils its perfection.[51] This point, seen from the inside, appears as purely formal excess that belongs to this very universe. Taken in itself, however, the point unfurls into a fully fledged inconsumable remainder, whose (ex/res)istance supports the apparent universality of the non-Whole. This remainder epitomizes the impossible outside. If there were any "real" outside, the remainder would be just a point of inscription in it—namely, a point, in which a seemingly universal world appears as a part of a higher order. The remainder stands for the place in which the purportedly universal is confined. of this confinement. It appears as the origin and the objective of this universe, as its source and inner goal.

As we will see in Chapter 3, modern sovereignty accounts for the construction of time and history. Just as the world that it creates appears universal, so does its time purport to contain and organize all events in one, universal history. This history, however, is, in fact, dependent on the previous confinement, epitomized by the tiny remainder. Historical time that we know is dependent on a point of curiosity whose existence has, once and forever, conditioned our time. Analogously to Badiou's event,[52] it occupies a borderline position: it appears as a normal event within our time, but, in truth, it conditions it wholly and thus seems to be a unit of some higher order.

Thus, modern sovereignty is a construct of radical dependence within the universe that rests upon, to recall Kant's idea, infinity of infinities. *Sovereignty separates and links an infinity taken as a unit with the higher order to which it belongs.* It is structurally located in a certain point of predetermination, from which it exerts unchallenged supremacy over a particular universe. It intermingles universality and particularity—embeds the latter in the former, thereby producing unprecedented structural effects reflected in all domains of reality.[53]

In the universe that it creates, it becomes a total and unsurpassable source of indebtedness. For this reason, sovereignty is accountable for specifically modern impoverishment, which stems from the omnipresent, structural predetermination of each universe within the modern era. Modern sovereignty is the reign of the recurring curse, of poverty which we struggle to overcome but only approach its end. Its name seals the epoch in which poverty, power, and messianism find their confluence in the point of indifferentiation.

2.18 The Polar Star of spirit appears to be opposed to the destitute universe because it took the power over it. *Der Polarstern* stands for this sovereign self-confidence and self-certainty which, once conceived, reshape all coordinates and irreparably cut the past off. Objectively, this new power has no ground, let alone a justification. But its self-referential structure creates ground and justification out of nothing. The past, which could provide a background against which this gesture would appear as unfounded, is transformed by the very appearance of sovereignty. All objectivity warps in contact with it. Everything which survives its emergence is already indebted, so indebted and feeble that sovereignty in its reign finds no peer.

Hegel's "ocean narrative" provides a poignant description of this new construction of reality. Against the sovereign Polar Star, we see only the bleakest and senseless mass of the ocean, whose passive and morbid half-dead existence contrasts sharply with the activity and unassailability of its star. We know nothing about the numb ocean; we do not know why it emerged and whether it had to emerge. Finally, we know very little about the origin of this reality. The only scrap of information that we have—namely, that this world appeared as a result of a catastrophe triggered off by a decision—actually coincides with the very notion of sovereignty. The little of knowledge we have may be summarized as follows: what exists, exists as a result of decision, which ruined the framework within which it was taken and constitutes the only passage to a new reality. This passage determines the history of the world it creates. For this reason, if we simply follow the history back to its origin, we find nothing more than a blind spot.

The seemingly unphilosophical tendency of Hegel to resort to rich metaphors—like the "Polar Star of spirit"—instead of conceptual work is, in fact, the only possible way to grasp the reality warped by the emergence of sovereignty. Ultimately, we have to confront the bare self-referential decision whose construction is so powerful that little of our ancient philosophical arsenal remains useful. The epoch in which this sovereignty finds its triumph, modernity, demands new intellectual tools, or rather paths,[54] since tools are hardly imaginable in the world without stable repetition. Thinking must resort to half-imaginary, half-conceptual mode of development, in which piled-up floes of thought must be cut through with extraconceptual linkage. The "ocean narrative" clearly draws a line for thought, determining where and how it might proceed. And sometimes it lifts the thought up and makes it overcome an obstacle which is foreign to its nature.

2.19 The Pole Star exemplifies the structure of modern sovereignty which, as such, *is given in advance*. It is in this sense that we should understand Adorno's and Horkheimer's famous claim that what they call the Enlightenment is totalitarian insofar not as it uses the analytical method, but "in its assumption that the trial is prejudged."[55] Modernity always forestalls our actions, playing a game whose result is already prejudged. Once we start the path of *Vernunft*, of reason, we immediately encounter and reveal the universe marked by sovereignty. Whenever we clear our flawed knowledge up in order to build it anew, we just expose the structure of sovereignty. Knowledge is imperfect due to its black sun; but by purifying it we only drift towards it. The characteristically modern tendency to simplification—tendency so rife in art and thinking of modernity[56]—is thus dependent on the predetermination of sovereignty.

But what is thought supposed to do once this basic structure of sovereignty is exposed? Thought is torn between the two poles: the senseless ocean, which is a great mass of inoperative differences—and the Pole Star, the shining self-confident star of sovereignty. Therefore, thought can either remain in the realm of the ocean and become a melancholic antiquarian of the past (or establish itself as a staunch partisan of ossified oppositions) or it can assume the position of sovereignty and find itself at home. This home is artificial, just as all sovereignty is. It is nothing but pure decision which takes the world in its grip and retroactively erases its own emergence in order to appear as an atemporal source of power.

Both solutions are desperate. The first one is bleak, subjugated skepticism. The second one, as we will soon see with particular reference to Hegel, is a self-constructed trap, as bitterly victorious as empty. But what is the most curious is the fact that *no choice made before sovereignty can turn into rejection of sovereignty*. Neither of the two options undermines its structure; on the contrary, they are fully determined by it.

What is even more stunning is that it is undecidable whether the structure of sovereignty "truly" existed before our move of reason or whether it was created by this move. Since sovereignty produces its past retroactively,[57] there is no objective point of reference which would provide us with a foothold to find the source of sovereignty. Its power always-already-exists once it is spotted, but if we spot it, we have already performed a gesture of sovereignty and established it retroactively.

In and around sovereignty, the concepts of continuity, discontinuity, and repetition lose sense and enter a zone of indifferentiation. It is for this reason that Kafka's parable *Before the Law*[58] conjures up an image of a gate which exists uniquely for the one that stands before it, whereas, in fact, structurally the very same gate closes the dead end of every modern path of thought.

Sovereignty: The most tempting of possibilities

4. Sovereignty is, first of all, a possibility. But it is a possibility of a special kind: neither a scenario which might or might not happen, nor an option which might or might not be chosen. It is more of a *Wirkungsmöglichkeit*, a working (meta-)possibility which exerts its influence on the very framework of what is possible and what is not. It transcends the framework in which it is put as one of the options. It reveals itself as some basic predetermination which is always already there, but simultaneously contracts itself into one of the seemingly equal options. Once chosen, it practically coincides with necessity, having been, retroactively, nothing more than the ineluctable self-choice.

This unique quality of *après-coup*-necessary-possibility marks the functioning of sovereignty. As a result, sovereignty is never truly absent; it always lurks in the background as a possibility. But, on the other hand, it is never fully present—it might not be fully achieved, since it is never just a complete, self-referential necessity. It preserves an element of potentiality, which, from an external point of view, appears as the possibility of choosing the path of sovereignty actively.

Consequently, even if sovereignty appears as an idea of tranquil self-grasp, whose self-grounded certainty takes the power over the world, it creates this illusion only at a distance, just like Hegel's Pole Star. In this position it exerts its influence, which, for all intents and purposes, coincides with theological idea of temptation. This temptation is nothing more than the transcending, centrifugal force of sovereignty, which, seen from the inside, makes it always incomplete. The very same force which accounts for the external power of sovereignty is an inner factor of destabilization. The path of sovereignty, once "chosen" (in the above mentioned sense), can never be finished.

It does not mean that this temptation cannot be resisted. Resistance is its inner possibility, dovetailed in advance into the emanating power of sovereignty. As Hegel and Foucault demonstrated,[59] all resistance is marked by what it resists. But, in the case of sovereignty, this remark is not enough. *All resistance against sovereignty draws its power from sovereignty itself*, even though it is perceived as something external. Consequently, sovereignty operates through constant displacement of the very same power which predetermines positions before it. In a strict sense, there is no place of sovereignty which would not be an illusion; but this constant displacement and indebtedness is its specificity. It is a highly negative power built on resistance[60] which, therefore, absorbs resistance into itself.

For this reason, sovereignty, in the broader sense, should not be conceived of as something which can be possessed, let alone possessed by someone; neither is it an occupiable place. Perhaps sovereignty should be approached through the image of a curve, which destabilizes all frameworks through which it passes and, more importantly, destabilizes itself into the bargain. It is a curve which traces a downward trajectory towards a fantasmatic total self-grasp. Whatever approaches this curve, finds itself sucked into the incessant move towards imaginary sovereignty. Not through some external influence, but through internal recomposition of the very being or thought, which suddenly finds this move at its core and cannot resist self-grounding.

In this sense, modern sovereignty is an eerie counterpart to Aristotle's *entelechia*: whereas *entelechia* is an inner movement-at-work of beings towards their perfection,[61] sovereignty is what pushes them to their self-grasp and self-certainty. The concept of *entelechia* is based on a phantasmatic vision of a harmonious universe in which the very same drive to perfection might be found in different beings and extracted as a philosophical idea. Modern sovereignty, however, is *a correlate of a shattered universe ruled by the basic, contentless difference*. Every piece of the universe is lured into assuming this difference as its own unique distinction opposable to all other pieces: and this lure is sovereignty. No overall harmony is to be found in this world; its central driving force pushes all its parts into utter singularity. Their relations become contentless, purely structural, and thus political. Nevertheless, this singularity of beings is materially impoverished: the universe ruled by sovereignty is not internally rich through diversity of its parts, but remains conspicuously poor, since it builds itself on repetition of the same contentless difference.[62] Therefore, sovereignty is always split between almost-identity and repetition, ostensible richness, and effective destitution.

It is not enough, however, to demonstrate, with a Derridean gesture, this inner inconsistency of sovereignty which makes all attempts of self-grasp impossible. The centrifugal force of sovereignty parasites on its outside, namely on the material content of the universe. It can never set itself free of it, but neither can it conquer it exhaustively.

Through demonstrating its inconsistence, we only spread its force towards new differences; we continue its work.

2.20 Modern thought can either succumb to sovereignty and accept the reign of an empty place which exerts its power over the entire universe—or it can attack this place and attempt to stand in the place of sovereignty proper.

Both options were outlined shortly after the dawn of modernity: Kant presented an exemplary form of the first approach, Hegel of the second. The years that passed between the publication of *The Critique of Pure Reason* and *The Phenomenology of Spirit* enclose the most basic cycle of modernity and set the thought free for eternal (ir) repetition. In Kant's thought, sovereignty is actually located in the unassailable shrine of *noumen*, which predetermines the universe, but can be actually accessed only through ethical self-legislation.[63] Hegel, in turn, holds the reserve to access the place of sovereignty for a grave philosophical error, the last frontier at which Kantian reason surrendered. In Hegel's view, philosophy must elevate thought to the place of sovereignty, so that it can conquer the universe.

This tension between Kant and Hegel, explored and trivialized to nausea, concerns, in fact, the decision taken before sovereignty. Thought, as we said, has two options: either to circumvent the black sun of sovereignty, thus remaining eternally dependent on its power, or to attack this place and take the universe as itself. In both cases, the result seems to stem from the pre-emptive decision. In a conflationist manner, one could even say that *the effect of sovereignty ultimately coincides with the decision which is taken before it.*

This trap for modern thought—the trap which is explored, circumvented or covered up with philosophical tricks for at least two centuries—stems from the structure of sovereignty, which is at work already when sovereignty appears within the framework of choice. Thus, with the advent of the retroactive power of sovereignty, all our history is gone.

From premodern transcendence to modern sovereignty

5.1 It is a common philosophical idea to conceive of modernity as an epoch in which transcendence fades or even disappears. Topoi of secularization, "death of God," the loss of "metaphysical hearing" are frequently used to refer to the specificity of modernity. But the disappearance of transcendence would be a fairly superficial observation if it were not framed within a broader picture. What is pivotal in this feature of modernity is not necessarily the loss of transcendence as a source of sense, moral injunctions or afterlife rewards, but rather *the structural displacement of transcendence.*

If transcendence is understood as the stable outside of the world, it requires premodern epistemology, in which two spheres of being coexist and might be referred to unproblematically. The separation of beings—their natural, independent existence—must precede any epistemological reflection. Consequently, transcendence necessarily falls into what Heidegger described as "ontotheology,"[64] a particular node of being and divinity.[65] It produces a naturalized, "calm existence" (to borrow Hegel's term)—namely, an existence based on natural separation from the world. Calmly existing transcendence has a natural and describable border with the world.

Modernity does not undermine this transcendence in itself. It simply rules out its epistemological foundation. The critical breakthrough of Kant posits each being in a constitutively epistemological relation: either it is conditioned by our cognition, or it extends beyond our cognition and becomes inaccessible. As a result, transcendence can no longer exist just as *the* other side of our world (whose position is so well captured by the German word "Jenseits"). Instead of two parallel worlds—ours and transcendent—modernity inaugurates one all-encompassing dynamic reality which has no true outside. As soon as this imaginary calm outside disappears, reality acquires paradoxical nature: it cannot have borders, since a border is what separates one space from another. But how could it be one if it has no borders? The united reality cannot be a tranquil totality. It pulses with incessant throb through which it demarcates and reabsorbs its outside, thereby constantly reassuring itself as a whole.

This transformation is not, as Quentin Meillassoux argued in his splendid book, a mere result of Kant's choice of "correlationism."[66] It is truly a confinement, Meillassoux' *Grand Dehors* (and also "*dehors claustral*").[67] The scope of the cut that separates us from premodern transcendence is of epochal nature; it is not a one-off philosophical mistake. Like the Big Bang, it is recognizable in our temporality and ubiquitous devices of sovereignty. Its ruling is far too immense to be crossed out with a single gesture of return. Transcendence disappears in reality, not just in philosophy.

Now that the possibility of calm transcendence vanishes, all that exists belongs to one reality. For this reason, Hegel's ocean is "boundless" (*uferlos*): it absorbed everything that had been outside of it. Such a reality, however, cannot be stable. It is as if *transcendence transformed itself into a dynamic remainder which ravages reality from within*. Transmogrified transcendence is no longer locked away in a designated place, but becomes a polymorphic excessive supplement which travels from one area to another and destabilizes all wholes, ones, relations, and beings.[68]

Consequently, it is not enough to claim that modernity "abolishes" transcendence. This is only a ripple on the surface of reality, nothing but a conspicuous effect of much deeper covert transformation. The very construction of reality changes, thereby excluding the previous place of transcendence, which, however, finds a new incarnation within reality. What in premodern thought was God, a firm and stable supreme being, now becomes a point of curiosity within the destabilized reality. It is a point that reappears in various areas, exerting constant und unabated power on everything that exists. Thus, it turns former beings into internally cracked things.

Therefore, with the advent of modernity the structure of transcendence is superseded by the structure of sovereignty. In this sense, sovereignty is transcendence that has been thrown into reality after its calm and demarcatable borders had dissolved. Consequently, *sovereignty is transcendence which changes its vector and no longer leads outside, but reflects all references back to the universe over which it reigns*.[69]

2.21 The Pole Star from Hegel's "ocean narrative" embodies this transmogrified transcendence, which has become an elusive place of sovereignty. Sovereign self-certainty is the new transcendence which appears as a mode to be followed and as a place to be occupied. Hegel grasped modern sovereignty because his philosophy chose its path.

Once this choice happens, it immediately makes the strangeness of the entire world deflate. The world is, fundamentally and in advance, conquered. Here, in this gesture of Hegel, we encounter another characteristic of modern sovereignty, which, parenthetically, is so well discernible in politics: a sovereign act never conquers its field fully and immediately, but first it makes it dependent on itself and thus thrusts it into a new time. This field might be still autonomous; it might still develop according to its own rules. But its structure has been irrevocably displaced and this development is in the ultimate instance conditioned by the sovereign center. The sovereign act, the act in which sovereignty takes power over a given field, has therefore a *structure of proclamation*, in which the general victory is declared, the cause is guaranteed, whilst the full subjugation of the field to the sovereign power is only a matter of time, of a new time which commences with the advent of sovereign power.

Proclamation and self-certainty: Taking the sovereign place

6. In the early hours of 7 November 1917, the future Great October Revolution looked more like a local Bolshevik insurrection in Petrograd, supported irregularly by Bolshevik adherents throughout Russia. The prosaic onset of the revolution, which had to be hastily mythologized in order to repress the oddly material and senseless sources of sovereign power, consisted in physical occupation of key parts of the city and some important buildings. Kerensky, the head of the Provisional Government, famously had to borrow a Renault from the American Embassy in order to summon soldiers supporting the old power. After his departure, even before the Winter Palace was captured, Lenin had issued the famed proclamation, "To the Citizens of Russia":

> The Provisional Government has been deposed. State power has passed into the hands of the organ of the Petrograd Soviet of Workers' and Soldiers' Deputies—the Revolutionary Military Committee, which heads the Petrograd proletariat and the garrison.
>
> The cause for which the people have fought, namely, the immediate offer of a democratic peace, the abolition of landed proprietorship, workers' control over production, and the establishment of Soviet power—this cause has been secured.
>
> Long live the revolution of workers, soldiers and peasants!
> Revolutionary Military Committee of the Petrograd
> Soviet of Workers' and Soldiers' Deputies
> 10 a.m., October 25, 1917.[70]

If present perfect is of any political use, it is this one: something has happened and it is irreversible. Even though the budding Bolshevik power was more than frail and this proclamation might as well have been ridiculed by the subsequent defeat of the Communist forces, Lenin wrote about an event that had happened and, whatever the future history would be, would not have been erased.

In this, it belonged to a higher order in time. It was a Badiouian intersection of the usual history (capture of buildings, streets, blockades of railways on 25 October 1917 Old Style) and the time of symbolic changes: the decisive point.[71] Whatever was to happen later, had been conditioned by the primordial victory of the revolution.

Lenin's proclamation embodies the act of sovereignty. Its pre-emptive conquer takes the field in advance, regardless of whether the earthly sovereign power truly controls the field it usurps to control. The struggle to gain real power over the field is a new epoch, which, at its core, presents itself as a contest accessory to the scope of the initial sovereign victory. From the point of view of sovereign power, no future events might detract from its victory because it belongs to a different order. Apparently, a new time begins, a time which intruded into history, rewrote it and will have no end. Lenin's words, "the cause has been secured," written at the moment when nothing yet could be guaranteed and all hopes might have been dashed, should be taken as an emblem of sovereignty. Because only one cause has been truly secured: the cause of sovereignty.

2.22 Hegel's idea of philosophy was to draw ultimate consequences from the destitution of the universe, over which the Pole Star of new transcendence shines. Philosophy should attack the place of the star and gain sovereignty over the universe.

Prima facie, this act seems usurpatory, if not preposterous, but in fact it is sober and logical. It stems from the feeling of utter impoverishment and loneliness. The universe became an area drained of transcendence, sense and privileged places. With the advent of modernity, we are alone in the world and must rely only on ourselves. This is the self-certainty of spirit: *there is nothing more beyond ourselves*. Just like Nietzsche's thought of eternal return, it is a thought that both wrecks all our hopes and gives us a boost to become masters of ourselves. This trap is a trap of sovereignty: we are thrown into its condition and must choose between desolation and self-redemption. Utter impoverishment reaches a point of indifferentiation with salvation—a point at which bare decision changes the vector between resignation and unshakable faith.

In the world without external transcendence the thought about the utter finitude acts as internal transcendence.[72] It throws the universe into radical tension: either the thought is avoided—and thus creates the distanced reign of sovereignty over the field of the repressed—or it is assumed and opens the spiral of self-enclosing sovereign path. Thus, Hegel's Pole Star is the star of ultimate finitude and loneliness which reflects the destitute universe back to itself. The ocean in Hegel's parable is the realm of dependence on the extinct transcendence, which now turned into a place of sovereignty. Whatever remains in this ocean is riveted to its past and thus subjugated to the very real and current sovereign power. Whatever finds itself in the place of the Pole Star, takes radical finitude for the source of its reign.

Hegel's project for philosophy is to turn the total destitution, and the ecstatic thought of finitude, into the foundation of new knowledge. If there is no transcendence—if knowledge fully belongs to the world that it concerns and this world fully belongs to the knowledge that it produces—then there are no substantial boundaries for cognition. The self-certainty of radical finitude gives philosophy the power to issue its proclamation:

Nur der *eine* Stern, der *innere Stern* des Geistes leuchtet; er ist der *Polarstern*.[73]

2.23 Smashed by Hegel's boldness, philosophical Kerensky ran away, but the whole new reign of philosophy is yet to be conquered. Let's return to one fragment of the *Konzept der Rede*:

> But it is natural that the spirit in its solitude with itself is seized with horror; one does not know yet where it's going, where one is heading. Among what has disappeared is much of what one would not give up at any price, and in this loneliness it has not yet restored, and one is uncertain whether it will find itself again or will be given back.

True, the world belongs to the spirit now, but everything must have been given up in order to reach this stage. The field which was gained is in ruins. Was it worth it? Will the world be restituted? Can the self-certainty restore all the material content of the previous world? To put this question in more precise terms: can philosophy, once it has entered the path of sovereignty, regain what was lost with the advent of modernity?

Such a doubt is not particular to philosophy: perhaps all sovereignty is gnawed by uncertainty. Since sovereignty is based on nothing more than its own decision, doubt gains the rank of the primary, if not the only one threat. The concern to fend off uncertainty produces powerful forces of resistance which contribute to this specific flavor of sovereign power which manifests itself in obsessions, overreactions and displacement of real targets that this power fights. Sovereignty, once conquered, creates a different world and a different time, and, in this sense, *cannot ever be lost*. "The cause has been secured" and no material adversities could threaten it. But, if there is anything that can undermine the victory, it is the very winner: whatever occupied the sovereign place must struggle with its centrifugal tendencies that aim to expel it from the center it attempts to occupy. Both sovereign power and thought, which, like Hegel's, attacks the Pole Star, position themselves in a virtually inexistent place, a place which is torn apart by its very construction. The most external coincides here with the most internal: attempting to occupy the place of sovereignty means to push towards an unachievable goal as well as towards one's most inner core, which are both an effect of parallax view. Sovereignty as such cannot lose or disappear; but whatever or whoever attempts to exert it, spirals into the fury of self-preservation.

Hegel's thought takes this path. It confronts material questions, stumbles upon them, sinks into doubt, but finally overcomes the obstacles and, with this act, subjugates its "positive material." In the very same manner, the philosopher dragged himself out of profound depression in Jena;[74] writing *Phenomenology of Spirit* was like following a ray of hope on the ocean of helplessness. Hegel's students noted[75] that during his lectures he used to attack new problem, lower his head, clear his throat, mumble, grapple with the riddle, go around in circles, only to finally lift his head up and pronounce *the* solution with self-confidence.[76] In this sense, we can say that sovereign power, or sovereign thought, develops itself in the continuous rhythm of self-abandonment and subsequent self-salvation. The structure of repetition, which incessantly recreates the initial act of conquering the place of sovereignty, marks everything which attempts to occupy this place.

Modernity's inner messianism: Reconstructing the universe

2.24 We remarked that with the advent of modernity all previous differences were put out of joint, lost their tranquil being and were reduced to a dead mass of "positive material." Hegel's philosophy uses the modern structure of sovereignty in order to breathe new life into this material, to recreate it on the basis of self-certain thought.

It is pivotal not to interpret this gesture as a personal stratagem of one German philosopher. On the contrary, it is a mighty new structure at work. It has the power of reviving the previous world (Hegel uses the word *wiederherstellen*, literally "re-produce")—the power that from the premodern point of view is just uncanny. This feature is not (just) a trait of aberrant idealism which paranoically usurps all creative power for thought. The German Idealism was the first current of philosophy which used this structure exhaustively, but the structure is much broader and far-reaching: it is the construction of modern sovereignty. Its existence first inactivates the existing world, pierces it through with a radically new dimension and makes it dependent on what appears as a pure, senseless decision.

In philosophy, this struggle culminates in Hegel's thinking, in which thought first purifies itself, discards all its intuitions, imaginations and comfortable truths in order to fight, in total loneliness, against the whole richness of the world it had previously extinguished. It has nothing left to lose: it may only push forward.

5.2 Modernity should not be considered, like it sometimes is, as an epoch in which metaphysics fell apart. Metaphysics exists and will never be eliminated by modernity. The specificity of the latter lies not in elimination of the past, but in its *reflexive deactivation*. As a consequence, metaphysics did not disappear, but was turned into content, displaced and played upon by modern grid of forces governed by sovereignty. In this sense, metaphysics exists, but became indiscernibly indifferent, which is a state much more complicated than mere inexistence or invalidity.

2.25 The final passage of the Inaugural Address opens as follows:

> As far as the *content* is concerned, that—that which is intelligible—is especially not present in the beginning; the feeling, the imagination have their *strong footholds directly ahead of them*; *faith, this natural certainty*, is satisfied with immediacy. But the *thinking that begins from itself* recognises *the same answers only in* [its/their] *developing necessity*, and it would only be *impatience that does not befit the thing*, [impatience] which *wants to answer its questions right at the beginning*, to want *to be at home already at the start*.
>
> Was den *Inhalt* betrifft, so ist jenes, das Verständlichsein, zunächst im Anfang allerdings nicht vorhanden; das Gefühl, die Vorstellung haben ihre *festen Haltungspunkte unmittelbar vor sich*, *der Glaube, diese natürliche* Gewißheit, ist mit der Unmittelbarkeit befriedigt. Aber das *Denken, das von sich ausgeht*, erkennt dieselben Antworten nur in ihrer *sich entwickelnden Notwendigkeit*, und es würde

nur *eine der Sache nicht gemäße Ungeduld* sein, die *ihre Fragen gleich im Anfang beantwortet, gleich anfangs zu Hause sein* wollte.[77]

Let us begin disentangling this dense fragment by first noticing that thought, having conquered the place of sovereignty, is deprived of understanding. There is nothing more senseless and less understandable than what is truly sovereign. It is not that what attempts to occupy the place of sovereignty is senseless in itself; on the contrary, *it is the very place that eludes all sense and understanding*. It cuts through all the symbolic universe but remains unassailable for its attacks.

Thought which locates itself in this place has therefore no material content: it has only its self-certainty and its movement. In a radically modern way, it dissolves thought from its material content. Thought becomes actually nothing more than pure power, a political device, indifferentiatable from conventional political power. The locus of sovereignty is a threshold of indifferentiation, in which the distinction between power and thought loses sense.

Confronted with all the world of inoperative material differences, the thought can rely only on itself: it must restore this world on its own conditions. But what it adds to the inert mass of positive material is not any new content, any new interpretation or explanation. It adds just the mere structure of sovereignty that plays out dead differences. The innovation of Hegel's philosophy is thought which does not bring new understanding to the previously inactivated world, but, on the contrary, *establishes its sovereign position, a position fundamentally deprived of understanding*.

This is the particular form of salvation in the modern universe, in which all creation that now lays bare and senseless covets proper explanation. Precisely this need is accountable for its eternal dependence and inertia. Modern world does not need understanding; on the contrary, it requires to have its understanding subtracted. And this is exactly what the place of sovereignty offers: a structure which makes all understanding dependent on an unbearably senseless decision. Modern understanding can function only if it is pegged upon a place of sovereignty which resists all understanding.

The above cited fragment of the Inaugural Address contrasts imagination (*Vorstellung*) and thinking (*Denken*). In the context of Hegel's thought, it clearly refers to the difference between religion—which generally grasps rightly the essence of things, but not directly and with the help of mediating images—and philosophy, which accomplishes religion through direct and conscious reference to the spirit.[78] But, apart from this particular context, the opposition of *Vorstellung* and *Denken* describes two possible approaches to the Pole Star of sovereignty which were mentioned earlier. Whereas *Vorstellung* clings to what it sees as external to itself, *Denken* redevelops the universe on the basis of itself. These two positions, into which the universe is split by sovereignty, may be associated with dependence and hegemony respectively. Hegel's philosophy chooses the path of hegemony structurally coincides with the hegemony of political sovereign.

2.26 Once thought occupies the place of sovereignty, it is apparently only a matter of time when it completes its work by subjugating all material differences, one by one, to its power. The task is, in fact, endless, as endless is the new time it has opened. From the perspective of the recently conquered place of sovereignty total and detailed hegemony seems to be a task which requires only a particular period of time. But, in truth, it can never end. It is for this reason that Hegel's philosophy is condemned to incessant engulfing new material, even though "its cause has been secured." This philosophy is unable to recognize its stalemate. Within the framework of sovereignty, its permanent impasse is viewed just as a temporary glitch. Accordingly, each sovereign is cumbersome, afflicted by its own structural imperfection, to which it cannot respond.

The Address ends with the following text:

The spirit must not fear to lose something that is for it of *genuine interest*; it is its . . . [?], on which rests that which for it emerges in *philosophy*. [Philosophy] will therefore *give* it *back all* that is true in the imaginations that the *instinct of reason* first produced; but it will . . .

Der Geist darf nicht fürchten, etwas zu verlieren, was wahrhaftes Interesse für ihn hat; es ist seine . . . [?], auf welcher das beruht, was sich in der *Philosophie* für ihn ergibt. Sie wird ihm daher *alles wiedergeben*, was Wahres in den Vorstellungen ist, welche der *Instinkt der Vernunft* zuerst hervorbrachte; aber sie wird . . .[79]

The spirit, namely the self-certainty of the newly appointed sovereign thought, is unsure whether it can have the whole universe subordinated to itself. If for Hegel the principal feature of sovereignty is the fact that it has always already won, why is this self-certainty mingled with self-doubt?

What we encounter here is *the inner split of sovereignty*. The certainty that it will conquer all material content is not the direct certainty of having all differences within; that would be already the total domination. This certainty is rather a promise that "the cause has been secured." Consequently, the sovereign must constantly remind itself about its victory and its position. In this self-assurance it appears that its current work—its true interest, as Hegel says, anticipating the core of Marxism—will never be in vain. Sovereignty seals the promise that whatever the spirit does in the future, it will never lose, neither itself, nor the world. Thus, the initial act of attacking the Pole Star predetermines the future of thought. It might be smashed altogether with its world, but as long as it exists, it cannot lose the world and the time it introduced.

This particular oscillation between the certainty of its own victory and the total self-doubt, which, whenever comes, requires a solid external foothold to be resisted, is responsible for the throb of modern sovereignty, so well discernible in Luther's faith.[80] The kind of faith that originated in Luther's formulation has no support not only in the external world (→ 2.3), but even in the subject. It has a divine promise, but to believe in it, it has only itself: it must rely on its volatile self-grounding in order to create a world which would support it, otherwise it loses everything. The world must be approached with faith, in total onslaught on its numbness. In this attack nothing is neutral.[81] Either victory or defeat, either the conquest of the world or ultimate failure among the realm of mute matter.

In this view, Hegel accomplishes Luther's intuitions: it is only in ultimate self-doubt and despair—in which there is nothing except for them—that an imaginary external foothold might turn these very same self-doubt and despair into unshakable faith. Utter desolation and total might overlap in their structure, being differentiated only by the tiniest remainder that switches the vector. In this sense, sovereignty binarizes whatever falls into its machinery.

The often quoted passage from Hölderlin's *Patmos*, "Wo aber Gefahr ist, wächst/Das Rettende auch,"[82] could be heralded as the motto of this binarizing device of sovereignty, if only it were hinted that, vice versa, wherever there is a hope of salvation, danger looms large, and, deplorably, the universe is caught in their oscillation.[83] Real modern dangers come from attempts of salvation, undertaken by victims or self-perceived victims. In this sense, Hegel's thought is the knowledge of the destitute modern reality, as ruthless as the modern universe itself.

Why sovereignty needs the law

7. The binarizing power of modern sovereignty sets the field over which it reigns in fundamental instability. Sovereignty first unifies the whole field, eliminating all instability which is due to the contingence of particular things. Against them, it is capable of unleashing power unrestrained in its blindness and brutality. The source of instability lies elsewhere than in things. It flows from the heart of sovereignty, which is its own "self-decision" that might be lost in a momentary feeling of self-doubt. Therefore, the reign of sovereignty is necessarily shaky, as if marked by the deepest neurosis. The sovereign is always concerned about its self-preservation, and it is right, because, essentially, it depends only on itself, even if the inner instability is projected onto the governed field. For this reason, the sovereign always has enemies, raised by its own construction.

It is for this essential instability that modern sovereignty is torn between endless postponement, in which the status quo appears as already won, once and forever, and moments of unpredictable sudden ruptures. This kind of instability is the constant tension between the acquired eternal tranquility and the obsessive return of rupture. The stability that might, temporarily, subsist under its reign, is unsurpassed in its demand for eternal continuance; yet, total uncertainty underlies its quietness.

In the construction of the modern state, this instability is reframed in the division between the sovereign and law. As Carl Schmitt demonstrated,[84] the self-restraint of sovereignty produced by establishing a legal order cannot put an end to the instability inherent in the exertion of sovereignty. The sovereign might, and must, intervene with the use of exception, suspending the legal order. In this sense, Schmitt's claims might be extrapolated towards perceiving *law as a device which governs the intrinsic postponement of sovereignty*. If so, the instability particular to sovereignty reappears in the tension between law and exception: law is a "solution" to sovereignty's dualism, the institutionalized tranquillity topped with the rupture embodied in the exception.

The sovereign requires law not necessarily as means of subordinating and governing the reigned field, but as a symbolic formation which embodies the preservation of the status quo. The existence of law, with its structurally embedded potential eternity of applications, provides a foothold for internally instable sovereignty.[85] Therefore, the proliferation of law and the emergence of modern sovereignty should not be taken for a mere coincidence.

2.27   As we already saw (→ 2.26), the rule of modern sovereignty engenders an illusion that *nothing can be truly lost*. More practically, it appears under the guise of ideology, which, as Žižek, among others, convincingly depicted,[86] offers a powerful force of denial under the scheme: even if it is true, it cannot be true enough as to change our actions; our world will continue forever. This sovereignty-based ideological construction is the very same mechanism that accounts for Hegel's unassailability of spirit. Sovereignty resembles a knob which fixes the world to a particular point of determination.

Hegel's thought, *crème de la crème de modernité*, cannot lose anything: no fact can ever resist its power of explanation, which will sweep across the whole universe and bring its content under the power of philosophy.[87] *The Phenomenology of Spirit*, *The Science of Logic*, *The Encyclopaedia of Philosophical Sciences*, and all Hegel's lectures are swollen with facts, historical narratives, and random pieces of natural science: the march of spirit can never stop until it assumes that it has its entire field subordinated to itself.

Sovereignty as a mode of governing the apocalyptic tension of modernity

8. The purely modern illusion of sovereignty, which lures us into being positively certain that nothing can truly be lost, is a powerful double-edged device. Apart from providing a foothold for self-certainty, it is also accountable for a particular form of stalemate which, after Kafka, might be called "paralysis before the Law." All truly crucial decisions, the ones which would reshape our world at its base, are shielded by the inviolable aura of sovereignty which deceive us into thinking that they should not need to be taken. If they were taken, they would constitute a traumatizing attack on the place of sovereignty. As a result, we stay paralyzed as Kafka's *am ha-aretz*, countryman, before the Law.[88] This particular form of sovereignty, taken in itself, seems to continue forever; it can be either altogether smashed or subjugated to.

This self-subversive nature of modern sovereignty produces a unique effect. Modernity is rife with apocalyptic visions,[89] in which the secular is, to all intents and purposes, indistinguishable from religious imagery. Apocalypses are anxiously awaited and often happen under the guise of political overthrows, wars and revolutions. Various ends of almost everything are proclaimed, from philosophy to art.[90] Total reinvention is a common mode of functioning. Yet, nothing is less believed in than a true apocalypse, a real end of the world in its current shape. The more we prepare for catastrophes, from global wars and physical destruction of life up to political revolutions and total paradigm switches, the more we dread them and the more paralyzed we are. The power of modern sovereignty attracts attention like a fatal danger at which we gaze with total, yet inoperative mobilization.[91]

Therefore, modern sovereignty may be construed as *a mode of governing the apocalyptic tension*. By establishing a block in the place of power it fuels the unease over the status quo, which appears as unsatisfactory, unjust and, most of all, permanently crumbling. Since the "normal" flow between the sovereign place and the subordinated field is obstructed, transformation might be imagined only as a local or universal apocalypse which will smash the entire construction. Nevertheless, the power of sovereignty itself organizes the flow of the apocalyptic tension and parasites on it.

Simultaneously, modern sovereignty seals the promise that nothing will be lost. And, indeed, in a most uncanny manner, the world still exists after mass murder and unimaginable orgies of ruthlessness and unreason that keep recurring in modernity. We can read about them. Whatever happened, is now meticulously written down and available to the public under the guise of writing. We thought the world would fall; but, miraculously and horrifyingly, it continues its existence.

2.28 Built upon the certainty that it cannot truly lose anything, Hegel's philosophy returns the previously forsaken universe back to us. It repeats the initial gesture of modernity, the inner destruction of material content, in order to revive the universe on its own conditions. This revival, however, is not innocent. It is possible only when philosophy assumes the universe as its own and takes it upon its shoulders, tainting itself by the condition of sovereignty, which, since Hegel, it must continually grapple with.

Hegel's thought and his "ocean narrative" demonstrate that modern universe functions as an inert mass of inoperative differences that requires a power that will govern and revive it. Consequently, modern reality is necessarily split into the "positive material" and the power of sovereignty which organizes it. Here lies the foundation of what might be called (with Nietzschean inspirations) modern perspectivism: *in modernity there seems to be no truly objective reality*. All content is subordinated to a sovereign place, either vivid or extinct, which, regardless of its condition, outlines a basic predetermination. The conclusion of Hegel's narrative would be thus the following: the world is returned to us, but always marked by a particular constellation of sovereignty.

2.29 The whole structure of Hegel's thought bursts at the seams when it attempts to engulf the whole reality. Although the Hegelian method applied to the positive material gives, from time to time, a truly original remark, it borders on the ridicule when it aims at grasping the whole reality. It appears in all its monstrosity, in a Real (in Lacanian sense) shape, where utmost understanding becomes coextensive with total unintelligibility, like in *The Science of Logic*.

The spirit purportedly finds itself in all its material content (unlike Aristotle's God, which contemplated only its empty content). Yet, Hegel's texts are not only factually incomplete, biased, and internally unstable (which was well played by Derrida's *Glas*[92]), but also take this incompleteness for the imaginative totality of spirit. In this sense, Hegel's work can never be truly accomplished. What it might do, and actually does, is completing the race through drastic shortcuts. It arrives at the finishing line by illusion.[93] As a result, it is not given the coveted solution, but merely the loop of self-referentiality which has been extended to some degree over the positive material, but definitely has not encompassed it all.

Once opened, the path of sovereign philosophy must engulf all that it encounters. The monstrosity of thought[94] which accepts this challenge is unbearable. Hegel himself was on the verge of a nervous breakdown during writing *The Science of Logic*,[95] when the text kept spilling out of its forms. What saves this never-ending spiral of thought is a grid of arbitrary cuts, which, under the guise of universality, preselects the material so that the whole construction might close at some point. And, as Derrida convincingly demonstrated, spectres of omitted material haunt the purportedly coherent totality.

The place of sovereignty cannot be simply occupied once and for all. Being in this place is tantamount to a permanent lunatic pursuit in which total subjugation of the field is the ultimate goal. It is for this reason that Hegel's philosophy cannot stop its run in the middle of the race. The beginning—the self-certainty of spirit, namely the decision to take the position of the Pole Star—determines the finishing line and makes other solutions just unacceptable half-measures.

2.30 The true finish is unreachable. What is possible then? Here lies one of the most misconstrued secrets of Hegel, the Real of his bold attempt, whose structure is indispensable to understanding the boundary conditions for modern thought. There are two names for the secret: the Absolute Knowledge and *Begriff* (this term, although it is literally translated as "notion," cannot be replaced with its English equivalent).

But before we look at them more closely (→2.31), it must be noted that the aporetic secret is coded in the very text of the Inaugural Address. The final promise it makes:

Sie wird ihm daher *alles wiedergeben*, was Wahres in den Vorstellungen ist, welche der *Instinkt der Vernunft* zuerst hervorbrachte;

[Philosophy] will therefore *give it back all* that is true in the imaginations that the *instinct of reason* first produced;

is supplemented with a stub of a sentence:

aber sie wird ...

There are at least two interpretative paths here. First, the full text of the sketch did not last to our days; second, it represents the cul-de-sac of Hegel's drifting into an uncharted territory that he did not want or could not explore any further. In both cases, the ellipsis at the end marks the incompleteness of the fragment rather than deliberately suspends the voice. But it is tempting to take this final cut for more than just a random ending. Philosophy, says Hegel, will return everything to the spirit; it will work in order to restore the world. "Aber sie wird," Hegel adds after a semicolon: and from this point on, an ellipsis cuts either the text itself or the possibility of the text itself. In this fortunate convergence, we can read *the failure of the promise of sovereignty*.

Philosophy attacking the sovereign place will return the lost world to us, *aber sie wird* ... This beginning of the second part of the sentence most likely introduces the passive ("but it [philosophy] is ..."), which might be variously completed ("supported," "subordinated to," "crowned with" ...). But, thanks to the specifically German construction of *Vorgangspassiv*—a type of the passive which refers to a process rather than a finished state—the verb used in the passive is not *sein* (to be), but *werden* (to become, to happen). As a consequence, the part "aber sie wird …" might be concurrently read as "but it [philosophy] becomes …" This formula might also have a double sense: either philosophy becomes something or it simply becomes, happens, occurs (the verb *werden*, which nowadays has in philosophy a distinctively Nietzschean–Heideggerian flavor, might stand on its own much easier than its English equivalent). Finally, there is a fourth interpretative option, in which the verb *werden* opens a future clause, just like in the first part of the sentence in which the promise is made, where philosophy is said to return everything to the spirit ("Sie wird ihm daher alles wiedergeben …").

Accordingly, the final sentence of the *Inaugural Address* might be read fourfold:

It [philosophy] will return to [the spirit] everything what is true in representations, which the *instinct of reason* first produced;

1. but [philosophy] is … [verb+ed]
2. but [philosophy] becomes … [something]
3. but [philosophy] will … [do something]
4. but [philosophy] becomes …

Whatever happens to philosophy after the ellipsis, these three dots of Hegel's either damaged or incomplete text coincide with the *inevitable failure of the path of sovereignty*. In this last stub, philosophy is suddenly set free. A while ago, it was still meant to deliver the retrieved universe back to the spirit and assumed a promise of immense proportions. However, with the unexpected "but," the promise is called into question. The unknown end of the sentence affects the promise, suspends it, and warps its sense, although seemingly nothing has been officially denied or disavowed. Philosophy becomes the sole subject, but its path is unknown: something might happen to philosophy or, perhaps, philosophy can become something or will do something. The final part of the sentence undermines, in fact, the division between activity and passivity: philosophy is open to what it becomes or will become what might happen to it. The text is suddenly interrupted and fails to hold up the narrative which supported the promise. *Philosophy falls out of discourse and confronts its fate beyond words.*

In this sense, the three dots of the ellipsis stand for the insufficiency of language to keep up with the becoming of philosophy. It has often been repeated (by Marx among others) that Hegel's Absolute Knowledge is an empty construct.[96] Yet, whatever it truly is, it still finds some expression in the text. Contrariwise, the ellipsis of the Inaugural Address puts across the final failure of philosophy even more tellingly. Instead of fulfilling the promise, philosophy is suddenly pushed out of discourse. The Absolute Knowledge, to which the ellipsis is a counterpart, is the point of the final demand and definitive failure of thought which took the path of sovereignty. Using Kant's[97] and Hegel's imagery, it might be described as falling from the Pole Star.

9. The Absolute Knowledge should constitute the final stage of philosophy, which has finally swept through the ocean of "positive material" (i.e., all differences which make

up the universe) and has once and forever taken the world upon itself. It is the promise which philosophy obtained when it attacked the place of sovereignty; it is also the promise that philosophy made to the destitute universe. Out of the inert mass of inoperative differences there should rise a new, coherent world, into which philosophy breathes life. In the Absolute Knowledge, all past knowledge should be preserved and reconciled in its contradictions. Since all differences are to be amassed within, there should be nothing left. The Absolute Knowledge, when realized, should be the totality without any outside.

The Pole Star of spirit, which, at the beginning, embodied the outside in the destitute universe, is now to coincide fully with it. The path of sovereignty promises that, once chosen, it will deliver the whole universe which had been forsaken by external transcendence and will locate it in the place of the new, ecstatic inner transcendence. The project of the Absolute Knowledge assumes that the excessive modern reality can finally equate with itself, precisely at the place of its former excess.

This promise has far-reaching consequences; some of them seem too bold even for Hegel himself. For instance, since after the emergence of the Absolute Knowledge there is nothing which could be external or transcendent to the united universe, time will be brought to an end:

> Time is just the notion definitely existent, and presented to consciousness in the form of empty intuition. Hence spirit necessarily appears in time, and it appears in time so long as it does not grasp its pure notion, i.e. so long as it does not annul time. Time is the pure self in external form, apprehended in intuition, and not grasped and understood by the self, it is the notion apprehended only through intuition. When this notion grasps itself, it supersedes its time character, (conceptually) comprehends intuition, and is intuition comprehended and comprehending. Time therefore appears as spirit's destiny and necessity, where spirit is not yet complete within itself . . .[98]

Hegel suggests that *time exists only insofar as we do not grasp the whole reality*. It seems to be only an effect of inner discordance within the universe, in which some elements claim to have independence and resist the stream of becoming. Time is an illusory background onto which we project contradictions that we cannot seize in their totality. But once these contradictions become solved in the Absolute Knowledge, there is no need to project them onto an external background. All elements of reality last in the very same pace; none distinguishes itself from the stream of synchronic existence. Therefore, time loses its sense: everything exists in absolute presence, in which the past lives in presentifying remembrance of *Er-innerung*.

The true impact of this idea, which rarely has attracted more attention (with the notable exception of Kojève[99]), is crucial for understanding modernity and we will analyze it in more detail (→ 51). For the time being, however, it must be said that it is in the dimension of time that the collapse of the Absolute Knowledge manifests itself most clearly.

Why does the Absolute Knowledge fail? The most common and intuitive answer would be: Hegel's discovery did not stop time, let alone prevented history from happening. We would be glad to claim it is preposterous, not to say insane, to argue that one philosophical idea might have such an impact. Therefore, the idea of the end of time lays Hegel's philosophy open to ridicule and proves the absurdity of the Absolute Knowledge. However, answers of this kind merely set aside the truly paradoxical dimension of modern thinking epitomized in Hegel's philosophy. The paradox demands more profound analysis.

It may be concisely formulated as follows: *the end of time is the finishing line of sovereignty*. Its understanding, however, requires something more than the cautious repression which is the other side of Hegel's self-eulogy.

10. The end of time is the finishing line of sovereignty. Once again, Hegel's thought will allow us to understand this claim. The Absolute Knowledge is like Aristotle's god seizing itself, although not in advance, in its perfect, formal and secluded solitude, but after a long path of history in which it turns out that everything that has ever existed, all the positive matter, has no true outside and it simply is what it is: itself. In the Absolute Knowledge everything grasps itself as everything and through everything. If so, time loses sense; everything already belongs to itself, so there can be no true outside and no real future.

Here lies the often analyzed tension between the achievement of philosophy in Hegel and the dialectical engine of this thought which still pushes forward regardless of the self-proclaimed end of philosophy. As it is well known, this inner imbalance, in its simplified reception, gave rise to the split between Hegelian left and Hegelian right. This split mirrors a tension inherent in the construction of sovereignty.

Hegel claims that time has ended as the spirit has finally grasped itself. He is tempted to pronounce the end of time, even though, obviously, no true end of the world has occurred and time has not been truly abolished. The end of time means that the course of thought has run to its end. The loop of self-referentiality, which was from the beginning planned as the final outcome, has extended, absorbed positive material and come to its finishing line.

The loop was intended to sweep through all positive material. That, however, proved impossible. What can be done is a drastic shortcut: selecting the material which should be absorbed and repressing the remainder. As a consequence, this thought arrives at the finishing line with a chaotic mix of positive material and, as planned, grasps itself. *Now, for the first time in the history of philosophy, thought confronts radical temporality*. All previous philosophies ended up with some claims, definitive or still tentative in some regard; but these claims related to reality as such. In Hegel's thought, however, philosophy absorbs the world and brings on one particular moment in which reality purportedly equates with itself. This moment is of truly messianic character and is nowhere near previous philosophical truths. The whole history is at stake here: not eternal truths, but one final truth arising at the unique moment in which the spirit grasps itself. The Absolute Knowledge lays a messianic and radically temporal claim. It uses up all time it was awarded when thought took the place of sovereignty. Now it lies bare when its time has ended.

This is a moment which might be given only once to each occupant of the place of sovereignty. The moment in which either thought or power reaches for total universality and claims that it has absorbed and united all its field.[100] It is the culmination of *a* time which was inaugurated with the advent of the new sovereign. As if forming an imaginary time loop, it re-presents the act of establishing the sovereign and rolls up all the history that has elapsed since that moment. From the perspective of the occupant of the place of sovereignty, its time has ended and furled itself into a circle, leaving the sovereign outside its time.

In this position all meaningful history that the sovereign has produced becomes coextensive with the sovereign itself. It appears in all its arbitrary character, as stark, meaningless usurpation. All justifications and senses fall off. The particular world and particular time which were produced by the force which took the place of sovereignty appear now as a totality which generates sense only within and for itself, but from an external point of view appears as a closed unit, senseless as a whole.

This is the finishing line which sovereignty holds in store for each force which attempts to put itself in its position. The end of time awaits for each sovereign as its inner necessity. Modern sovereignty is all about eluding and pushing this end off. Hegel was bold enough to face it for the first time, but he mistook the modern fatum for his own privileged position.

Philosophy's day after, or a failure of modern messianism

11.1 When Hegel lays the claim to end history, his thought gets suddenly stranded. It has exhausted the time it was granted: now it has no resources to move on. Even though it ended its time, time as such continues and overruns it. One can hardly imagine a more difficult position for thought. It is comparable only with embarrassment and physical pain of continuing existence that a self-proclaimed messiah feels after declaring her mission and failing. Hegel's thought, once it reaches its final point, cannot endure the bare time of mere existence which it is abruptly confronted with.

Such existence appears as a senseless whole which merely subsists. It resembles a piece of matter, timeless-and-pierced-through-by-time, something like a pebble on the roadside of the real, inexorable time. Its nightmarish subsistence epitomizes a "morning after" of a failed messianic claim. At this point, after having played the highest stake, philosophy starts its afterlife, whose spectral nature might manifest itself in three different strategies.

11.2 The first strategy is the silence of the text. The failure of philosophy is manifestly visible in the fate of philosophical writing. The first book which delivered Hegel's messianic message to the world, *The Phenomenology of Spirit*, ends with a proclamation of the spirit grasping itself, but then, most ordinarily and most traumatizingly, *the text simply ends*. As Kojève[101] (and Mallarmé before him[102]) perspicaciously noted, the history culminates in one book, in *the* Book.[103] But what can be more stunning than the utmost contradiction between some mass of paper and time which still, mercilessly, goes on? The Book, or rather, quite plainly, some piece of text, might be published, reproduced, read, reread, cited, and interpreted, but in terms of real time it is just a material object which, like all others, lasts in time. Kojève surprisingly easily shunned away from this paradox, claiming that once the Book is created, its further fates are non-problematic:

> Obviously, the Book, to be a Book and not a mass of bound and blackened paper, must be read and understood by human beings. But the future readers do not change anything in the Book. And if, to read the Book, the Human Being must *live*, that is be born, grow up and die, with his/her life reduced essentially to this reading …—[he/she] does not create nothing new …[104]

For Kojève, the Book is not just matter, or not properly a piece of matter: it has sense, being therefore "an intellectual entity" (une entité spirituelle).[105] For this reason it is not only eternal, it is eternity itself.[106] Kojève takes Hegel's time for the only one that exists: in order to explain what comes after the Book, he must assume that the Book is of the purely virtual character. It is like a static concept of revelation, which may be infinitely replayed leaving the original untouched.

But the Book ends with a blank page which opens the dimension of incomprehensible progress that Kojève so futilely wanted to cover. Time goes on, despite the creation of the Book which aims to engulf it. The greatest of Hegel's triumphs conceals in fact a shattering debacle: a Book which ends with white pages, unable to perpetuate itself. Hegel claimed to muster all forces in order to prepare a messianic jump. But the whiteness of the sheet[107] afterwards opens up the traumatic Real, which, however, apparently is not referred to by the text itself. The text prepares its finish, rallies all forces, cuts the history and itself at the same time. The Book, once written, attempts to pass for a philosophical victory. But in its inconspicuous material aspect it supplements its triumph with a bitter truth: the messianic attempt has failed and what has left is dead matter.[108]

This strategy is most telling about the fate of philosophy which took the path of sovereignty. It resembles the history of Jewish messianism,[109] which is a row of failed messiahs who go on living, from Bar Kochba till Sabbatai Zvi, in the silent, but unbearably clear excess of time which overruns each messianic attempt.

11.3 The second strategy is the priesthood of the dead truth. Hegel proposes it at the end of his *Lectures on the Philosophy of Religion*:

> For us philosophical knowledge has harmonised this discord, and the aim of these lectures has just been to reconcile reason and religion, … and to rediscover in revealed religion the truth and the Idea.
> But this reconciliation is itself merely a partial one without outward universality. Philosophy forms in this connection a sanctuary apart, and those who serve in it constitute an isolated order of priests, who must not mix with the world, and whose work is to protect the possessions of Truth. How the actual present-day world is to find its way out of this state of disruption, and what form it is to take, are questions which must be left to itself to settle, and to deal with them is not the immediate practical business and concern of philosophy.[110]

This fragment was noted down in 1824, seventeen years after Hegel finished his *Phenomenology*. That Book already lies like a piece of dead matter brushed by time and points to the failure of the project. Now, after almost two decades since the discovery of the Absolute Knowledge, Hegel decides to try out a different strategy. Instead of keeping up the mortal silence of the text exposed to time, Hegel clearly refers to the fate of his project. In the *Lectures on the Philosophy of Religion*, he detaches the truth of the Absolute Knowledge from its strictly temporal and material anchoring in the text: from now on, *it becomes simply truth whose embeddedness in text is purely accidental.* Truth is eternal. Once discovered, it does not require the text in which it first appeared: the afterlife of thought and its material remainder are repressed as inconsequential, because truth lives beyond them.

This strategy allows of saving the face of philosophy after its messianic claim. In close affinity with the structural mode in which failed Jewish messianism turned into otherworldly Christianity, Hegel decides not to stick by the utmost temporality and reality of his truth. Instead, he changes it into an eternal truth which drifts above the reality and remains unassailable. That this trick is Christian by structure is corroborated by the language of "priesthood" and "sanctuaries," which clearly points to the detachment of the truth from what it previously strived to subjugate. Philosophy is to turn into an almost monastic order, conserving once established truth, whose immaculate existence has little to do with events in the outside world.

In fact, this strategy contradicts the very concept of the Absolute Knowledge. In order to repress its truth, it attempts to sanctify it, just as Christianity repressed and sublimed the failure of some Jewish messiahs.

11.4 The last strategy consists in recognizing that the messianic attempt was not unique, but may be ventured in the future. This possibility consists in assuming that *each occupant of the place of sovereignty has its own unique moment—its messianic attempt—which cannot be overcome and which brings its rule to an end.*

The moment of completion repeats and seals the initial act of taking sovereignty, but it also reveals its emptiness and hopelessness. It can no longer rule as before. It might subsist only as its own spectre, through loyalty to the failed messiah. Nevertheless, it is open to be replaced by another potential occupant of the place of sovereignty.

This strategy might be the boldest and it is probably the only one that saves philosophy from total failure. It seems the most honest, if honesty is of any sense here. Hegel flirted with this option at the end of his *Lectures on the History of Philosophy*, when, parting with his students, he summoned them to undertake the task of constant actualization of philosophy, of continuous making Spirit concordant with itself:

> Our standpoint now is accordingly the knowledge of this Idea as spirit, as absolute Spirit, which in this way opposes to itself another spirit, the finite, the principle of which is to know absolute spirit, in order that absolute spirit may become existent for it. I have tried to develop and bring before your thoughts this series of successive spiritual forms pertaining to Philosophy in its progress, and to indicate the connection between them. This series is the true kingdom of spirits, the only kingdom of spirits that there is—it is a series which is not a multiplicity, nor does

it even remain a series, if we understand thereby that one of its members merely follows on another; but in the very process of coming to the knowledge of itself it is transformed into the moments of the one Spirit, or the one self-present Spirit. This long procession of spirits is formed by the individual pulses which beat in its life; they are the organism of our substance, an absolutely necessary progression, which expresses nothing less than the nature of spirit itself, and which lives in us all.[111]

This succession does not seem to stop with the discovery of the Spirit which encompasses them, because time goes on, a new, particular spirit arises, and, accordingly, the Spirit would have to be found anew. Hence Hegel's call:

We have to give ear to its urgency—when the mole that is within it forces its way on—and we have to make it a reality. It is my desire that this history of Philosophy should contain for you a summons to grasp the spirit of the time, which is present in us by nature, and—each in his own place—consciously to bring it from its natural condition, i.e., from its lifeless seclusion, into the light of day.[112]

It is nothing less than a call for permanent repetition of messianic attempts in philosophy. If philosophy does not overcome its time, but brings it to the light of spirit, it should be acknowledged that each time *might* find its completion in the work of philosophy which lays it to rest. If so, the true novelty of Hegel's thinking would be not a particular solution he gave to this epoch, but the discovery of this incessant necessity to keep up with the spirit and bring it to light by attacking the place of sovereignty in each sovereign constellation.

Perhaps "epochs" do not exist elsewhere than in this messianic attempt to bring them to ultimate sovereignty. In this sense, Hegel's philosophy did not grasp history, but only traced the path of opening and closing *a* time—and laid it open for future attempts.

12. All these strategies confirm that it is not possible to hold up the place of modern sovereignty. Whatever thought or power attempts to occupy it, it enters the spiral path with the end of its time as the finishing line. Thus, collapse is inherent in the very structure of sovereignty.

Even though at the beginning the place of sovereignty promises the unification of the inoperative and shattered universe, this promise becomes a lure of sovereignty, always postponed and displaced. When it finally appears that the unification is at hand, when, as in the case of Hegel, everything begins to coincide with everything in a self-referential point of time, the whole construction collapses. Total unity, as soon as it is reached, turns out to unite only the thought that aspired to sovereignty. It is not the universe, the ocean from Hegel's speech, that finds its peace under the sovereign. It is merely the sovereign that closes the pre-established circle of its own illusory trajectory and finds itself in the position of fundamental insufficiency. This unique moment opens up a crack through which the fundamental perspectivism of modernity is discernible.

It lays bare *some real and unbearable dimension of lasting*, which overruns each attempt to unify and grasp modern reality. This dimension is always more powerful than any particular thought or power aspiring to sovereignty. It foils and ridicules all endeavors fueled by the structure of modern sovereignty, and in this sense it constitutes its other side. Sovereignty lures us into undertaking an attempt which, unbeknownst to thinking, is condemned to failure; at the moment of failure the very same place which thought has so far occupied expels it. This place is unbearably empty and lasts in an incomprehensible and unbearable way. Thus, sovereignty always overruns the sovereign. Whereas the sovereign appears retrospectively as a particular contender who failed, sovereignty lasts.

In this sense, the not-yet-clarified entanglement between sovereignty and time demands further elaboration. It accounts for the obsessively modern categories of *belatedness* and *postponement*, whose murky rule afflicts so deeply our (late, all-too-late) times. The inertia of our politics, dead forms of the exertion of power, as well as the growing despair over lasting, which becomes the hopelessness at its purest, are deeply rooted in the relation between sovereignty and time. Their interplay requires urgent insight, perhaps not to stave off another inevitable catastrophe which will attempt to break through the dead end of our times, but, primarily, in order to be cautious about what we celebrate as our main philosophical meal since deconstruction.

In other words, it is not the catastrophe that should interest us in modernity. Uncountable modern discourses are built around some more or less apocalyptic view of this epoch. Modernity has been repeatedly condemned, to nausea, for the fall of metaphysics and tradition, the disintegration of coherent morals, the reign of barren reason which churns out still new abstract justifications that cannot guide anyone. Another branch of these discourses depicts the inevitable doom that lurks in the horizon, always almost-ready to throw our civilization into some fatal ending. Much as their prophecies are sometimes close to the real threat, it cannot be omitted that it is the very structure of modernity which generates, and will generate, tensions of apocalyptic flavor. In this incessant throb, which pronounces the end times only to return to the disillusioned status quo, *modernity replays the structure of catastrophe on which it is founded*.[113]

Instead of focusing on apocalyptic tensions, it is much more enlightening to confront the actual lasting: what goes on despite still new prophecies of the end (of capitalism, of philosophy, of humanity, etc.). Evidently, lasting forms up the very same device which is responsible for the repetition of messianic/apocalyptic movement. But its work is more subterranean, cloaked by ideology, and, primarily, senseless and unbearable. It is in this sense that we should understand Walter Benjamin's words: "The notion of progress should be founded on the idea of catastrophe. That it 'goes on this way' is the catastrophe. It is not the each time imminent, but the each time given."[114] In modernity catastrophe is our daily bread; the real miracle is lasting.

11.5 Sovereignty lasts and outlasts the sovereign. Therefore, the place of sovereignty appears as a quasi-divine dimension of the unassailable and the unbearable, even after its occupant was expelled. This relation is well discernible in the strategies of failure of the sovereign thought that Hegel outlined. Each of them is marked by the difference between the time of event (creation of the Book, gaining the truth, self-recognition) and the meaningless, empty time of repetition in which the thought that risked everything and failed, lasts. Sovereigns rise and fall, and then live their afterlives, but sovereignty never crumbles. Thus, sovereignty shines like the unassailable Pole Star, from which all contenders must fall off.[115]

2.31 Hegel's "ocean narrative" is thus a poignant chronicle of a tremendous philosophical failure. Far from being an errant path of one thinker, it is a catastrophe of thought which had struggled to overcome the consequences of the initial disintegration of the world. The new universe is indelibly marked by the structure of sovereignty: the figure of the Pole Star remains its emblem. In this universe, thought might either bow down before the place of sovereignty or seek to take its place by force. The second path opens up an attempt which is, in fact, messianic by nature. It fails, just like all messianisms fail, only to find itself outlasted and overrun by sovereignty. This particular relationship between sovereignty and the structure of messianism inherent in modernity demands further elaboration.

"Aber sie wird ...," read the last words of the Inaugural Address. If they are to be translated as "but [philosophy] becomes ...," we might pose a sober question: what does philosophy become? What is its fate? What is its sense if not—let us dare a tentative answer—to provide the whiteness of paper[116] on which the throb of modern messianism is to write itself down?

In this sense, philosophy would be a counterpart to the Pole Star of sovereignty. Just like the Pole Star, it lasts, but not on its own ground: it simply cannot die despite numerous attempts. But in this Blanchotian undeadness, philosophy accompanies the unassailable Pole Star of sovereignty and charts its tales in modernity.

13.1 Hegel's failure is the practical discovery of what, since Lacan, is known under the name of *jouissance*, the inaccessible excess of the Real beyond the split.[117] If Aristotle's god—the thought thinking itself—appeared possible and uncontradictory, Hegel's Absolute can grasp itself only in a fantasmatic place.

The momentary fulfillment of the Absolute, which seizes its own hand precisely in the place in which Hegel's pen touches paper, is nothing less than Lacan's picture of *jouissance* as the mouth kissing itself.[118] The purely fantasmatic nature of this climax appears immediately afterwards: it is "possible" only if the Absolute is incomplete, if, in truth, it is a stump whose partiality allows of leaving behind some veiled area that sets the stage of the fantasy. In fact, it is not a totality, but just a part that touches itself, although with the mediation of the repressed totality which secretly supports the scene. The inevitable partiality is created by the distance between the Pole Star and positive material, which, once and for all, makes totality an impasse. But it is the irremovable alterity of the Pole Star that lends, for a moment, the power to repress the rest of reality and stage the self-grasp.

Nevertheless, the position of the Pole Star cannot be held: it outlasts the attempt to reach *jouissance* and reveals its insufficiency. The dimension of inexhaustible lasting, which cannot be halted by the self-grasp of the Absolute, comes to the fore. The whole staging transpires and, in the heart of the expected reconciliation, the starkest rift re-appears. What is crucial, and what Lacan's description of *jouissance* does not focus on, is the problem of lasting as the key feature of *jouissance*.

13.2 Hegel's claim that his discovery puts an end to history has been all too often misunderstood and ridiculed.[119] But in its actual sense, as pertaining to modernity, it is perfectly true, albeit with a minor correction. *History, as we know it, emerged with the advent of modernity and was finished from the very beginning.* In this sense, Hegel's thought only repeats what had already (un)happened. The discovery of the end of history is like finding that the person we deemed alive is already a corpse.

The novelty of Hegel's thinking was finding that meaningful history is not open—contrary to real time—but is, in fact, a loop that can be traversed. Viewed from this perspective, modern history will always have a blind spot, the point of *jouissance*, Hegel's Pole Star. As a meaningful narrative of the past, history revolves around its founding insufficiency which acts as a tempting agent, luring us into proclamations of the end of history. Modernity is therefore marked by constant returns of the structure of *jouissance*, of desperate pursuits of the point zero, in which senseless lasting appears with all its might.

In this sense, Hegel's discovery is both original and utterly trivial. Original, because it was for the first time that the structure of modern history was explicitly displayed. Trivial, because the end concerns not the very philosophy of Hegel, but modern history itself, regardless of any philosopher's work. It is the structure of *jouissance* that we keep experiencing in paradoxical repetition, and beyond any conditions allowing of acknowledging repetition. Hegel traces the *nec plus ultra* of modern thought and, for the impoverished gaze, makes all "future history" redundant.

Consequently, Hegel's thought might be described as ec-static monotheism: a view of the universe as one totality, always opposed to the tiniest, but irremovable remainder. This remainder acts as divinity in the world without transcendence. By constantly shifting its place, gives to this universe its unprecedented momentum.

Stars in modern philosophy: "Us" and solitude on Earth

2.32 The universe of modernity has no true outside, it borders no otherworldly space. Its boundaries include themselves, as they do not separate two areas but outline, only from the inside, the outer limits of modernity. No wonder that modern philosophy, from Kant and Hegel, through Franz Rosenzweig's *The Star of Redemption*[120] and Heidegger, up to Peter Sloterdijk's *Spheres*,[121] so often reaches for astronomical imagery in order to portray the fate of the world in modernity.[122] Perhaps only metaphors of astronomical origin are potent enough to support the modern vision of reality as the excessive unity supplemented and troubled by the remainder.

Among these visions, Hegel's "ocean narrative" is distinguished by the consistent stress on the irreducibly excessive position of the Pole Star. As we already saw, its place might be attacked, but in an attempt which is in advance doomed to failure. The Pole Star appears either as something most external—a guide for the destitute universe, its only transcendence—or as, in fact, something most internal, the core of spirit, which can never be lost, no matter how far the disintegration went.

In Hegel's description the total impoverishment of the universe and its redemption through the self-certainty of spirit are separated only by a tiny difference which, in fact, is a change of perspective. Just as the two aspects of Wittgenstein's famous duck-rabbit,[123] the very same totality appears either as a hopeless dark ocean of dead differences or as the united universe in which the spirit recognizes itself in most stunning contradictions, accepts them and rules over them from the point of sovereignty. The existence of this tiniest difference—which separates total powerlessness from infallible hope, damnation from salvation,[124] bourgeoisie from proletariat, necessity and dependence from freedom—is the most clear sign that modern sovereignty is at work. When Benjamin claims (after Scholem) that the messiah will not change nothing except for a small amendment,[125] his thought is motivated—above and despite all "inexhaustible",[126] but constructed oppositions of Athens and Jerusalem[127]—by the same structure which led Martin Luther to his discovery of *sola fide*. This obsessively ruminated "tiny difference", whose size is completely disproportionate to the influence, is the ultimate remainder of modern reality and the sting of sovereignty.

2.33 Alenka Zupančič noted once that Nietzsche's nihilism means, in fact, that "All has become One."[128] If so, the modern universe is inherently nihilistic, not in the sense of the views which it begets, but in its very tissue. Part of the price for unity is being ravaged by the sovereign exception which underpins the One.

2.34 Therefore, Hegel's Pole Star stands both for the utmost externality and the utmost internality. It is either the guide of the destitute universe—its only stable point of reference, whose calm light signals that reality is never even with itself—or it is the very core of the universe, the "thing" which bears more affinity with the universe than any of its parts. In both cases, the Pole Star constitutes a privileged place whose constant oscillation between externality and internality exerts unabated influence on the universe. It has no actual content; its position remains purely structural. The existence of the Pole Star puts all material ("positive") content of modernity in constant tension: no sense or truth can stabilize itself, let alone escape from its structurally imposed position.

It should not be believed that it was some more or less vague postmodernity that shackled our stable construction of socially accepted truths.[129] *Modernity has never had any actual truths*: it just has enormous positive material which is played upon by the structure anchored in the Pole Star of sovereignty.[130] It appears in every serious opposition as the irremovable excess, which cannot be explained in terms of material content.

2.35 In the line of Hegel's admiration for Protestantism, one could see in the discovery of the Pole Star a sign of liberation from human authority.[131] Indeed, the Pole Star gives us a foothold for resisting all external power. But this liberty is based on total dependence on the Pole Star itself. That might seem negligible if the Pole Star represents *our own* spirit: why should we not be dependent on ourselves? Is not that what freedom is about?

Yet, the Polar Star does not emancipate from power and dependence. It only displaces the sovereign instance, taking the loop of the cord from the previous sovereign and putting it on our own neck. In this manner, the old nineteenth- and twentieth-century paradox—how can ultimate liberation turn into utter enslavement— finds it conceptual frame.

14.1 In the famous passage from *Überwindung der Metaphysik* (*Overcoming of Metaphysics*), Heidegger calls the Earth "the errant star" (der Irrstern).[132] The Earth is purportedly lost, being nothing more than a desert forsaken by Being. Once again, the astronomical imagery seems at hand to chart the relation between everything and nothing.

The utterly melancholic, passive and impoverished view of Heidegger aspires to be the *nec plus ultra* of modern thought. The forgetfulness of Being (*Seinsvergessenheit*), the withdrawal of Being—which leaves the Earth to its fate of the desert[133] colonized by will and technique—seems to grasp well the disintegration of late modernity. But the point which Heidegger finally reached after his strenuous fight for destitution, namely the desert land in which all that had been pure and bright faded into inoperative, mute shadows, only patchily ornamented with shackles of poetry and art, is, in fact, the bleak ocean from Hegel's Inaugural Address. The ocean, which, however, is not the only thing left in this reality. *Melancholy is one step; disillusion is another; but there is hope, and hope is our despair.*

The hope of Heidegger, a dim reflection of the previous imperialism of philosophy, embodied in Hegel's path of sovereignty, is the last, but indelible mark of the Pole Star. Hope never dies ultimately and this is the strength of sovereignty. The existence of the tiniest glitter of transcendence supports the structure in which this universe portrays itself as a desert. As long as modernity lasts, hope must fade, but cannot disappear.[134] It transmogrifies into the weakest self-celebrating forms in which it subsists although it claims to have actually already withdrawn.[135] Even the hope of the hopeless, the tiniest, Gnostic-like mere possibility of salvation, expropriates the universe from itself, denigrates it and provides the external point of view. In §13 of his *Zürauer Aphorismen*, Kafka wrote:

> A first sign of incipient insight is the desire to die. This life seems unbearable, another one seems unattainable. One is no longer ashamed of wanting to die; one asks to be taken from the old cell, which one hates, to a new one, which one will only learn to hate. A remainder of faith contributes to that, because during the transport the Lord may accidentally happen to come through the corridor, look at the prisoner and say: "You should not imprison this one again. He comes to me."[136]

This is the weakest of all hopes, "the remainder of faith": that the Lord might, by accident, pass through when the prisoners are transported and take one with himself. Being nothing less than an empty possibility, detached from the real probability of occurring, it is the last sign of the exterior: the last glimmer of the Pole Star.

Because no matter how its light would fade, the existence of the Pole Star remains unendangered.

14.2 As long as there is a remainder to this destitute universe, as long as there is any foothold for hope, the Pole Star lures us into its place. It seems as if this place must be taken, so that all differences suddenly match each other and the whole universe appear in its totality. Therefore, the very construction of modern reality produces the irreducible structure of faith, whose actual locus is the remainder. Modern faith is not about believing in the otherworldly. It is about the directly observable power of the remainder, the power present in thinking, which seems to offer the new self-constitution of the universe on the basis of the remainder. It is for this reason that modern faith is so adamant and sober at the same time. We believe in something both closest and most demanding that usually takes the form of *ourselves*.

14.3 If Heidegger calls the Earth "the errant star," he might do it only with reference to Being. Being survives the destitution as its ground and abyss (*Ab-grund*, to quote Nietzsche's[137] and Heidegger's word play). It is what lasts and grounds, even in the most drastic impoverishment of the Earth. If it had not been for the mysterious relation between Being and the Earth, the Earth could not have been grasped as such, let alone portrayed as the errant star. In this light the relation between the Earth and Being appears as the distinction between the non-Whole and the remainder, its unassailable and inassimilable part/non-part, both external and internal, and neither, its ground and supplement,[138] the Whole bigger than the (non-)Whole itself and, simultaneously, the last, tiniest obstacle to the self-constitution of totality.

Quite naturally, in the logic of modern thought, Heidegger seeks access to his version of the Pole Star. His *Gelassenheit*,[139] the releasement, is a late form of approaching the place of sovereignty, which in vain attempts to dissolve sovereignty itself. In the measureless extension of the dimension of lasting—which Heidegger's path effectively boils down to—thinking seems so close to reaching its goal: the merciless and always-outlasting place of sovereignty. If not through bold attack, the place might be approached in stark but steadfast humility, assumes the thinker. If this humility is appropriately developed and practiced, the place of sovereignty might disappear and the clearing of Being might open for longer. Utter hopelessness mixes with ultimate hope, like in Luther's confession: the Earth is either the errant star condemned to eternal wandering or it might be, out of a sudden, saved. But humility does not dissolve sovereignty; it only celebrates and ornaments it with new myths. Lasting might be only desired, and with this desire Heidegger's thought returns to the cult of its Pole Star, which takes the place of *es* in the "es gibt" of the *Er-eignis*.[140]

In this cult, what Nietzsche called the "dancing star" becomes fixed and turns into Heideggerian "the only star" toward which one must head.[141] This star, shining with the light of Being, is never reached by the darkening of the world.[142] Thinking is therefore nothing more than confining oneself to the only thought, which supports the world just like a star in the sky.[143] It is the very same star whose wooden model Heidegger cherished so much[144]—the same whose representation ornaments Heidegger's tombstone in Meßkirch, thus bringing the darkness to the ground.[145]

14.4 To last, like the place of sovereignty lasts, to shine like our Pole Star over the destitute universe, is the desire of late modern thought. But, in fact, in modernity we have always been late, modernity is late by nature, and we have never desired anything else than lasting.

15.1 The definitive and unbearable feature of the modern universe is its *utmost structural solitude*. The incommensurable scale of this solitude is visible only against the background of previous epochs which did not know the universe in its proper sense, namely as the all-encompassing, but uneven and unstable totality.

In this regard, Hegel's *Inaugural Address* relates, for the first time, the piercing feeling of total desolation which awakens after the catastrophe of immense proportions. In this catastrophe, the universe inflated to include everything that exists or is conceivable. It sucked into itself all otherworldly imaginations, all divinity and transcendence. As a result, the universe stands alone, for there is almost nothing else. It is trapped in its all-encompassing character, carved out by its own snug boundaries which overlap with what defines them. In this regard, the modern universe is, in fact, unthinkable, for it seems to have no external foothold so that it could relate to itself.

15.2 How can this universe be experienced in its utter solitude?[146] If the modern universe could be truly all-encompassing, so that its boundaries would never be noticeable, it would never appear as solitary. On the contrary, just like the ancient Greek κόσμος, it would be simply everything what exists, the stable totality which could not be distinguished from anything else; we would know things, always in plural, but not a singular totality. Yet, the modern universe is in constant tension, because after each of its attempts to engulf everything, there is an irreducible, structural remainder, epitomized by Hegel's Pole Star. Its unassailable position sets the universe in constant tension and makes it visible for itself.

As long as the Pole Star is present, the universe cannot overlap with everything that exists. Consequently, the modern universe is always solitary in relation to its mysterious and elusive outside/inside, whose constant mobility incessantly traces the boundaries of the universe. As long as there is something that resists its absorbing power, the universe will appear as conditioned by and indebted to some unknown source. In this sense, the existence of the Pole Star is coextensive with a *permanent illusion of presence*, even if it is "presence" reduced to a half-absent trace of some vague presence which seemingly evaporated a long time ago. This illusion makes the modern universe look like a desert, separated from what it is conditioned by.

Even the weakest of all remnants of some past transcendence—which now, in its new form, should be called sovereignty—seems to save the universe from its solitude. It leaves some outside, which is enough to sustain thinking in terms of source, absence, trace and unstable totalities. In this light, the self-certainty of Hegel, his unfailing ability to lift up his head after unbearable contradictions took hold of thinking, is structurally equivalent to the practice of deconstruction, which might rely on the ubiquitous work of difference and will always find some trace to carry on.[147] All that the Pole Star requires is *a* difference—not a presence, let alone more developed forms of transcendence. Here lies the key distinction between the premodern transcendence and modern transcendence-sovereignty: the latter's functioning does not depend on its content, scope, position or strength. It might subsist in the weakest of forms, but even then it functions as well as if it were God in person.

This last, irreducible difference throws the modern universe into absolute solitude. No matter how it would be dressed up, the remainder cannot be eradicated. Therefore, it ostensibly refers to something that has been, in all appearance, irretrievably lost. Some structurally generated illusion/obsession of origin, self-dissolving in endless avatars—in traces to be found, errors to be mended and crises to be overcome—throws modernity into perpetual musing on its own desertification and desolation. Thus, with the Pole Star hovering over it, the modern universe will always appear in post-apocalyptic and melancholic light.

15.3 In one of his more esoteric writings, the volume *Das Ereignis* ("Becoming") written in the dead of Second World War (1941–2), Heidegger muses on the term "passage" (*Vorbeigang*).[148] As usual in this period, it appears within a cluster of other key words, such as *Ereignis* or *Seynsverlassenheit* ("leaving-by-Being"). One of these words, however, strikes an uncanny resemblance with Hegel's ocean narrative: "constellation" (*Konstellation*). Heidegger writes:

> *Die Konstellation des Vorbeigangs*
> Die Lichtung dieser Kon-stellation (Unstern—zu Stern). Was ist ihr Zwischen?
> Die sich vorbereitende Ortschaft—das Da-sein.
> Aus diesem Zwischen bestimmt sich das » *Inzwischen* «, und dieses bestimmt das *Jetzt* und das Jetzige der Geschichte des Seyns.
> Die Notlosigkeit.[149]

> *The constellation of passage*
> The clearing of this con-stellation (unlucky star—to star). What is their between?
> The locality which prepares itself—the Da-sein.
> On the ground on this between determines itself the "inbetween," which determines the *now* und the current of the history of Being.
> The lack of distress.

The con-stellation (*con-stellatio*) is the set of stars, "stellar togetherness." In Heidegger's thinking, the passage, a close relative of becoming, extends between two poles of a constellation. A constellation rules the passage and determines it. Once again, the sidereal terminology gives language to speak about becoming within the modern realm.

According to Heidegger, we are but in-between trapped between the two stars, one unlucky and one that we seek. The unlucky star in German is *Unstern*, literally an "unstar": negation of the star. If so, do we not travel between the absence of the star—the absence which shines above like an ominous star itself—and the proper star? It is a permanent travel organized by one and the same star, disappearing and appearing, remolding itself into its own absence and thus shining with a promise of salvation and dark light of distress. Within this "in-between" that we inhabit human existence becomes a Da-sein, whereas the Earth, as Heidegger concludes,[150] is a desertified "errant star" (Irrstern). This portrayal does justice to the modern Mirror Star: it reigns over an epoch which combines utter desolation with greatest hopes for salvation.

15.4 The remainder, the irreducible difference, throws the modern universe into absolute solitude. It is perhaps in this sense that in his late thought Žižek attempts to develop the idea that the normal state of the world is not of zero, but of minus energy.[151] This concept is accurate, however, only if it is strictly confined to the modern universe. It is only with the collapse of transcendence and its transformation into sovereignty, embodied by the Pole Star of modernity, that the concept of the universe as a below-zero totality is at all conceivable.

The Pole Star embodies total expropriation, in which the place which saps the universe's energy appears simultaneously as the core of this universe. In this sense, total exploitation and ultimate self-management of flows of energy, in a more than surprising manner, enter the threshold of indifferentiation in modernity. Therefore, what is truly crucial is not the below-zero energy of the modern universe, but rather the unique ability of this minus point to move freely through positive material and permanently reorganize relations between its parts.

16.1 But, if there is truly no transcendence, if there is only us, if all our hopes, postponements, all uncertainties which open up finitude, are, ultimately, only ours, and, if all the time in which we see future improvements, development or, even, rescue, is nothing but our projection which veils the unbearable present, where everything is just what it is, where the universe overlaps with itself, then it would be the Pole Star that saves us from ourselves. The Pole Star is also us: that is why we attempt to take it. But the Pole Star, in its unassailable nature of the remnant, is what introduces into the universe *the minimal displacement* which pushes us off from ourselves.

Thus, the Pole Star, embodiment of sovereignty, is the paradoxical inner transcendence of the modern universe deprived of confines in the proper sense. As long as sovereignty subsists, the universe is an unstable, protean totality, haunted by its apparent insufficiency and indebtedness. The structure of sovereignty postpones and displaces, creates multiple times and produces, as their common core, the unbearable dimension of lasting, into which they all fall. The structure of sovereignty dissects the totality from itself and sets the cut-off part against the rest, creating an illusion that there is something except beyond it. Yet, in truth (which is, in the properly Lacanian sense,[152] impossible), there is nothing but us. Naturally, the certainty that there is something such as us and that, *in fact*, it is all us, is nothing else but the miraculous work of sovereignty. In its deflecting power, it creates certainty out of nothing, props it up against a subject and opposes the latter to the inert mass over which it is supposed to rule. Hence the strictly modern affinity between (self)certainty, subject and subjectivity.

The work of the Pole Star produces, as its culmination, the temptation to acknowledge that all there is, is *us*, that there is nothing external and the universe is a field of *our* rule.[153] But, as we already saw, this temptation creates the sovereign. And the sovereign is the first victim of sovereignty: it falls off its promontory, leaving behind itself the unbearable dimension of lasting, whose characteristic silence is still hearable in places-remnants of past atrocities of sovereign powers. In other words, "us" is not a solution, but the core of the problem.

16.2 In her famous essay *Personal Responsibility under Dictatorship* Hannah Arendt argued that, in principle, those who are able to refuse consent to totalitarian power are not motivated by the staunch loyalty to cut-and-dried moral rules, which the regime wants to infringe, but, on the contrary, are skeptics, "because they are used to examine things and to make up their own minds."[154] This statement reflects the disillusioned powerlessness in which post-war thought woke up. How can we, intellectually, morally, and legally, deal with the existence of total regimes of sovereign power that not only commit crimes, but also change the very framework of the symbolic which defines crimes? How can we demand responsibility, if laws, newly enacted by the sovereign, change what hitherto had been crimes into acts morally indifferent or even commanded by the power?

Arendt concludes: "Best of all will be those who know only one thing for certain: that whatever else happens, as long as we live we shall have to live together with ourselves."[155] Indeed, in the modern universe we are thrown back on ourselves. Much disillusioning and calming as that is, it cannot be omitted that our absolute solitude might be equally the cornerstone of new ethics and the foundation of absolute crime that ruins even the possibility of naming it a crime. At the end of his notes from the dark years 1931-4, Max Horkheimer remarked bleakly that "[a]lso humankind is all alone":[156] now we cannot be nothing but "us."

"Us" remains like dregs after drinking the infusion of modern history. It seems as if in the convoluted modern universe this short, simple "us" provided some foundation, something which cannot be denied, something which allows to debunk social myths. But it is no true foundation. "Us" is a product of sovereignty, in whose inner contradiction it finds its fuel. We actually never know what "us" is: me, my past, my fears, my community, humankind, all animals, dwellers of the Earth,[157] the modern, the living or the present? "Us" sparkles with its undeterminable contents. That what it actually means is unclear and subject to political interception, but the certainty that "us" exists is—under the bleak sun of sovereignty—indestructible.

16.3 In this endless drudgery of creating, recreating and falling of "us" we seem trapped in a gallery of mirrors, which make us emerge out of nothing only to be played on against some inert mass. Yet, this entrapment is naturally nothing else than the work of sovereignty at its best. Through its power of deflection, reflection and creation, this remainder, the cornerstone of sovereignty, epitomized by Hegel's Pole Star, deserves a more subtle name: *the Mirror Star*.

16.4 The work of the Mirror Star is clearly discernible in the theory of the modern state. At the end of his *Lectures on the Philosophy of History*, Hegel notoriously deducts the status of the nation-state as Reason embodied and the true object of religious worship. This seemingly disgusting loyalist plea for the Prussian autocracy announces a much deeper paradox of modern sovereign state. Hegel begins with noticing that the true nation-state may be only Protestant or at least based on the Protestant principle, because only Protestantism seeks unity of belief and practice, state and religion. And it is precisely this unity that modern state requires as its inner will. Let us look closer into Hegel's reasoning:

> Consciousness that has received an abstract culture, and whose sphere is the Understanding can be indifferent to Religion, but Religion is the general form in which Truth exists for *non-abstract* consciousness. And the Protestant Religion does not admit of two kinds of consciences, while in the Catholic world the Holy stands on the one side and on the other side abstraction opposed to Religion, that is to its superstition and its truth.[158]

In this portrayal, Protestantism repudiates social abstraction and seeks not understanding, but Reason, which is nothing else than a claim to unity. It is based on the already familiar self-identity. The Protestant state finds an answer to the Rousseauian dilemma of how to construct a totality out of atomic individual wills:

> An *intellectual principle* was thus discovered to serve as a basis for the State—one which does not, like previous principles, belong to the sphere of opinion, such as the social impulse, the desire of security for property, etc. nor owe its origin to the religious sentiment, as does that of the Divine appointment of the governing power—but the principle of Certainty, which is identity with my self-consciousness, stopping short however of that of Truth, which needs to be distinguished from it. This is a vast discovery in regard to the profoundest depths of being and Freedom.[159]

How, if at all, can individual wills of citizens be reconciled and joined into one state will?[160] In this regard, Protestantism brings one crucial novelty: it establishes the principle of Certainty, "identity with my self-consciousness." It is nothing else than the self-confidence which we already analyzed as the Hegel's Polar Star. But how can it unite colliding individual wills? The answer is to be found a few pages further:

> This collision of subjective wills leads therefore to ... *Disposition* [*Gesinnung*]—an *ex animo* acquiescence in the laws; not the mere customary observance of them, but the cordial recognition of laws and the Constitution as in principle fixed and immutable, and of the supreme obligation of individuals to subject their particular wills to them. There may be various opinions and views respecting laws, constitution and government, but there must be a disposition on the part of the citizens to regard all these opinions as subordinate to the substantial interest of the State, and to insist upon them no farther than that interest will allow; moreover nothing must be considered higher and more sacred than good will towards the State; or, if Religion be looked upon as higher and more sacred, it must involve nothing really alien or opposed to the Constitution.... But although the aspects of Religion and the State are different, they are radically *one*; and the laws find their highest confirmation in Religion.[161]

Hegel's argumentation may be recapitulated as follows.[162] Modern society is necessarily pluralistic. Different views and opinions spread across the population. Every individual has her own will. If a state is to be born out of such a chaos, there are two options—"Catholic" and "Protestant" solutions—but, the first is flawed from the beginning. In theory, there may exist Catholic states, based on abstraction and Understanding, which artificially separate the state and the holy, and therefore never can form a truly united nation-state. Yet, Catholic states will never reach the unity and spirit of a nation-state.[163] The second, true option, is seemingly Protestant insofar as it concerns a state in which religion and statehood, albeit formally different, are equal in their content. This Protestantism in question is nothing but a reign of the principle of Certainty and self-identity of the state. The state is built upon its own sovereign conviction, upon the force of Spirit. It is possible, however, only if each and every individual has, underneath her particular will, *the disposition to recognize and follow the interest of the state as unity*.

This disposition is purely formal. It does not require the subjects of the state to adopt one worldview. They may as well believe in everything they want, if only at the bottom they preserve the disposition. Thus, it does not limit opinions as to their content; it merely suspends them if necessary. Citizens enjoy freedom, if only they are ready to suspend it at some point at the state's request. In this sense, such a disposition is a matrix of sovereignty within subjects of the state. It squares well with their private lives, it does not impinge on their interests and desires, but, *if necessary*, renders them inoperative so that the subject acts for the interest of the state.

It is in this sense that Hegel claimed, in the previously cited fragment, that the modern state is no longer based on opinions, for example concerning the deity of the ruler or legitimacy of state apparatus. It is, on the contrary, based on a contentless disposition to suspend opinions, views and desires, and to succumb to the state as unity. Disposition is to opinion what a sovereign is to the ruled: a (potential) suspension.

Modern state, based on the principle of sovereignty, does not have to intrude upon someone's freedom of thought. On the contrary, as long as this freedom is safely in the grip of disposition, modern state flourishes from it. Yet, ultimately, all opinions must be put in the dim apocalyptic light of the ultimate mobilization, in which disposition will have to suspend opinions. It is therefore clear that Hegel's opposition between Catholicism and Protestantism is just a disguise. What is truly at stake is the difference between the imaginary premodern state, ruled through opinions, and the modern state, ruled by disposition:

> Here it must be frankly stated, that with the Catholic Religion no rational constitution is possible; for Government and People must reciprocate that final guarantee of Disposition, and can have it only in a Religion that is not opposed to a rational political constitution.[164]

Thus, disposition is elevated to the role of a cornerstone of modern sovereign state. It is a final guarantee that the Government owes to the People and the People owes to the Government. Unsurprisingly, the word "state" is absent from this fragment: *the state is what emerges from reciprocity of promise between the Government and the People through the disposition*.

The disposition, let us remind, is a plea of ultimate loyalty, based on recognition of self-identity. To whom are we and are supposed to be loyal? In Hegel's language of sovereignty the answer is clear: to ourselves. With this very word we return to the paradox of planetary solitude embodied in the Mirror Star. In the disillusioned Hegelian gaze, the state is what remains after transcendence collapsed and left us stranded. *The state is utmost solitude*. To understand that there is nothing else than "us" means, in Hegel's logic, to accept the state as bitter perhaps, but all-too-real factuality. After all, whom should we be loyal to, if all the rules have crumbled? To "us," because "us" is the last, purely structural foothold of loyalty.

The state, just like all devices supported by the structure of sovereignty, displays features of the Mirror Star. On the one hand, it seems foreign to its citizens, being an estranged point which reigns over them. On the other hand, it appears nothing else than themselves. From an "external" perspective, it creates their identity through displacement—which is a source of recurring vibrating self-doubt as to who is "us" that reigns and "in whose name" the reign takes place. Perhaps, then, the sovereign state may be created in its "unity" with the people only through the work of the Mirror Star, but it is precisely this work that leaves the state identity open and prone to plunging into the temptation of total overlap between the people and the government.[165]

This temptation is of course brought to its limits by extreme nationalism, but its roots are well embedded in the very construction of the modern state. Already Thomas Hobbes remarks in his *Leviathan*:

> every subject is by this institution author of all the actions, and judgments of the sovereign instituted; it follows, that whatsoever he doth, it can be no injury to any of his subjects; nor ought he to be by any of them accused of injustice. For he that doth anything by authority from another, doth therein no injury to him by whose authority he acteth: but by this institution of a commonwealth, every particular man is author of all the sovereign doth: and consequently he that complaineth of injury from his sovereign, complaineth of that whereof he himself is author ... It is true that they that have sovereign power, may commit iniquity; but not injustice, or injury in the proper signification.[166]

In this fragment, Hobbes pursues full identification of the sovereign and the subject. As the latter allowed to be reigned by the former, s/he cannot raise any meaningful claim against the sovereign. Both are welded by identity. As a consequence, even though the sovereign exercises ultimate power over the subject, the term "injustice" does not even apply to their relations. Hobbes' principle of self-preservation, a natural law of each human being,[167] is an *external* principle, whereas the sovereign and the subject are treated as internal parts of one totality. For this reason the production of identity hands life over into the power of sovereignty.

The state is utmost solitude of "us," but, simultaneously, it is the device that produces "us" in the displacing reflection of the Mirror Star. As long as this displacement is active, citizens are linked to the state only through a latent disposition which ordinarily lets them engage in private acts and express opinions freely. But as soon as the contractions of sovereignty are triggered, the state, the government and the people veer towards the dark center of impossibility, where the three are supposed to melt into each other. "Private worlds" are suspended through disposition. There is a moment of seemingly sober realization: we need to fight for ourselves. The disposition to this way of thinking seals the unholy pact between the government and the people under the name of the state.[168] Thus, capitalist personal freedom is, above the apparent contradiction, squared with the demand of state nationalism to sacrifice one's life for the "fatherland."[169]

It is for this reason that Hegel needs his pseudo-Protestantism as the key foundation of the nation-state. According to his suggestions, Catholicism is opposed to the rational constitution because it presupposes abstraction and separation. In other words, as a shadow of premodern transcendence (even if already ineffective), it is detrimental to the unity of the state. The nation-state requires a religion which overlaps with the disposition that safeguards the reciprocal pact between the government and the people. It is a religion founded on self-recognition of planetary solitude, which, conflated to the boundaries of a nation-state, produces "us" that we are supposed to be loyal to. There is nothing more tempting than the self-indulgent tautology of being "ourselves," fighting for "ourselves," defending "ourselves" and working for "ourselves."

Yet, what eludes Hegel's attention is precisely the mode of construction of the stifling natio-state by the Mirror Star: that is, all the practical devices that give to particular and oppressive devices of power the unbridled power released by self-identity. The key feature of the Mirror Star's work lies precisely in producing the effect of apparent ineluctability of the path between the subject and the identity it is supposed to pursue. With this tension between self-realization and irremovable, endless postponement, the Mirror Star disguises the most contingent circumstances of the whole device in which it is used.

Against Hegel's critique of "Catholicism" there is a powerful counter-narrative which eulogizes Rome as the embodiment of universality against the particularity of Protestant nation-states.[170] But what truly deserves in-depth critique is the device which, in the spiral fall into the abyss of self-identity, lets itself be determined by most trivial and contingent circumstances of power. In other words, the self-recognition through the "Protestant" state religion is a staged trap: once the possibility of self-identity appears on Earth, sovereignty has us in its grip, in this garb or another.

What remains at bottom is another "us." But what makes and determines "us" holds power over a particular constellation of sovereignty. "Us" is organized by the cornerstone of sovereignty: the Mirror Star.

Creation of modern identity: From the Polar Star to the Mirror Star

17. With the advent of modernity, the intellectual imagery veers towards astronomical metaphors. Kantian "starry heavens" (→1.6) explode over human heads. All these heavens, stars and planetary erring are not imagined as something utterly distanced from us, but, very close to us. Here lies a stunning paradox: modernity thinks and

imagines itself through figures which connote the vastest and most all-encompassing relations, but, simultaneously, these relations constitute the innermost structure of the modern universe. Just as Nietzsche[171] and Heidegger[172] hinted, relations between the farthest and the closest became displaced. Yet it is not a result of some primordial error that might be mended, but a *permanent disruption of distance* that characterizes modernity. The farthest melts into the closest and vice versa. Stars, which for Aristotle epitomized most estranged and nearly perfect entities, began to live among us as symbols of stumbling blocks in most earthly relations. Being nothing but ourselves, we appear to ourselves as something most estranged, whereas both the closest ("us") and the farthest (the unassailable position of sovereignty) are indifferentiable positions created within the modern universe.

The modern universe cannot think itself otherwise than in categories of unstable totality, but it needs to think itself even in the tiniest bits of knowledge concerning most prosaic things. Here lies the power of what Marx portrayed as concrete abstraction[173]—namely, a point of indifferentiation between the most abstract and most concrete, in which local knowledge is always general and total knowledge is always flawed by the particularity of the local. In this sense, the Mirror Star is ubiquitous. It is what remains the most distanced and unimaginable—and the closest. All the modern universe, if it might be imagined at all, is its playground.

What is "us" then? Who are "we" that due to some kind of objectification turn into "us"? Maybe nothing else than—to make a pun on Heidegger's sombre concept[174]— nothing but *Arbeiter des Sterns*, "workers of the star"? If so, working for "ourselves" is nothing else than working for the star which holds our identity. This toil is deeply entangled in dependence on sovereignty. Heidegger himself either "worked" in either frenetic, but vague mobilization (in the early 30s) or in *Gelassenheit*, the patient "process" of releasement. In both cases, he awaited *die Sternstunde*, "the hour of the star"—mentioned in the seminar on *Der Ister*—slowly prepared by "the concealed spirit of the beginning in the West."[175]

"Us" would then be a working set of projections on distant mirrors. It is straddled between emptiness and identity which is always promised, deferred, and projected onto the place and time of the Mirror Star.

5.3 We already saw that modern sovereignty might be interpreted as transformation of transcendence. Whereas transcendence appears outside the world, as its stable counterpart, sovereignty appears within the universe and deflects all impulses directed at the outside back to the universe. But now we might notice how the figure of the Mirror Star epitomizes this paradoxical position: forces which led from this world towards its transcendence were bent in a circle and started to operate directly on the mass of positive material of the universe. In this sense, the loop of *jouissance* is the precise projection of the process of self-encirclement of transcendence in modernity.

The former frontier between the world and the otherworldly was not removed. On the contrary, it was preserved as a moving point which seems to mark the boundary of the universe, but, in fact, only reveals its impossibility to overlap with itself. The true problem of modernity, therefore, is not the disappearance of transcendence, but the structural displacement of transcendence into the position of the Mirror Star. It is in this, and only in this sense, that Heidegger's claim that modern thought is the age of completion of metaphysics[176] might be continued. Metaphysics dropped its content, transmogrified into a powerful, purely structural mechanism and thus brought its history to a standstill whose repetitive throb makes an impression of the almost-already reached end.

To paraphrase Kant,[177] the realm of transcendence has come among us. We do not need to watch metaphysics burn out, let alone guard its fading. Fading is the essential and atemporal condition of sovereignty—modern transcendence—through which it rules.

18.1 The Mirror Star accounts for the primordial instability of all beings within the modern universe and their structurally embedded temptation to constitute themselves in the place of the impossible.

The mirror captures the image of a being. It produces an image in which a being might, for the first time, perceive itself as one whole. But this whole does not appear in the place of this being; in this sense, it is not its own. It appears upon the seemingly supplementary surface of the mirror, which purports to act only as a material, external support, not intervening into the constitution of the image as such. Thus, the Mirror Star, which works accordingly, epitomizes the paradoxical entanglement of identity and its disruption in the modern universe.

All beings need a mediation in order to constitute themselves as wholes; but this mediation must come from the outside. A distinct whole might be constituted only outside beings, in the place which does not belong to them, but seems to act as a mere prop. In the modern universe beings do not overlap with themselves, but are torn between their existence and their (imaginary) wholeness which requires some outside point in order to be formed. And it is the Mirror Star that appears to offer an external place in which beings might constitute themselves. In this place, they might, for the first time, recognize themselves in their independence, in the furthest possible estrangement from all relations. In other words, through the existence of the Mirror Star—or sovereignty, as we called it—within the modern universe all beings are offered their solid, independent identities, but at the furthest, almost impossible point.

18.2 All mirrors expropriate; they extract the complete identity from a being. Once we catch our image in the mirror, we are tempted to think about ourselves as something complete, unitary and independent. Our identity was extracted and formed at the surface of the mirror. Nevertheless, it is still an external place, even if the emptiest. The Mirror Star, which is the inner transcendence of the modern universe and its ubiquitous remainder, acts in this manner. It lures beings with the possibility of self-constitution, which will cut the being from the unbearable turmoil of constantly shifting grounds.

This lure is the promise of independence, of control over one's boundaries, of being finally oneself, beyond all the entanglements of the modern universe. It constitutes the structure of modern identity, which functions as a *split temptation to become oneself*: if followed to the end, it veers towards the most external and empty place, thereby ruining the being. If not followed, it shines over the being's world as a postponed possibility, which, in its congealed state, acts as identity itself. Therefore, modern identity exists as a deferred promise, whose power lies in its luring capacities. It is this promise and the resistance against it that makes modern beings exist. But, if this resistance fades and the promise is taken seriously, all identity falls apart leaving only dregs of negativity at its bottom.

19. As a consequence, all that we are tempted with in the modern universe is "us"—our identity. "Be yourself!" or Nietzschean "become who you are!" are nothing but sweet temptations of sovereignty. In this sense, the lure is helplessly tautological and stubbornly defies the need for its justification: why should not we become ourselves if it is possible? Is it not something that we, somehow, already possess, and, beyond any demand for explanation, have an unquestionable right to? If we already are, we are who we are, why should not we become who we are? The apparent tautology eliminates in advance any questions about the sense and ethical calculus of "becoming whom one is."

The constitutive curve of modern identity would be then constituted by the split between "us" and "us-in-truth." The split which is, in fact, nothing, a mere switch of perspective, the tiniest difference embedded in identity; but its force, the force of modern sovereignty, which pushes beings into themselves so that they finally overlap with themselves, is hard to overestimate. The split is so small, so insignificant, that it seems as if its removal demanded only a minute effort. Yet, it is structurally irremovable: it suspends the relation between efforts and goals, thereby excluding the possibility of assessing how much effort was effectively spent. The goal belongs to a different level than the effort, so they can never meet. As a result, the effort loses all external measures and might be spent endlessly and uncountably.

The suspension of effort through a structural blockade is a fingerprint of sovereignty, which reigns over the modern universe not as transcendence—with external revelation, sense and injunctions, juxtaposed with the world—but with the contentless difference and displacement. It seems as if the universe reigned over itself, but this relation presumes that something differentiates the universe-as-reigning from the universe-as-reigned: this miraculous power of dissolving, creating identity and, finally, of setting off the potential accumulated through inner differentiation of beings, is, precisely speaking, modern sovereignty.

20. If sovereignty acts through displacement and difference, it is dependent on the existence of *space*. Yet, the space in question should be understood in a conceptual, not ordinary sense—that is, an overarching, all-encompassing possibility of bare difference created by moving a being from itself.

This space is necessary for the always-external position of the Mirror Star, which never coincides with beings, but presents them with their own image constituted in another place. In this sense, space is the factor which introduces into beings a basic, contentless difference—which makes two beings different even though all their substantial features are the same. In this light, Leibniz's defence of the premodern *status quo*—the identity of indiscernibles[178]—demonstrates how modern difference already intervened into the smooth and transparent premodern universe not based on some fundamental unsettling negativity. Apparently, modernity originates a kind of overarching, inexplicable difference, which cannot be meaningfully described, but might be only acknowledged and referred to with the concept of space. Modern space not only differentiates two identical beings (that is fairly intuitive), but even one being, separating it from its identity that has been constituted elsewhere.

In this sense, it is rather the Lurianic concept of צמצום (tsimtsum)—the divine contraction[179] (or, in Gershom Scholem's modern interpretation, withdrawal of God[180])—that captures the emergence of modern space as *a possibility of creation through basic differentiation*.[181]

21. Space and the Mirror Star create altogether a device of modern difference, which bears only superficial affinity to the premodern difference based on substantial content.

The principal feature of this modern device consists in the specific position of material content which is no longer the natural locus of difference (e.g., two things are different because one is green, the other is red), namely the substance from which difference arises. In modernity, material content turns into *passive material* on which the device of difference plays. In this sense, difference precedes the material content and arranges it in such a manner that some material differences are fueled by the power of negativity and become significant, whereas others become almost invisible.

The previously unitary substantial difference is now, within the modern device, split into space—which provides the basic, contentless difference, indiscernible from the very possibility of difference—and the Mirror Star, which turns the spatial difference into the mirage of constituted identity. Spatial difference is inexplicable and primary; the mirror seems to stabilize it and reduce it to insignificant distance. Into such a device the positive material is caught and then it is played upon. Modern difference might be therefore considered as *a play of spatially distanced mirrors*, which seize the material content, reproduce it, enriching with the potential of mute, spatial difference, and then juxtapose it with itself.

As a consequence, in modernity two contradictory statements enter the threshold of indifferentiation: that difference is something most basic, inexplicable and ubiquitous—and that difference is something most insignificant, which may be almost disregarded with the institution of identity. And, perhaps it is the dual device of modern difference that accounts for the modern simultaneous obsession and repression of sight as a figure of one-sidedness, of geometrical, systematic and thus blind approach to reality which creates objects only to still and kill them.[182] Sight is often intuitively viewed as insufficient in juxtaposition with the irremovable excessive difference that founds reality. But it was not until the dawn of modernity that this approach was made possible—and it is from the dual device of space and the Mirror Star that it might draw its force.

The Mirror Star: Modern universe in motion

22. The figure of the Mirror Star demonstrates that, ultimately, we are left with nothing but ourselves. This remainder simultaneously creates and dislocates every gaze, making everything project itself outside everything in search for itself. Thus, the universe

reigns over itself in a form which resembles a Möbius band, but with a permanently shifting separator between its two sides. In this world without causes, reasons and justifications everything might pass for a cause.

The category which might best grasp this specificity is the old Freudian-Althusserian term:[183] overdetermination. The existence of the Mirror Star distorts every relation by overburdening it with irremovable excess. As a consequence, excess and remainder are central obsessions of modernity. Just as in the Middle Ages philosophy compulsively ruminated about universals, so is modern philosophy fixed on the problem of relation between totality, remainder and excess. The early modern rise of epistemology and its break into an ontological-epistemological complex in the Kantian critique prepared the ground for what we have been musing on for over two centuries. The thirty years that passed between 1788, when Kant published his second *Critique*, and 1818, the year of Hegel's *Inaugural Address* in Berlin, bear the first marks of the new, inertly cyclical nature of modern time, in which pure, unpredictable happening mysteriously re-traces the circular move around the remainder.

23. What is surprising in the universe reigned by the Mirror Star is the frugality of its mechanism, so stunningly and visibly poor. It does without all ornaments of transcendence—all gods and otherworldly powers—which were indispensable in the previous epochs. It moves by itself, regardless of any external impulses. In its construction, it is always on the verge of absolute standstill, since it cannot be anyhow pushed outside. But this standstill is never reached, it is always near, it has always almost happened. The seemingly ultimate moment of accomplishment is, however, permanently postponed by an apparently unimportant last obstacle. The universe governed by the structure of sovereignty is always running out of time. It is permanently on overtime, on this senseless extra time which is borrowed as a supplement, but extends to become the basic mode of temporality.

This universe is destitute and solitary. Through the work of constant displacement and subsequently produced illusion, it creates still new unreachable goals. But as soon as the mirror moves further away, the stark, senseless materiality of what had been done appears as almost painful.

24. Modernity is the epoch which the figure of the Mirror Star both sets in motion and explains, to the point of their indifferentiability.

2

For a Derridean-Copernican Revolution

Modernity Before History

25. It is now time to look closer at the terms "modern" and "modernity" that we used in the previous chapter. What do we do when we refer explanations to one particular epoch, modernity? It is almost as if by adding the adjective "modern" or the expression "in modernity" the phenomena in question underwent a substantial transformation and "modern" meant nothing less than "historically discontinuous."

Countless authors, from Hegel himself, through Marx, Nietzsche, Adorno, Blumenberg, Heidegger, up to Foucault, Arendt, Agamben, and Žižek, investigated the *differentia specifica* of modernity and conceived of it as a more or less radically new epoch.[1] However varied their approaches would be, they saw modernity as an unprecedented cut in the tissue of history. But we accept it, common sense runs to our help (and desolation) claiming that over and above all discontinuities which might exist between modernity and the premodern era there is some basic dimension of continuity, at least in terms of social relations, technique, memory, etc. Fernand Braudel's concept of *longue durée* manifestly defies the vision of a total cut.[2] But in this manner the debate falls into a fruitless opposition between quasi-metaphysical supporters of modern specificity against "rational" adherents of natural and observable continuity of history. In this context opting for particularity of modernity seems to be equivalent to taking the metaphysicians' side.

But, what if this opposition is distributed so skilfully around the shatters of truth that each side is hopelessly entrenched in its own justifiable position? What if the opposition should be broken and reconfigured in order to shed light on modernity? Perhaps what is unique about this epoch is that it itself produces the conditions of possibility of perceiving it: *there would not be history if modernity did not already operate*.[3] In this sense, even supporters of continuity act within the field of the possible opened by modernity.

History as a presupposition of modernity

26. History, as we know it currently, bears little resemblance to what it might have been before the advent of modernity. Our history is not a short tapestry of myth which links divine beginnings of the universe with its possible future end. It is not a screen

whose frames would be given once and for all or which would provide total sense for everything which is displayed within them. Our history has no ruler, no personal will, let alone a reasonable one. It can no longer be smoothly pigeonholed into a universal scheme of sense. Happening has now its own value, and in the meantime all other values crumbled. We feel, almost palpably, the raw matter of happening. Before modernity, we seem to have been able to tame it with meanings. But now they arrive and smash the very fundaments of our understanding. The most powerful constructions that we produce to domesticate history are ridiculed by their own collapse.

In other words, history as we know it has emancipated from the grip of meaning. As such, it is no longer a solid meaningful construction potent enough to render time irrelevant for the very framework of our understanding. It is not that time became a dangerous device, it has always been so; but now, more than ever, it is visible how this device is capable of eating away at the fundaments of meanings. In this light, modernity could be seen as time-related general neurosis, in which the bare difference of time comes to the fore.

Therefore, history as defined in modernity is significantly different from anything that might have been previously called history. In modernity, historicity pervaded the entire imagery of the epoch. Our historical position is enquired obsessively and to little avail. We desperately seek for the meaning of history and with absolute certainty of its impossibility. In short, history has never truly become a real philosophical problem until the advent of modernity.

27.1 The problem of history grows out of mycelium[4] of *the possibility of historical self-differentiation*—that is, of the very possibility of perceiving difference based only on time and not on substantial content. History, as we know it, arises when time becomes a real destructive power which holds priority over meaning. Meanings no longer grasp the flow of time; on the contrary, they pass *in* time. This new, destructive time makes A different from B on the ground of mere temporal difference, and this difference precedes and undermines all substantial determinations. Therefore, the core of mechanism that builds up our meaningful history is meaningless.

In this sense, history is a symbolic device dependent upon temporal self-differentiation which it neither understands nor grasps. What we contemporaneously call history has a structure of the symbolic that revolves around the real of time—contrariwise to premodern historical narratives, in which meanings were able to grasp happening and domesticate it. As a consequence, (modern) history is always partial, fragmented, and not in possession of its own mechanism. It is marked by indebtedness to its own elusive core, and, for this reason, *it has the structure of ongoing catastrophe viewed from the position of a latecomer.*

27.2 The shift in the work of the concept of history did not pass unnoticed in eighteenth-century thought.[5] It profoundly marked Hume's philosophy, which, for this reason, gained much more importance than it could have received as a form of luxurious skepticism. The focal point of Hume's thought lies in his critical reassessment of causality. It is well-known that he vigorously opposed causality construed as the necessary linkage between events.[6] In his view, what we perceive as relations between causes and effects boils down to our mere habit. Yet, in truth, Hume argues, there is no objective link between them and only our remembrance of event sequences leads us to consider them intertwined. This argumentation is the first sign of the fundamental reconfiguration which made time precede before meaning.

It is visible as soon as we penetrate into the engine of Hume's reasoning. According to Hume, the idea of causality stems from our memory: we remember past accidents and infer from them how causal links will work in the future.[7] If so, the only truly grounded empirical data must come from the present. As a consequence, even the most reliably observed and logged experience that already belongs to the past cannot be fully trusted. For Hume all the past is nothing but our recollection; all the future, nothing but our anticipation.[8] Naturally, it does not mean that thinking of past and future events should be discarded altogether; they should be treated with skepticism grounded in the recognition of the primary role of the present.

Due to this primacy of the present Hume comes to a conclusion that memory and imagination are effectively of the same nature[9] and the only difference between them consists in liveliness of perceptions that memory presents:

> And as any idea of the memory, by losing its force and vivacity, may degenerate to such a degree, as to be taken for an idea of the imagination; so on the other hand an idea of the imagination may acquire such a force and vivacity, as to pass for an idea of the memory, and counterfeit its effects on the belief and judgment.[10]

Whereas there is no qualitative difference between memory and imagination, such a difference exists between memory and present impressions. Consequently, present impressions constitute a privileged source of knowledge. If we do not experience hallucinations, imagination cannot produce impressions equally convincing as our senses.

This "solipsism of the present" is not just an errant path of skepticism; on the contrary, it is a sign of a tectonic reconfiguration. What Hume dubs as "ideas," produced either by memory or imagination, is nothing less than the whole structure of our language-based knowledge. This skepticism, therefore, claims that all our statements, all memories and anticipations, are always dependent on the shifting "present."

Hume may be understood as arguing that a statement is true as long as the state of affairs which it describes is still present. "I see a messiah now," is true as long as I see a messiah, but becomes a dubious memory if the messiah disappeared. Yet, this reading does not do justice to the scale of Humean skepticism, because it assumes that the very structure of language is unchangeable and its eternal presence always corresponds to some "present" which corroborates the veracity of statements. But what makes us assume that the content of statements passes while statements are still understandable? Why should we think that the "solipsism of the present" spares language itself? If it does not, then we should assume that past statements are unreliable by the very fact of their past quality, not only because their reference might have disappeared. In other words, consistent Humean skepticism should assume that *there is no understanding between the past and the present, because time ravages the very work of meaning*.

Naturally, thus construed skepticism is far-fetched and self-contradictory, as it is itself couched in statements that belong to the past. Moreover, it must rely on a hard-line logocentrist form of presentism. But the sense of Hume's discovery is nonetheless crucial. What he stumbles upon is the repositioning of relations between time and meaning. Meanings no longer can be unproblematically conserved in time: in their very functioning, they are being undermined by the flow of time.

Humean "present" is only an undeveloped rendering of the new relation between time and meaning. At the very core of the symbolic universe a permanent time-related crack appears. It seems as if our whole language and knowledge were dependent on a purely temporal difference, and thus undermined in their claims to producing eternally valid statements. In their very construction they depend on what ravages them.

In this context, Hume's presentism would be a desperate attempt to grasp the elusive center which seems both to give and preclude the only solid anchoring for language and knowledge. The whole tentative is manifestly erroneous. But, as such, it is a testimony to an obscure event which shattered the symbolic framework and let the genie of temporal self-differentiation out of the bottle.

27.3 What we know as history is a symbolic device that emerges in relation to the appearance of contentless temporal difference at the heart of the symbolic. In this regard, history is a mediating instrument through which the symbolic refers to the temporal crack in its own tissue. That history obsessively pervades modern thinking would be then a consequence of time-induced erosion of the symbolic.

Deconstructing history: Self-differentiation and time

28.1 The problem of history, as we remarked (→ 27.1), grows out of mycelium of the possibility of temporal self-differentiation—that is, some new, basic form of differentiation, contentless and based purely on time. This self-differentiation is a mechanism that introduces basic difference into the universe. It does so by whirling around an ungraspable residue which ultimately makes the symbolic possible.

As demonstrated Hume's example, this self-differentiation—as a result of which time precedes the symbolic—is not, in itself, a mechanism that has always existed. It is not eternal, but has emerged at some point. Can this moment be pinpointed? Such a question concerns the murkiest issue of the origins of modernity. We can definitely track some traces, but the whole event is shrouded by mystery—in the line of Heidegger's remark on thought's inability to reach beginnings.[11]

Why? Because we are already *in* history, propelled by the emergence of temporal self-differentiation. We attempt to recognize boundaries of the event in whose stream we are immersed. Once triggered, temporal self-differentiation continues its work and, in this sense, is an ongoing event. It ultimately splits the epoch "before" from the epoch "after" its emergence. Thus, it allows of perceiving its origin only through its own mechanism. But contentless self-differentiation always produces nothing else than pure difference; how then its emergence could be different from its usual work if not through this very same pure difference?

Here we encounter a fundamental paradox of modern temporality and history: the emergence of pure difference differs from what it is preceded by only through pure difference, that is, by itself. For this reason, the origins of modern self-differentiation cannot be differentiated from its continuous work. It seems as if it neither emerged nor existed for ever. Through its very functioning, it continuously repeats its origin from which it is indifferentiable.

Therefore, if the emergence of temporal self-differentiation is linked to (if not identified with) the origins of modernity, it becomes clear that despite all our intuitions modernity cannot be understood as "an epoch" which simply emerged. Contrariwise, *modernity should be considered a proto-condition of history*. It seems as if it never started and, simultaneously, always kept starting anew.

28.2 Perhaps then modernity is to history what Derrida's *différance* is to language: that is, "the pure movement which produces difference," "before all determination of content."[12] Modernity allows of history and builds its basic framework of differentiation. What we know as history is already modern history.

Yet, modernity offers us a much more fascinating riddle. It is not only a proto-condition of history, but also "an epoch" that appears *in* history. It appears in what it has allowed of. Having opened the dimension of history, it returns to what is has conditioned and inscribes itself in it as a point of particularity. For this reason, modernity occupies a paradoxical overdetermined position: it both conditions the very perception of history and locates itself within it.

Therefore, all features commonly associated with modernity—its reflexivity, historical consciousness, self-problematization, constant attempts to overcome itself and demarcate itself from the outside—would be conditioned by a much more stunning proto-structure. Modernity is bound to enquire about its nature and position, because it does not fully fit the continuous array of epochs. Not due to its special features or distinctive characteristics, but because of the primordial constructing link between modernity and history, which would make modernity stand out in the portrayal of epochs even if this "epoch" had almost no distinctive traits. For this reason, modernity attempts to pass for an "epoch," but simultaneously allows of the whole history understood as a chain of "epochs."

When relating to modernity, history enters the field of its own conditions of possibility and grapples for its own boundaries. Symmetrically, modernity needs the dimension of history in order to search for its self-constitution. But this search is futile,[13] since history as we know it is a by-product of modern self-differentiation—and cannot be an answer to the question of what modernity truly is. Modernity is a problem in itself, in its dual embedding in and outside history. It cannot be understood without history, but history is not the key.

29.1 The specificity of modernity lies in the overdetermined link between its two forms: it is both (1) a field of possibility of historical self-differentiation, and (2) an epoch within a temporal sequence. This link might be described as a collapse of the proto-difference into a restrained symbolic form, "an epoch."

Traces of this collapse haunt all forms of thinking about modernity under the guise of irremovable excess. On the one hand, when we stick to circumspect historiography, modernity dissolves into a series of events and long-term transformations which step by step lead to the creation of our contemporary world. Ruptures disappear from such history. Even the most spectacular upheavals which we tend to associate with the beginnings of modernity—such as, for instance, the French Revolution—might be (and must be) causally linked to earlier developments (the rise of the *tiers état*, corruption of the institutional system of absolutism, new currents of thought, the example of the American Revolution, etc.[14]). In this way, the uniqueness of the event is blunted. Even if we agree that apart from all the conditioning circumstances such events have their own unique dynamics (thus bringing historiography a bit closer to Badiou's concept of event), there is no obvious link between such dynamics and the specificity of modernity. True, modern revolutions are unique, but does it anyhow reveal the uniqueness of the whole epoch? Evidently, historiography which assumes that history is continuous remains haunted by the spectre of rupture which it can either ignore totally or dissolve in local novelty of particular events. Modernity is too excessive to be pacified within a continuous sequence of epochs.

On the other hand, all searches for the *differentia specifica* of modernity border dangerously on metaphysical speculation, because they usually presuppose that history in itself is meaningful and gives, to this particular epoch, a distinctive shape. In this understanding, there is some "modern excess" which precedes all events in modernity and manifests itself in them. In other words, the French Revolution, for instance, does not inaugurate features of a new epoch, but embodies the change which already happened.[15] But, in practice, this "excess"—rationalized under various names, from the instrumentalization of reason up to secularization—cannot be isolated in itself; it always appears in a necessary link with concrete processes in modernity. The structure cannot be dissociated from positive historical material. If we seek the specificity of modernity in this way, we necessarily extrapolate *some* features of *some* events into a broader framework. Then we attempt to return with them to other events and seek out, to the detriment of objectivity, "the truly modern" traits, which are in fact nothing more than characteristics of one event transposed onto another.

The rift between continuous and discontinuous view on modern history uncannily resembles Kant's antinomies of pure reason:[16] either modernity can be dissolved into a finite (even if not known entirely) chain of causes, and thus flows from what precedes it historically, or there is some radical, ungraspable novelty, which we might only recognize in some events, but which does not boil down to them.

29.2 This antinomy shows that the essence of the dilemma does not consist in the difference between modernity-as-one-of-the-epochs and modernity-as-uniqueness. Such a difference is a result, not the ground of the problem. That we might see modernity either as continuing previous history or introducing a radical cut is already the key differentiation. Modernity resists unequivocal descriptions. It multiplies and warps all attempts to grasp it. Therefore, the true problem does not consist in deciding which of the two options is true, but in the very fact that the zone of ambiguity always shrouds the origins and character of modernity. What we perceive as modern is inextricably linked with our decision to break the stalemate: and then it appears in the form that we have determined ourselves.

To sum up: the specificity of modernity does not necessarily lie in its radical originality. On the contrary, it consists in the fact that modernity, as one of the epochs of the imagined continuous history, overlaps with modernity as the very field of possibility of history. For this reason, in a certain sense, *history is mediation through which modernity investigates itself*. Obviously, having such a role, history cannot provide any answer on the character of modernity: it only gathers a lot of objective material which will never solve the problem, since it has little to do with it. Modernity as a concept is an overdetermined loop, which eventually, after all historical ruminations, simply returns to itself. But, what is undoubtedly given, is the differentiation between perceiving modernity either as unique or fitting into the scheme of history. The rift here is not an argument about facts or interpretations, but a real antagonism in the post-Lacanian sense. The very existence of this rift suggests that at the basic level, available only to abstraction, modernity is nothing but a field of differentiation which allows of history. Therefore, it is itself ahistorical, or rather proto-historical. From the point of view of history, modernity is its Real, in relation to which it is always deferred. Perhaps then the real specificity of modernity might be then grasped only if it is treated, in a paradoxical manner, as situated completely outside history.

Modernity as a proto-historical space

30.1 If so, we may need to discard the opposition between continuous history and discontinuous history ripped open by modernity. What we should do is investigating the tension between the basic difference operating under, in and upon history—and the positive historical material which the difference organizes and then inscribes itself in it. It must be stressed that this positive material is in itself created by the work of difference, which, by its apparent withdrawal,[17] creates the impression of objectivity, or even materiality of "mere facts."

But can we actually think in this line? We have always already nearly-thought so. Great philosophies of the modern era, starting with Kant and his theory of time and space as forms of sensibility,[18] presuppose, at some level, that modernity is ahistorical—namely, that it is some mass of "factual matter" only organized into histories. It is for this reason that modern philosophies obsessively think about history and produce historical (counter)narratives. Among them the story about "the Greek error"—that is, Socratean/Platonian collapse into metaphysics from which Western philosophy must constantly awake itself—probably enjoys the greatest popularity.[19] Others demand radical historical transformations, either Idealist, like Hegel, or materialist, like Marx, or post-/non-/metaphysical, like Heidegger. But their true problem is not the historical position of modernity, let alone modern specificity. They obsessively return to the way in which *some a/historical difference produces and cuts through history*. For them, this difference is palpable, it is almost here and now, like, for Kant, the Kingdom of God. They predict a radically new epoch and would like to deliver it, thereby witnessing how the difference smashes the dead present. The historical narratives in which they dress up the whole division between the difference and the positive material are moveable decorations, pushed to and fro.

Therefore, modern philosophy attests to the work of a device composed of the basic difference, the positive material and historical narratives which fly out like sparks from the hammering of self-differentiation.

30.2 What we then ought to seek is thinking modernity in its ostensibly and consistently a/historical or proto-historical character. Our natural convictions about the continuity of history, our searches for crucial events, our endless debates on what is modern and what is not, and to what extent, deserve to be suspended. There can be no determining event that may be linked with the "onset" of modernity. It is rather always the same time-cutting event which keeps occurring that pierces through the mass of positive material and gives an impression of "specifically modern" happenings.

In this sense, from the proto-historical point of view, modernity has never begun and will never end, since its "existence" conditions the only vision of history that we know. If the field of self-differentiation which governs our historicity changes, it will do so in a discontinuous manner. *Modernity will then disappear, but will not end, for it itself imposes all conditions of historicity that allow of perceiving "beginnings" and "endings."* Yet, it might be equally possible that in this respect modernity as a proto-historical grid is a trap absorbing all forms of history. If it were so, then we should not expect any radical cut that will eliminate our current historicity.

If, therefore, modernity is to be thought in all its seriousness, it should be perceived as a space within which not only time operates, but is also rendered possible. If so, time cannot be the ultimate "container" for all events, as Kant wanted,[20] a container to which modernity were to belong only as a unit. Time is such a container only to a limited degree: beyond it there is—*in* modernity—some broader space of mediation in which time itself is located. Perhaps then, modernity, from a strategic point of view, should be rather understood as our (conceptual) universe. In itself it would be timeless, since it has time "in itself."

Overdetermination of modernity: A trans-epoch

31.1 Yet, even if we perceive modernity as the proto-historical field of self-differentiation which has time in itself, we cannot get rid of the initial problem. We remarked that modernity is overdetermined—being, simultaneously, the grid of conditions of possibility and an epoch inscribed in the history it itself allows of. By treating modernity proto-historically we simply disregard the fact that modernity is also, in a certain respect, an era. Is then any chance of understanding modernity in both of these aspects?

If we have to deal with a proto-condition which allows of history and then inscribes itself in it, we might take different paths. The first one, manifestly deconstructionist, would be to scrutinze carefully how particular narratives on modernity perform this inscription. It would involve tracking great stories on the beginnings of modernity, from the Cartesian one up to the French Revolution, in search of manipulative gestures through which the positive material is first posited and then "revealed" as a sign of epochal breakthrough. But this path, however necessary and illuminating, shows only the work of *the modern inscription,* that is how the whole device achieves its results. We do not learn, however, how the proto-historical field functions and why modernity has a self-differentiating propulsion at its heart. If we want to address these questions, we would need to take a different path.

This alternative path, that we had already begun to outline, starts with suspending the dimension of history. Since history operates within modernity and serves as the mediating term between modernity-as-proto-history and modernity-as-an-epoch, modernity might be grasped not through its inscription in history but in the inexhaustible movement of self-differentiation that constantly and necessarily produces history. In this sense, (modern) self-differentiation seems—but only seems—to be ubiquitous and transhistorical. It is precisely for this reason that Derrida might have tracked the work of *différance* not only in modern, but also premodern works. But the fact that he could undertake his project does not mean that self-differentiation was "in itself" eternal, that it "already was" in past texts. By its very definition, self-differentiation works as if it were eternal, as if it "were always already there," but, in fact, it simply clings to positive material from which it becomes inextricable.

If so, we should be aware that the dimension of history is an indispensable part of modern thinking. It might disguise itself as a supplement, as a grid for narratives, even as a purely neutral or technical frame of reference. In all these roles, it attempts to appear as objective as possible—that is, as a mere framework, obvious and taken for granted. In this sense, it performs a stabilizing function: since modernity is a realm of relentless difference, there needs to be a "container," some inactive, neutral—and, most of all, "external"—matter which does not take part in the constant game of differentiation.[21] The dimension of history appears as such. Among the permanent transformation, which is the daily bread of modernity, the very framework of transformation—history—appears as the only invariable. We might witness nothing but change, but at least it is change that can we notice: this is the conviction that founds the dimension of history. It is particularly visible in the contemporary humanities, which—as if in a Hassidic tale collected by Shmuel Yosef Agnon and famously cited by Scholem[22]—cannot repeat the former magic of thought, because it sees too many aporetic places and differentiates its substance to the point of loss of sense, but at least it can narrate how the magic worked in the past. Since the nineteenth century, thought has been permanently collapsing into history which seems to have crept in between "reality itself" and thought once and for all. Thus, history cut us off from the "naive" attempt to describe the world and supplemented it with history of ideas.

The alternative path that we outline here must therefore suspend the dimension of history. In other words, history can no longer pass for an objective, transparent-as-air framework for thought; it must be perceived as part and parcel of the very same device which triggers constant self-differentiation. Suspension means that we can neither lament over the loss of directness by the establishment of history (this lament, as the Derridean lure of origin,[23] would be itself produced by the historical framework) nor unconditionally immerse in history as the necessary mode of our thinking. On the contrary, history should be understood as the indispensable part of discourse and, as such, rendered inactive in its claims for neutrality in relation to the play of difference.

In this sense, it would be necessary to rethink the usage of historical or quasi-historical elements of philosophical narratives at least from Rousseau[24] onwards. The historical framework which founds various discourses of the humanities (with intellectual history at the forefront) cannot be the neutral milieu veiling the inherent emptiness of modern thought: it must appear as the core of the problem. Yet, this is precisely what is the hardest to reconsider, given that historical research has become the main (even if not always conscious) mode of the contemporary humanities.

31.2 Setting aside the necessity of re-evaluation of the historical framework, we still need to seek an answer for the underlying problem: how can we think modernity as both proto-history and an epoch? We are already aware that the very possibility of historical discourse as we know it is modern in its provenance. For this reason, modernity as proto-history must be conceived of as a term which applies to both modern and premodern times. We have already suspended the dimension of history as something which is necessarily produced by modern discourse. What we obtain is modernity as a unique mix of universality and particularity: modernity is both ubiquitous (since it founds the very possibility of the dimension of history) and delimited (as an epoch within this history). Modernity epitomizes the rift between universality and particularity, which both coincide in what simultaneously divides and links them: history.

This paradox has far-reaching consequences. It is modernity that allows of conceiving continuous history, but at the same time such a history is tainted by modern characteristics. What we know as objective is possible only through a founding, non-objective delimitation. All (temporal) universality that we construct is haunted by an element of particularity. This entanglement of universality and particularity resembles of what we already called perspectivism (→ 2.28).[25] Perhaps then modernity should be perceived as necessarily perspectivist—as the inherent perspectivism of the very conceptual universe that we are in.

In this sense modernity would be "the perspectivism of all perspectivisms," the ultimate curve of the space in which modern discourses are produced. If all of them are necessarily particular and biased, but nevertheless posing for a universal symbolic framework, modernity would be the broadest possible description of perspectivism. It would constitute the last frontier that we can reach in the perspectivist universe. There is no such thing as "objective content" in modernity: even as a whole it is subjected to some basic predetermination.

31.3 In this construction, it becomes clear that a given history acts as mediator between universality, to which a given perspective pretends, and particularity of its basic predetermination. In case of the whole modernity, the role of the mediator is played by history as such. Modernity as the ultimate case of perspectivism, its framework of possibility, links universality and particularity through the very dimension of history and inscribes all positive material in this framework. For this reason, modernity is both the (universal) proto-history and a (particular) epoch—with history as such acting as its field of operation.

Consequently, in modernity, everything is structurally historical. History enters each and every part of modern life, language[26] and thinking, like an unstoppable flood.

Within the boundaries of this trans-epoch eternity might never appear otherwise than an ephemeral moment of messianic halt. This has nothing to do with the premodern eternity, in which gods were born. The messianic attempt only accentuates particularity of the moment; then history only gathers its momentum. If history is the ultimate mediator between universality and particularity of modernity as a trans-epoch, then feeling helplessly historical and painfully thrown into modernity are one and the same thing.

3

Modernity as a Construct of Sovereignty

32. The deconstructive results of the previous chapter demonstrated the profound ambiguity of modernity in its relations to historicity. Modernity revealed itself to be both a condition of possibility for history and "an epoch" inscribed in it. Now it is time to confront the role of sovereignty in this structure.

Modernity, history, and sovereignty

33. If modernity is the ultimate structure of perspectivism, it must be related to the functioning of sovereignty, which, as we remarked, founds the perspectivist bias. According to one of the previous definitions (→3), sovereignty is what makes infinity particular by turning it into a unit within a seemingly existing higher order. If so, *modernity would be the ultimate infinity particularized by the work of sovereignty*. It would be the definitive field reigned by sovereignty, the field which encompasses all other fields. In this capacity, it would be the ultimate horizon of the sovereignty-governed universe.

But, in this role, modernity would have to be a unit in a higher order, in which the place of sovereignty is embedded. In case of all other sovereignty-ruled fields we can pinpoint the root through which it appears as a (non-)whole delimited by its basic predetermination. Modernity, however, understood as the ultimate, all-encompassing field reigned by sovereignty, leaves us no access to this elusive "higher order," in which it is embedded. Modernity cannot simply be a unit within the chain of "epochs," if it itself produces this order as we know it. Therefore, it must belong to an order that we are not aware of because until this form of sovereignty elapses, we will never learn what may lie beyond. This order, which is, in an unclear manner, of temporal character, can be only assumed to exist, but not grasped directly. With all complex connotations of the world "real," it might be called *real time*.

34.1 The concept of "real time" grasps, by its very name, a few important characteristics of the order to which modernity seems to belong. First of all, it is real (in Lacanian sense[1]), namely: (1) it is inaccessible for cognition and all symbolic (meaningful) narratives, but also (2) it functions as a haunting present/absent dimension which constantly exerts its influence upon sense. Second, it creates an impression of being more real than anything else that we know through symbolic mediation. Third, it is somehow temporal, because we can expect that its units might supersede each other. It augurs some possibility of change. Given that it is located outside all the symbolic frameworks, it seems to link them by a contentless dimension, which, for this reason, is very close to temporality. Due to modernity's "belonging" to real time, and only in this sense, we might perceive modernity as a framework of possibilities that can pass.

Moreover, real time is strictly bound with the functioning of sovereignty as the overarching mechanism of modernity. *Real time is, and must be, imagined as space in which sovereignty is inscribed.* Therefore, we cannot know this space, since its existence is for us only an effect of sovereignty.

34.2 "Real time" has also one more feature. In the Lacanian doxa the Real is both covered and pointed to by the Symbolic.[2] The Symbolic is born in the resistance to the Real and tainted by its influence. If so, real time would also have its symbolic counterpart. This cover is nothing less than meaningful history. Just as in Zupančič's portrayal the Real constitutes "the internal fracture or split of representation, … its intrinsic edge on account of which representation never fully coincides, not simply with its object, but with itself,"[3] so is real time closer to a rift in meaningful temporality rather than a fully fledged separate "dimension." It is through history that modernity disguises its position—delimited by sovereignty embedded in real time—with the illusion of continuous order of epochs to which modernity seemingly belongs on equal rights with others. History that we know would therefore be marked by an indelible scar of real time, in which modernity reveals its sovereignty-based construction.

If modernity appears as an epoch within the historical framework, it is not entirely an illusion: modernity is not eternal and there is some temporal order in which it might be viewed as a unit that will pass.[4] But the history that we know—the one in which modernity starts, for instance, in the eighteenth century—is a symbolic cover of this order, of real time. If so, it must be split by an inner incoherence organized around its real core. This inexplicable contradiction fuels yet new narratives on the correct "origins of modernity." But, if we have in mind mechanisms of sovereignty, we will immediately recognize that this aporia has deeper roots. Meaningful history, produced by modernity as its very tissue, bears scars of real time. We can see them as scars within universality which is, at its bottom, delimited and anchored in the unknown, meaningless dimension.

It is perhaps this dimension that Walter Benjamin's Angel of History[5] is drawn into, without having the chance of looking in the direction it heads towards. In the rhythm of recurring irruptions of sovereignty that mark our times we would be happy to see *a real change*, the change which will put an end to this throb of sovereignty. But, in fact, we can imagine real change only through its throb. With every new historical catastrophe some contours of real time seem to emerge, as if sovereignty repeated constantly its pre-limitation and thus pointed to the source of its impoverishment.

35. For these reasons, modernity will not pass in the common understanding of the term. It will not be superseded by another epoch just like all the "premodern epochs" which we currently imagine to have superseded each other. Meaningful

history covers a tectonic rift through which modernity installed itself and reassured its reign as the very possibility of historical narrative. Whenever we look at history, modernity is already there, although it still needs to re-inscribe its initial delimitation. For this reason, in the tension between history as a universal framework and modernity as an epoch modernity repeats symbolically its embedding in real time. The general uneasiness that makes modernity so different from other "epochs" is the proper trace, although often misunderstood, of its sovereignty-governed position in real time.

36.1 Coming back to the initial question we might ask again: given the specific construction of modernity, how can we think it in its relation to sovereignty?

Let us first recapitulate our conclusions. We know already that due to the proto-historical character of modernity it cannot be thought as simply "one of the epochs." It is still inscribed in the history which it itself allows of producing, and this inscription embodies the perspectivist nature of modernity as the ultimate crossing between universality and particularity. It renders symbolically palpable the embedding of modernity in real time, that is, in the meaningless order imagined and covered by symbolic narratives of history. In this sense, the "premodern epochs" of history epitomize, in an impoverished manner, the radical otherness of real time.

Modernity, as a structure wholly reigned by the device of sovereignty, is, in its own rights, cut from the very same framework of history that it produces. This self-referential cut is precisely the point of sovereignty. For this reason, the inscription of modernity in the historical "continuity" should not be simply rejected as an error. Contrariwise, it should be understood in the impossibility of its claim, and reinterpreted as the only trace of real time that we might ever grasp. In the constant tension amidst which modernity aims to redraw its relation to "previous epochs" we might therefore observe the rift of real time affecting the symbolic history. In other words, whenever we try to pinpoint "the origins of modernity," we struggle with the empty point of sovereignty that quilts history with a reflection of real time.

36.2 Given these conclusions, modernity must be simultaneously described as unique—as the whole and only universe that we know—and as an epoch, but in real time that we cannot understand. Beyond any doubt, it is difficult to do justice to such specificity of modernity. Perhaps "doing justice" should be understood very much in the sense of the final message of the torturing machine from Kafka's *Penal Colony*, which engraves on the living body of the former torturer the lethal injunction: "*Sei gerecht!*"[6] "Be just!"

How then should we use the terms "modern" and "modernity"? First of all, both must be viewed as signs of radical cut. What is modern has no predecessors.[7] Not because there were no events before modernity or there was nothing in the past that resembles modern phenomena, but because *modernity is a universe shielded from the past by its construction based on sovereignty.* The very word "modern" carries some potential of radical novelty, of something which, regardless of all resemblances, introduces a structural displacement into the dimension it describes.[8]

Still, "modern" and "modernity" have a distinct connotation of referring to an epoch, one among others. Despite all the falsity of this referral understood literally, it preserves the potential of grasping the non-totality of modernity. It points towards the possibility of something other than modernity, of time which is outside the modern framework of history. It reintroduces into the core of modern universe an element of radical otherness. Thus, it opens modernity by the very same gesture which, through the power of sovereignty, cuts it out from any historical continuity.

Therefore, the words "modern" and "modernity" preserve some rudimentary ambiguity. If we are ever to grasp the construction of modernity in a more adequate manner, we need to re-evaluate this ambiguity and treat it not as an unfortunate by-product of linguistic inconsistency, but as a dynamic paradox.

36.3 If so, we should understood modernity as the total universe in which we are trapped. It is the universe to which history belongs, and not the universe which is in history. All the past that we look at is already structurally modern; it is exposed to the play of differentiation and sovereignty. But what is modern is so unique that this uniqueness must appear against the background of what we called "real time"—an ungraspable dimension which both contains and eludes temporal and spatial determinations. Therefore "modern" means simultaneously: (1) belonging to a total universe which is radically cut from whatever could be imagined as non-modern, and (2) pointing to the dimension of real time, that is of radical, non-modern otherness, in which modernity is embedded through its sovereignty-governed structure.

In this sense, the history that we know—the symbolic narrative which uses the concept of "epochs"—is too deceiving in its simplistic continuity. But its inner scars reveal the complex device of modernity, which both allows of history and inscribes itself in it, thus repeating its embedding in real time.

37. There is one important objection, however: if we understand the terms "modernity" and "modern" in this way, do we not encounter a blatant logical flaw? If we define sovereignty by being modern, and then describe modernity as structurally determined by sovereignty, do we not produce a form of *petitio principi*?

In simple logics, it would definitely be a flaw. But the overdetermined realm of modernity is a self-referring curve which makes separate concepts coincide. While we describe this realm, we encounter the zone of indifferentiation between modernity and sovereignty: the structure of sovereignty cuts modernity from all historical continuity, whereas modernity, through its cut, displays the structure of sovereignty. Both concepts preserve the trace of some radical rupture—and in this rupture they coincide.

Naturally, it does not mean that "premodern sovereignty" or "sovereignty as such" are senseless concepts; their indispensable role in grasping the devices of power is obvious. But, insofar as they conjure up a vision of continuous history of sovereignty, whose modern form is only one among others, their usage totally falsifies the specificity of modern cut. Modern sovereignty is not a form of sovereignty concretized in one of the epochs, but part of the very construction of modernity. In this sense, *petitio principi* is necessary: only through the entanglement of modernity and sovereignty can we approach the structure of times that we are thrown into.

Temporal and spatial aspects of modernity as a trans-epoch

38.1 Modernity, if it is thus understood, reveals some unexpected traits. One of the most fascinating is the unique interplay between spatial and temporal imagery that applies to modernity. It has three intertwined aspects: two temporal and one spatial.

The first temporal aspect is obvious: modernity is an "epoch." But, in this role, it seems constantly undermined by excessive ruminations about the beginning and essence of such an epoch. Modernity can never find its peace in assuming the role of a tranquil unit in the flow of historical time. There must be some atemporal structure which accounts for this seemingly temporal entanglement of modernity in history.

We already encountered this atemporal structure: it is modernity understood as the *proto-historical structure*. Seen from this perspective, modernity appears as uniquely atemporal: it gives the conditions of historicity but is not subjected to them. Hardly any concepts from our limited imagery could do justice to its status. But in the dialectic pair of "time" and "space" it is "space" that seems to better suit its character. Therefore, as a set of conditions of historicity, as proto-history, modernity appears as a kind of space, in which time develops and is anchored. This is precisely the spatial aspect of modernity.

Its "spatiality" stems from the fact that it immobilizes all possibilities of referring to time. It seems as if all the time that is possible developed within it. All the history, once recognized as allowed of by modernity, resembles a screen on which the positive material of the past is played by modern devices of difference. Therefore, the set of conditions and devices that accounts for this play appears timeless. As space, modernity has never begun and will never end. It is taken for granted as a precondition of our understanding.

The spatial metaphor, applied to modernity as proto-history, connotes a few characteristics. First, it portrays modernity as a universe which *contains*: time, symbolic narratives, histories, etc. Modernity construed as space is very simple; it is nothing but a common frame, which in itself is not temporal. Whatever exists in modernity as proto-history is synchronic: narratives or histories cannot be ordered chronologically, there is no "earlier" and "after," everything coexists beyond the dimension of time. Second, modernity as space is generally undecidable (in early Derrida's sense[9]): it allows of play of difference but itself is not drawn into it. The spatial metaphor guarantees this effect of neutrality by establishing a framework which contains, but does not interact directly with the contained.

Third, modernity as space produces an effect of materiality. Setting aside the task of confronting the real foundation of modern materialism, let us settle here for a provisional remark: the spatial metaphor allows of cutting the play of difference by providing a dimension in which difference appears as something rudimentary and taken for granted. Anchored in this dimension, the difference might be referred to without the further process of differentiation. This dimension is matter, which, by its purely spatial character, seems to contain no additional determinations subject to the play of difference. The most telling example of the role of spatiality in anchoring difference is nothing less than Derrida's *différance*,[10] which, by replacing "e" with "a" and thus changing only the spelling, not the pronunciation of the word, resorts to the utter dimension of embodying difference: material arrangement of signs on the surface. If difference is the final *explanans* we can find, it cannot be referred to in a "pure," not difference-contaminated manner. It can be only *anchored in space as the ultimate and most meaningless framework of displacing and differentiating*. For this reason, matter and materiality become a true modern obsession,[11] as they allow to produce the fetish of the difference which is ultimately embodied and referred-to-without-differentiation-in-reference-itself.

38.2 But even the spatial character of modernity as proto-history cannot be entirely closed. The modern universe, referred to with spatial imagery, is not everything. Much as we cannot think outside the modern framework, we might still rightly suspect that it itself appeared at a certain moment and will possibly pass. The modern universe is not an eternal space. It contains temporality, but itself is marked by some unknown temporal scar. When Heidegger kept grappling with the idea of the horizon of Being,[12] he attested to the existence of an irremovable aporia, which, read in its modern sense, is the following: modernity shapes the time that we know and therefore itself appears as timeless, but it itself remains marked by some peculiar "higher" temporality. Thus the spatial and atemporal character of modernity as proto-history points, through its cracks, to its second temporal dimension: real time.

If it were not for real time, modernity as proto-history could become the whole universe without any outside. But the existence of real time ruins this perfect self-sufficiency of the ultimate poverty. If modernity is based on the structure of sovereignty, it might appear as almost-the-Whole only at the price of being embedded in a different order: and the very mirage of this different order dissociates modernity from reality. What slips in, is real time, the second temporal dimension, in which the spatial and atemporal modernity as proto-history reveals itself as marked by some overarching, unimaginable and traumatizing trace.

At this point, the spatial and temporal imagery, as applied to modernity, become inextricably entangled. In its spatial aspect, modernity appears as synchronic, allowing of history, which is born within the atemporal framework of differentiation. But, in its second temporal aspect, modernity seems undercut at its bottom, its atemporal structure being dependent on the overarching inexplicable real time. It seems as if this whole symbolic universe could simply disappear and become superseded by another one. *Modernity trembles with the ungraspable possibility of its own disappearance.*

Real time is nothing but a trace: it is not a directly perceivable dimension, but the ultimate possibility of total, "overepochal" upheaval. For this reason, modernity as proto-history experiences its embedding in real time not directly, but from a parallax view. It is always a haunting trace located in the self-inscription of modernity into the history it produces, that is, in the first temporal aspect. Modernity experiences its own undermining temporality as a trace inscribed in the historical framework that it itself produces.

38.3 Knowing how the second temporal aspect is inscribed into the first temporal aspect, with the mediation of the spatial one, we should venture, perhaps, another term for modernity conceived as an "epoch." Instead of marking each time its overdetermined character, we may just call modernity a *trans-epoch*. This term preserves its double character: first, it is deliberately (and artificially) constructed as one of the epochs within history; second, it contains a mark which opens it up to the spatial and second temporal aspect.[13]

All ruminations about the beginnings, nature and specificity of modernity should be understood as pertaining to thus constructed notion of trans-epoch. By coining this category, we can safely delimit all quasi-metaphysical claims as to what modernity "truly" is. Thus, for example, when Agamben associates modernity with the epoch of concentration camps,[14] we can avoid embarrassing debates between those who point out to the fact that quite a lot of people live currently outside of actual concentration camps and those who claim that "in reality," everything around us is a concentration camp. There will always be "metaphysicians" against "empiricists" in the debate on modernity; their existence is part and parcel of modern specificity. But, instead of arguing who is "right," we should simply delimit the "metaphysics" of modernity to the trans-epoch. Agamben's claim pertains only to modernity as the trans-epoch.[15] Thus corrected, he is "right" as much as empiricists are when they point to undebatable facts from the rich and complex history of modernity conceived as an epoch.[16]

Nevertheless, modernity can never be enclosed in a set of events,[17] and not due to their inexhaustibility, multicausalism or abundance; not even because the very term "modernity" implies a simple excess of connotation over designation, which leads us to futile enquiries into its meaning.[18] The true excess of modernity, viewed from its epochal position, crystallizes in the fact of its being a trans-epoch.[19] For this reason, no exhaustive histories of modernity, rich in facts and causes, will ever satiate our thirst for exploring the boundaries and characteristics of the modern age. That we still believe in some traits that underlie every phenomenon which appears within the modern universe is a proof of the radical cut that separates modernity from any other epoch.

38.4 Ultimately, both temporal aspects are almost one and the same device, but irreconcilably split by the atemporal, spatial character of modernity as proto-history. In turn, from the point of view of proto-history, it is time that prevents the final and perfect self-constitution of modernity as the all-encompassing space. The entanglement and exchange of modern temporality and spatiality attest to the fact that *modernity always appears as non-perfect, almost-constituted; it seems to require an external supplement that practically it almost-already has*. Spatiality demands projection into temporality, but temporality, in its turn, demands projection into spatiality, whereas both form an internally broken device.

This map of displacements, constitutions through non-constitutions, supplements being no-supplements, identities projected onto other places or times, additional dimensions (either temporal or spatial) being necessary for the self-formation—and, most particularly, of absolute usurpations made at the price of the smallest remainder—are traces of nothing less than a device that rules through sovereignty, the device we already called the Mirror Star.

Historicizing modernity with the Mirror Star

39. Despite the common legacy of Nietzschean, Heideggerian, and Derridean thought, there is still a common pattern of intuitive thinking which separates ontological, "ontological," ontic or post-ontological problems from the problem of historicity. We

are eager to assume that how the world, or its text, functions, is one thing, whereas our historical position is another. Even late Heidegger might be read in this way: there is hardly anything more self-indulging than accepting that the ontological field of possibilities is each time determined by "an epoch of Being," and, simultaneously, believing that Being somehow runs through the sequence of epochs and in each one of them constitutes a different framework of ontological possibilities. Such thinking once again collapses into perceiving time as a sequence, in which particular forms of something more atemporal appear. Yet, as long as we dissociate time from what "appears" or "changes" in it, we have not properly grasped the modern entanglement of temporality and spatiality. The Mirror Star makes "ontology" and "historicity" fold into each other in a zone of indifferentiation.

40. The entanglement between the Mirror Star and the construction of modernity deserves a tale of its own. Undoubtedly, this is the moment when we enter the murkiest waters. What we seek here is the paradoxical foundation of modernity as the sovereignty-governed trans-epoch.

Let us first recapitulate our previous conclusions on the character and functioning of the Mirror Star. In Chapter 1, we described the Mirror Star as, first, a figure of sovereignty, which deflects the impulses that used to be directed towards transcendence back to our universe. In this sense, sovereignty might be described as "transformed" transcendence, a form of transcendence proper to modernity. Second, the Mirror Star, through its inward-directed power of deflecting, lures beings with the promise of self-constitution in an impossible, projected place and thus introduces basic difference (Derridean "spacing") into the heart of beings. Third, the Mirror Star puts modernity in the condition of a virtual standstill, in which everything is always already decided upon, but one last step, always deterred—Sade's "*encore un effort*"[20]—is imagined as needed to reach this condition in full. In this aspect, the Mirror Star constitutes the true engine of modernity, in which the effort which is needed and demanded is necessarily excessive, because it has no measure and must be spent in a *sui generis* zone of exception.[21] All these three characteristics of the Mirror Star mark the construction of modernity. Let us look at them more closely one by one.

40.1 Construed as a figure of sovereignty—that is of "transformed" transcendence—the Mirror Star allows of thinking in deep the key problem of modern philosophy: the link between temporality and the collapse of transcendence. Naturally, this link was grasped by philosophy very early in the modern era. Hegel, in the preface to his *Phenomenology of Spirit*, acknowledged the disappearance of the "thread of light" (*Lichtfaden*) which linked all that had existed with heaven.[22] This concept, however, had not gained prominence until Hegel's own Protestant appropriation of the death of God[23] dissipated and made a place for Nietzsche's proclamation of the same event, which is always something that happens and is never complete.[24] It is worth noting that "the death of God"—a generic term for the disappearance of transcendence and its supporting power for earthly things—is therefore an event, just like the collapse of Hegel's *Lichtfaden*.[25]

We have grown too accustomed to this concept so that it could still astonish us.[26] But what can be more astonishing than a radical transformation of the metaphysical structure of the universe which happens as an event in time? The inexplicability of such event might find its parallel, perhaps, only in the act of Creation, in which nothingness turns into being. How can the broadest metaphysical framework simply collapse in a particular moment of our history? How can there be a moment which cuts history in two, establishing metaphysical "before" and post-metaphysical "after"?

Obviously, one could object that this whole event is nothing but a transformation of human perception, whose mechanism would not be shocking. But such an objection not only flattens the whole problem, but also, in a mystified manner, relies on the very paradox it denounces, because the possibility of seeing "a transformation of human perception" is already located at our side of the "transformation." Whatever this transformation really was, we know it to be all-encompassing and still affecting our conceptual universe.

The Mirror Star in its first aspect—connoting the new form of transcendence, a deflected one, which we called sovereignty—would not then belong to a static structure, but would be a mechanism of somehow temporal character. *Modern sovereignty preserves a trace of an event*. In this regard the first aspect of the Mirror Star is closely linked to the spatio-temporal construction of modernity.

This link is complex. First of all, contrary to simplifying historiosophical narratives, the collapse of transcendence cannot be simply an event of "objective history." There can be no continuous history in which this event would be recorded as one happening against the background of a neutral scale of time. The collapse of transcendence is inscribed into our continuous historical narratives only insofar as they both cover and display the scar of real time. All our myths of the-already-happened fall, so cherished among modern philosophers/writers, from Rousseau to Heidegger, are simply symbolic historical narratives which attempt to disguise the scar of real time. As a consequence, "the collapse of transcendence," has never happened as a simple transformation in continuous time. This collapse describes rather the self-referentiality of the modern universe, to which history belongs. There is no "objective," let alone meaningful history which could render this event. It is rather rendered by the whole construction of the modern universe.

But the self-referentiality of modernity is punctured in one particular place of singularity, in the place of the temporal scar, which makes an impression that this collapse truly happened in time. The dimension in which it is located is not history, but real time, which seems, and simply seems, to precede the very construction of the modern universe. Real time is, in itself, unattainable. What we might perceive is only its inscription into history. For this reason, we are tempted to see the collapse of transcendence as an event that happened in our time, event which can be pinpointed and objectively referred to. But what we indeed see is the scar of real time inscribed into historical narratives.

If so, what about the link between the collapse of transcendence and historicity that we constantly reconsider in modernity? What about this event that both Hegel and Nietzsche saw as taking place in history? Given our previous considerations on the construction of modernity, we might tentatively approach the answer. The event in question is just an effect of the entanglement of spatiality and temporality in modernity. What we indeed grasp with the category of event is the very existence of the modern universe and its sovereign cut. The structure of modernity appears as something which emerged out of a dramatic collapse; it seems to exist only insofar as it is temporally traumatized. In this sense, *whatever is modern, here and now, already belongs to the past, as if it were temporally expropriated by a powerful structural force.* And this temporal expropriation is equivocal to being governed by sovereignty.[27] Whatever is marked by the structure of sovereignty, remains temporally indebted, set "out of joint," to use Derrida's favorite Shakespearean term for times of confusion.[28] Under sovereignty, everything is induced into a state of permanent tension between temporality and atemporality.

For this reason, the atemporal structure of modernity is something that we necessarily experience as a past event. The entanglement of temporality and spatiality in modernity constantly displaces our gaze, turning the synchronic into diachronic, atemporal into temporal, current state of affairs into a past catastrophe. We experience the whole modernity not as a closed universe—which, in a certain regard, it is—but as an event.

It was of Nietzsche's profoundest intuition that Gods die slowly, or, at least that the message of their death comes to our ears with disproportionate delay.[29] But, the delayed event will never come; the death of God will never have happened once and for all. This inner tension of the supposed "event," which simultaneously has happened, is happening and has always been there, remains the most conspicuous feature of modern spatio-temporal entanglement. A time of no time, something temporal which never passes, an event without beginning or end that set the temporal throb of the whole universe are all traces of real time.

In this way, *modernity experiences its construction as something which is an ongoing, but always-already-delayed event.* Therefore, the Mirror Star, which stands for "modern transcendence," that is—sovereignty, appears as: (1) the founding element in the structure of modernity, (2) a result of some profound transformation, which can be only speculated upon, and (3) as ongoing process which keeps remolding the universe it governs.

40.2 In its second aspect, in which the Mirror Star is construed as the power of deflection that projects and constitutes identities, it sheds light on the status of history in modernity. It demonstrates that *history is the imaginary place, in which the mirage of identity of modernity is constituted.* It seems as if modernity had an "identity," a "nature," an "essence," or at least, humbly, a "character": but all that it truly has is the lure of self-constitution, supported by the Mirror Star.

Our previous considerations on the work of the Mirror Star (→ 18–21) brought us to the conclusion that, together with space, it creates the device of modern difference. We remarked that space differentiates beings from themselves, while the Mirror Star projects identities of beings on an imaginary, impossible place. But if modernity as such is the realm of the Mirror Star, should it not be also affected by the process of differentiation and the constitution of identity? Indeed, whenever modernity is attempted to be understood as a Whole—namely, as a symbolic universe of spatial character—there is a tiny senseless remainder. Its existence, on the one hand, hinders the perfect constitution of the Whole, but on the other hand, makes it visible. This remainder is the scar of real time, which, above the whole modernity construed as a symbolic universe, leaves the possibility of dissociating modernity from all-that-has-ever-existed. Therefore, it is real time that provides modernity with the possibility of differentiation from itself. It is real time that opens up the musty enclosed construction of modernity and points to the possibility of reality beyond the modern realm.

Modernity becomes therefore differentiated from itself through the work of real time. But differentiation is just the first condition of establishing identity. The second one, as we remarked earlier, is the deflecting power of the Mirror Star, which projects identity onto a certain place—a place which is separated by senseless difference from the "being" whose identity is to be constituted. In this sense, real time constitutes an abyss against which modernity might be perceived. This abyss is covered by the mirror surface, on which identity of modernity appears. The name of such a mirror surface is well-known: it is history. History appears as the symbolic cover of real time, as part of the process in which modernity constitutes its identity.

Therefore, it might be said that the Mirror Star creates the identity of modernity by producing a mirror surface which covers the abyss of most radical differentiation, that is, the abyss of real time. And onto this surface the "identity" of modernity is projected. This "identity" relies on the portrayal of modernity as "just an epoch," one among others, which appears in the continuous sequence of history. In this sense, a meaningful history is a by-product of the work of the Mirror Star as applied to modernity. It acts as a surface in which identity might be inscribed. Perhaps then there would be no history as we know it without sovereignty and the universe over which it reigns. It allows modernity to create its own image, as if anything like "the identity of modernity" could have ever existed.

To sum up, meaningful history is nothing more than a cover of the abyss of real time. It rises as an effect of the Mirror Star only to give support for imaginary "identity of modernity." For this reason, the constant musings over the exact beginnings or end of modernity cannot stop. It is in this pursue towards its "identity," projected onto the dimension of history, that modernity attempts to constitute itself. And, as usual with all the works of the Mirror Star, this attempt might end up twofold: (1) either the rift remains unbridged and the identity of modernity keeps to be an unresolved mystery and a subject of relentless, obsessive ruminations, (2) or thinking on the nature of modernity reaches its imaginary goal and the "essence" of modernity evaporates: what remains is just the abyss of real time. The second path is clearly visible in messianic contractions of modernity, through which—both in theory (from Rousseau, Sade, and Hegel onwards) and in practice (for instance, in revolutionary Marxism)—the strangest of all "epochs" struggles to overcome itself. As a consequence, modernity is marked by the unquenchable thirst either for its own self-recognition (demarcation of its beginning and end)—or, in the more radical path, for its (self-)overcoming. In psychonanalytic categories, the first one is desire, while the second one is drive.[30] Both, however, attest to the framework established by the Mirror Star.

Modernity cannot be overcome. Here Heidegger's remarks on the *Überwindung der Metaphysik*[31] should be read as pertaining precisely to the status of this "epoch", the most peculiar of all. Modernity can disappear, that should be taken for granted; but it will never put an end to its rule on its own.[32] Modernity is not only the space in which the Mirror Star acts, but also the space which the Mirror Star entirely organizes, closes and supplements. For this reason, only the scar of real time preserves the possibility of modernity's disappearance and, through its work, makes modern thinking so prone to negative theology.[33] "The identity of modernity" painfully points to this structural block: *modernity can be visible, as such, only against real time, but in order to constitute itself meaningfully, it must create the dimension of history which covers the abyss.*

The device of historical narratives is created by the Mirror Star operating on the whole of modernity. Hence, it is modernity that gives us an unprecedented historical perspective and, for the first time, *equals being with event*. But this gain comes at a price, a price of living in a spatio-temporal universe sealed off from the outside. In this sense, history is a reel on which our imaginations are projected, but the abyss underneath never ceases to haunt us.

40.3 The third—and perhaps the most obscure and fascinating—mode of the Mirror Star's work is the fundamental structural deferral (→ 22, 23). In relation to modernity, the Mirror Star is accountable for the unique, sovereignty-governed functioning of temporality.

Sovereignty distorts the very framework of time. Usual perception of time which dominates in the industrial era identifies time with the continuous flow of time units, which may be counted, summed up and used to measure the length and timing of events.[34] There are smaller and larger units, which can be converted into one another. All in all, this vision of time assumes that as soon as the calculated number of units elapses, the estimated goal will be achieved. Thus, all change that happens might be framed in the grid of time units: *change converts into time units losslessly*.

Sovereignty, however, distorts the very relation between the countable set of time units and the goal. In sovereignty-marked temporality change cannot be fully and losslessly converted into time units. This distortion stems directly from the construction of sovereignty that we described earlier. Sovereignty brings with itself a fundamental split between what is governed—within the grid imposed by the particular construction of sovereignty—and the reigning sovereign center.[35] The split between them is impenetrable from the side of the governed. Whatever happens within the governed area, happens within an *a priori* determined framework. But as such, happening does not affect the center. From this split, flows the fundamental distortion of sovereignty-governed temporality, which breaks down into two modalities: (1) countable, summable, organizable set of time units within the governed area, (2) the time in which the very structure of sovereignty comes to existence, lasts and disappears. From the perspective of the former, the latter time is *real*: meaningless, unattainable, but marking the whole temporality device. This is the real time in which the very meaningful framework of time appears as temporal and changeable. Contrariwise, the first temporal modality that we described—meaningful and countable—is nothing less than history.

The split between real time and history is inherent in sovereignty. Whatever field is reigned by sovereignty, it is torn between these two modalities of temporality. Consequently, it needs to be assumed that *each particular form of sovereignty, each sovereignty-reigned area necessarily has its own, particular history, as part of its very structure*. For this reason, there are as many histories as there are sovereigns. Moreover, each history is biased by the basic determination imposed by the sovereign. In this sense, histories are multiple and perspectival.[36]

If there were only histories—if their condition of possibility could be erased from the view—we would not experience deferral. But real time at the background of each sovereign center distorts the functioning of the otherwise simple and losslessly convertible time of histories. The historical framework functions properly insofar as its units are used to count time related to events which are entirely subjected to the sovereignty-reigned field. As soon as within the historical framework we attempt to refer to the defining moment of the sovereign center—thereby reaching outside the field which is entirely governed by it—the time of our history gets out of joint. The historical framework cannot grasp temporal relation to the sovereign center itself and becomes deferred.

What appears in the deferral brought to the extreme, is some mute, unintelligible dimension of lasting. It appears when something seems to resist the meaningful time, something which is apparently immutable. Freud attempted to understand this immutable distorting obstacle as the death drive.[37] But, perhaps instead of extending its existence to all "epochs," as Freud implicitly did, we should confine it to modernity, in which, *not by mere coincidence*, the death drive was discovered. Lasting appears when the structure of sovereignty becomes visible within the field of history. It is as if a foreign body were thrown into a mechanism, which then gets stuck on the unsuspected obstacle. Therefore *lasting can be described as a structural block of history around the irruption of real time.*

Once again, astrophysical imagery might help us here. As Einstein theorized, around huge masses time slows down due to curvature of spacetime. This effect is particularly noticeable around black holes. For external observers, objects falling onto black holes take infinite time to reach the event horizon. Metaphorically speaking, points of sovereignty behave like black holes: time slows and warps around them. History becomes stuck in its collapse onto the singularity of sovereignty, but in this entrapment it reaches, suddenly, its infinity of lasting.

Whenever history becomes stuck around its sovereign center, meaningful time can no longer comprise a whole. What appears is some dead—or rather undead (in Žižek's sense[38])—senseless time which cannot be used, explained or used as a run-up to an event. It augurs some event, which, however, never comes. Lasting is a dimension of the unbearable: of intolerable continuance that goes on although it has no cover in sense. Within it, the ultimate non-event becomes coextensional with event. That nothing is really happening is experienced as the most powerful and traumatizing happening. This unbearable present might be only seen from askew, under the guise of a major, ground-breaking event that looms on the horizon: but, in fact, there is, and there will be, no event in time. *This dead time as a whole is already the event in question.*

Since the dimension of lasting is inherent in the very framework of history embedded in sovereignty, each and every form of sovereignty has lasting as its looming possibility. What lasts, dead-and-undead, finished-but-not-yet-finished, suspended between existence and disappearance, is most clearly dependent on some sovereign power which dies a slow (in its own perspective, endless) death. The sphere of lasting circumscribes every sovereign as a transitional zone between the perfect functioning of its history and realms of other sovereigns. In lasting sovereign, power reveals itself in its utmost, naked senselessness and groundlessness. For this reason, fading regimes of truth and/or of political power resort to the same gestures, in which they can offer no meaningful justification for their existence but still demand loyalty for the sake of loyalty. In this sense, *the quality of undeadness is a clear mark of (decaying) sovereignty*.

Regimes built on deferral are useful frameworks for exploitation of what is governed by it. They raise demands which concern the goal located on the level of the governing, not the governed. As a result, these goals become unachievable. All such demands of the governing center are by nature measureless, because the system of measuring and converting, offered by meaningful history, warps in contact with them. For this reason, lasting, as the utmost form of deferral, creates conditions for total and disproportionate exploitation which cannot be even appropriately measured or discerned. Sade's "encore un effort," the call for one more, yet most demanding effort, perfectly embodies the reign through lasting. The luring proximity of the definitive goal—always almost present, but always deferred—entices the governed to spend the final reserves.

Therefore, deferral and lasting determine the structure of each sovereignty-reigned field. As we remarked earlier, modernity itself might be seen as the ultimate regime of sovereignty, as the all-encompassing field organized by sovereign power. If so, what would be deferral and lasting at this highest level?

Modernity, as a sovereignty-reigned universe, is subject to deferral in relation between its own internal time and the real time outside of it, which is experienced as a fundamental delay of most crucial transformations that we await. Consequently, the question of the end of modernity always permeates the modern universe as its irreducible possibility.[39] In this sense, modernity is the first and only "epoch" which is aware of its radically temporal character. That this whole universe lies on shifting sands is a conviction which belongs to its constructive elements. Yet, modernity cannot understand its "end" in its own temporal relations, let alone count down the time to its finishing line. For this reason, *modernity lasts confronted with the threatening verdict of its unknown sovereign rule*. It is ravaged by its inherent deferral, by the excess of (un) dead time which cannot be channeled into meaningful historical narratives. No historical explanation can grasp the beginning and the end of the modern universe. Modernity has no sense and no boundaries: its irruption opens into the mass of histories which cannot cover up the dimension of lasting that appears between them.

Lasting allows of most radical forms of sovereign power. A structure which keeps recurring in modernity is a promise that "this epoch" can be overcome; yet the fulfillment of the promise depends on present effort, which is incommensurable with the goal towards it is ostensibly directed. Messianic and revolutionary currents of modernity rely on this promise, thereby often, all-too-often becoming tools of sovereign power.

Heidegger's obscure cult of lasting

41.1 In this light, Heidegger's late thought should not be understood as an in-between stage between twenty-five centuries of metaphysics and the new beginning, whose auguries glimmer in the wreckage of our post-metaphysical conceptual devices.

Heidegger's path is consistently and inherently modern: the star which pierces through the murky clouds of his late writings is not, and cannot be, the awaited star of redemption, but the archmodern Mirror Star. The putative promise of hope is nothing more than a sign of lasting.

For this reason, Heidegger's late philosophy cannot be overestimated in its importance to outlining the structures of modernity. It is not the end, but the pitch-black bottom of modern universe—a point in which its bare construction elements that are at work since the "onset of modernity" become more visible than they have ever been before. In a sense, it is an endless dead end: Heidegger opens up a reservoir of (un)dead time, in which everything lasts without conclusion and awaits the perpetually deferred final cut that is supposed to be administered by the unknown sovereign center. Meanings evaporate and histories dry up; only indelible dregs of lasting remain. Although this dimension finally makes modernity's contours discernible, it cannot bring any salvation.[40] *Sticking to it is tantamount to the most obscene surrender to sovereignty.* It is a form of devotion to the dying sovereign with the hope of receiving its last will and the nomination of the new one.[41] In this light, Heidegger's political "erring" is no accident. Perhaps it was the suspension of loyalty to brutal political power of the Nazis that lead him to the state of lasting, in which the final dying-undead sovereign was sought and pleaded allegiance to.[42]

If so, Heidegger's *Ereignis*,[43] happening, is the category that ultimately grasps, albeit unconsciously, the ongoing structural block inherent in modernity. As we already remarked, in lasting happening enters a zone of indifferentiation with non-happening, while event becomes coextensional with being.[44] *Ereignis* captures precisely this experience. Yet, contrary to Heidegger's expectations, twenty-five centuries of Western metaphysics cannot melt away into tense awaiting, mainly because there are no twenty-five centuries of Western metaphysics. There is only modern universe, in which they were molded from the premodern past. The structural bottom of modernity is, and has always been, within the reach of our hand, although it usually appeared under the guise of millennial transformations. Heidegger's late thought is pivotal in this regard: even though it attempts, once again, to portray the *basso continuo* of destitution—towards which it heads itself[45]—as a fundamental change at the heart of continuous Western tradition, the obscenity of such gesture finally transpires. The scale of Heidegger's calamity demonstrates, however, the purest state of modern lasting and the trap it sets for thinking. For this reason, any thought that attempts to address the question of modernity adequately must take Heidegger's *Denken* for its crucial point of reference.

Perhaps then Heidegger's thinking is the only true counterpart to Hegel in modern philosophy. Both represent the two extreme positions in relation to sovereignty. Hegel, in an answer to the structural block revealed by Kant, wants to take the place of the sovereign, leaving no remainder. Late Heidegger goes the other way round, extrapolating the Kantian distance to sovereignty into the position of perpetual waiting. Where Hegel is a philosophical warrior, Heidegger treads water. But in both of these positions they are fundamentally reactionary to the work of sovereignty.

41.2 Reducing Heidegger's thought to correct proportions demonstrates that *modern philosophies may be viewed as different forms of waiting.*

Heidegger's thought is located at one end of the continuum, at the pole of nearly infinite lasting. But, in reality, it is built around nothing, like a magic castle that surrounds a celebrated empty point, a point of sovereignty. When at some point of his late thinking Heidegger ventures acknowledging that "Being is nothingness" ("Das Sein ist das Nichts"[46]), he reaches the short circuit between the two poles whose distance was the only source of tension that allowed of building the elaborate field of his analyses. And this short circuit is precisely the basic framework of modern thought, the very same that Hegel reaches, through other paths, in the Absolute Knowledge. Modernity conjures up whole fascinating worlds, but when its poles are too close to each other, short circuit puts an end to the miraculous spectacle.

Therefore, the only philosophical skill that is of true use in modernity is the ability to withstand and defer one's own end. When at the end of his *Beyond the Pleasure Principle* Freud alludes to the figure of limping Jacob-Israel,[47] suggesting that scientific investigation must inevitably go through detours, he outlines the very specificity of thinking within the modern universe. In this regard, the Jewish imagery of life-as-deferral strikes a surprisingly concordant tone with characteristically modern feeling of melancholia. This link is clearly discernible in Walter Benjamin's short text, *Agesilaus Santander*,[48] in which he described his life as developing under the black light of Saturn, "the planet of ultimate detours."[49] In this manner, Benjamin blended two seemingly contradictory currents: Jewish appraisal of life and modern "gift of death" that reduces the richness of life to almost Blanchotian bare survival. But perhaps this blend points to yet another modern specificity: it does not matter how the deferral is reached—under the vitality represented by the Star of David or under the dark star of melancholia, which paralyzes even the possibility of death. What counts is deferral against the inevitable cut. In this kind of modern Kabbalah, the Mirror Star would be Saturn: the Blackstar. The modern requirement to last would thus blend life and melancholia.

In its only viable skill, to last, modern philosophy mimics the sovereign. Philosophical discourses rise and fall like sovereign powers, all built around the short circuit of nothingness and supported by their own decision. It is for this reason that philosophy is so tempted to flirt with political power and is able to preserve loyalty to political positions long after they evaporate from reality.

41.3 In the opening lines of his *Contributions to Philosophy*, Heidegger remarks:

> Contributions to Philosophy enact a questioning along a pathway which is first traced out by the crossing to the other beginning, into which Western thinking is now entering. This pathway brings the crossing into the openness of history and establishes the crossing as perhaps a very long sojourn, in the enactment of which the other beginning of thinking always remains only an intimation, though already decisive.[50]

What he means to do is an endless work of preparing, "grounding," which might trace the passage to the other beginning. Thus, Heidegger's thinking awaits Western philosophy as a point in which revolutionary thinking undergoes two transformations: it begins to concern the whole (trans-)epoch of modernity, not just a politico-social system, and gets mired in utter passivity. In such a constellation, the passage is permanently looked for, but never found. It is nothing but revolving around the empty positon of the sovereign when the sovereign itself is gone.

Perhaps then Heidegger does something totally different to what he officially intended. The more "grounding" work he does, the more the constellation which produces the perception of a passage is perpetuated. It is true that we have probably no means to leap into the non-modern: yet, awaiting the non-modern is more modern than anything else.

Modernity and the Mirror Star

40.4 Lasting awaits modernity as its final outlet. Wherever historical narratives are blocked and time gets out of joint, folding around the question of the end of modernity, lasting reappears, bringing with itself the notorious modern sense of malaise and exhaustion. Bare structures of sovereignty make everything appear as if before the Law. But lasting is no destiny: it might be equally broken through by a new, powerful sovereign structure which covers up the deferral inherent in the modern universe. Late modernity's shortage of sense, however, makes it particularly prone to encountering lasting. In this light, the upsurge in quasi-apocalyptic musings on the end of modernity which we witnessed since at least the 1960s[51] would have their roots in the malfunction of historical narratives, which are no longer potent enough to veil lasting.

That the dark center of malaise contains a promise of its imminent end is a spurious assumption; much more likely the malaise is here to stay. In this regard Heidegger's path is nothing short of abject spiritual poverty, whose artificial disguise makes it pass for late philosophical wisdom.

42. Sovereignty, once discerned in all its overwhelming power, should be viewed by Marxism as its primary problem. As long as sovereignty is reduced to its purely political aspects, it may be deftly relegated to the position of a disturbing factor in the generally undisputed realm of economy. Even Lenin, otherwise well versed in the pragmatics of political struggle, was blind to the overarching power of sovereignty, for which politics is only one field of articulation.[52] The shock caused by the nationalist turn of social-democratic parties at the dawn of the First World War, only aggravated by the total fiasco of "socialism in one country" —a sombre prelude to all nationalist regimes of the twentieth and twenty-first century—cannot allow Marxists to deceive themselves any longer. It is astonishing how little attention broadly construed Marxism devoted to nationalism, so eagerly setting it aside as erroneous ideology which defends the ruling class or, worse still, tacitly taking for granted its elements.[53] Much as this is true, nationalism is not a passing fancy: cruel as it might sound, in terms of practice it is much more powerful than Marxism itself. Its emergence at the crossings of modern state and population clearly points to the fact that is a direct product of modern sovereignty. Marxists criticized it at pivotal points of history (as, for example, Lenin and Sorel[54] during and after the First World War), but almost never taking it for their direct enemy and much more often flirting with it.[55] What Eric Hobsbawm[56] did to

Marxist history must be done to the very core of Marxism: political power organized by and around sovereignty must be its new object of critique.

Sovereignty must be first recognzed in its totality, namely as a structure underlying modern knowledge, ontology and history. Its characteristics—especially deferral and lasting—must be taken into account as boundary conditions for analysis and social praxis. Marxism should be reconsidered as part and parcel of modern sovereign thinking, with its central tenets being, perhaps, the most crystal elaborations of near-sovereign illusions.[57]

Marx's vision of unlimited productivity, unleashed from the fetters of capital and coupled with the total flexibility of human beings' time (in the morning I write, then I plough, make music and, at the end of the day, I sharpen sickles ...) is the hope of *living in the freedom that may be found only in the eye of the hurricane*. It is a life without deferral or delay; a life in which immediacy extends between my will and its realization. Deferral, from the Marxist perspective, is the curse of modern world: a device ruthlessly used as a tool of exploitation. But perhaps it is deferral—and lasting—that define the *nec plus ultra* of Marxism, as long as modernity continues its sovereign reign.

40.5 To sum up: the Mirror Star is discernible on three levels of the modern universe. First, it accounts for the mysterious beginning of modernity imagined under the guise of "the collapse of transcendence." As we remarked, this beginning is not an event in objective history, but a trace of sovereign cut which determines modernity. The modern indifferentiation between ontology and historicity makes existence co-extensive with event. Therefore, the collapse—or "the death of God," in properly Nietzschean sense—continues to happen as an ongoing event.

Second, the Mirror Star is accountable for the displacement of gaze which creates imaginary "identity of modernity." This identity appears on the artificial construction of history, which veils real time. Unstable, but necessary, unfathomable, yet still promising to be found, identity of modernity is sought within the historical framework. Nonetheless, all identity that modernity might ever have is a volatile construction, never equal with itself; it takes the shadow of its existence from a parallax view, but can never exist directly.

Third, the Mirror Star is responsible for modern deferral and lasting. It warps temporal relations within sovereignty-governed areas. In its ultimate form, as the reign over the modern universe itself, it is accountable for modernity's tendency to be suspended in its never-ending process of self-overcoming.

If only the inadequacy of our language were not so tricky, a summary of these reflections might sound as follows: *modernity had no beginning, has no identity and will have no end to speak of*.[58] But its whole universe is pervaded with a near-apocalyptic feeling of exhaustion, as if the accumulated mass of real time were to take vengeance on everything what is modern.[59] Still, the indecidability of the temporal mark that haunts modernity draws the line of both our freedom and our seclusion.

4

The Unfinished Time of Modernity

43. In the previous chapter, we brought modernity to radical historicization in its links with sovereignty. This allows us to make one step further and ask: what is the proper temporality of modernity?

The spectral democracy of modernity

44. Modernity might be viewed as paradoxically continuous space in which histories rise and fall. As such, it does not provide overarching linear time.[1] Linear time might be locally created within particular histories, but never as the global time for the whole modernity. In this sense, modernity has no meaningful time of its own: it is only a space in which particular times may emerge.

The emergence and decline of particular time was first discernible in the French Revolution. The revolutionary calendar was designed as a permanent notation for a definitively and irrevocably inaugurated era. Nonetheless, it fell into disuse after only twelve years.[2] It might seem that it perished, but the French Commune revived it, even if only for eighteen days.[3] This example demonstrates that the time which starts counting never stops: it might be rendered inoperative, but its future always remains open. It might be revived as a reigning time, but if the rotting sovereignty loosens its grip, it may equally give way and exist manifestly parallel to other times.

Every time, even at the peak of its reign, begins to decompose. In the areas where sovereignty wanes, the undercoat of how modern histories are constructed becomes visible and spectres appear stronger than ever. It is *interregnum, a period when the ruling time becomes struck with a powerful blow, opens up past times and revives spectres.*

This is also the fate of our times: until sovereignty starts its another round of uncontrolled discharge, spectres come to life. They return beyond the rational framework of history, producing unexpected links and re-asserting the singularity of event.[4] Post-war thought gave them more than new blood—a whole new science of hauntology. It seems that waves of history withdrew and left us stranded, comfortable enough to admire the immense seabed of temporality. And all this admiration flourishes in the shadow of a powerful recurring wave.

45. If modernity is the universe of never-finished and never-accomplished worlds, which are only put on hold and can be later revived, the political nature of modernity

is best grasped by the concept of democracy. Nevertheless, democracy must be here understood in a specific manner: not (only) as a general form of a political regime, but as *a condition of turning time into a space of political practice.*

What distinguishes modern democracy is its open avowal of the unlimited time horizon.[5] No one who wields power now can claim any right to wielding it in the future. In this way, the current balance of political influence between parties or rulers is just a conjecture that must be always read in a broader timeline which, within the democratic discourse, opens up into infinity. In modernity, the future is not only open and uncertain, but, in this openness and uncertainty, it actively shapes the here and now. The future works as a gap within the present, separating it from the moment of total victory, but promising the eternal possibility of revival. As a consequence, democracy should be viewed as a political incarnation of the modern universe: not a regime per se, but a basic condition on which political regimes are built. Within it, nothing is lost forever, but also nothing is truly gained. In this sense, totalitarianisms may be seen as desperate and reckless attempts to use the democratic position against itself, to block it by closing the time horizon with imaginary millenarism. If so, the trite and all-too-abused opposition between democracy and totalitarianism[6] mystifies the existence of the democratic predetermination, which makes "democratic" and "totalitarian" regimes alike stand on shifting sands.

Democratic predetermination irrevocably undermines legitimacy of any claim to one truth or one authority. By definition, it produces a field of political options. Due to their indeterminacy, none of these options can truly win. Thus, the almost natural propensity of modernity is not to settle political, ideological or historical disputes, but to conserve them in their entirety. Modernity displays a universal drive to conserve, amass, collect and freeze all conflicts—with an empty illusion of their future resolution.

If "totalitarianisms" struggle to erase everything except for them, it is precisely because they intend to restore premodernity by artificial elevation of one particular option to the position of self-evident and eternal power. Surely, history is not more favorable to "democracy" than to "totalitarianism," but the former better matches the morning after when another heap of ruins sees the light of day.

Democratic predetermination makes modern politics an art of managing the heap of rubble. This image, echoing both with Kantian irony on a cemetery as a place of perpetual peace[7] and with Benjamin's vision of the Angel of History, conveys the essence of modern incommensurability between perspectives and their histories. The heap of rubble can be either openly preserved or smashed and re-used. These three options correspond generally to the division between liberal democracy and "totalitarianism." In this respect, modern politics must be supplemented by new ethics which does not think about whether to accept reality as it is (that is structurally impossible), but analyzes the price of each move in the field of ruins.

46. The nonchalant mastery of Francis Scott Fitzgerald's *The Great Gatsby* culminates in the famed final line of the novel, whose popularity equals the degree of its misinterpretation: "So we beat on, boats against the current, borne back ceaselessly into the past."[8] There is nothing more deluding than reading it as a description of perpetual tension between the future that we are pushed into and the past that drags us back. This

sentence, in all its poetical depth, has the paradoxical power that bears an uncanny to Benjamin's theses on the concept of history.

Contrary to the Angel of History who, pushed into the future by the incomprehensible storm of history, looks at the mounting ruins of the past with horror, Fitzgerald's aphorism, read philosophically, suggests that *the current of history drives us straight into the past*. What history has for its goal is its past. Contrary to common intuitions, the past is not something that has been lost and, as such, is overshadowed by the present or by the future. The progress that in modernity became our obsession does not lead to any future, to any future novelty, but drags us all the more into the past.

The true future is, however, not lost: it is that tiny edge that we momentarily gain over the current. Even if it seems that by "beating on" we act, just like the main character of Fitzgerald's novel, only to restore the past, we effectively draw the future from the past in which it was concealed. In this sense, being stuck to the past may be less conservative than progress itself, because *progress, if let loose, recurs to the origins of a given history*. The past, in itself, reigns without further help. But if the past is actively pursued, the spell of recurrence is broken. It is only the force which makes us experience history as not-yet-completed that brings into history a spectre from its own guts: namely its own projected future, which—though initially constructed as an empty luring point—may be taken seriously and thus used to force this history open.

To put it differently, our "beating on," seemingly having for its aim the restoration of some lost and never actualized past, disturbs the mechanism of smooth recurrence of the past inscribed in every perspective. Therefore, the struggle for the past, as noted—differently—by Benjamin, Žižek,[9] and Badiou, has a truly revolutionary potential. In this struggle, the device which veils the embedding of every history in modernity-as-space becomes dismantled and the foundations of perspectivist history transpire. It appears that what enticed us as our future and accompanied us as our present was nothing but the past, which recurs incessantly to its murky point of sovereign exception. By being obdurate on realizing the promises of the past we may gain an edge over the current and, in advantageous circumstances, unravel it into the smoothness of modernity-as-space.

47. In his sixth Zürau aphorism Kafka writes:

> The decisive moment of human progress always lasts. For this reason the revolutionary spiritual movements that declare everything preceding as nothing are right, because nothing has yet happened.[10]

Under no circumstances should this aphorism be read ahistorically, that is in abstraction from the "epoch" which it describes from within. Once the contours of modernity are discerned, there is nothing that has truly happened. The onset of our times is indubitable, though unknown. What happens since then, what has happened, *seems nothing, really*, even though factually events have been abundant. The fact that modernity splits the inoperative content from the powerful machinery of abstract forces makes all the particular histories just turns of the same screw. In this incommensurable blindness and unprecedented waste, modernity desperately demands radical novelty only to reveal it as its own next convulsion.

48. In this sense, since the beginning of the historically embedded history, that is since the onset of modernity, we have not yet made a single step. We are still on the threshold. Whatever was revealed at the very beginning, for example between (Kant's) 1788 and (Hegel's) 1818, has never been overcome. Modernity constantly puts us in the still-lasting decisive moment, as if everything were still to be overcome and the final leap were still to be done. It always seems that the decisive is yet to come. Since the beginning of modernity nothing has truly happened and nothing will, because the only happening that counts under the modern logic is the end of modernity. It is, paradoxically, the only event that cannot be registered within the modern logic, because it will put an end to it. And, however we may lure ourselves that it has occurred, or will occur shortly, the decisive moment keeps lasting.

From this perspective, the most tremendous and traumatizing events of the past are still, in the light of the modern construction, nothing. Therefore, we are helplessly caught in a kind of historical double bind: *modernity brings the past to a disturbing level of visibility with the same gesture that pronounces a judgment over this past as being, essentially, nothing.* For this reason, our obsessive rumination about the past is part and parcel of the same device that gives us the lure of being at the forefront of history, which awaits, at any moment, a thorough Messianic reconstruction.

Thus, we live in a borrowed time, to quote Zygmunt Bauman's phrase.[11] Since the beginning of modernity the knowledge about history is more of a burden than a tool for understanding. Within the framework which produces modern history the past is essentially incomprehensible. The more it is visible—and the more it is enticing—the less it is intelligible. Our indebtedness is mounting as we push on further away from the murky beginnings of modernity. With each attempt to understand our historical position, we dig a deeper grave. And perhaps it is along these lines that Benjamin's description of the Angel of History should be read.

49. The return of an unfinished history is usually gradual. It slowly creeps in, just as if a powerful storm already loomed at the horizon, opening an *interregnum* whose stillness marks the spatial tissue of the modern universe. In these times, richness of old mature cultures is abundant, whereas the pre-past histories return in the guise of absolute novelty and augur a fundamental change. Perhaps cravings for the past golden age, like the European pre-1914 times, are, in fact, nothing else than a passion for eternity that glimmers in the *interregnum*. In this sense, *interregna* have tales of their own and myths that last long. Histories might return, *interregna* do not: their myths stay forever bound to one particular moment that can never be repeated.

Thus, *interregna* provide us with a model modern time. Within their boundaries it seems that the first step is coming. It is for this reason that suddenly we might feel relieved from the unresolved burden of modernity and enjoy its emptiness without tension, whose accumulation gradually brought about the rich stillness of the *interregnum*.[12]

50. According to Marx's famous quip, the bourgeois think that "there has been history, but there is no longer any."[13] In their ideological (mis)representation, they conceive of history as something that had to function in order to establish the *status quo*, but later left us quietly, inaugurating an eternal kingdom of "freedom, equality, property and Bentham," as Marx wrote ironically in *The Capital*.[14]

Yet, from their structural point of modernity, the bourgeois are right in this regard. In a sense, we cannot experience history otherwise than as something that has been completed. Only the obsession of origins, of mounting indebtedness, of a tremendous tectonic change that looms at the horizon and gives our jaded palates a new excitement, contradicts their version. In this tension we never catch history as such.

We owe the fragmented and displaced perception of history to the work of sovereignty. *Its unique power of creating through suspending applies primarily to history.* We know history only in its inoperative, spectral glory, which Kierkegaard recognzed so well in his despair over the structural impossibility to believe in something that happened in history.[15] It is in the *interregnum* between particular histories that the real spatiality of modernity becomes discernible. What modern philosophy—with futile efforts—attempts to grab under the category of "happening," is nothing else than the crystal surface of modernity in which sovereigns are embedded.

Therefore, we know history only as well-anchored in the past and constantly threatened by a fall of the current sovereign. It is for this reason that every current power keeps fighting its past enemies. In one of his Collège de France lectures Michel Foucault deftly reversed Clausewitz's trite proverb and claimed that it is politics in nominal time of peace that should be viewed as prolongation of war with other means.[16] In a more metaphorical sense, every sovereign is miserably tied to the war from which it emerged. It is always, at the fundamental level, ontologically belated. Sovereign power never targets its actual enemy, because at bottom its view is distorted through its own existence-through-history. Through this distortion, every modern sovereign narrative has, in its construction, an element of self-perceived error, a fundamental flaw that determined our origins and warped our present. It is the very same error that is searched at the origins and expected at the end. For it is nothing else than projection of a sovereign's position on the surface of modernity-as-space.

It is this bare whiteness of modernity-as-space that, upon confrontation, appears to us as a shadow of traumatizing and impossible "real history." What we perceive as happening, as real history at work, is nothing else but a total collapse of a given device that constructs the present with a representation of the past. For this reason, the more we convince ourselves that we know history, the more we are exposed to the ravaging impact of happening. *It is precisely our understanding that is lured into a trap and turned against us.*

Just like the Mirror Star bends transcendence inwards and thus turns the vector of pressure, blocking the whole construction from the inside, so is historical understanding posited against happening. Historical understanding demands, by its very emplacement, that what it cannot reach and what defies it. In this sense, the Mirror Star produces the fundamental historical tension at the heart of modernity. Therefore, history is precisely what makes us obsessive about happening. It promises to bring us to the threshold of understanding and, in this very moment, leaves us stunned before the inconceivable spectacle. What modernity brings about is a total reconfiguration in relations between temporality and sense, which leads to the emergence of, on the one side, histories, and, on the other side, happening.

51.1 With the benefit of hindsight that the last two centuries gave us, it may be claimed the epicenter of Hegel's desire to have relief from historical understanding is located in the obscure concept of *Begriff*. In Hegelian sense it is not simply a "notion,"[17] as this term must be, somewhat mechanically, translated into English. Contrary to the Latin static etymology of "notion," which is an abstract projection of an intellectual category onto reality, *Begriff* conjures up the dynamics of "grasping" (*be-greifen*), an act engaged in its own movement. It must be underlined that Hegel's *Begriff* is a strictly original concept which has little to do with common understanding of "notions."

What *Begriff* captures, in fact, is a moment of perfect loop, in which everything that is conditioned appears in connection with everything that is conditioning, and thus leaves no inexplicable element within the scope of reasoning.[18] A useful example of how *Begriff* works concerns causation. Philosophy, at least since Aristotle, separated causes from effects, investigating relations of causation between them. In Hegel's view, the very language in which these ruminations had taken place were not neutral categories, but a particular opposition based on a perspectivist assumption. We see causes and effects only when we have already assumed that "reality" splits into causes and effects. We can produce knowledge with them, but its original assumption is inseparable from the positive material that it absorbed. Once this predetermination is spotted, the original assumption begins to be problematic.

Naturally, Hegel cannot offer any disentanglement from being always thrown into a particular constellation of language. His unmistakably modern answer is to push forward. To see *Begriff* is to understand how the void of indetermination splits into a grid of notions, passes through positive material that it itself posited and then refinds the original division in strict correlation with the knowledge that has been thus produced.

51.2 The Absolute Knowledge is a *Begriff* at the highest level, at which everything that existed as a presupposition has been inscribed into the content.[19] As we already demonstrated (→ 9, 10), time for Hegel is an illusion produced by the fragmentation of the universe into innumerable perspectives with their own historical narratives. To each one of them *Begriff* is a salvation, because it inscribes the particular history into its content and thus grasps it from the atemporal side, with time rendered inoperative *within* the grasped content. It is in this sense that *Begriff* in the Absolute Knowledge gives them freedom:[20] they appear without external references, with their own time reabsorbed into their circumference. And, as Kojève noted with great perspicacity, their time becomes effectively dissolved.[21]

Hegel's argument is understandable only if we distinguish meaningful histories from the real of happening. He struggles to look through the particularity of each perspective in order to see how its time is constructed and dependent on a set of contingent assumptions. Once all perspectives are viewed with their time included, time stops. Nothing meaningful can happen; all epochs, with one gesture, are put to the grave. What appears in this moment is the timeless surface of modernity-as-space. It is timeless, because no time can be counted in relation to it. It knows no units, no epochs or standstills. *But, knowing no time, it is still a form of temporality: the real experience of happening which smashes all meanings and stable frameworks.*

51.3 But what stems from suspending meaningful time and standing before the real of happening? Nothing, basically, just as each return of the death drive is a stubborn recurrence to the same position of eternal vigilance before the void. And so is Hegel a priest of permanent vigilance before modernity-as-space. His legacy, as underlined in *Lectures on the Philosophy of Religion*, consists in one task: restoring the real of happening each time when new meanings blossom and produce times that begin to shroud the once reached null point of history. In this sense, Hegel's drive is a permanent "chimney sweep" that attempts to clear happening from history that keeps sedimenting upon its surface. In the truly modern spirit of aestheticizing destruction, this work, despite its effectively negative character, acquires a positive aura.

51.4 Hegel's drive is a quest for respite from the modern burden of historicity. It attempts to relieve the consciousness from the influx of historical signifiers that permanently posit the present as part of a broader, perspectivist narrative on history. In a sense, Hegel repeats the Descartes' gesture of presenting the content to consciousness; but the real novelty consists in the loop of presentation, in which the content overlaps with the consciousness. *In other words, each history is presented to itself and thus reduced to a place on the surface of happening.* And, in the reversal produced by the Mirror Star, respite is to be sought in the eye of the tornado. It is then, in fact, nothing but a passing fold on the surface of modernity.

52. From Hegel onwards we are permanently tempted to do away with positive historical content. The spasms of modern historicity are nothing else than the throb of this negative drive to remove the necessarily "falsified," perspectival history whose subsequent forms reign each time. It is just as if by removing history and standing before the meaningless modernity-as-space, experienced as happening, we felt relieved from a terrible burden of perspectivism. Therefore, the very same instance which shields us from the emptiness of modern surface, is—through a double bind sealed by the Mirror Star—experienced as unbearable indebtedness that we are tempted to reject. Apparently, modernity establishes a peculiar state of exception in which *protection* against historicity is perceived as hypocrisy that one needs to repel, even if to one's own detriment.

53. Marx's, and not only Marx's, vision of revolution embodies the Hegelian logic of *Begriff*. It struggles to unite reality once more, to get rid of particular histories and inaugurate "proper time," which would not be dependent on perspectivist narratives. It is in this sense that we should understand Marx's claim that all history that leads up to socialism is just prehistory of humanity.[22] The revolutionary breakthrough permanently separates prehistory and the new, proper time, which must be of a different character.[23] This "proper time," ushered in by the revolutionary act, is, effectively, atemporal: it is

not even vigilance before happening, it is timeless happening as such. Precisely for this reason, Benjamin's revolutionary "tiger jump"[24] brings back and unites all the dispersed past.

Yet, happening is an empty point of *nec plus ultra*. Where perspectivist historical narratives are annihilated, there is only way back—and this way back to meaningful world leads through the pain of Thermidor. What ultimately remains is the silence of a failed messianic event, the very same which Jules Michelet describes in the opening pages of his *History of the French Revolution*. While walking through desertified summer Paris, he stumbles upon *le Champ de Mars*, which he perceives with a gaze of profound melancholy found only where history dared play for the highest stake:

> The Revolution is in us, in our spirits; it has no monument in the outside world. Living spirit of France, where will I grasp you if not in me? ... So I go to the Champ-de-Mars, I sit on the dry grass, I breathe the great spirit which hovers over the arid plain. The Champ-de-Mars, this is the only monument that the Revolution left ... The Empire has its column, and it almost entirely appropriated the Arc-de-Triomphe; the kingdom has its Louvre, its Invalides ...
>
> And the Revolution has for its monument ... the void.
>
> Its monument is sand, as plain as in Arabia ...[25]

54. Finally, Hegel's *Begriff* describes precisely the relation between time and sovereignty. The link is simple. Meaningful time elapses only under the umbrella of a sovereign. Wherever the sovereign begins to crumble, time gets out of joint and turns into lasting. But, at the farthest point, in which the demise of the sovereign is indistinguishable from the empty center of its rule, time dissolves into uncountable and indiscernible happening. And this happening is a crack that allows us, for a little while, to see the common space of all sovereigns and all their histories.

Descartes' demon of historicity: Is there history outside modernity?

55. In the third of his *Meditations on the First Philosophy*, Descartes opens his reflections on *le malin génie* (the evil genius)—the assumed powerful deceiver to whom, perhaps, I own all illusions of sensations and knowledge—to the riddle of temporality. The famed reasoning assumes that a deceiving God might have created everything that we perceive, experience and know. But, bad enough, the power of deceit may concern even time itself:

> For the whole time of my life may be divided into an infinity of parts, each of which is in no way dependent on any other; and, accordingly, because I was in existence a short time ago, it does not follow that I must now exist, unless in this moment some cause create me anew, as it were,—that is, conserve me. In truth, it is perfectly clear and evident to all who will attentively consider the nature of duration that the conservation of a substance, in each moment of its duration,

requires the same power and act that would be necessary to create it, supposing it were not yet in existence ... I interrogate myself to discover whether I possess any power by means of which I can bring it about that I, who now am, shall exist a moment afterwards: for, since I am merely a thinking thing ..., if such a power resided in me, I should, without doubt, be conscious of it; but I am conscious of no such power, and thereby I manifestly know that I am dependent upon some being different from myself.[26]

Consistent doubting undermines not only the existence of the world, but also the continuity of time. What can guarantee, asks Descartes anticipating Hume's skepticism, my continuous existence? Am I not, in fact, created anew in every moment? And, more importantly, *have I not been created just a while ago, with all my memories of the past being created with me*?

This well-known Cartesian riddle embodies a fundamental doubt that was cast on temporality in the modern era. Even if Descartes himself may be variously posited in his relation to modernity,[27] this aspect of his thought surprisingly well resembles the profound cut that modernity introduced into temporality. By asking the very question of what supports continuity, temporality is both created and rendered problematic, that is, created through emergence from its own wound.

The structural affinity between the epoch of absolutism (and the first emergence of modern sovereigns) and Descartes' thought is evident. The Cartesian *ego* occupies the same empty peak of sovereignty that absolute rulers of the time attempted to conquer. In this sense, the profound tectonic creation/reorganization of temporality that Descartes' thinking attests to is a sign that sovereignty entered the world and marked it with its own temporal devices.

56. In the spirit of Descartes' doubting reasoning, we might equally ask: what if there was nothing before modernity? What if modernity was created out of nothing? Out of no history? What if it emerged with the already constructed past that we take for real, but with no justification? Would not all the premodern past be just an internal organization of history by the modern framework? And, what if, in fact, there was no actual premodern history?

What if there is an evil genius, a *malin génie*, who deceives us as to the solidity of history? Were not all the artifacts of the premodern past delivered and deliberately placed in our *lieux de mémoire*, so that we live under the illusion that there used to be a world that had not been modern? Is there a guarantee that the testimonies about the premodern past, all the numerous texts of our history, are not a sham? What could give us certainty that modernity is not equal with the entire universe, but that it began,[28] and, perhaps, will disappear one day?

57. The apparent absurdity of these questions, whose skepticism is brought to the very end, does not allow, however, to disregard them easily. Wherever there is a sovereign cut, doubt penetrates the freshly opened crack and persists in it until the rift of sovereignty closes. The uncertainty as to the origins of modernity—or even the total doubt in its difference from the universe as such—is a sign that this unique trans-

epoch is carved by the blade of sovereignty. *Thereby, the other side of modernity is known to us only under the guise of possibility, never as factuality.*

Sovereignty colonizes factuality by suspending it into possibility. Once factuality becomes one option of the many other possibilities, an abyss opens under its existence. Hovering above the precipice, with no meaningful justification, no material support, only by the virtue of a contingent, arbitrary decision, it is a perpetual state into which sovereignty plunges the universe.[29]

For this reason, Kantianism, together with its consummation, Hegelianism, are the proper philosophies of the modern era. Descartes discovered the abyss, but it was Kant who gave the basic ideology describing how to dwell upon the abyss—in a realm where possibility precedes factuality. Kantianism is a way of acting in suspension of knowledge, with active reference to the emptiness that is left after this suspension. In this regard it is *the* proper philosophy of modern sovereignty. In the whole domain of knowledge it inaugurates a state of exception, which Agamben unnecessarily reserved to the domain of the law by defining it as "an anomic space in which what is at stake is a force of law without law."[30] *This state of exception applies equally to history.*

58. The very threat, absurd as it may sound, that modernity was begotten out of nothing—that nothing can eliminate the zone of indistinguishability between the existence of continuous, premodern history and the instantaneous creation of its projected image—sets history in the perpetual tension of possibility. By claiming that there is no history except for modern history we do not negate that continuous premodern history might exist or, quite reasonably, might have existed. "Modern" does not mean that history can rise only under modernity. It is rather a signifier that remarks the indelible possibility that the modern universe was created out of nothing and all history belongs only to it.[31]

History that we know hovers over the abyss of unjustifiable possibility, once and forever opened by sovereignty. For this reason, its links with any "premodern epochs" are irrevocably suspended. In this sense, the Cartesian *malin génie* does not have to exist "really." The very possibility, understood ontologically,[32] that it might exist is enough. Its work is done not through real acts, but through planting possibilities that will never be eradicated. Perhaps then *le malin génie* has a familiar name: sovereignty.

59. What sovereignty brings about is a new type of temporality, based on a structural cut with the past. It does not mean that "the past"—"premodernity"—disappears. On the contrary, for the first time it gets salvaged and viewed in its entirety. But, as such, it is rendered inoperative, suspended on the sovereign cut. Becoming just a mass of positive material, it is, in a paradoxical manner, visible and inconsequential, both present and spectral. It may be, and must be, arranged into histories, but, at the same time, these histories are ravaged by primordial doubt as to their epoch-irrelevant validity. *In this and only this sense, there was no history before modernity.*

60. As if in some unsettling fulfillment of Isaac Luria's Kabalistic intuitions, modern universe sprang out of nothing. Whatever had given rise to modernity, must have withdrawn. The true paradox lies in the fact that we have all elements of the riddle, and

all the keys, in our hand. The premodern world has been well preserved around us, in countless artifacts, testimonies and traces. It had withdrawn in its validity, but not in its meanings, which still have been preserved like Lurianic *reshimu*, remainders. The perpetually suspended subsistence of the premodern world founds the greatest modern myth, namely that modernity is one of the many epochs.

Consequently, any premodern history is just an image projected onto the abyssal rift opened up by sovereignty.

61. We cannot refrain from such projections, which is well attested by all the fake histories that philosophy attempted to present as descriptions of its development. Nietzsche's Greeks and Heidegger's Presocratics are late stages in this self-deceit, in which premodern history is marked, at an arbitrarily selected point, with a projection of the modern cut. What we keep reliving in this manner is, however, nothing more than a slash of sovereignty which puts us on the historical map that we cannot see. Therefore, we require a new Copernican revolution in order to understand that it is not modernity that depends on history, but the other way round.[33]

62. Therefore, it would be false to perceive modernity as an epoch of secularized history which, nevertheless, would still preserve its eschatological-theological component (in the line of Karl Löwith,[34] Carl Schmitt or even, occasionally, Giorgio Agamben[35]). There is no theological structure that would withstand the emergence of modernity and still reign over it, even if under the secular disguise. The sovereign cut which stands at the fictitious origins of modernity is more powerful than any theology. It gives rise to theology—lost in the helpless hall of mirrors that our thinking has become—but is more indifferent to its claims than a dead body to *kaddish*.

To claim otherwise and to build the picture of modernity upon a reference to the made-up corpse of theology is nothing less but concocting a false story that belongs to סטרא אחרא. Our history did not start with revelation and will not end with redemption, as Jacob Taubes wanted to believe.[36] Our history is not continuous and has never become "secularised."[37] The only form of it which is accessible to us arose among the turmoil caused by the sovereign cut—which, for the sake of theologizing, should be held for the (new) Creation. In modernity, histories are always multiple and subjected to the rules of the modern field. And, as demonstrated earlier, seeking history above modernity is precisely what is barred.[38]

For this reason, if there was indeed the Löwithian *Heilsgeschehen* ("the becoming of salvation," as one could translate it, awkwardly but literally, into English), it would not include modern history. No modern event would stand in an individual position to the becoming of salvation. What would count would be only modernity as a non-Whole totality, which makes all its content subservient to its *a priori* construction. From the impossible point of view of *Heilsgeschehen*, all ages of modernity would look as one twinkling of an eye.

63. The realm that we inhabit, only rarely finding traces of the outside, is ravaged by *the possibility of possibility*. It is not only that this universe each time offers us a possible

alternative to what "really" is. Into everything that exists creeps in a permanent structural element, which always makes another possibility, possible. This seemingly pointless wordplay should not deceive us: the possibility of possibility connotes some fundamental destabilization at a much more fundamental level than just the emergence of simple alternative to everything. Even if there were no alternatives to some factuality, the possibility of possibility would already dismantle and decenter it, creating alternatives out of nothing. This is the true sense of modern *creatio continua*: permanent nothingness at the heart of things is already a working, though empty alternative, which makes positive existence appear as a feat of resistance.

64. Common modern *doxa* gives priority to factuality over possibility. Within factuality, it seems that everything that exists has emerged out of an array of possibilities that had collapsed and given up their weak modal ontology for a much stronger ontology of existence. Yet, perhaps modernity relies on a reverse relation: each factuality is, at its heart, dismantled by a ravaging set of possibilities. Perhaps then factuality is not necessarily stronger than the spectres of possibility. Each factuality stands against the emptiness of possibilities and is paralyzed with its own shattered existence. In modernity, factuality hovers over the abyss filled with possibilities. They do not dispel in sunlight, because there is no sunlight. Under the light of the Mirror Star they may be easily mistaken for beings.

65. Histories are born out of the tremor fueled by the possibility of possibility. Modern history is nothing else but the constant attempt to castigate difference and to set aside the horror that what we see as solid was different and will be different. By deliberately narrating the genealogy of today, we desperately conceal the traumatizing absurd of the sovereign cut. Modernity emerges as a universe in which everything *could be different*. This indelible possibility produces histories and separates us, forever, from what they purportedly say about the premodern past.

66. But is not the possibility of possibility, which was introduced by the modern sovereign cut, just an instance of the age-old doubt *that the universe we perceive is merely an illusion*? The history of thought offers us hundreds of conceptions which reduce the world to some kind of veiled essence. Yet, what separates them from the possibility of possibility, introduced by the sovereign cut, is their essentially ontological character. The world they portray is in truth something else than our perceptions suggest, but since time immemorial and forever. Thus, premodern ontology is the domain of eternity and even if it views the world as created, its basic ontological framework remains unchangeable. Meanwhile, the modern sovereign cut operates differently. It strikes out ontology as an independent domain. At the lowest level it melts ontology with temporality to the point of their indifferentiation. It does not simply suggest that the world might be something different than we think it is. The situation is much more complicated: the sovereign cut always produces an inerasable aspect of temporality at the heart of existence.

Therein lies the originality of Descartes' "evil genius." Not in assuming radical skepticism which claims that the world may be ruled by the "evil genius" who deceives us. Not even in assuming that something different may have happened in the past. The true weight of Descartes' invention lies in the recognition *that possibility not only undermines ontology and not only sets temporality in tension, but makes these two inseparable in their possibility-based oscillation.*

After the sovereign cut, the world can no longer be described in abstraction from history. The possibility of possibility colonizes and dismantles the distinction between ontology and temporality: what may be different might equally have been different. There is no synchronic view. No world can be established without history. Therefore, history is, at the deepest level, part and parcel of any ontological framework. Changing ontology means changing history and vice versa.

Thus, the spectres of what may be are the spectres of what may have been, and conversely. In the domain of possibility, time is just another dimension that we can traverse freely. For this reason, in modernity one cannot cast a fundamental doubt on a world without undermining its history. And, the other way around, no history may be changed without shattering the ontology of what purportedly is.

67. Whoever would like to take pride in the fact that modernity did away with old metaphysical gods must be reminded that this act was not done by our hands. It was the sovereign cut that suspended the validity of metaphysics (although not its meaning[39]). Our only virtue was to sit comfortably in the hall of mirrors and wallow in the dim light of extinct suns.[40]

The same fact is responsible for our inherent powerlessness towards metaphysics. We are ruled by dead gods because we are satisfied with them being dead; their continuing rule *is a different matter* that we hope to tackle later.[41] In this "later" that never comes lies our permanent entrapment in the device of sovereignty.[42] The empty place of ancient rules is being occupied by yet new sovereigns, each time temporarily, and each time with a definite certainty that we could destroy this construction in a twinkling of an eye, if only we wanted. Our possible, but never realized desire to demolish the modern universe remains a possibility that, in truth, founds the sovereign reign.

68. Sovereignty is very much of a drug, whose application aggravates our condition. It undermines all certainty by instilling the ubiquitous possibility. Under its black sun, everything can be different and/or could have been different. But the sovereign reign is, ultimately, the only thing we can be sure of. Therefore, what ruins our certainty is eventually the only certain foothold upon the ocean of disactivated past.

The Mirror Star comes to us under the disguise of innocent possibility, whose influence, however, can never be eradicated once it lets itself in. It suspends all our past. It renders inoperative every positive content. Its low light lures us into thinking that no positive thing can stand on its own.

For this reason, we no longer accept simple explanations. Premodern philosophies were satisfied with explaining phenomena by juxtaposing them with some positive determination. They had the power to settle for claiming that the world is explained by the highest Good or by positive God. Yet, modern philosophy is eager to reject all theorizing that explains something by producing another independent instance that is purportedly accountable for it. What we seek now are explanations that emerge out of nothing. The purely modern gesture in thinking is *to explain the world only with reference to the world*, in a closed, autopoietic loop. Hegel, who explains each phenomenon with its own "other side" and, ultimately, elucidates the universe as *interpretandum* only with the universe *as interpretans*—but viewed from the "right" angle—is the unsurpassed master of this art. It is just as if all things had been ravaged at heart by some indelible negativity which commands us to pass through independent, positive determinations and seek "serious," structural devices.

69. Deep inside, each modern philosophical discovery is based on a short circuit, a tiny spot where modernity touches itself. It is hardly anything more than a fold, observed in most contingent circumstances. And then the power of thinking comes, which blows it up to the proportions of the universe. Yet, still, at the very heart of this universe, *modern philosophy is based on nothing, really*—if by nothing we can denote the tiniest remainder through which modernity both separates and contacts itself, producing a spark.

Our philosophical knowledge in modernity is surprisingly fragile. And perhaps the decomposition goes as far as to threaten the very possibility of understanding. Do we really know anything? Do we really understand? Do we not just munch on past texts in hopeless and repetitive tentative to grasp the thought that passed through and left nothing but a trace? Heidegger was right in calling for "paths, not work": there is no work we can write, read and understand. We just keep collecting traces, start anew and draw our paths inconclusively.

70. As long as modernity builds up our universe, the structure of sovereignty cannot be overcome. Nevertheless, it may be at least effectively ignored, as long as we manage to remain in the fragile balance between the subdued positivity of things and the temptation of radical negativity. The ubiquity of modernity cannot make us passive, resigned or entrapped. All positivity that still exists needs our active support, which compensates the lack of breath that was evacuated from it by the sovereign cut. The gentle art of *tikkun* is yet to be reappraised.

71. This active support of positivity should be the cornerstone of modern ethics. In modernity, the fundamental critique of sovereignty is a prerequisite of ethical thinking proper. No ethics may be devised until the powerful forces of sovereignty rule over our universe. Without taking them into account, we are prone to ramble on within the field a priori circumscribed by the sovereign power. Levinas is an ominous example here: his ethics of unconditional responsibility for the other, so trivialized in its numerous later recitals, is inherently dependent on the sovereign staging of negativity.[43]

Therefore, ethics that could claim to be adequate to the challenges of modernity may come only after the contours of sovereign devices are well explored. There are no illusions to be harbored in this regard. Modernity is a realm of unprecedented possibilities, unleashed powers of immense proportions, practical miracles happening continuously before our eyes. Whatever ethics could exist in this universe must be modest, sober, and demanding. Its inconspicuous humility must, however, be resilient to the most powerful tricks of mind so often practiced by modern philosophy—tricks which promise everything, leave us standing and then dispel like mist in the open sun.

72. With a touch of Blochian intuition it could be easily believed that possibility is what liberates us by smashing the closeness of an oppressive world. But what possibility truly demands is sobriety, because only by being sober, even ruthlessly sober, we may draw the line between the possibility that is an entrapment of sovereignty and the possibility that liberates. Possibility builds for us whole worlds on shifting sands, but simultaneously gives us neither the audacity nor the perseverance to inhabit them. This sobriety should also whisper to our ear that, perhaps, under the modern sun we will never experience the universe otherwise. We will always get carried away by myriads of possibilities, taking our curse for our blessing.

5

Sovereign Suspension and Provisionality

73.1 In the spring of 1917, soon after the death of Franz Josef I, who had reigned for 68 years, and not long before the ultimate fall of the three European empires—Franz Kafka composed a short parable which was originally intended to be part of a larger whole, but was later published independently under the title "Eine kaiserliche Botschaft," "An Imperial Message":

> The emperor, so a parable runs, has sent a message to you, the humble subject, the insignificant shadow cowering in the remotest distance before the imperial sun; the Emperor from his deathbed has sent a message to you alone. He has commanded the messenger to kneel down by the bed, and has whispered the message to him; so much store did he lay on it that he ordered the messenger to whisper it back into his ear again. Then by a nod of the head he has confirmed that it is right. Yes, before the assembled spectators of his death—all the obstructing walls have been broken down, and on the spacious and loftily mounting open staircases stand in a ring the great princes of the Empire—before all these he has delivered his message. The messenger immediately sets out on his journey; a powerful, an indefatigable man; now pushing with his right arm, now with his left, he cleaves a way for himself through the throng; if he encounters resistance he points to his breast, where the symbol of the sun glitters; the way is made easier for him than it would be for any other man. But *the multitudes are so vast; their numbers have no end.* If he could reach the open fields how fast he would fly, and soon doubtless you would hear the welcome hammering of his fists on your door. *But instead how vainly does he wear out his strength*; still he is only making his way through the chambers of the innermost palace; *never will he get to the end of them*; and *if he succeeded in that nothing would be gained*; the courts would still have to be crossed; and after the courts the second outer palace; *and so on for thousands of years*; and if at last he should burst through the outermost gate—but never, never can that happen—the imperial capital would lie before him, the center of the world, crammed to bursting with its own sediment. *Nobody could fight his way through here even with a message from a dead man.* But you sit at your window when evening falls and dream it to yourself.[1]

What strikes the reader at first sight is the mounting cascade of obstacles that hinder the delivery of the message. Even the smallest of them is powerful enough to detain the messenger. Yet, above each hindrance, which in itself might somehow give a false hope of victory, immediately appears another, in a seemingly endless chain of difficulties. For the messenger, the game is not only unequal, it gets constantly redefined in order to multiply inequalities. It would seem reasonable that the messenger should concentrate on one obstacle at a time, apply himself and hope for the best, not caring about the next steps. But the very perspective of next hindrances eats away at his strength—and worse even, paralyzes him.

It is not only that the obstacles are incommensurable in relation to the messenger's powers. This incommensurability plays with his strength. At first it suggests that there is a maybe slight, but real possibility of reaching the goal. Otherwise, the journey would never have been undertaken. The journey has already started, a step has been taken and some distance has shortened—therefore, there is some hope. But, soon it turns out that the incommensurability lurks in the dark. The obstacles multiply, the powers wane and, most importantly, the scale of difficulties starts to appear in its overwhelming hopelessness. The messenger becomes enmeshed in a trap which is, in fact, a direct consequence of his own initial blindness, *of his nonchalant hope*.

Yet, what is worse, even the arrival of the messenger, already a thousand times impossible, is not the goal. The goal is to transfer the message. One can imagine that the messenger finally conquers all hindrances and arrives at our place: he opens the door and drops dead. In this situation all his toil turns out to have been utterly pointless. The message sets in motion the whole universe. First, it kills off the old emperor, because without the hope of its delivery the old ruler would not have had the power to turn into nothingness. Then, the message propels the "indefatigable man" to push through the realm in your direction.

Ultimately, however, matter takes over. The message cannot be delivered. Even the most potent symbols cannot overwhelm the inertia, the vastness and the stubborn indifference of matter. And if the message is not delivered, then the whole undertaking becomes incomprehensible. It will have been nothing but a local stir in the ocean of inert matter, no more significant than a landslide or erosion of a dune.

73.2 What is even worse is the last sentence in which the whole story turns out to be a trick of the mind. Someone, say you, made the story up. Two consequences should be drawn from this final twist.

First, the whole story was conceived in the symbolic. It describes the fate of a symbolic message that becomes fatally ensnared in the undeadness of matter. But, if so, it is the symbolic that describes to itself its own eventual failure. Before it makes any real move, the symbolic already envisages its own debacle. Thus, there is no need to confront matter. Matter arises within the symbolic as its own perpetual deferral which paralyzes even the first move. It does not have to be any "real" enemy. Matter is intrinsically embedded in the symbolic and thus its final victory is nothing but a walkover. The symbolic, instead of really acting, anticipates its own route. By doing so, it reveals matter. And once matter appears, the whole potency of the symbolic dissipates.

Second, if you make the history up, "when evening falls," then what if there has been, in fact, an imperial message that will never have been delivered? What if the message was sent and the story accidently coincides with it? If so, is not our seemingly delusional dream the only true narrative about what has happened, but a one which will be never become known in a normal way? The delivery of the message overlaps with the delivery of the story of the message. If the latter is not delivered, then the whole route also becomes wiped out of any symbolic memory. So perhaps our daydreaming is the only means of learning what really happened. *Being, at its core, just a possibility, it might be more real than any fact solidly backed up by testimonies and credible narratives.* The whole "imperial message" is just a product of imagination, but, as such, it may be the only way to find out the truth. Thus, possibility melts with reality to the point of indistinguishability. As long as the universe is impermeable—and the message cannot be delivered—possibility is the only way to inquire into reality. But there is a price to be paid for this: reality conflates with possibility.

73.3 But it is not even you that made this story up. It was born in Kafka's writing. Contrary to the message that it describes, it has been delivered to us and, seemingly, it has not failed. We can read it, *it is here*. If so, was it really lost on its way?

It is. Because ultimately the apparent delivery of the message is the utter form of deception. We still dream it to ourselves. But contrary to the "humble subject" who will never learn about the failed message, we feel entitled to know it. We know that it has been delivered and, basing on this deception, we imagine its way. We stage all possible difficulties, we imagine all impossibilities of delivery, all lost letters, but we do it after the message has been delivered. No wonder that it has been delivered, if it has always been there. We have never moved from the window. We only staged the whole trip, imagined the unimaginable efforts and now return to the very same point that we have never left. Nevertheless, we do not return unscathed, but with mortal fatigue.

In other words, we were ready to pay the price, but only if our position—the place "by the window"—would not be endangered. We are eager to dispose of all our powers in advance, we agree to fall from exhaustion, if only the whole staging guarantees us a safe vantage point. *We can wander through the vastest spaces, we can admit all defeats and insufficiencies of our thinking, but ultimately we remain safe in our position by the window.*

Kantian sublimity and incommensurability of the modern universe

74. Since Kant, the position by the window has a philosophical name: the sublime.[2] Let us cite the favorite quote of all interpreters:

> Bold, overhanging, and as it were threatening, rocks; clouds piled up in the sky, moving with lightning flashes and thunder peals; volcanoes in all their violence of destruction; hurricanes with their track of devastation; the boundless ocean in a state of tumult; the lofty waterfall of a mighty river, and such like; these exhibit our faculty of resistance as insignificantly small in comparison with their might. But, the sight of them is the more attractive, the more fearful it is, provided only that we are in security; and we readily call these objects sublime, because they raise the energies of the soul above their accustomed height, and discover in us a faculty of

resistance of a quite different kind, which gives us courage to measure ourselves against the apparent almightiness of nature.³

In Kant's view, the sublime, both in mathematics and in nature,⁴ is an experience of incommensurability:

> But, if we call anything not only great, but absolutely great in every point of view (great beyond all comparison), *i.e.* sublime, we soon see that it is not permissible to seek for an adequate standard of this outside itself, but merely in itself. It is a magnitude which is like itself alone. It follows hence that the sublime is not to be sought in the things of nature, but only in our Ideas; but in which of them it lies must be reserved for the Deduction.
> ... *The sublime is that in comparison with which everything else is small.*⁵

> *The sublime is that, the mere ability to think which, shows a faculty of the mind surpassing every standard of Sense.*⁶

> Nature is therefore sublime in those of its phenomena, whose intuition brings with it the Idea of their infinity. This last can only come by the inadequacy of the greatest effort of our Imagination to estimate the magnitude of an object.⁷

We experience the sublime when our finite faculties of comprehension become overwhelmed with incommensurable potency. The *jouissance*-like intensity of this feeling that mixes pain with pleasure brings Kant so close to Sade:⁸

> The feeling of the Sublime is therefore a feeling of pain, arising from a want of accordance between the aesthetical estimation of magnitude formed by the Imagination and the estimation of the same formed by Reason. There is at the same time a pleasure thus excited, arising from the correspondence with rational Ideas of this very judgment of the inadequacy of our greatest faculty of Sense ...⁹

The sublime is not some extreme possibility at the margins of our experience; it is, suddenly, something most cherished and sought. Almost as if we revelled in our finiteness being brutally disclosed, we pursue the sublime. But it is possible only if two conditions laid down by Kant are met. First, the sublime must belong not to the object that provokes it, but to the judgment, which reflectively finds itself overwhelmed by incommensurability. Second, the sublime may be properly experienced only from a safe position, as a trick of the judgment which is not required to be directly involved in the tumult of incommensurability.

75. If "the boundless ocean in a state of tumult" provokes the experience of the sublime, it is because it provokes the painful/pleasant intuition of our own finiteness, which, nevertheless, is safe and may play the danger only for itself.
    Here, Kant's pictures of wild nature could be much more metaphorical than he may have assumed. Kantian sublime is not necessarily about the actual oceans, waterfalls or

storms. What this "boundless ocean" may primarily stand for is the defused modern universe from Hegel's narrative (→ 2.2). *If so, then modernity as a whole would be experienced within the structure of the sublime.* In other words, modernity appears as a permanently opening rift of incommensurability.[10]

It is this feature that gave modern thinking and modern art its unprecedented potency. Their perspicacious depth owes to the unique ability to play the rise and fall of whole worlds, without our getting even slightly bruised. True, modernity has brought real horrors on which previous "times" could not have even speculated. But on the top of that modernity is experienced as a continuous, unbearable "tumult" from which, however, we return surprisingly unscathed.

Perhaps even all relation of proportionality between real atrocity and the feeling of horror has been irrevocably disturbed. On the one hand, whenever real horror appears, we have no language for it and act like mute indifferent dummies. Actual suffering comes not from the experienced tremor, but from an inconspicuous, absurd and almost gratuitous source. On the other hand, what we are excited by is the horror that we can narrate. And it is in such narratives that modernity conflates with the ongoing, overwhelming catastrophe.

76. The modern universe is experienced—within the framework of the sublime—as incommensurable, but only from a safe position. Incommensurability and safety of the finiteness are inextricably entangled.

The experience of incommensurable vastness, which points to our finite, determined position, only apparently sets us in tremor. There is always an undertone of cozy self-indulgence. It is well visible in Heidegger's enquiry into the finiteness of *Dasein* ≥— in the period of *Sein und Zeit*[11] and shortly afterwards. Discovering the abyss that finiteness is set against simultaneously outlines the contours of the local musty world. The more we stare into the vastness, the more entitled we feel to our temporal finite realm. We always feel out of joint, condemned to live in perpetual tension with no permanent abode, in a profound disturbance brought by modernity. Yet—and in this "yet" lies the gist of the sea change—we turn temporal misery into a perpetual state, in which we feel comfortable. We revel in homelessness. We continuously relive the groundlessness of our condition. The vastness around us adds some dirty comfort to our finite and temporal dwellings.

Paradoxically, the deepest precipices make our bricked-up vantage points all the more solid. *The tremendous incommensurability of modernity may be experienced only from the position of finiteness*. Only there it appears and only this position it creates as its spectre.

Permanent provisionality: Modernity as a universe of exception

77. If in modernity everything is makeshift, our actions lose visible consequences. Until a solid ground is finally reached, we act provisionally. This is the proper dimension of the state of exception that Agamben discovered with truly exceptional perspicacity, but theorized it atemporally.[12] The state of exception, however, should not be treated

as a generalized state, applicable to all epochs, but rather as the ultimate peculiarity of modernity as such.

Its first traits appear early, in Descartes' makeshift ethics. In the famous inaugurating gesture of early modern philosophy, Descartes attempts to rebuild science and knowledge after they were exposed to radical skepticism. But, while the reconstruction is *in progress*, some provisional rules of conduct must be applied:

> [A]s it is not sufficient, before beginning to rebuild one's dwelling-house, merely to throw it down and to furnish materials and architects, or to study architecture, and to have carefully traced the plan of it besides, it is also necessary to be provided with some other wherein to lodge conveniently while the work is in progress. Thus, in order that I might not remain undecided in my actions, ... I provisionally made myself a moral, consisting merely of three or four maxims ...
>
> 1. The first was, to obey the laws and customs of my country, keeping always to the religion in which, by the grace of God, I had been instructed from my childhood ...
> 2. My second maxim was, to be as firm and as resolute in my actions as I could, and to follow the most doubtful opinions, when I had once determined on them, no less constantly than if they were very certain. In this I acted as travelers who find themselves astray in some forest should do, for they ought not to wander about, turning now to one side and now to another, still less to remain in one place, but walk as straight as they can in one direction, and not change it for trivial reasons, although it were chance alone which determined their choice to begin with; for by this means, if they do not go precisely where they desire, *at least they arrive in time at some place where they will probably fare better than in the middle of the forest* [emphasis added]. And as *the actions of life seldom permit of any delay* [emphasis added], it is a very certain truth, that when it is not in our power to discern the most truthful opinions, we ought to follow the most probable. *And even though we remark no more probability in these than in those, we ought nevertheless to decide upon some, and then no longer consider them doubtful, in so far as they correspond to practice, but as very true and certain, because the reason which has made us decide upon them is so* [emphasis added].[13]

As Žižek rightly pointed out, this fragment augurs the future Heideggerian ontology "of provisionary existence," in which morality consists not in a particular set of rules, but in sticking to one's ungrounded decision.[14]

What is perhaps the most astonishing trait of Descartes' move, is the fully conscious—and let us venture this thought, inevitable—dissociation of acts from judgments. As to the latter, we are helplessly lost and we cannot be sure what we should do. Until the edifice is finished, we do not know what our life truly consists in. In theory, we could wait for judgments, but the construction—as Descartes himself counts with—drags on with no foreseeable closure on the horizon. Yet, *life does not permit of any delay*, therefore we need to act without having any substantial ground.

Thus, our actions are nothing but a chain of uncoordinated rash decisions, whose only justification is our obstinate sticking to a choice which, in fact, hovers over the abyss of senselessness.

Dissociating acts from judgments ruins the basic coordinates of time. There is no true time as long as we wait; we live in provisional time that spurs us on to decisions. Yet, we are still under the deception that a moment will arrive in which the ground will be found and we will put our past actions under close scrutiny in order to undo what was wrong. Until it comes, we need to supplement the material content of right opinions with only one thing: an ungrounded decision. In this manner, a structural act replaces the material content.

Descartes' argument for this replacement is simple: until the work is done, it is better to move in one direction, even erringly, because otherwise we linger in the middle of our loss without any conclusion. But, if we get lost, we have two options: either we go in one direction, hoping for not getting lost any more, or we stay put waiting for help or sudden revelation. Descartes does not even consider the latter option, which, parenthetically, has a late-Heideggerian flavor.[15] As if the pressure of provisional time were too strong for him, he needs to push forward, in one direction, on one decision.

78. What can be learned from the juxtaposition of Kafka's parable and Descartes' makeshift ethics is that in modernity even the most serious acts—to which we allocate greatest resources and which we precede with very long period of consideration and preparation—ultimately cannot be realized properly. Resources are easily exhausted. The period, carved out according to our sense of temporality, turns utterly incommensurable with the dimension of lasting that opens up in the process. No act can be carried out in its groundedness. What do we do then? We leave its empty shell, pretending that we act according to all principles and plans, only to effectively supplement it with *provisional measures*.

In acting, the abyss opens up. We lose acts as we go along. What we leave behind is nothing but debris of principles, plans and grounds, perpetually suspended by each and every provisional measure. For this reason, nothing is resolved once and for ever. To each act, it appears, we may return in a borrowed time; but the perpetual stream of provisionality pushes us on. We move on, because, as Descartes noted with manifest resignation, we think we will fare better in a place that we finally reach than in the middle of the forest. But perhaps we keep arriving still deeper and deeper in the very same middle.

If gods could die, our situation would be much simpler. Yet, gods do not die, not even are properly undead. It is rather that we tell ourselves a provisional tale about their death, waiting for the arrival of the message. Thus, *modern life emancipates itself only through provisionality*.

79. The message of Kafka's messenger will never reach us. What we get, makes its way to us, however, is a parable on his coming, structurally different from the message.

The message is targeted at its addressee and, coming from the source of power, is manifestly valid. It is produced by the center and goes to a particular recipient. Its authority is universal, just as its uniqueness. Contrariwise, the parable comes out of nowhere. It simply is; no one knows when and how it is transmitted. It slips into one's mind as the putative explanation of reality. To use Bloch's expression, it "blossoms from its own matter [*Sache*]."[16] Ultimately, the parable is the knowledge of the dispersed: it propagates itself without any proof or sign of validity, is not backed up by any confirmation, its power relies only on possibility,[17] never on certainty. In this sense, parable slips doubt into every reasoning: it is enough to hear it once in order to lose certainty forever.

Whenever the deliverance of the message is suspended, a space for parables is opened. The world of law and power is superseded by a realm of provisionality, whose basic principle is permanent dispersion. Each region of this realm awaits the message, but until it arrives—and it never arrives—lands of provisionality conceive their own explanations under the guise of parables. But, through parables, they are effectively expropriated from any stability and autonomy. Once a parable emerges, the place in which it originated always turns to the distant center from which a supposed message is to arrive. Visions of the outside never cease to haunt this place. In this manner, the parable rearranges and brings to light the purely spatial relations between places: a place is carved out in its singularity, put in relationship with the receding center and exposed in the growing distance. *This mounting dispersion in perpetual deferral is the new space produced by sovereignty.*

Among these places, modernity itself is an overarching space of dispersion, in which parables and possibility correspond to the permanently deferred arrival of the message. Needless to say, this vision is a parable among others.

80. Premodern thinking, in the form we are bound to see from our position, eagerly links the temporal with the transcendent. Whatever happens here and now, "on Earth," has its roots in the metaphysical framework of the otherwordly. The vector of influence may vary: either the metaphysical determines the temporal, or the other way round. Yet, the influence, even if mediated, is structurally undisturbed. Modernity works differently. It disposes of the metaphysical by opening in its place a yawning abyss. Interestingly, such a catastrophe of the otherwordly does not entail, as we could suppose, the shattering of the everyday life. On the contrary: life is put in a state of provisionality, in which it is both deprived of metaphysical support and continuously existing. *Questioned at its bottom, wrenched out of regular temporality, the here and now of modernity subsists in some provisional state which turned permanent.*

The post-metaphysical abyss no longer influences it directly. It rather outlines its borders, being accountable for the state of permanent provisionality. The earthly modern life is granted its own autonomy. Nothing that happens within modernity stands in a direct relation to any transcendent principle. In this sense, no deed has a real ethical value. No wonder that the only legitimate ethics seems to be the Kantian one, which finds the ethical in the ultimate self-groundedness of an act so clearly marked against the abyss of former transcendence. The abyss is acknowledged, the most shattering intellectual depictions of the precipice are elaborated, but ordinary life heaves a sigh of relief when the ex-transcendence may be paid only lip service.

Still, the undeadness of permanent provisionality is a continuously experienced burden, freedom without freedom, autonomy without substance. Last but not least, most hideous cruelty may rise when everything is provisional, even if—or especially if—forever.

81. Among many definitions that modernity may be approached with this one is extraordinarily potent: *modernity is the provisional turned permanent.*
Commonly, we ignore the provisional and wait for the permanent, because the provisional should pass and make place for the permanent. In the ordinary ontology, the provisional is subsidiary to the permanent. It draws its specificity from the relationship to something that will last and defines itself as such. The provisional should be transient. It only fills the void between something and something, covering the abyss of transformation. Yet, in modernity, all these intuitions become not only useless, but also detrimental: reality uses them against our interest. The provisional does not pass; the permanent, seemingly just at the reach of our hands, still does not come. Thus, the most insignificant, contingent and makeshift fiber of here and now gains the provisional power of premodern eternal gods. What we finally need to learn is the ability of seeing how each moment of modernity, emancipated-through-suspension from the metaphysical harness, wields the full sovereign power.
It is not that we are "just" governed[18] by the slightest and contingent conjectures. Under the sovereign suspension we are blocked from assessing their real weight and meaning. Most serious decisions, which, in other circumstances, would be considered crucial, are taken as if they meant nothing. Under the black sun of sovereignty, the inconsequential may take the vacant seat of power, seemingly just for a while, but, in reality, to hold unprecedented sway.[19]

82. It is for this reason that usually so-called totalitarian regimes are not, contrary to intuitive expectations, smooth machines of power which carry out hideous, but bold decisions of their leaders. The opposite, namely chaos, is not the rule either. What is typical for a totalitarian regime—and embodied fully in the functioning of the Third Reich—is creating a vast zone of suspension, within which the most contingent circumstances turn into decisions of highest importance. Thus, they are neither ordered not chaotic: where ground principles are suspended, a contingent act is, in an ironically late-Wittgensteinian manner, coextensive with the whole symbolic order in which it is supposedly purported.
How the suspension produced by modern sovereignty ends may be imagined with the help of a telling example. In 1944–5, when the Red Army forced its way westwards through Eastern and Central Europe, the Third Reich needed to resolve the remaining problem of death and concentration camps. The total defeat of Germany loomed large on the horizon. The Nazi pseudo-utopia lay bare in its hideous usurpations. But there were still numerous prisoners detained in camps. Except for those whom the Third Reich deemed necessary to kill in order to protect "das Geheimnis" (the secret of the perpetrated genocide), such as the Sonderkommando members, lives of prisoners were utterly indifferent to the state. They could provide little work force, and even when it could be used, it was, in fact, of no purpose. Primo Levi, who described himself as fortunate to be "employed" as a chemist in the laboratory of the Auschwitz III-Monowitz, grasped well the essence of this time of purposeless work, in which the

product of one day was destroyed by Allied bombers the next day and finally the factory functioned only by absurd inertia.[20] Nevertheless, the camps functioned until the Red Army was really close. Then the prisoners were often evacuated in death marches. Some, being too ill to march, or making a risky choice, remained in camps.

Their life or death was of utmost indifference to the Third Reich. There was even no guiding principle that could decide on their survival. Killing them off would make for the state no bigger difference than letting them live. Needless to say, the state did not feel obliged to follow any moral rules. It ran the final stage of its evacuation, suspending all norms and effectively letting the utmost contingency take the place of the order. Under the effective Nazi administration, Jewish prisoners were bodies to be exterminated. Yet, in this zone of suspension, even this injunction disappeared. The prisoners depended on pure conjecture of an appalling form of the state of nature. They could be killed on a whim by a guardian or let live.[21]

Primo Levi thus described the final days in the camp, in which the utterly contingent and groundless choice of prisoners decided about their life or death:

> Outside the hut the camp sounded unusually excited. One of the two Hungarians got up, went out and returned half an hour later laden with filthy rags.... One could see that they were in a hurry to have the matter over with before the fear itself made them hesitate. It was crazy of them to think of walking even for one hour, weak as they were, especially in the snow with those broken-down shoes found at the last moment. I tried to explain, but they looked at me without replying. Their eyes were like those of terrified cattle.
>
> Just for a moment it flashed through my mind that they might even be right. They climbed awkwardly out of the window; I saw them, shapeless bundles, lurching into the night. They did not return, I learnt much later that, unable to continue, they had been killed by the SS a few hours after the beginning of the march.[22]

Levi's choice to stay in the camp, although finally saving, led to a terrible experience of groundlessness of SS-Männer's decision:

> Nobody knew what our fate would be. Some SS men had remained, some of the guard towers were still occupied. About midday an SS officer made a tour of the huts. He appointed a chief in each of them, selecting from among the remaining non-Jews, and ordered a list of the patients to be made at once, divided into Jews and non-Jews. The matter seemed clear. No one was surprised that the Germans preserved their national love of classifications until the very end, nor did any Jew seriously expect to live until the following day.
>
> ... It was soon night but the electric light remained on. We saw with tranquil fear that an armed SS man stood at the corner of the hut. I had no desire to talk and was not afraid except in that external and conditional manner I have described. I continued reading until late. There were no clocks, but it must have been about 11 p. m. when all the lights went out, even those of the reflectors on the guard-towers.... Then the bombardment began. It was nothing new: I climbed down to the ground, put my bare feet into my shoes, and waited.

> ... But then there was a near explosion, and before one could think, a second and a third one, loud enough to burst one's ear-drums. Windows were breaking, the hut shook, the spoon I had fixed in the wall fell down. Then it seemed all over.
> ... The Germans were no longer there. The towers were empty.[23]

Sovereign power disappears as a kind of miracle and against its own logic. But, in its final hours, the link between provisionality, contingence, and decision reaches its peak. In the abyss of suspension, no decision is predictable and no consequence can be credibly linked with a choice. Permanent provisionality governs with a power of a thunderbolt.

The latest and utmost form of Agambenian bare life appears where the sovereign power withdraws even from defining its relationship to it. Records and punishments vanish. The news about our death or survival can never reach anyone. The message gets permanently stuck somewhere in the vast plains, though, potentially, it could arrive someday. But, even if it did, it would not mean anything to anyone.

83. Naturally, it is equally possible that there has never been a real center, not even in the most severe premodern imaginations. Perhaps the sun that we know now as black had never been bright. Thus, a cunning subterfuge of modern sovereignty would be to mask its origins by suggesting that it had had its "proper" or "positive" form. Nevertheless, darkness, in a negative suggestion, may only produce the reference to the putative original state.

Modernity in parable

73.4 The emergence of opaqueness and impermeability to universal messages is coextensive with the creation of space. That a message cannot be delivered emancipates, although provisionally, a place from all other places. It creates the notion of space as something which insulates and blocks. Within space, a given place is never anchored; it simply is, sustained by the surrounding impermeability.

Naturally, there has never been and there will never have been a message proper. That we await it, producing parables, is only a structural mechanism of our universe. But, this is precisely what cannot be said, or, at least, cannot be said otherwise than in a parable. A well-known Kafka's parable *On parables* reads as follows:

> Many complain that the words of the wise are always merely parables and of no use in daily life, which is the only life we have. When the sage says: "Go over", he does not mean that we should cross over to some actual place, which we could do anyhow if the labor were worth it; he means some fabulous yonder, something unknown to us, something too that he cannot designate more precisely, and therefore cannot help us here in the very least. All these parables really set out to say merely that the incomprehensible is incomprehensible, and we know that already. But the cares we have to struggle with every day: that is a different matter.

> Concerning this a man once said: Why such reluctance? If you only followed the parables you yourselves would become parables and with that rid yourself of all your daily cares.
>
> Another said: I bet that is also a parable.
>
> The first said: You have won.
>
> The second said: But unfortunately only in parable.
>
> The first said: No, in reality: in parable you have lost.[24]

This parable entices us not only to believe, but also live in parables: such a life is of unsurpassed comfort when compared with the uneasy position of skeptics. Skeptics are precisely those who denounce parable as parable, because they seem to have reality as a counterpart to parable. They win, as the real always wins, but by a walkover, having first paralyzed the field of parable.

Agamben expresses the ultimate tendency of modernity when he claims that the true, and desired, lesson of Kafka's *On Parables* is to see the disappearance of the difference between the discourse and reality.[25] Yet, whether we win or lose is of hardly any importance: what counts is that *the parable has always already been here*, from the beginning of modernity, and gives itself as the only accessible knowledge on the dispersed universe. The choice between daily life and life in parables is equally always here, it never comes to pass. The insignificance of what we actually choose to the position of parable is that of matter.

84. With the engulfment of authority by the modern rift, all texts of our tradition, most notably of the premodern tradition, turn into parables. In this sense, their origins are properly inexplicable. Obviously, we can pinpoint the exact moment in which they were produced, we can determine authors, circumstances, manuscripts and even writing utensils, with greater or lesser accuracy, but it never brings us to their exact origins. In modernity texts appear as parables: always out of nothing.[26] The creation of a text is an irremovable riddle. Texts refer to some outside, but it remains beyond our reach. They summon the message, often picturing its way in great detail, yet the message never arrives in our place.

It is from this rift that modern humanities spur from: hermeneutics is perhaps the most obvious example, but not the most telling one. The search for the inaccessible origins is painfully epitomized by the continued effort of philologists and interpreters to seek out the tiniest pieces of writings by a famous author to determine the context of their creation and publish them with excessive commentary. The blatant discrepancy between the actual value of such a text (to say nothing about its "veracity," if such a criterion could still be of any avail) and the fetishistic toil to put it on the map is the sign that this text is already a parable. Any success in determining the context of its emergence tells us nothing about its origins.

The origins could be only pictured, in a momentary epiphany, if the message, like a lightning, struck the exact place we occupy. Without it, we are like the person from

Wittgenstein's parable who bought a few copies of the same newspaper in order to verify whether the reported news are true.[27]

85. In this perspective, modernity is not inherently atheistic in a sense that it would be a universe deprived of divinity. On the contrary: God may equally still exist. But the circumstances of its existence change. Any message that it could produce would have to travel the vastest distance, in which obstacles mount geometrically. Therefore, its message would become suspended in the impermeable fabric of modern space, which *never promises anything without inscribing the promise into the framework of perpetual delay*.

Thus, all theology turns into the position of a parable. As a local, wild knowledge, it buzzes with all the energy that only infallibility can yield. With this step, God becomes properly immortal: once a parable slips in, there always remains a touch of possibility. In this possible form, as a rumor, God is irremovable. For the price of its effective disappearance and being stuck in something much more powerful than itself—the opaqueness of modern space—God transforms its life into an ineradicable parable.

One question haunts post-war theologians: where was God in Auschwitz? It cannot be easily set aside with a pseudo-Lurianic theories of God's withdrawal, such as the one propounded by Hans Jonas.[28] Properly speaking, God has never withdrawn. It has never left the universe for our freedom, let alone to give us the chance for ethical development. God has not disappeared. On the contrary, it perpetuated itself by turning into a parable. Where was God in Auschwitz? Not in suffering victims: such an answer is a rather tasteless mythology. *It was precisely in this question*, which is an irrepressible parable that demands the arrival of the message. The message, in turn, is stuck in the impenetrable space of modernity.

A certain philosophical anti-Semite claimed that only God can save us. Some theologians claim that it is "us" that can save God by continuing its legacy after its disappearance. Yet, both claims are, in fact, meaningless, even if the first one is hideous and the second is noble. Until the space is broken, no side can make a saving move.[29]

Critique of provisionality

86.1 That texts turn into parables gives law its distinctly modern flavor. Let us bring forward another well-known story by Kafka, *The New Advocate*:

> We have a new advocate, Dr. Bucephalus. There is little in his appearance to remind that he was once Alexander of Macedon's battle charger. Of course, if you know his story, you are aware of something. But even a simple usher whom I saw the other day on the front steps of the Law Courts, a man with the professional appraisal of the regular small bettor at a racecourse, was running an admiring eye over the advocate as he mounted the marble steps with a high action that made them ring beneath his feet.
>
> In general the Bar approves the admission of Bucephalus. With astonishing insight people tell themselves that, modern society being what it is, Bucephalus is

in a difficult position, and therefore, considering also his importance in the history of the world, he deserves at least a friendly reception. Nowadays—it cannot be denied—there is no Alexander the Great. There are plenty of men who know how to murder people; the skill needed to reach over a banqueting table and pink a friend with a lance is not lacking; and for many Macedonia is too confining, so that they curse Philip, the father—but no one, no one at all, can blaze a trail to India. Even in his day the gates of India were beyond reach, yet the King's sword pointed the way to them. Today the gates have receded to remoter and loftier places; no one points the way; many carry sword, but only to brandish them, and the eye that tries to follow them is confused.

So perhaps it is really best to do as Bucephalus has done and absorb oneself in law books. In the quiet lamplight, his flanks unhampered by the thighs of a rider, free and far from the clamor of battle, he reads and turns the pages of our ancient tomes.[30]

Setting aside the usual and obvious interpretations, let us focus on the status of law. Under the guise of practicing law, Dr. Bucephalus carries out only one Agambenian duty:[31] he studies law books. Law is to be studied, not applied. Why? Once the past turned into a parable—and we, Drs. Bucephales, also acquired this status—law equally is based on presumption. It never arrives as a commanding message. It simply is, written in books, deprived of its immanent support, *sustaining in its position of a parable that draws all force from the deferral of the message*. Studying law is nothing else than waiting for the message. This seemingly messianic delay is, in fact, well inscribed in the mechanism of modern law, which never exerts its power directly but only entraps us in the threat of its application. As a consequence, Agamben's greatest, not to say Heideggerian mistake, was to take the arch-modern suspension for a messianic promise of the outside.[32]

Modern legislative procedures cover, precisely like the ratiocinations of "people" from Kafka's story, the immanent deferral at the heart of modern law. The legislative decision is properly empty, based on nothing, but in the dusklands it casts a long shadow, long enough to create an impression that the message is already looming on the horizon. Sovereignty is a reign of shadows, which cover the murky origins of the emergence of a given law.[33] The law is before us seemingly without the tyranny of the former lawgiver. But in this withdrawn legal presence the sovereign reign is perpetuated. In the prolonged period of studies, in which everything—even the greatest atrocities of human invention—may and have to be studied, our empty, provisional time is governed by anything that claims even the weakest and most irrational power, to which we yield out of our fatigue.

To think freedom without sovereignty is the key to future non-modern thought. Quite probably, it is also a local illusion of modern devices and another dead end, already traversed a thousand times.

86.2 Nevertheless, imagining freedom beyond sovereignty is of highest importance, especially for Marxism. The Marxist tradition never undertook a systematic critique of provisionality, which is acutely in need if any revolutionary movement is considered.[34]

Otherwise, we will only stumble, once again, into the pitfall of Lenin's "withering state" which actually never withers, quite the contrary, perpetuates its transitionality against all pious declarations.[35] The fact that the dictatorship of the proletariat, supposedly aimed at dealing away with the state, produced one of the most powerful and oppressive states of the world should be the central paradox that Marxism is summoned to reconsider. All justifications of "real socialism" shamelessly yield to sovereignty which eagerly covers each epochal failure with explaining that "it was not so bad, actually." If it was not, why should we care about revolting anyway?

Today, more than ever, the socialist tradition is hearable as a silent murmur of the parable. We know more than Lenin; as such, we are much more skeptical, doubtful and paralyzed to take any decision than he was. Marxism precipitously falls off the rank of message (if it ever was one) into second-hand parables. Reprinting them, crucial as it is, only fuels the fire. The realm of provisionality takes it all, so more than anything else we need *a substantiated critique of provisional government*.

73.5 Kafka's *An Imperial Message* depicts a universe of total mobilization, in which only the exception would be potent enough to reach its goal. The messenger's strengths are unique; it seems that everything privileges him in his mission. All others may fail, but not him. In this prearranged arena, where all forces are mobilized against us, we may trust only in qualities of the exceptional man. Thus, everything which is ordinary, non-exceptional, is sacrificed in advance, without even being recorded in the books. Only the exception counts as able to perform the demanded task. Thus, without any dispute, the whole universe of non-exceptionality is given up, for the sake of a fetishistic pseudo-salvation by the exception.

Confronted with the total failure, whose incommensurability in relation to our powers only keeps mounting, we are ready to turn a blind eye to the primordial injustice and sacrifice the whole universe. What we abide by is just one exception, the only thing we deem capable of fighting the catastrophe. The exception, embodied by the messenger, is nothing else than the Mirror Star of sovereignty: our last hope and fetishistic support that allows us to subsist among the catastrophe.

But this last hope always remains suspended. If we were capable of a sober calculation of our strengths and weaknesses, we would have to assume it had been effectively lost. Its very construction relies on the deferral. As long as we can project it outside, we live our lives among the dark boundless ocean, though, properly speaking, we are only spectres supported by their fetishistic device. We gave everything up in advance, but this is precisely what we do not want to face, as long as the exception can still make it. We put all our money on it, and now it lingers. So we tell ourselves—next to the window, when the evening comes—the tale of the potent *remainder, last hope, a structural-secular Messiah* that keeps lingering.[36] Truly, the Mirror Star is us, projected: it is as empty as "us," but at least still glimmering from afar.

6

The Big Bang of Modernity

87. In the previous chapter we described the modern universe as reigned by the deferred message and effectively governed by parables expands to giant proportions. In this sense, modernity is a symbolic Big Bang, a constantly growing space. This is what Kafka's *An Imperial Message* (→ 76) presumes implicitly: the symbolic space keeps expanding. The pace of the expansion always exceeds the ability to traverse the space and deliver the message. The messages have been sent, yet the goalposts keep shifting, and even if messengers are still moving, they will be always overtaken by the speed of expansion. Consequently, the delay not only keeps mounting, but on the top of one delay immediately another one appears.

This process takes place even in pure thinking: as Kafka demonstrates, it is enough to make a turn of the thought in order to see how it bogs down in the infinity that all of a sudden opens before it. Confronted with this expanding abyss, we can only shortcut the proper path—now unavailable due to its swelling—and act haphazardly. We keep setting aside our confrontation with this fundamental trauma and construct the provisional world. What cannot be disentangled must be cut if we are to move forward; and since Descartes, we are persuaded to move on, cutting yet new knots.

It is for this reason that "solving" philosophical problems became so insufficient and, in fact, ridiculous for anyone who would like to boast having done it. *All steps of the paths that we traverse in thinking no longer sum up to one whole.* The expansion of the symbolic space of modernity yields to every place its unique materiality and inertia. Nothing can be counted up losslessly anymore. It is for this reason that writing attracts our attention as the basic tissue of thinking: it preserves, spatially, each tiny element apart. Thus, the expanding space of modernity blocks us from solving problems and condemns us to producing a perpetual commentary on what has been written.

In writing—as understood in the tradition of *écriture*—nothing has to be resolved once and forever; it seems that everything may be preserved in its integrity until we find the correct answer. It is not an accident that writing attracted philosophical attention in the second part of the twentieth century: it is the most basic level of recording. In fact, writing epitomizes the work of the parable: its creation is shrouded by mystery, it simply is, and calls for the message, whose arrival is still delayed.

Modernity as an expanding universe

88. Even Benjamin's vision of Klee's *Angelus Novus*—"[h]is eyes are staring, his mouth is open, his wings are spread," as "he sees one single catastrophe which keeps piling wreckage upon wreckage and hurls it in front of his feet," while "this storm irresistibly propels him into the future to which his back is turned, while the pile of debris before him grows skyward"[1]—does not give full justice to the paralyzing fear which we experience when confronted with the pile of misunderstandings, unresolved disputes, unsolved dilemmas, unrevenged wrongs, and lost chances for salvation that modernity makes us perceive as our past.

To get a grip on the present is one of our greatest, but irresistible, illusions within the modern universe. As long as it is harbored—as long as we demand radical justice (but how could we renounce it?[2])—our bills of frustration can only mount. In the meantime, it seems that not only we have not yet made even the first step, but a mere return from the closest place would irreparably exhaust our forces. So, we sit at the window when the evening comes.

89.1 As Foucault once perspicuously noted, our language, having engulfed infinity at the onset of modernity, keeps expanding.[3] It is leaking into the vast space that slips in between our words and spreads them apart.[4] The meaning of each word is therefore coupled with a tremendous echo of spaces—Kant's infinities of infinities (→ 1.2)—in which it reverberates. Perhaps then deconstruction would only be a method of reflexively re-inscribing this echo into the stream of language, which desperately and hopelessly tries to hew itself out from the mass of writing. In this sense, deconstruction would be the closest approach to the bottom level of modernity.

89.2 Each being thrown into the modern universe should be seen as exposed to the most extreme power of negativity that can easily rip it up. The strength of identities that keep beings in their shape is just negativity with the opposite vector.[5] The cohesion and existence of modern beings depends on the interplay between negative forces. That explains why the strongest identities, which push that interplay into imbalance, are nothing but rampant force of destruction. Destruction and aggression appear in the universe, in which no being can even last a while without getting hopelessly dissociated from itself and being internally interspersed by a distance that its whole life would not suffice to traverse.

89.3 The distance that immediately parasites the dissociation of each being makes modern politics inherently fetishistic.[6] As soon as a given political opinion or proposal is formulated, it is wrenched from the context of its emergence and dissociated from the context of its application. Even if—and this "even if" must be understood Kafkasquely—we managed somehow to apply a given political idea, it would come from an untraverseable distance and appear as a foreign body. From this perspective, *political fight is fetishism applied*: it sticks to principles that are already older than themselves at the moment of their emergence. For this reason, any political formation which has at least some experience renounces its principles and turns into a circumscribed, but yawning void, sewn to the apparatus of power. Against this background, the Leninist politics, focused on permanent re-evaluation of its core and always keen to recount its position against the perpetually shifting center, may have claimed to understand the political fetishism of modernity. Which does not mean, obviously, that this fetishism did not smash it in the moment of trial. But, as Kafka noticed, "there are opportunities too great, in a certain way, to be exploited; there are things that fail only of their own volition and for no other reason."[7]

Even the greatest effort is still helplessly small in comparison with what is demanded. At the most untoward hour, we need to drop the calculation and push forward, leaving heaps of rubble behind us.

90.1 Yet, the world is, of course, going on. None of our concerns about the leakage of language, expansion of the symbolic universe, deferral of the message stops the world, now governed provisionally, from heading onwards. The price we pay is incomprehensibility of this development. *In its core, the world appears foreign to us.* This perception stems directly from its provisional governance. There is always a mediating device between us and the world, a device which takes upon itself the role of temporary power. But it means that all that we encounter, including ourselves, appears as geometrically mounting incomprehensibility. Modern incomprehensibility has a life on its own, a life with which a truce can be declared.

The principal condition of this truce is to renounce any attempts to understand the ongoing expansion and dispersion. It must be taken as a fact. With its inherent unsurpassable irony, sovereignty promises us that in the last instance the world is ours. That it is temporarily out of comprehension and governed by a supposedly transient device should not, sovereignty claims, discourage us from thinking that once the finiteness of the world is discovered, everything is essentially on our side.

As Maggie Nelson put it with unsurpassed tranquility of recognition, "We cannot read the darkness. We cannot read it. It is a form of madness, albeit a common one, that we try."[8] Darkness is what it is and can be neither looked into nor passed by.

Fetishism of modern politics: Lessons from Heidegger

91. The inherent fetishism of modern politics—as determined by the sovereignty-governed field—crystallizes in Heidegger's thinking. The debates between his accusers, who point to his well-known arsenal of pro-Nazi, anti-Semitic,[9] or at least dubious statements and acts—and his defenders, who accept Heidegger's own motto: "Wer groß denkt, muss groß irren" ("Whoever thinks big, must err big")[10] and highlight the limited scope of his entanglement in Nazism—usually do not confront the possibility that Heideggerian thinking and political choices are parts of one and the same position on a much deeper level. Thus, the "flaw" is not in one erroneous political choice, but in the whole framework that allows Heidegger to present this choice as inconsequential.

In 1945, Heidegger attempted to recapitulate his actions during the Nazi era, particularly at his position of the rector of the University of Freiburg, in a brief statement written for university authorities:

> Because the will of the overwhelming majority of the German people expressed in free elections affirmed at the time a foundations work in the sense of the National-Socialist movement, I considered it necessary and possible to cooperate also in the area of the university in order to confront the general confusion and the threat to the West in a decided and effective way. And precisely because in the field of science and the humanities so-called "impossible" people from the "movement" often pushed for influence and power, it seemed to me necessary to make visible essential spiritual goals and horizons and to attempt, out of Western responsibility, to take care of their emanation into reality.[11]

In this light, all actual deeds were either committed with noble intentions or, eventually, engulfed by the ocean of Western nihilism:

> The in itself meaningless case of the rectorate 1933/34 is probably an indication of the metaphysical essential condition of science, which can no longer be determined by attempts at renewal or held back in their essential transformation into pure technology.... The rectorate was an attempt to see in the "movement" that came to power, in all its inadequacies and coarseness, the far-reaching, which might one day bring about gathering of the Western historical essence of the German. It should in no way be denied that at that time I believed in such possibilities and renounced the very own profession of thinking in favour of official activities. In no way it should be diminished what my own inadequacy in office caused. However, with only these perspectives one does not grasp the essence of what made me take over the office. The different assessments of this rectorate in the horizons of a usual academic business may be correct and right in their own way, but they never strike the essential. Today there is even less chance than ever to open the horizon of this essential to the blinded eyes. The essential thing is that we are in the midst of the completion of nihilism, that God is "dead" and that every period of time for the deity is buried.[12]

If the tale of modernity is presented as an ongoing catastrophe[13]—which, as we dare think, it indeed is, but provided that there had been no Eden from which it fell—then, all actual deeds melt in the general desertification and the reign of "technics." Within this non-logic, exercising the function of the rector, dismissing Jewish academics, holding public pro-Nazi speeches,[14] deplorable "in their own way," are then, in truth, nothing. That in this portrayal ultimately "all cows are black" is an obvious argument against Heidegger.[15] Yet, what demands much more thorough reconsideration is the link between *the suspended waiting for Being to intervene and the paradoxical, both permanent and temporary, government of the provisional.*

In the post-war self-portrayal, Heidegger alluded to the deep motives that had made him join the Nazi movement. They were allegedly much deeper than those of the common Nazis, so as soon as Heidegger realized that Nazism was not only by far shallower than he had expected, but also resistant to any profound philosophical attempts to guide it, he withdrew into the silence of his work.[16] There is no need to deny that Heidegger actually had these deeper reasons—in fact, he ventured having a quasi-

Hegelian moment of recognizing himself as part of a profound historical change concerning Germany and the world[17]—but the problem is precisely in them. With the advent of *die Kehre*, all reasons become much too deep to be ever reached.[18] Thinking approaches the level of *Seyn* and *Er-eignis* which will never be grasped, but only incessantly circumscribed, traversed, half-discerned from the position of full receptive passivity.[19] At the same time, this passivity gives the provisional power all earthly might and exculpates it in advance from all its responsibility.[20] The profundity of Heidegger's thinking after *die Kehre* is therefore entangled in a hideously limited device of provisional power. As Sloterdijk rightly noted, his "depth is without breadth."[21]

In this sense, Heidegger enters the familiar, though murky waters of the bleak ocean from Hegel's narrative (→ 2.2). Apart from applying a different metaphor—Heidegger prefers, after Nietzsche, "the desert" and "desertification" (*Verwüstung*)—the pivotal difference is that whereas Hegel recognizes that the Mirror Star which shines over it is, in fact, *us*, Heidegger posits the Star in its absolute and sovereign refusal (*Verweigerung*) to beings. And, although without this portrayal we would not be given the picture of the Mirror Star in its fullness, it is marked by the most profound misjudgment: while renouncing the legacy of German Idealism, which assumed the possibility of self-recognition in the Mirror Star and thus set the dialectics in motion,[22] Heidegger in advance rejects any responsibility for the Mirror Star and, in consequence, allows to be led by unrecognized forces in his passive blindness.

Perhaps Being, *das Seyn*, is the stillness of the bleak ocean under the distant Star, whose mirror-like surface Heidegger covers with opaqueness of irresponsibility. In this sense, his philosophical position is a step back from a much more responsible understanding of the Mirror Star paradox offered by the German Idealism. Obviously, it is a step back that we need in order to appreciate the scale of catastrophe.

If, therefore, Heidegger claims that all worldly assessments of his rectorate, though in a certain sense justified, elude what is essential, he occupies the position of the provisional government turned permanent. His "provisional" actions had most real repercussions and were ethically unjustifiable, which he himself implicitly concedes. Yet, in the figure of *Ereignis* he pushes the modern provisionality to its very end, withdrawing importance from everything that takes place upon the desert of contemporaneity. Until the Mirror Star makes a decisive move, all actions may be presented as inconsequential and thus erased from actual history, just like Rousseau's blood after the fall did not seem to him to be his own.

In this manner, Heidegger—read against his repression of the Shoah—is a *nec plus ultra* point for modern thought, its lowest point and, simultaneously, a point of epiphany. Which means that within the modern universe, all knowledge has a high price.

Heidegger was a master of awaiting. He turned language—through incessant repetitions, reformulations, re-posed questions[23] ("a favourite prerequisite of the jargon," as Adorno noted,[24] formulated in a style both "terribly dangerous and foolishly funny"[25])—into a machine for awaiting. All that may have been decisive was expulsed from it and supplemented with grounding a *possibility* of decision. He ploughed through the whole philosophical realm as the staunchest agent of modernity. Thus, all happening was elevated to the position of the Mirror Star; within the bleak ocean, no true decisions were taken and everything lost its consequence. In this sense, Heidegger fulfilled Descartes' demand: he pushed on through the forest as long as to end up in the deepest jungle, from which only a miracle could save us.

Grasping modernity through writing: Mallarmé and the Septentrion

2.36 When Mallarmé concludes his arch-modern poem *Un coup de dés . . .* with the famous line:

Toute Pensée émet un Coup de Dés[26]
Every Thought emits a Throw of Dice,

he plays on a unique chance that each thought might have once and only once: the chance to seize infinity of which its own emergence is a momentary disturbance. The unrepeatable moment of creation stands before the Mirror Star, almost-already at its place. Dice are thrown, with a hope of ground-breaking victory and the ominous shadow of ultimate debacle; dice are being thrown, as if to stave off the moment when the place triumphs once again in order to become the only thing that *has place*.

In his bravely brilliant book[27] Quentin Meillassoux demonstrated that *Un coup de dés* might be read as inherently coded, but with an undecidable code: the very tension between the existence of the code, the deciphering of the code and the inexistence/ illegibility of the code embodies the ultimate contingence of the chance to which the poem refers.

Extrapolating Meillassoux's conclusions, it can be noticed that *Un coup de dés* performs a perfect contingent self-referential loop. In many regards similar to Hegel's, this loop is nonetheless of negative character. Hegel's *Phenomenology* discovers itself as the moment of revelation of the Absolute: within it, the Absolute finds and asserts itself in its presence. It can speak clearly in the name of what it embodies. In *Un coup de dés*, however, the poem embodies and refers to a "contingent Absolute." For this reason, it cannot speak in its name otherwise as through Chance: *that the poem is "truly" the expression of the new Absolute is in itself undecidable, just like the new Absolute*. The self-reference between "the Absolute" and its expression is maintained, but just as "the Absolute" turns into pure chance, so does the overlap between the expression and the expressed must become contingent.

Un coup de dés, precisely in this messianic attempt to give a unique and paradoxical self-assertion of chance, demonstrates the paradox of the Mirror Star. In the poem's struggle for expression in the short-circuit between itself and chance, it attempts to invade the very place the Mirror Star occupies: the critical point at which the modern universe fully overlaps with itself. At this point, all modern throb would cease, modernity would appear just as it is, with no outside and no remainder. It would be the place of absolute sovereignty over the modern realm and for this reason *Un coup de dés* is a struggle for total and irrevocable power.

"RIEN N'AURA EU LIEU QUE LE LIEU," reads the poem, "Nothing will have taken place but the place," with a notable hypothetic exclusion: "EXCEPTÉ PEUT-

ÊTRE UNE CONSTELLATION"—"except perhaps a constellation." The smooth surface of modernity, the place understood in its self-referential and self-asserted certainty, or, otherwise, the ocean without a tiny difference, "ces parages du vague," where there are only waves and vagueness, "en quoi toute réalité se dissout"—"in which all reality is dissolved"—that is, the darkest ocean from Hegel's narrative that engulfs everything that has ever existed—*has one undecidable exception.*

Hegel was "the master" of the ocean, the one who knew that the Polar Star of the spirit could never be shattered and that the Star was, in fact, the spirit in which he partook. But since Hegel ages have lapsed and our modern world grew older in an astonishing pace. What we took for youth of spirit was already the secret of old-age lasciviousness. After Hegel's debacle—the one which revealed in a nutshell the failed messianism of modern sovereignty—*we are nothing but late*. This lateness pervades our universe, as if there was nothing new.

In this light, Mallarmé is already a late master, the one which throws dice desperately, amidst the waves of nothingness that seem to prevail. The catastrophe which Hegel first described seems here much more tremendous: from the bottom of the shipwreck dice are thrown, for a unique occasion, to be an unrepeatable sign of what happened. The possibility to reach the Star is much more oblique. Waters of the ocean overflow the player and instead of being saved through the Star, he might venture only one contingently successful throw. To wait, like Heidegger, perpetually lingering in search of new paths, or to throw the dice once and for all, like Mallarmé, the belated completion of Hegel, are the two poles of the modern game. We all keep fighting at the front and we differ only in bravery, which explains why this apparently purely intellect-existential game ultimately has an ethical stake.

The Mallarméan exception to the modern ocean—in other words, the ubiquity of the place—is what he calls a "constellation." It traverses the last page of the poem, written in capital letters. But small letters that it is intermingled with cannot attack it. The constellation seems to be at inaccessible heights ("à l'altitude // aussi loin qu'un endroit / fusionne avec au delà"). The approach to the constellation means groping for a place which melts into the outside, but does not reach it.

Mallarmé names the constellation: the Septentrion. The word is an old Latin name for the seven stars of Ursa Minor, the constellation which contains the Polaris—although in some variants it was also used to designate the nearby Ursa Maior. Its etymology combines *septem*, "seven" and *trio*, "oxen"—probably referring to the nightly cycles that seven stars of both constellations perform around the North celestial pole. For this reason, *septentrio* used to be a Latin name for the North. Preserved in Romance languages, it also began to denote the northernmost of the north, the inaccessible subpolar regions of the Earth. As a constellation, the Septentrion connotes moving around the impossible center which cannot be reached.

In *The Antichrist*, Nietzsche famously refers to another term associated with the North. He calls "us," whoever "us" are, "Hyperboreans,"[28] those living far-off, "beyond the (usual) north." But what is north of the north? Where is the place that the whole existence of the modern realm points to? How can we be Hyperboreans, if not in a failed sense, as fellow travellers of the immutable and unassailable Star that shines above the universe which is ultimately left to itself?

In the nightly tread around the Pole Star, we might only believe in what Mallarmé suggests: that "quelque surface vacante et supérieure"—"some vacant and higher surface" will preserve the count we perform. If the Star is ultimately unreachable, we may only hope that *from its perspective our gestures are seen and recorded*. For this reason, the Star is the mirror, which gives nothing but super-external assertion of what we present to it. All our modern messianisms ultimately fail, because ultimately, having almost-won everything, they demand the far-off place to help us, see us, *reflect and constitute us*. And the Star, "veillant / doutant / roulant / brillant et méditant"— "watching / doubting / rolling / shining and meditating"—remains intransigent, until it will have finally given way to what comes after modernity disappears.

Modernity can be reached only through a failure of writing in its relation to itself. Each time with a one-off throw. For this very reason, the question whether there was anything before and beyond modernity is now properly undecidable.

Endless life: Why modernity produces biopolitics

92.1 Modernity is a space in which all statements are manifestly produced within certain perspectives and shaped by references to the boundaries of their perspectives, even if only tacitly, through their "inter-dits" (to use Luce Irigaray's term[29]). Expansion and lasting are two names of this space.

When the expansion of the modern realm is taken into account, two potent intellectual devices developed by Spinoza and Nietzsche, respectively—*conatus*[30] and will-to-power[31]—should be read not as "descriptions of reality" (as if philosophy could do that), but as first-hand testimonies from the expanding universe of modernity. When Spinoza claims that "[t]he striving by which each thing strives to persevere in its being involves no finite time, but an indefinite time,"[32] he grasps in fact the eternity which opens before any modern perspective and its correlative history. That both Spinoza and Nietzsche attribute this eternal push to single beings is a sign that between the deep perspectival structure of modernity and beings that populate its realm there is a secret affinity sealed by what we call biopolitics.

Equally, the three early modern theories of state power—Hobbes', Locke's, and Rousseau's—are built around the assumption that the basic goal of human life is self-preservation.[33] Among all imaginable goals, it is the strangest one, because it adds nothing to the quality of life and does not make it meaningful, but rather demonstrates its lasting. Thus, in modernity, *life conflates with itself*, resounding with the same *basso continuo* that is otherwise hearable as lasting. And on this meaningless, self-referential loop of life stands the edifice of modern power.

93.1 It is only against the background of this modern "Big Bang" that we may understand precisely the emergence of biopolitics. Biopolitics, as the set of techniques aimed at governing life, requires, first of all, to determine its object. In this regard Agamben's remarkable feat was to seize the basic coordinates of this object in the concept of "bare life."[34] Yet, perhaps we should venture a thought that what gives the bare life its anchoring point are traits of the modern universe itself. Modern "are life" (if it has ever been any other than modern, which is undecidable), conceived as life entrapped in the device of law, is strictly correlated to the properly modern *strive to survive*.

In the universe of provisionality turned permanent, where no definitive decisions are taken and no final cuts are made, *also life cannot end*. What this claim means is that there is no meaningful end of life: life cannot be not only meaningfully cut, but also understood in this cut. Therefore, until the meaningful end appears on the horizon, we tend to perceive life as permanent and empty prolongation of lasting. As an unexpected consequence, life in itself becomes a value. Buried deep in the evidently progressive and humanitarian motives of human rights, there is a hidden premise which does not form any rational presumption, but remains rooted in the very construction of the modern universe. This presumption treats life as a result of a provisional truce: since we do not know how to end life or how to give it a meaning, we need to prolong it eternally.[35]

It is in this respect that the hypocritical Catholic ethics, opposing medical interventions in terminally ill lives, professes a maxim that has nothing to do with its own original doctrine, but embodies properly modern biopolitics: modern life was expropriated from its meaning and, consequently, its end. Since we are not in its possession, we remain confined to prolonging the status quo.

93.2 It is just as if we did not have enough power to make decisions and had to push forward our growing inheritance without the chance to settle the score. Ongoing surviving is a blood-curdling experience. Yet, it is the price to be paid when the confrontation with intolerable incommensurability cannot be resolved.

To perceive the ongoing history as a catastrophe seems to be a particularly modern experience. Believing in a certain direction of history which transforms it into "progress"—a *credo* of the epoch of "great narratives"—is perhaps nothing else than a fetishist move to cover the abyss that keeps mounting day by day. Contemporaneity does not have enough power to settle its own, limited conflicts, to say nothing about the past which is a heap of rubble upon rubble. If we think that our time is a failure in comparison with the world twenty to thirty years ago, we would need to notice how that each epoch already saw itself as a collapse from a previous local balance, even the post-war *les trentes glorieuses*.[36]

As the bubble of history keeps expanding, griefs and injustice take hold of the overall calculus. The burden of the past is irresolvable. In the case of human beings, death cuts the life which withers with the unsupportable weight, yet modernity knows no end. Thus, our culture is sick unto life, it lives against its will, against its perpetuated survival. We forgot how to die, which is a radically good change, but we still do not know how to live. It is as if we still learned how to live finally—which, parenthetically, is the last message of Jacques Derrida.[37] We have been set free and we still do not know how to be free. To call a temporary truce we hail life as such, refusing to lose, decide or die, *but is that really perpetual life?*

93.3 Lasting is not on our side. Within its device, it always seems that there is some adjourned trial and a suspended sentence. But it is also lasting that within the modern universe gives an extra value to life as such. Thus, whoever wants to break the spell of lasting and make a decision out of nothing, confronts the problem of life, which appears as an insurmountable impasse. In this precise sense, mass killings are dead-ends of hideous attempts to put an end to lasting.

Lasting would be, therefore, the defining metapolitical space within which modern politics takes place. It is extra-political, as the infrastructure of politics, but indirectly determines political actions by bending the space within which they take place. For this reason, biopolitics emerges as one of the forms of *politics of lasting* which is a necessarily plural and internally disparate set of political formations appearing within the metapolitical space of lasting.

93.4 With the advent of modernity, the perception of what constitutes a basic, minimum state of things undergoes a transformation which has already been quite well described. In premodern, Aristotelian physics, things were perceived as tending to immobility.[38] Immobility in their natural place was the origin and goal of things. It was only by applying an external force that they might have been set in motion; nevertheless, as soon as the force was exhausted, things returned to their natural state. In early modern physics, however, inaugurated by Galileo and Newton, the basic state of things is identified not with immobility, but with inertia.[39] Things no longer have a "natural state" or natural tendencies. They are inert, which means that they preserve the state determined by the last acting force until a new force affects them. Consequently, they may be equally in perpetual motion if only there is no force that influences their movement. It is in this way that lasting—a purely modern device, never to be confounded with premodern immobility—emerges as a new mode of thinking.

93.5 What Freud identified as the death drive, namely a tendency of all animate nature to reach the zero-level of energy,[40] does not, in fact, have death proper as its object. Death itself is an event, so the zero-level energy must lie elsewhere. *The properly understood state of zero-level energy is bare life*, that is, a state in which an organism which merely lasts, but still clings to its existence.[41] Just as the inert thing in Galilean physics preserves the state determined by the moving force, so bare life, once it emerged, continues its existence waiting for external stimuli. In itself, *bare life is a machine for experiencing.* The state of zero-level energy is tantamount to mere living in a monadic state and experiencing what comes from the outside.

In this sense, we are ravaged by lasting from within. It constitutes the basic framework of living in the modern universe, making "us" monads structurally built upon confrontation with external stimuli. From this construct comes the temptation to manifest one's sovereignty—which is, in fact, nothing but an illusion of a monad that takes control of its outside. The potency of this illusion, however, is painfully real, because bare lasting constitutes the *basso continuo* of our existence within the modern universe.

In the modern universe, we are still things, though equipped with language. And as things, we are exposed to lasting which ultimately presents itself as a space for the broadest community of everything that exists. Heidegger's *Gelassenheit*,[42] Blanchot's *communauté inavouable*,[43] Nancy's *communauté désœuvrée*,[44] Agamben's *communità che viene*[45]—and, to a certain degree, Jabès' *hospitalité*[46]—all conjure up the vision of this community.[47] Nevertheless, even if it appears as a (weak) messianic hope, it is nothing more than a structural feature of modernity—in a certain sense, a trap that was planted in the beginning and will be present until the final cut.

Such a community is naturally impossible. It assumes both the last stage of distinguishability of things and the first stage of their indistinguishability. It must be imagined as a barred place, like Lacan's *jouissance*, in which things simultaneously melt into one and retain a minimal separation. They are, in fact, like objects in the bleak ocean from Hegel's narrative: already seeable as one, but still minimally outlined. Therefore, the twilight cannot end, because in the darkest night they would lose their liminal status. The bleak ocean requires at least a dim light, a light which does not come from the mass of things, but from above.

To stay within the reworked Hegel's imagery, we may claim that this light comes from the Mirror Star. In this way, the final community, an allegedly messianic goal, is nothing less than a basic structure of modernity finally exposed. By running away from sovereignty, we arrive at its bare reign. The community of things let be refers to the final, unified place of sovereign power.

93.6 For this reason, the emergence of (modern) sovereignty inaugurates biopolitics proper. Biopolitics may arise only when the power believes in an uncanny affinity between its own principles and the core of life. All power based on biopolitics is born out of this peculiar sticky gaze, with which sovereignty looks upon life as only formally independent, but at its essence bearing an unsupportable kinship with the mode of sovereign power. It is only against this background that sadism proper may arise: and it is no accident that de Sade was even over-present at the outburst of modernity, also in its most political form, the French Revolution. And, contrariwise, biopolitics is not understandable without this intrusive, paralyzing gaze that sovereign power holds life with, peels it from all the richness of world entanglement and displays it, with intolerable ruthlessness, as bare life. Both Rilke's *Malte*[48] and Kafka's *The Trial*[49] are pervaded with the sense of despair that a world-entangled life experiences when confronted with the gaze of the power that knows "who we really are."

The community that links the sovereign power with bare life within the framework of biopolitics is built on lasting. In this sense, it is an experience of empty prolongation of status quo, to which all richness and differences of the world are meaningless external intrusions. The disgustingly familiar wink which the sovereign power sends to its subordinates marks the supposed community of nihilism: of nothing which, at the very core, beyond all illusions, builds things. In this wink, all subtlety of the world evaporates: what remains are bare things and, among them, bare lives.

Therefore, modern politics cannot abstract from this proto-biopolitical relation that the sovereign has with bare life. *The sovereign is to the universe what bare life is to life: radical impoverishment, a seat of empty power that crosses out all the richness of the universe or of meaningful life.* If so, then the relationship between the sovereign and bare life is a matrix of impoverishment, a core of ravaging lasting, against which the inexhaustible abundance of the universe and life rooted in it appears as field to be subjugated, exploited and abolished in its validity.

93.7 In his perspicacious essay, *Egoism and Freedom Movements: On the Anthropology of the Bourgeois Era*, Max Horkheimer remarked that at the beginning of the bourgeois era self-preservation began to be perceived as the foundational characteristics of beings.[50] This sharply contrasts with medieval views on human beings concentrated on norms and nature. The latter was construed as providing a harmonious place for humans in the meaningful universe under God's rule. In early modernity, however, the status of norms not grounded in the human nature itself became dubious. Nature ceased to be a moral harmonious whole. Self-preservation, as the natural goal of each being, replaced moral norms received in God's revelation. Horkheimer explains this transformation as a manifestation of the dawn of capitalist individualism, which transplants its bourgeois perception of human beings onto general anthropology.[51]

Yet, perhaps such an explanation, although illustrative, does not grasp the emergence of bare life and capitalism as two manifestations of the same tectonic displacement. Capitalism does not in itself explain the sudden rise of self-preservation. Both require to be put on the map concurrently. Capitalism operates on bare life,[52] just as bare life makes capitalism possible. This vicious circle may be broken only when the two are seen in the perspective of the shift, which makes lasting a principal device of the modern universe.

93.8 It seems almost as if in biopolitics we had an insight into a mirror universe in which everything that is bright and rich turns gray under a black sun. This mirror universe is the one of sovereignty. Once the critical exception on which sovereignty builds itself enters the universe, it turns beings into their shadow forms, "neither being nor not being," to quote Heidegger.[53] Therefore, the position of the sovereign is helplessly boring: the sovereign never finds anything new; it always, by definition, finds itself. This self-recognition is what Hegel described as faith. The sovereign center is therefore constructed upon permanent repetition, which lasts as long as it can recognize itself in things, but in this reign it loses all the meaningful differences of the universe.

If, according to the most simplified handbook extract of Kantianism, Kant claimed that we find in things only what we put into it, it is not an epistemological statement proper, but rather one of the first discoveries of what (modern) sovereignty consists in. The universe reigned by sovereignty—and, as we once remarked, modernity is the ultimate one of them—is bleak. It is pervaded by the same principle whose main activity is unceasing recognition of itself and drawing from this procedure a dark *jouissance*. We, as human things, may equally join this operation insofar as we reduce our lives to bare lives. As meaningless lasting bare lives we can observe everything from afar, waiting for the real difference to come.

This is perhaps the greatest secret of Heidegger's *Denkweg*: first, to push impoverishment as far as possible to stage one's bare life—bare before the sovereign—then, to turn all the sense of the universe into a mass of blackness and finally await the pseudo-messianic event to come. Yet, under the harness of sovereignty, the event is just a mirror reflection of bare life. If it came, it would be by pure accident which has nothing to do with our waiting.

Marx's biopolitics

94.1 Modern biopolitics, as grounded on lasting, found one of its most brilliant analytics in Marx. Key moments of his mature thought—the theory of surplus value, time and labor—recognize precisely the link between lasting and bare life. Many streams of popular and vulgar Marxism (including the so-called real socialism) put this theory on a back burner, highlighting rather the issue of ownership of means of production rather than the truly biopolitical issue of the modern labor power. The reason is evident: whereas concentration on means of production and distribution finds its counterparts in various political practices—through revolution, expropriation and/or nationalization—Marx's theory of labor and time is, in fact, much more pessimistic, as it does not offer intuitive means of abolishing exploitation. In this respect, it is much closer to critical theory which can do hardly anything but to decry injustice and unreason as inherent parts of a large social formation, whose boundaries overlap with modernity itself. In this manner, it dashes the hope that a major change may happen without the whole (trans-)epoch to pass.[54]

One of the cornerstones of Marx's philosophy of economy is the often disputed[55] assumption that only work creates value.[56] Socially objectified work is therefore not only the source, but also the only common measure of value of commodities. Therefore, each commodity is work embodied, "solidified" in its body.[57] The ultimate common measure of work, purified from empirical distortions, *is time*. Thus, equal work in equal time produces the same value, Marx claims.[58] Market exchange does not add to the once created value.[59] Value of a commodity may be increased only if another commodity's utility value is consumed[60] (for example, coke, itself a commodity, is burned to produce steel), so, ultimately, all value can be reduced to some expenditure of labor. All local perturbations aside, prices tend to reflect the proportions of value as time of work solidified in commodities.[61]

Within the framework of capitalist production, there is no free labor: labor takes the form of labor power—a product that is sold and bought on the market. As long as means of production are controlled by one class, the expropriated cannot undertake free labor that would have a real market significance; they have to sell their labor power to capitalists. Consequently, the existence of value requires labor power to be spent. And in the labor power lies the dialectical engine of capitalist exploitation (so well discerned later by Lacan[62]). The truly unique character of labor power lies in its dualist structure:[63] on the one hand, it is a commodity among others, sellable and buyable, effectively sold and bought, like grain, steel or cloth; but, on the other hand, it is the only commodity that, while its use value is consumed, produces value. The capitalist buys labor power of a worker as a commodity, yet by consuming it (that is, by applying worker's labor to their own ends) s/he produces new commodities—and new value.[64]

In this way, labor power becomes the crucial exception in the world of commodities. Every other commodity, while consumed, loses its exchange value and brings to its owner a particular use value (for example, satisfying natural needs such as hunger): thus, the world of production sinks wholly into the world of consumption.[65] But labor power is a unique commodity, which, while its use value is consumed, produces new exchange value. Thus, it is a short circuit between exchange and use values, between production and consumption: *the more labor power is consumed, the more value is produced.* This point of curiosity warps the ordinary relation between production and consumption, turning them into two sides of a Möbius band.

If labor power is a commodity, it must itself have exchange value. In defining it Marx makes another revolutionary step. Generally speaking, as with all other commodities, it is determined by the time required to produce this commodity. Yet a subtle Marx's twist consists in replacing "production" with "reproduction."[66] Labor power is the only commodity which is not produced, but re-produced. In other words, it is not a solid object, produced one after another (like in Deleuze's and Guattari's portrayal of schizophrenic capitalism[67]) but rather a potential that must be permanently kept ready for use. To keep labor power in use, the worker must eat, rest somewhere, have a shelter and basic objects of everyday use. Therefore, the value of labor power equals the average maintenance of a worker.[68] In this moment, Marx discovers the truly biopolitical device: in the revealed capitalist logic, *each day every human being dies a bit—and this bit equals 24 hours.*[69] Therefore, for the global reproduction of labor power, its value must include the cost of reproduction of workers (giving birth to and upbringing their children who will replace the workers that finally die for the world of production).

It is then enough for the capitalist to pay the value of reproduction of a worker—just the minimum necessary to maintain his/her ability to work—while the value produced through the application of labor power is much higher. The difference between the value of reproduction of a worker and the value s/he produces is, naturally, the notorious surplus value, which is appropriated by the capitalist and constitutes the cornerstone of exploitation.[70] Surplus value is directly correlated to the surplus time of labor that the capitalist demands from the worker, that is, the unpaid time that exceeds the time needed by the worker to obtain the value of goods necessary for his/her maintenance. As such, surplus value is irremovable under capitalism, even if wages are raised.[71]

94.2 What Marx discovers is, in fact, the biopolitical framework of lasting, within which the worker is permanently reproduced.[72] The worker is not reproduced as an individual person, having his/her name, character or preferences, not even nationality: *the reproduction pertains to bare life*. It is for this reason that capitalism, according to Marx, always returns to the ideal situation in which the worker is paid only in order to sustain his/her existence. In other words, capitalism is a system which is evil to workers not by harming or killing them directly (usually), but insofar as it lets them live and sustains their life. The worker is sustained in the barest of all forms, only as a machine able to work. Moreover, Marx claims that inasmuch as the worker is to be replaced by another, capitalism must rely on the instinct for self-preservation and reproduction.[73] It might therefore seem that the fate of capitalism is determined by factors external to it, namely by the social system and individuals' preferences. Yet, miraculously, the goal of capitalism and instinct for self-preservation coincide.

From this biopolitical perspective, *bare life is something which has no end*. Lives end in death; but bare life is perpetually sustained and whenever one living creature falls out of the system, it is immediately replaced by another, thus sustaining the perpetual reproduction of bare life. Even if capitalism after Marx mellowed—at least for a certain time and in certain places—and allowed workers to lead lives which are richer than mere subsistence, it still perceives the worker as a device to be reproduced and maintained in its perpetual readiness to work. And in this regard, as a life that needs to last and always be in disposal, the worker is still, biopolitically speaking, bare life.

94.3 If so, we may ask whether it is (and was) capitalism that is responsible for the emergence of bare life. Yet, precisely this question is inadmissible, because capitalism and bare life are parts of the same sovereignty-reigned system based on lasting.

The lasting of bare life and within bare life makes from it a continuous point of reference for cycles of production and consumption. In this sense, within the capitalist framework, human beings are only bare lives that produce and are reproduced—by production and consumption—while permanently surviving capitalist cycles. Lives are converted into potentially infinite reservoirs of time, from which yet new time units may be permanently drawn.[74] And, as Agamben perspicaciously noticed, in modernity inactivity (or contemplative life) is defined as negation of work, whereas in antiquity work (*negotium*) was conceived of as negation of *otium*, contemplative inoperativeness.[75]

Thus, it seems as if life in the modern realm turned into a stone which is constantly tossed from side to side by the cycles of capital. Even if it is alive, it must remain immutable in its perpetual disponibility. In the whirlpool of external distractions and exchanges, a life is a helplessly isolated monad. In itself, it never experiences a real change that would shatter its impoverished essence. The shock of waking up as a piece of animated matter, first discovered by Descartes, is, indeed, the dawn of modern capitalist universe.

What is left for stony lives is the miracle of total passivity as the ultimate illusion that radicalizing one's misfortune brings the salvation closer. Yet, the salvation has nothing to do with them. If it arrives, it will have to smash them equally with the whole system of re-production. The bare life of an animated stone, once produced, is perpetually in the trap of its own construction.

It is for this reason that in modernity—as bare lives—we feel a peculiar affinity with things.[76] Just as material things are produced only as vehicles of exchange value and become useless after they perform their function in the production–consumption cycle, so do we gain sense only insofar as involved in the circular movement of capital. Yet, both bare lives and things share the position of vehicles, in themselves permanently disponible, passive, and lasting, alien to the world of meaning and speaking a secret common language between themselves.

94.4 In the 1980s and early 1990s, just as institutional footholds of Western Marxism were shrinking and its intellectual vigor continued to fade, Moishe Postone offered a thorough and thought-provoking rereading of Marx's mature thought.[77] In his presentation, he passes over the problem of distribution of products, as secondary, and attacks the theoretical complex of a few concepts: labor, time, value, and labor power. This readjustment is based on the fundamental realization that Marx launched his critique primarily against labor under capitalism.[78] Therefore the questions Postone asked reveal, on the one hand, how the so-called really existing socialism mirrored capitalism,[79] having little to do with Marx's idea of communism, and, on the other hand, how all-encompassing Marx's project truly is, as it opposes modern society in its totality.[80] Communism is fight in the tension opened up by the Mirror Star; socialism is, in all irony of this sentence, just about the *Lustprinzip*.[81]

In Postone's reading, the crux of the passage to communism does not consist in gaining the economic affluence, justly distributed among the free human beings, but in *attaining the state of free labor, undertaken in free time*. If, therefore, Marx wants to replace value with real affluence,[82] it is only in order to free life from the constraints of being posited and expended as labor power. In this regard, the nexus between labor power and time, which measures it and converts it into value, must be broken.[83] Time needs to be freed from the role of measure of value,[84] that is from its status of "an abstract form of compulsion."[85]

Translated into biopolitical terms, Postone's remarks may be interpreted as pointing to the fact that Marx's intention was to wrench life from its condition of bare life. Within it, life is induced into permanent lasting, thus having no time of its own, but, in its perpetual suspension, is used in the externally imposed mechanical and convertible time. The condition of bare life within the cycles of capital should be imagined as the subsistence of the country man before the gate from Kafka's parable *Before the Law*, but with a small supplement: thus suspended, his life is exploited while it awaits its alleged salvation.

Marx demands, therefore, that life have its sense within itself, that it not be bare. It should become, become in its own terms and its own time. It cannot be frozen like a stone that is pushed to and fro in capitalist time cycles. Life is to bare life what affluence is to value: *primordial abundance which is non-posited and non-disponible, united with its differences, and has its own time dynamics*. Life, unlike bare life, does not wait for salvation while being suspended to create abstract time.

In this biopolitical twist of Postone's reading of Marx, the abolition of bare life is strictly correlated to what founds it: abstract time. If surplus value, the source of all capitalist exploitation, is, in fact, accumulated and expropriated surplus of time,[86] then it is only by tearing down the framework in which labor is expended through time that exploitation can stop. The time that capitalism produces is to "real," rich time what bare life is to full life. Therefore, the impoverished time in which bare life is generated and in which it subsists is the necessary condition of capitalism.

As Postone rightly points out, capitalism converts all historical time into the present, disponible time.[87] This claim should be understood biopolitically as following: *capitalism, through its structure of sovereignty, holds life in the perpetual present*.[88] That is why in modernity all provisional temporality turns permanent. It is not a shortcoming, let alone a mistake, but the crucial element of the whole modern universe. Life, held in perpetual present, is transformed into bare life. For this reason, what Marx imagines as communism consists not only (or not principally) in material affluence, but in human beings having disposable time,[89] living in time, actively using it, and not being its "country men."

Yet, who can be sure that by waiting for the transformation we are not the ultimate bare lives? Modernity always deflects our efforts to overcome it back into its own realm. In this sense, even Marx's expectations may be just the noblest hopes of the human spirit, turned, against his will, into Gnosticism. But, if it were so, would Gnosticism be the fault of the alleged Gnostic?

94.6 Marx would be then the first thinker to recognize that modernity introduced a new relationship between life and time. In the framework of the modern universe, life is not lived, but it subsists and reproduces itself. *Life is principally something that is, is at hand, something that continues itself.* It overflows any content that it may have—which, in fact, sticks to it in total contingence. Life is not meaningful or meaningless, it eludes all determinations: life lasts. It is then no accident that philosophy of life emerges as one of the most influential currents of modern thinking.[90] At least from a certain angle, it is only dressing up Marx's discovery of labor force in the Romantic mystifying garb.[91] It perceives life as source of all meanings, but ungraspable in itself,[92] thus repeating the paradox of labor force, both a commodity and source of value.

As long as modernity is in force, life will appear as an elusive manifestation of pure lasting, as the mystique of time embodied. Marxism is the first intellectual current to confront the stupefying relationship between the excessive remainder of modernity, embodied in the Mirror Star, and capitalist exploitation.

Perhaps one of the greatest miracles of capitalism is its radical immanence ravaged simultaneously by momentary transcendence: *in capitalism, the world is ultimately just what it is, in its utter sober and material existence, but at the same time it produces an exploiting position of transcendence which pretends to be nothing but "us."*[93] Examples were given by Marx himself: we know that money is ultimately just a sign, but we still dance according to its play. We know that commodities are, in the last instance, just fetishes, but we still relate to them in a fetishistic manner. There is nothing "truly" transcendent (in the premodern sense) about them, but, somehow, they manage to rise above the immanence to rule over us. Recognition of these facts does not change anything, or even makes it worse: the split which produces transcendence works even with greater cynicism when we are aware of it.[94]

Marx was keen on repeating that the problem of capitalism does not consist in the distribution of products of labor, nor even in inadequate wages. Workers might be remunerated quite well, yet the exploitation is still at work. Surplus labor, which is the crux of Marxism, is nothing less than the counterpart of the sovereign framework. Workers are exploited not because the capitalist underpays them, but because they are thrust into a framework of sovereign dependence. Liberation may come only when surplus labor disappears and labor squares with itself, without the addition of the sovereign sting. Therefore, *the crux of Marxism is in its anti-sovereigntist power.*

Capitalism turns modern split of beings to the purpose of exploitation. What we need now more than ever is a general theory of how the position of a remainder, produced by sovereignty, leads to exploitation. As Žižek rightly pointed out, today's capitalism does not exploit just workers, as in classic Marxist theory; it exploits us whenever we need to hand over parts of our lives to those who are in the position of controlling resources and gaining rent for selling them again to us (especially in the domain of common goods, such as knowledge or software).[95] Today, more than ever, dependence appears to be the basic condition of exploitation. In here lies the potential to join two theories that are as separate and dialectically tense as quantum theory and theory of relativity in modern physics: namely, Marxist theory of exploitation and theory of sovereign power (in the line of Hobbes, Rousseau, Schmitt, and Agamben).

Modernity, as seen through the concept of the Mirror Star, might be the vault of this conceptual edifice. Foundations may be discovered in the condition of life under capitalism, seen as subsistence. But, in order to do that, we need to rearrange Marxism a tiny bit so that it confronts modernity as such.

95. Thus Marxism would be one of the most potent parables of modernity. Beneath its originality lies a deeper layer, much darker, simpler and more common. Perhaps Marxism only elaborates a certain intuition which borders on the verge of hope: an intuition that something is coming, the messenger is on his way, delivering us the resolution of the riddle. In this regard Marxism is far-off from being a sober realization of our planetary solitude: *its radicality and call for action stems only from the hope of deliverance that comes from beyond.*[96]

For this reason, Marx was particularly lucid when he refrained from speculating on the future communism. As we said earlier, parable is not necessarily untrue: it is the knowledge of the stifled universe, to which some external reality may in fact correspond, but precisely that is undecidable. So, Marx was right in explicating the parable whose veracity lies beyond the boundaries of modernity.

94.7 If so, then the end of hope of deliverance is, to all intents and purposes, the end of Marxism. And, the other way round, the end of Marxism is the end of hope of deliverance within the boundaries of reason.

Ronald Aronson, formerly one of the staunchest academic Marxists in the United States, published in 1995 his resounding book, *After Marxism*. The aura of disappointment and loss of the sense of direction that permeated the time when this text was composed[97] led him to conclude that once Marxism irrevocably died, we are now "on our own," remaining "without the guidance of any holistic theory, without being directed by an authority . . ., without the faith that our actions for a better world join in a larger current destined to become an overwhelming force."[98] Thus, "the condition of being 'on our own' means, for better or worse, that we are thrown back on our own powers and energies."[99]

At that moment, it seemed that the cycle of the Mirror Star was accomplished: what appeared from afar again returned to Earth.[100] We suddenly realized that we are here alone, in utmost solitude, relying only on ourselves. Hope did not disappear in its entirety, but was simply displaced from its faraway position into an imaginary conflation with the ones whom it was supposed to save. Yet, through its return, it only strengthened the illusion that there are "us," that there are identities, and, most importantly, that we can make a sober account of what we are and have here and now.

Ethical critique of sovereign identity

96. Well, one could say, why do we not discard metaphysical and post-metaphysical illusions and build upon realistic here and now, as the Internationale enchanted us:

"producers, save ourselves!" Yet, what if within the modern universe all sober "here and now" is nothing more than the realm of provisionality turned permanent, that is, waiting before the gates of sovereignty? What we need is *the critique of provisionality, in which ethics will play the crucial part*. Given that perpetual provisionality inaugurates a new kind of possibility—a world-shattering, all-encompassing and irremovable one—we need to reorientate ourselves in the universe that ceded all solid existence to the sneaking mole of possibility.

Under no circumstances should we believe that in today's era sovereignty is diminishing or even disappearing. Such beliefs, fueled by the shift from modernity to so-called "late modernity" or "postmodernity," are based on an erroneous imagery of sovereignty as unlimited state power. If, as claim their adherents, in today's world globalization entangles states in webs of mutual dependences, state power is no longer unlimited. But, in truth, never, even in absolute monarchies, has state power been unlimited. Such a concept is manifestly self-defensible, given that power demands limits to define itself. Sovereignty is not about actual power, *but the suspended possibility*. In this light, even the most defenseless state apparatus still retains sovereignty. As long as it *might*—ontologically, not practically—suspend all relationships of "civil society" and subject them to its command, it is sovereign. To the realm of facts, sovereignty comes as a metaphysical force.

Furthermore, sovereignty is structurally based on a split. That it seems weak is not a historical conjecture, but its inherent trait. It always seems as if sovereignty crumbled in confrontation with reality, even in case of the most solid and penetrative systems of power. It does not govern, it reigns: and reigning assumes elementary withdrawal. Between sovereignty and the reigned field there is no direct relationship. Thus, sovereignty retains itself in the depths of its apparent weakness.

Therefore, "crumbling" of sovereignty is a view that is doubly limited: first, sovereignty is a much broader phenomenon than its political incarnation and, second, as long as actually diminishing forces of state power do not concern the possibility, the realm of sovereignty is untouched.

97. The ongoing modern Big Bang fuels the dimension of lasting, which is in principle incommensurable with the dimension of history. History is a futile attempt to enclose becoming in the realm of sense. Contrariwise, lasting acts as a centrifugal force which displaces the meaningful portrayal of "events" and links between them.

Perhaps for this reason we are doomed all the more to the experience of fundamentally insufficient history. History either ensconces itself in a comfortable zone of self-reference or astonishes us with its sudden twists. Thus, the true aporia lies not in the fact that we do not have a history which would be adequate to becoming, but in that history still holds sway over us despite its manifest inoperativeness. Therefore, the very construction of history must be reconsidered.

98. If the modern universe is viewed in its proper dimensions, then the need of salvation appears just as a reflection of ourselves in the Mirror Star. But it is a reflection at a far-off point which lures us with the spell of the outside. It is not that there is no outside: the outside exists, but only as a tain for the mirror, a point that produces a

displacement from which we see ourselves as "us." Therefore, as long as we believe in our identity, whatever it is, as long as we believe in "us" or at least in the possibility of constituting "us," we are—with the very same gesture—expropriated and promised salvation.

Thus, sovereignty—the very same device which creates the lure of identity—is responsible for the hope of deliverance. For this reason, we should not confound the modern hope for salvation with any previous kind of messianism. Here we are, only "us" and this "us" is the core problem. The everyday waiting for the message is our reality, not the palace, in which the messenger has been detained for perpetuity.

99. Perceiving "ourselves" as lost castaways upon the bleakest of all oceans—modernity—would therefore be the ultimate lure. What we need is richness of the universe that, once again, will make "us" just one of its swiftly passing constellations.

Conclusion

On 18 August 1897, over eight years after his breakdown, the mentally ill Nietzsche attempted to put pen to paper for the last time. He began by writing down in his notebook a phrase from *Beyond Good and Evil*: "Oh Lebens Mittag. Feierliche Zeit! Oh Sommergarten!"[1] ("Oh midday of life! Solemn time! Oh garden of summer!"). His handwriting is childish and sloppy. He missed some letters, others were disfigured, but his memory still managed to preserve the quotation from his own book and associate it with the correct season of the year. When one looks at Nietzsche's notes, it seems as if an extinguished mind had echoed with the summits of its own spirit. The height of an otherwise somber German summer must have borne at least a slight resemblance of the French south, a resemblance potent enough to spark off the last effort of a ruined mind. It was only a month after Nietzsche had been moved from Naumburg to Weimar. In April 1897, he reportedly did not even notice the death of his mother, who had been looking after him,[2] but then he suddenly managed to recall a few verses which give the briefest account of his thought and its overall *Stimmung*. These words, apart from being a poignant testimony to the fall of a great spirit, shine like sparkles of transcendence in drab and dreadful conditions.

Perhaps Marx was right that history repeats itself as farce. But, if so, what is the repetition of philosophy? Philosophy withers faster than it blossoms, but it can repeat itself, all of a sudden, after its fall. In this sense, *philosophy repeats itself as afterlife*. Or perhaps even it is the art—although not of dying, as Plato held—but the art of afterlife. It casts long shadows, in which it can grasp both the fall and what comes afterwards.

Would not philosophy therefore be privileged to discover the boundaries and structures of modernity, our "trans-epoch," a "time" of unexpected wonders and longest shadows? In modernity, we all live our afterlives, having been cut from the premodern past by a tectonic rift. We have all collapsed, like Nietzsche on Piazza Carlo Alberti in Turin, and now we wander through a deserted universe. In this sublime, but dreary reality, *philosophy is something that can happen to us in its sudden repetition*, just like the above cited verse happened to Nietzsche. Philosophy does not give any answers and obviously is not able to penetrate the boundaries of modernity. Its realm is imaginary, just like a summer garden, say, on the steep slopes of the path to Nietzsche's beloved Èze.

But what philosophy can do is re-marking our position in modernity. The basic contours of modernity emerged already in writings of Hume, Rousseau, de Sade, Kant, Fichte, and Hegel. But even if we are bound to return to them, we keep retracing our path. We wake up like a mentally deranged person in the middle of the night just to scream out a few verses anew and thus sustain the continuity of our journey through the modern universe. In this sense, philosophy, though long dead, keeps happening to us.

If so, we should not be afraid that, in modernity (and most particularly, in the so-called late modernity), philosophy sounds hollow, like an echo resonating in a desertified landscape. This echo is like a philosophical sonar which explores the boundaries of the expanding universe that we have found ourselves in. Feelings of exhaustion and debt, especially to those who had the privilege of outlining the basic coordinates of modernity in the first place, are inevitable. With the advent of modernity, philosophy was given an unprecedented promise, a power that it had never previously had; the arrogations of Hegel and Marx best epitomize what suddenly became possible. But the greater the promise was, the bitterer must have been the disappointment afterwards. With the advent of modernity, we opened a universe so vast, powerful and overwhelming that—contrary to Nietzsche's wishes—we were never able to rise to its challenges and just ran for cover, cowardly and haphazardly. Thus, we exhausted the greatest promises and live philosophy in its afterlife. It is a *par excellence* modern condition, straddling between vitality and inoperativity, greatest hopes and most prosaic powerlessness.[3] Philosophy is now neither knowledge nor beauty,[4] a spectre hovering in abyss, undemanding and unrequited, still yearning for everything, but obtaining just shards of what it believed to hope for.

Are we not, like Nietzsche in August 1897, haunted by these past moments in which philosophy reached its imaginary peaks? If so, it would be a gross misjudgment to dismiss philosophy for its dreams of the summer garden. We should rather look at the moments in which dreams return, once again revealing the boundaries of modernity, just like bolts of lightning illuminate the darkening sky.

If philosophy lives its somber afterlife and only occasionally wakes up with a sudden recognition, it can, perhaps, discover the boundaries of modernity more aptly than other discourses. Is modernity not just such a bleak desert on which wonders happen from time to time? If so, we would be able to think of it only in these sudden lucid moments of awakening, when the unexpected return of the past illuminates the traversed path. In comparison with other discourses, the recognition that philosophy produces may be found empty or even preposterous. But, ultimately, do we not need a discourse that is in itself internally broken to recognize the strangest features of our trans-epoch that other discourses all too often follow in a stupor?

*

What could philosophy discern, therefore, in the modern trans-epoch?

Modernity is a rhisomatic entanglement. Wherever we look, we find nothing but connections. One of them makes modernity inextricably intertwined with sovereignty, to the extent that the two would not exist without each other. Sovereignty acts as a new, dislocated transcendence of the modern universe. Seen from the outside, it cuts modernity from real time and organizes into a space of multiple, perspectival histories based on different centers of sovereign power. Within this space, sovereignty appears as the Mirror Star: the point which is a remainder of the whole universe and attracts it as if it were its true outside. Thus, modernity is propelled by the interminable lure of this point. In its both reflecting and attracting power, the Mirror Star creates the vision of identities. All modern beings are, on the one hand, promised to have a strong identity and, on the other hand, are always put on a quest for the Mirror Star in which it is to be found. Contentwise, all beings are "themselves"; but it is the split which opens up in them that sets them in tension of self-search.

The same applies to modernity as the "trans-epoch." Its identity is always projected onto the Mirror Star and deflected in it: always ungraspable, displaced, but irremovable in its luring power. We will never settle the dispute on the boundaries and features of modernity, but the fact that we need to investigate this hopeless question testifies to the submission of the whole modernity to mechanisms of sovereignty. In modernity, we are ultimately nothing but "us," deprived of any true external references and thrown back on our own "trans-epoch." Yet, at the same time, this seemingly utmost solitude is internally displaced by the work of the Mirror Star which keeps splitting it into "us-now" and "us-to-become." It keeps pushing us into an unrelenting circular movement of "self-becoming."

Thus, modernity appears to us as a plastic universe which can, and should,—be fundamentally transformed, not in its particularities, but in its general overarching structure. And it is in this tension between "can" and "should" that modernity gains its propelling structure. The motto "Become what you are!" would be, therefore, the injunction that directly covers up the inner instability of modernity which mingles existence, modality, and obligation at the heart of each being. The change that modernity demands is very particular: rather than bringing a total novelty, it is realization of what, in a certain sense, already exists. Nothing grasps this trait better than Benjamin's remark from his Kafka essay, in which he ascribes (after Scholem) to the Messiah not the total overhaul of the world, but a small correction, a tiny displacement that will finally put all things in order.[5]

It is for this reason that modernity is a trans-epoch of perpetual instability, self-questioning and tension. But, counterintuitively, the more it is ripped by internal rifts, the better it is rooted. Capitalism, as the fundamental form under which modernity appears to us, has been already well-recognized in its protean and almost indestructible nature that engulfs its threats to its advantage.[6]

*

Modernity is therefore characterized by an incessant throb, in which the Mirror Star plays the pivotal role. There are times when modernity appears to us as nothing more than a destitute universe awaiting its own salvation. Lights fade, things lose sense, and time turns into unbearable lasting. The status quo is perceived as something worse than even the most destructive novelty. The content of the possible new is reduced to the tinniest glimmer of difference: nothing is known about what may come, except for its possibility. In such circumstances, we may rightly suspect that the currently reigning sovereign is utterly rotten. Its whole realm has become exhausted, nothing can be simply amended and what has left is just the mere possibility of difference: the distant shimmer of the Mirror Star, the ultimate unknown.

In these times, "our" sovereign world (or rather "us") closes in its almost total immanence to the point that the Mirror Star is utterly estranged from it. It becomes the final remainder that prevents the world from overlapping with itself. We know these moments, like the French 1789, 1792, and 1794, the European summers of 1914 and 1939, the Russian 1917, or the German 1932, when the world seems to turn into a desert with only a glimmer of luring promise on the sky. The greater the desert, the brighter the star, and, finally, there is nothing left to do but jump into the unknown. The impetus of the leap is fueled not only by pangs of exhaustion, but, primarily, by the paradoxical and vague feeling that *we are not what we are*. It is not only the world that has become unbearable: we can no longer look at "ourselves" without a disturbing sense of inner rift, of most profound uncertainty that is somehow linked to the condition of the world.[7] It is for this reason that liminal moments are never confined just to a particular state of the world, but to the whole construction of a given sovereign which involves "us" as well. We are equally split as the world: our identity, the most "own" and "our" as possible, is suddenly far away, at the other side of the leap. We need to jump towards the promise of the Mirror Star. Allegedly, we do it only to gain true ourselves, but, in reality, we simply leap into a bubbling vortex of modernity that will spit "us" out in a faraway and unpredictable point.

Pseudo-theologians in Löwithian or Taubesian style would be therefore almost right by tracking a theological moment in modern revolutions, if it were not just the opposite: *what we know as theological in our trans-epoch is simply modern, or even arch-modern*. It is not theology that returns in revolutions: it is the purest modernity at work that some inaptly attribute to secularized premodern sacrum. But, in fact, it is safer to imagine that all gods which appear to us within the modern universe are just figures of modernity and, therefore, simulacra of sacrum. They are not, by any means, representations of some "eternal Real"[8] in our epoch: they appear in the place where modern negativity reveals itself by thrusting the past into a zone of indifferentiation.

Modern revolutions are thus strictly linked to the acute need of becoming that is experienced by all beings split between "themselves" and their identity. Not only in modernity we are necessarily expropriated, but what has been expropriated appears to us in a distant mirror, creating the illusion that there can be something like "us." The illusions of strong identity are possible only on the basis of the original expropriation. Together they fuel the inextinguishable movement of beings towards becoming, towards the change in which "they" will finally appear. But becoming is, in fact, nothing but managing expropriation and shifting the remainder with occasional moments of epiphany, when, for a brief moment, the Mirror Star seems to overlap with a given being. It is for this reason that whenever becoming seems to have been grasped, it already stands still out of time.

One of the most important books about modern politics that still demands a thorough re-reading, Nietzsche's *Ecce Homo*, renders this paradox in a short, almost consciously kitschy fragment:

> On this perfect day, when everything is ripe and the grapes are not the only things that are turning brown, I have just seen my life bathed in sunshine: I looked backwards, I looked out, I have never seen so many things that were so good, all at the same time.[9]

Nietzsche's experience—which directly precedes the fall into insanity—exemplifies one of the rare moments when the Mirror Star seems to return to "us," putting an end to the perpetual split. All appears reconciled under the same sky. Just as Hegel first noted, time stops: all moments of time are like stops on one road, traversable to and fro. We approach the liminal point, in which *we are finally "us"*: "ecce homo." It is a momentary coincidence of "us" with "us," in which the projected identity seems to square with the subject. In this respect, Nietzsche's rapture is strictly equivalent to liminal moments in each true revolution, when, in a sudden release from a sovereign's fetters, the subject temporarily squares with reality.

It is, simultaneously, the moment of utmost imaginable freedom and total solitude, in which exultation and despair blend inseparably. We seem to exist as "us," but this "us" overlaps with the world, being for the first time truly outlined, but at the same time—dissolved in everything. It appears as if we opened an over-epochal passage and travelled between whole ages of the universe. We travel through a total constriction of the world towards another one. In this passage, the Mirror Star momentarily coincides with our position and we lose all guidance. The past, the present and the past—like in Nietzsche's note—lie frozen as parts of the very world that we are leaving. We no longer move along the imaginary line from the past through the present towards the future: the whole history crumbles and we traverse it diagonally. We are moving towards unexpected future, the one that our history did not outline, the one which was some other's, if not no one's, future. In some anachronist bitter irony, Nietzsche inadvertently noticed that in such passages not only grapes turn brown.

This travel takes place without any guiding principle. In such moments we are truly "us" and no Mirror Star shines over us. What we call "us" reveals itself just as an empty structural position of movement, pushed to and fro by any content that happens to influence it. The history of each such passage—greatest revolutions in particular—demonstrates how tiniest and most contingent factual details change the whole configuration of future history because they got stuck in the passage like a grain of sand in an oyster's shell.[10] Coincidences are elevated to the rank of historical necessities. Thus, in the moment where we would be expected to finally capture "us" in its essence, it turns out to be most dependent on accidental external impulses.

To use Lacanian language, the passage takes place in the Real, hence its traumatizing effect. It is in these rare moments that we fully experience that modernity has lost its transcendence. Under the sovereign power, the yawning gap in the point of former transcendence is covered by a sovereign; yet in the passage, when we leave the shelter of a sovereign, *the absence of any external reference point is acutely palpable*. This is the mystery of "us": "us" is a projection of sovereign power and once actively demanded, it dissolves in emptiness of the immanent universe. When we find "ourselves," it is just the universe constricted in its passage from one world to another.

The passage ends with "us" stranded in a completely accidental point, in which the Mirror Star, once again, is thrown out to the outside. We are no longer "ourselves." The universe sinks in the fetishistic construct of a new sovereign power. It is as if we woke up in a particularly bitter morning after, in which the liminal point of almost unlimited possibilities dissipates and leaves nothing but a new formation of sovereignty and a hangover after the carnival. All mirages of possibility are intercepted by the new sovereign, whose artificial mystery conceals the constriction of the universe that we have traversed. In it is in this manner that modern revolutions end up in a system of state power, once again intercepted by sovereignty.

*

The incessant throb of the Mirror Star makes one concept a key problem of modernity: *identity*. Identity is always paradoxical: if we are "us," why should we learn who "we" are, what "we" need, how "we" are different from others? If we are "us," that should be enough. Identity is nothing but a downward spiral that pulls us in the deadly maelstrom of modern fights. Its construction—possible only within the modern universe—promises utmost particularity, but is, in fact, inextricably intertwined with universality. Identity, even if it seems self-sufficient, is always turned against the whole world in which it is immersed, from which it gains its meaning and wants to differentiate itself. For this reason, the path to discovering and strengthening one's identity—the path into "oneself"—is always a path that drags the whole world behind. The lure of identity is the contraption of sovereignty: the deeper we go, the more we need to sacrifice, but the yawning gap at the bottom only grows.

It is probably futile to think about any form of power, and of living, outside of the spell of sovereignty. As long as modernity is not gone, we can only make our best of it. Perhaps we need to learn how to live with the concept of identity instead of hoping for its eradication. But what we are morally obliged to is recognizing *the temptation of being "ourselves" as one of the most fundamental and dangerous motors of modernity*. Politically speaking, it is most clear in the deadly poison of Fascism (as the derailed misinterpretation of communism) but liberal democracy, being a permanently transitional regime particularly conducive to the development of temptations, knows it as well. And, finally, communism, being the most ethical elaboration of the Mirror Star's work, must undertake the most serious confrontation with its failures that end up in entanglement in sovereignty. The impulses of the Mirror Star are impossible to eradicate: instead of debating whether to withhold or to engage, we need to learn how to frame its work ethically.

What we always need to pay attention to is how the "us" is constructed, who is included and who is excluded, where the boundaries of identity are traced. Contrary to Luter's and Hegel's unquestioned and pre-established certainty that, ultimately, we will find ourselves, we should not be afraid of losing "ourselves." Greater things have been lost than this lure, for which there is always a price to be paid. Paradoxical though it may sound, *we should embrace the condition of being lost, being nobody or existing as something that does not square with itself*. Dismemberment caused by the modern forces must be assumed and not turned into a trap of "us." And finally, no *katechon* in the Schmittian style should be imagined: it is nothing but giving to sovereignty its full provisional government.

We are thrown into the modern universe and subjected to dark forces that tempt and push us. Instead of denying them or trying to get rid of them, we need a completely new kind of ethical reflection that gives us a standing point to assess the transformations and mirages of "us." Marx's hope that the humankind can take control of the forces it is subjected to was part of the lure—what we need instead is finding an ethical calculus in the universe that splits into structures and content. We need to find out how to protect the richness of the inoperative modern universe against the looming destitution and desertification that are all too often contained in the promise of becoming. Under the modern spiral of identity, there is no overall perspective on the costs and advantages of what we sacrifice in order to "reach ourselves"; the loss of the calculus is part and parcel of this temptation. New ethical thinking must inhabit this lack and teach us how not to lose the world in the process of becoming.

But how is ethical thinking possible, if it is also subjugated to the reign of the Mirror Star? How could it offer us a solid overall assessment of temptations and imbalances inherent to our existence in the modern universe? Levinasian ethics, which attempted to overcome Heidegger, but, in fact, used the same modern ultimatum as Heidegger— although with an allegedly ethical purpose—clearly shows how ethics fell into what we would like it to save. What we need then, perhaps, is not yet another ethics, but a more powerful term which could grasp the relation of forces that shape philosophical thinking (and ethics, in particular): *the ethical*. In order to explain it, it is necessary to recall briefly its counterpart, the concept of the political formulated by Carl Schmitt.

Schmitt's "the political" names a division of a fundamental kind. It is a division which transcends all divisions based on content, such as the division between good and evil (in the moral sphere) or beautiful and ugly (in the aesthetic sphere).[11] It might accidentally coincide with them, but in its functioning, it remains independent. In its groundlessness, the political fuels the ultimate and passion-generating opposition. Schmitt associates this fundamental division with the distinction between friend and enemy.[12] But, in fact, the nature of the political cannot be explained as such, since it is a primordial division which anticipates concrete "friends" and "enemies."

Abstracting from the thick history of this concept, it might be rightly claimed to be an expression of modern tendency to simplification at its purest. It is created to assert one's identity. And, accordingly, both "us" and "the enemy" are empty structural positions. All material justifications can neither determine nor change the nomination of the enemy once it is settled. This division is the foothold of negativity and, if sufficiently aggravated, its utmost product. The tendency to reduce all material differences, to order and subjugate them to one, elementary, all-encompassing division—in which the whole reality becomes encircled in one either/or—is the structural movement towards "ourselves" as reflected in the Mirror Star.

If there is to be any revival of ethics in the modern universe, the field of ethical reflection must be extended in order to include the functioning of the Mirror Star and the problem of the political. Instead of ethics, perhaps we should think about the ethical: the type of philosophical enquiry which calls into question the work of the Mirror Star and its usage, particularly within the framework of the political. Old ethics is no longer possible without gross philosophical blindness: since ethics is itself ravaged by negativity, it cannot confront it. The ethical, however, provides a counterbalance to the political: just as the political subsumes all differences under one, definitive category and falls into the vortex of "becoming ourselves"—thereby cutting off all sensible reasoning on its sense—so the ethical must derail, foil, and judge this process. *The ethical involves questioning each argumentative step as a potential work of the Mirror*

Star. Naturally, the Mirror Star and the field it creates, namely the political, cannot be eradicated; but their silent influence might be recognized and subjected to ethical reflection.

The Mirror Star wins over ethics by a walkover. When ethics makes its claims, the Mirror Star creates an impression that ethics simply does not apply to situations, in which we simply discover and assert ourselves. If we are already "us," becoming "us" is just a little bit more than a mere tautology, a purely formal move, not the one, which should be viewed in the light of ethics. In modernity, asserting of one's identity is an open gate to most atrocious deeds. The political consists in obstinate sticking to a fundamental division—to one's "identity" and the irremovable position of "the enemy"—which forces its way through the growing impoverishment of the world that contracts into an empty binary opposition. If so, the ethical should also be obstinate in resuming the ethical calculus of each move: it should stubbornly remind us that each time that the political begins to ravage our world, there is a price to be paid. No political blindness, no temptation will ever cancel the bill. There is richness of each world that may be haphazardly lost and no fervor to reach "oneself" is in advance entitled to sacrifice it. The Mirror Star tempts us to jump into the political; but, in modernity-as-space, each move is counted against the whole trans-epoch and it is the ethical that allows us to see that count in advance. It is true, as Lenin held, that all revolutions are made according to Napoleon's formula: *On s'engage et puis on voit*.[13] But the ethical reminds that *On aura été vu après qu'on s'engage*.

The ethical would therefore be a complex net of thinking, whose aim would be to respond—as well as we can—to the discontents of modernity. Among all functions that it might have, three seem the most important. First, it needs to add ethical calculus to the ongoing process of impoverishment that the modern universe is subjected to. As long as modernity is not gone, we need to learn how to live in perpetual tension—with lures of identity, temptations of becoming, and the unabating readiness to annul everything that exists by claiming its emptiness. In darkening times, the ethical would provide the only reference point for observing and judging the process. The work of the Mirror Star, even triggered in most noble reasons, is structurally prone to degenerate into a senseless spiral movement into itself. The ethical, in all its helplessness, would demand that each contingent content that might get in the way of this movement be carefully assessed. In this manner, the ethical is the utmost unpolitical and impractical, as it attempts to break the constricting loop that the world is turning into. When the storm comes, negotiating between its center and the outside world seems futile, but ultimately this is where the ethical must position itself. And perhaps this is the method that allows to defend Marx's hope that humanity can reappropriate and save the whole richness of the world.

Second, the ethical must provide a *cordon sanitaire* against the modern logic of permanent provisionality. Modern ethics is, as Descartes claimed (→ 77), temporary ethics for the time when we reconstruct our knowledge undermined at its bottom by modernity. But, in modernity, provisionality turns permanent and the supposedly sought goal is never achieved. As a result, rules adopted for the temporary world are here to stay. Descartes' idea of ethics becomes the celebration of what is most contingent as the new law of the world, even if it officially heralded as just "provisional." Against such ethics, which has no power against the political, the ethical must stand up with thinking that takes provisionality seriously and does not allow it to suspend the ethical judgment. Provisonality is never neutral, let alone ethically indifferent: it is an entrapment for ethics as such. The ethical must break the deadly blackmail of taking the provisional world for unimportant and temporal and therefore not worthy of deeper reflection. Against the movement of the political, which usually pays lip service to some hypocritically established ethics and suspends it in practice ("after we win over the enemy, we will behave as we are supposed to, but now we must reckon with demands of daily fight"), the ethical must obstinately reveal the ravaging power of the Mirror Star. It is principally opposed to sovereignty and its illusions. It cannot and should not prevent the constricting worlds in their modern spasms: but it must restore the overall ethical account of it. As a gesture of rejecting the provisional, the ethical needs to take for granted our solitude on Earth and make its peace with it. The ethical should be a cloud that hovers over finitude and negotiates the overall calculus of beings,[14] so that power and resources cannot be usurped in the name of provisionality.

Third, the ethical must assume the last and crucial task. Modernity is ravaged by the logic of sovereignty, which makes each position biased, perspectival, and dependent on an empty sovereign center. Such a position, however, cannot be easily referred to, as there is no perceptible common space between perspectives and histories. To make the situation worse, the whole modernity as the trans-epoch is organized within the logic of sovereignty which cuts it from its outside. It is for this reason that in, modernity, our position is described not by messages, but by parables (→ 79). In other words, modernity excludes one common map on which our position could be put. Equally, we are lost as to the position of modernity in real time: neither the origin nor the end of modernity are cognizable. There is no framework that would describe our position from top to bottom. We are left in total singularity that absorbs and deflects into itself all external references. In other words, modern sovereignty causes utmost solitude that we cannot even logically refer to.

Under such circumstances, how could we describe our position? There is no sign in the universal language that could refer to it by passing from universality to particularity. Therefore, what we need is *a sign that would work contrariwise, passing from particularity to universality*. At least since Derrida, there is a name for it: re-mark.[15] Here re-marking will be understood as paradoxalization of the sign, which does not refer from something particular to something universal in which it is to be interpreted, but the other way round: re-mark circumscribes the particular and leaves the power of reference in suspension. Thus suspended, it calls for the outside by taking the referent for its starting point. It takes particularity for what is referred to, but from the unknown outside. And perhaps this is how Benjamin wanted to portray in his *Passagenwerk* the present as the response to the unknown utopian call from the past.[16]

When we re-mark the position shielded and biased by sovereignty, we denounce the sovereign. We reach to the outside which remains concealed, but is appealed to in our re-marking. Naturally, re-marking is a by-product of sovereignty; it shares its closure. But simultaneously it is what allows to denounce the elementary violence and bias of the sovereignty-governed universe.

The ethical should embrace re-marking as its final task. If the overall ethical calculus is not possible due to the universe warped into perspectives, we are left with re-marks. Re-marking is thus a properly metaethical move, because it reveals the very framework of ethics.

*

Ultimately, what desperately needs re-marking is modernity itself. Although it attempts to hide its character under the guise of "one of many epochs," it governs the whole apparatus within which history is produced. Due to its work, continuity of history appears to us as most natural and self-evident, just like air that we breathe. To say it is an illusion would be imprecise: *actually, we have no language to denounce the illusory character of continuity of history*. It is produced by the very same language we use to describe or negate it. But believing in continuous history is nothing less than succumbing to sovereignty.

Therefore, the nature of modernity cannot be referred to. It can be, however, re-marked. This path is tantamount to utmost solitude, in which we are left with the meaningless claim that something which appears to us as eternal or atemporal is, in truth, strictly modern. Adding the adjective "modern," empty though it seems, cuts through the dense tissue of obvious eternity that shrouds modern beings. This is re-marking: leaving modern phenomena in the suddenly revealed solitude of their sovereign character. We cannot truly know what modernity is, but at least we have been given the weak force to re-mark it. Therefore, the ubiquity of the modern cut should be re-marked and denounced as a gesture of the ethical.

Re-marking is like trying, in the middle of the desert, to write down a few words of an old rhyme. A *summer garden* will suffice. It adds nothing new. But like Nietzsche in Weimar, re-marking pierces the night with "long, rough, moaning-like sounds,"[17] thereby denouncing our current position upon the bleak ocean of modernity and calling for a life beyond survival, modernity, and sovereignty. Beyond the cult of the star, which should be left to its distance, and with all the sobriety of revolutionary movement that knows the price and the possibilities.

Notes

Unless stated otherwise, all translations from non-English texts are the author's.

Mottos

1 Jean-Jacques Rousseau, "Les Rêveries du promeneur solitaire," in *Œuvres complètes*, ed. F. S. Eigeldinger, Vol. 3 (Genève and Paris: Slatkine & Champion, 2002), 477.
2 Paul Celan, *Ansprache anlässlich der Entgegennahme des Literaturpreises der freien Hansestadt Bremen* in *Gesammelte Werke*, Band 3 (Frankfurt am Main: Suhrkamp, 2000), 186.

Introduction

1 Cf. Fredric Jameson, *A Singular Modernity: Essay on the Ontology of the Present* (London and New York: Verso, 2002), 2; Slavoj Žižek, *Lenin: The Day after the Revolution* (London and New York: Verso, 2017), xiv.
2 A good account of the Left's intellectual and practical malaise—much greater today than it used to be even fifteen years ago—was given by Stephen Eric Bronner in his famous book *Reclaiming Enlightenment*. Stephen Eric Bronner, *Reclaiming Enlightenment: Towards a Politic of Radical Engagement* (New York: Columbia University Press, 2004), ix–xiii.
3 Stéphane Mallarmé, "Un Coup de dés jamais n'abolira le hasard," in *Œuvres complètes* (Paris: Pléiade, 1998), 363–89.
4 Cf. Henri Lefèbvre, *Introduction to Modernity: Twelve Preludes*, trans. J. Moore (London & New York: Verso, 1995), 316–18.
5 Cf. David Harvey, *The Condition of Postmodernity* (Hoboken, NJ: Wiley, 1992), 116. Žižek convincingly holds postmodernity just for "a self-relating repetition of the modernist break, its application to itself, it is modernity brought to conclusion." Slajov Žižek, *Disparities* (London and New York: Bloomsbury, 2016), 112.
6 It is perfectly understandable, yet still deplorable, how far the reaction against deconstruction and revival of dialectics went: new realism often falls into all the pitfalls of phenomenological naïveté, but this time naïveté is much harder to justify than it was a century ago.
7 Giorgio Agamben, *Qu'est-ce que le contemporain?*, trans. M. Rovere (Paris: Payot & Rivages, 2008), 19–23.
8 Cf. Jacques Derrida, *La Bête et le souverain. Séminaire*. Vols 1–2 *(2001–2002)* (Paris: Galilée, 2008/2010); ibid., *Voyous. Deux essais sur la raison* (Paris: Galilée, 2003); and ibid., *La Solidarité des vivants et le pardon. Conférence et entretiens* (Paris: Hermann, 2016).

9 On the uneasy gender calculus of deconstruction, see Catherine Malabou, *Changer de différance. Le Féminin et la question philosophique* (Paris: Galilée, 2009).
10 Peter Sloterdijk once argued that: "For a century now philosophy has been lying on its deathbed, but it cannot die because it has not fulfilled its task. Its farewell thus has been tortuously drawn out." Peter Sloterdijk, *Critique of Cynical Reason*, trans. M. Eldred (Minneapolis, MN, and London: University of Minnesota Press, 1987), xxvi. Yet, against Sloterdijk's conclusion, philosophy is not a reservoir of empty words: it is precisely in its otherworldly form that it corresponds, even if weakly, to the spectral character of our times.
11 "È come quando guardi qualcosa al crepuscolo. Non è tacito che la luce sia incerta, ma che sai che non potrei finire di vedere, perché la luce viene meno. Così appaiono ora cose e persone: fissate per sempre nel non poter finire di vederle." Agamben, *Autoritratto nello studio* (Milano: Nottetempo, 2017), 10.
12 See Jacques Lacan, *Le Séminaire. Livre XIX—... ou pire* (Paris: Seuil 2011), 27, 76.
13 Cf. Peter Trawny, *Adyton. Heideggers esoterische Philosophie* (Berlin: Matthes & Seitz, 2010), 62. In such proceedings, as Heidegger notes, "all concepts are once again created from the beginning." Martin Heidegger, *Gesamtausgabe, Band 94, Überlegungen II–VI (Schwarze Hefte 1931–1938)* (Frankfurt am Main: Vittorio Klostermann, 2014), 217.
14 Cf. Agamben, *La potenza del pensiero. Saggi e conferenze* (Torino: Neri Pozza, 2012), 22.
15 Freud notices in his *Traumdeutung* that:

> There is often a passage in even the most thoroughly interpreted dream which has to be left obscure; this is because we become aware during the work of interpretation that at that point there is a tangle of dream-thoughts which cannot be unraveled and which moreover adds nothing to our knowledge of the content of the dream. This is the dream's navel, the spot where it reaches down into the unknown.

Sigmund Freud, *The Interpretation of Dreams*, trans. J. Strachey (New York: Avon Books, 1965), 564.
16 Agamben, *Homo sacer. Il potere sovrano e la nuda vita* (Torino: Einaudi, 1995); ibid., *Stato di Eccezione. Homo sacer II, 1* (Torino: Bollati Boringhieri, 2003); ibid., *Il regno e la gloria. Per una genealogia teologica dell'economia e del governo. Homo sacer II, 2* (Torino: Bollati Boringhieri, 2009); ibid., *Stasis. La guerra civile come paradigma politico. Homo sacer II, 2* (Torino: Bollati Boringhieri, 2015); ibid., *Il sacramento del linguaggio. Archeologia del giuramento. Homo sacer II, 3* (Roma-Bari: Laterza, 2008); ibid., *Opus Dei. Archeologia dell'ufficio. Homo sacer II, 5* (Torino: Bollati Boringhieri, 2012); ibid., *Quel che resta di Auschwitz. L'archivio e il testimone. Homo sacer III* (Torino: Bollati Boringhieri, 1998); ibid., *Altissima povertà. Regole monastiche e forma di vita. Homo sacer IV, 1* (Vicenza: Neri Pozza, 2011); *L'uso dei corpi. Homo sacer IV, 2* (Vicenza: Neri Pozza, 2014).
17 Agamben's work, although indispensable in recognizing the contours and essence of modernity, profoundly obfuscates the novelty that modernity brought. The philosopher's notorious propensity to explain modern phenomena with either ahistorical mechanisms of language or alleged ancient or theological genealogies detracts from the originality of the modern era. In this respect, Agamben is too much indebted to the Schmittian-Löwithian-Taubesian school of thinking, as demonstrated in his claim that probably all philosophy of history is constitutively Christian. Cf. Agamben, *Il mistero del male. Benedetto XVI e la fine dei tempi* (Roma e Bari: Laterza 2013), 15.

18 On Jewish thought and modernity, see Agata Bielik-Robson, *Jewish Cryptotheologies of Late Modernity* (Abingdon: Routledge, 2014).
19 Derrida, *Marx & Sons* (Paris: PUF/Galilée, 2002), 69–71; ibid., *Foi et savoir* (Paris: Seuil, 2001), 30–1.

Chapter 1 The Mirror Star

1 See Fernand Braudel, *Civilization and Capitalism, 15th–18th Centuries, Vol. 2: The Wheels of Commerce*, trans. S. Reynolds (London: William Collins, 1983), 240–2.
2 In such periodization, there is always a problem of how to classify the so-called "early modern period," starting roughly with the late Renaissance and continuing up to the "properly modern period." In this context, Descartes, as the proto-father of modern thought, always poses a dilemma. Given that the whole problem stems from modernity's paradoxical nature, no solution is correct. We can either associate the beginning of modernity with the sixteenth–seventeenth century or settle for half-baked conceptualizations, in which there is a supplementary "early modernity," a kind of run-up to the actual one. Alternatively, we can repress the doubt like otherwise subtle and perspicacious Marshall Berman, who divided modernity into three phases. The first (sixteenth–eighteenth century) is the time when "people are just beginning to experience modern life; they hardly know what they hardly know what has hit them. They grope, desperately but half blindly, for an adequate vocabulary; they have little or no sense of a modern public or community within which their trials and hopes can be shared." Marshall Berman, *All that is Solid Melts into Air: The Experience of Modernity* (New York: Penguin Books, 1988), 16–17. The awkward position of this run-up period is the best evidence for how futile the direct attempt is to determine modernity's origins.
3 Immanuel Kant, *The Critique of Practical Reason*, trans. T. K. Abbott (London: Longmans, Green & Co., 1879), 376–7.
4 Louis Auguste Blanqui, *L'Éternité par les astres* (Paris: Germer Baillière, 1872).
5 Blaise Pascal, *Pensées* (Paris: Gallimard, 1969 [1670]), 58–60.
6 Robert Pippin noticed this modern breakthrough introduced by Kant, but he concentrated on the level of rationalist self-determination which founds Kantian thought. Robert B. Pippin, *Modernism as a Philosophical Problem: On the Dissatisfactions of European High Culture* (Malden, MA, and Oxford: Blackwell, 1999), 11, 45–60. What is most fascinating, however, is not the Kantian manifesto, but the first traces of a new world that Kant's thinking is dependent on.
7 Aristotle, *On the Heavens*, trans. J. Leofric Stocks (Oxford: Clarendon Press, 1922), parts 6–8.
8 Just like, according to Foucault's remark, modernity in Kant ceases to be a part of opposition with ancient times and becomes a problem in itself. Michel Foucault, *Le Gouvernement de soi et des autres. Cours au Collège de France, 1982–1983* (Seuil: Gallimard, 2008), 15–18.
9 Terry Pinkard, *Hegel: A Biography* (Cambridge: Cambridge University Press, 2000), 419–435.
10 Cf. Slavoj Žižek, *Less than Nothing: Hegel and the Shadow of Dialectical Materialism* (London and New York: Verso, 2012), 1–8.
11 See Slavoj Žižek, *Sex and the Failed Absolute* (London and New York: Bloomsbury, 2020), 6.

12 See Karl Rosenkranz, *Georg Friedrich Wilhelm Hegels Leben* (Darmstadt: Wissenschaftliche Buchgesellschaft, 1977), 315–20; Pinkard, *Hegel*, p. 430.
13 Rosenkranz, *Georg Friedrich Wilhelm Hegels Leben*, 327–8.
14 Ibid., 327.
15 It is accessible in the English translation, G. W. F. Hegel, *Political Writings*, trans. H. B. Nisbet (Cambridge and New York: Cambridge University Press, 1999), 181–5.
16 It was published in the German edition of Hegel's collected works under the title *Konzept der Rede beim Antritt des philosophischen Lehramtes an der Universität Berlin (Einleitung zur Enzyklopädie-Vorlesung)*, in G. W. F. Hegel, *Werke*, ed. E. Moldenhauer and K. M. Michel, Band X (Frankfurt am Main: Suhrkamp, 1969–71), 399–417.
17 Ibid., 416.
18 Interestingly, over a century later, Heidegger refers to the same imagery, saying that in the era of godlessness, "All lights on heaven are extinguished" ("Alle Lichter am Himmel verlöschen"). Heidegger, *Gesamtausgabe, Band 71, Das Ereignis* (Frankfurt am Main: Vittorio Klostermann, 2009), 210.
19 Hegel, *Lectures on the History of Philosophy*, trans. E. S. Haldane and F. H. Simson, vol. 1 (London: Kegan Paul, Trench, Trübner & Co., 1892–6), 73–4.
20 See Pippin, *Modernism as a Philosophical Problem*, 63–4.
21 When in his *Introduction to Metaphysics* Heidegger interpreted Parmenides' three paths for thinking, he made the famous wordplay of the German word for "decision," *Entscheidung*, by adding a hyphen in the word. *Ent-scheidung* stresses the fact that a decision is a way out (as connoted by the prefix *ent-*) of a situation of division [*Scheidung*]. In a post-non-Hegelian perpetuation of a clinch, Heidegger points to the tension and reciprocal conditioning of division and the decision that cuts it:

> The human being must distinguish among these three paths and, accordingly, come to a decision for or against them. At the inception of philosophy, to think is to open up and lay out the three paths. This act of distinguishing puts the human being, as one who knows, upon these paths and at their intersection, and thus into constant de-cision [*Ent-scheidung*]. With de-cision, history as such begins. In de-cision, and only in de-cision is anything decided, even about the gods. [Accordingly, de-cision here does not mean the judgment and choice of human beings, but rather a division <*Scheidung*> in the aforementioned togetherness of Being, unconcealment, seeming and not-Being.].

Heidegger, *Introduction to Metaphysics*, trans. G. Fried and R. Polt (New Haven, CT, and London: Yale University Press, 2000), 116. Accordingly, in Hegel's narrative, the decision is ubiquitous. But it leaves only an aftertaste of division. In fact, division is viewed only as a spectre of possibility that passes through a crack opened up by decision.
22 The abyss of decision was obsessively investigated by Schelling. One of his greatest strengths was perhaps the ability to think the decision, *Entschluß*, as a radical cut that irreparably collapses the array of possibilities and puts them, somewhat retrospectively, into an order. For example, in his *Weltalter* Schelling theorizes with profound perspicacity on how the decision puts an end to actual simultaneity of the past, the present, and the future, opening up time as such: "Hence, the contradiction only breaks with eternity when it is in its highest intensity and, instead of a single eternity, posits a succession of eternities (eons) or times. But this succession of eternities is precisely what we, by and large, call time. Hence, eternity opens up into time in this decision." Friedrich Wilhelm Joseph von Schelling, *The Ages of the World*, trans. J. M. Wirth (Albany, NY: State University of New York Press, 2000), 76.

23 Even in Schelling's *Weltalter*, with all the subtlety of its theory of decision, there is still an external subject: God:

> But it is inconceivable that there could be compulsion anywhere in the Godhead. Everything must rest on the highest voluntarism. Hence, God, to the extent that God is the eternal No, cannot be overwhelmed. God can only be overcome by the Good such that God yields to Love and makes Himself into Love's ground. We must imagine the course in this way, although this cannot be conceived as actually having happened in this way. For God as the Yes, as the No, and as the unity of both, is still one. There are not separate personalities. Hence, one can think that everything occurred just as if in a lightning flash, for it is epitomized as a happening without actually *(explicite)* being something that happened. This resolution *[Ent-Schließung]*, coming out of the innermost unity, is only comparable to that incomprehensible primordial act in which the freedom of a person is decided for the first time.

Ibid., 77-8. In other words, the existence of the subject of the decision, be it God or a human being, gives Schelling's philosophy a paradoxical unity, but, in exchange, deprives it of what Hegel succeeded in: understanding the modern collapse as a fully autonomous and all-encompassing process.

24 In *Was heißt Denken?* Heidegger famously sums up this intuition in one recurring formula: "Most thought-provoking in our thought-provoking time is that we are still not thinking." Heidegger, *What is Called Thinking?*, trans. F. D. Wieck and J. Glenn Gray (New York, Evanston, NJ, and London: Harper & Row, 1968), 6. See also Heidegger, *Gesamtausgabe, Band 66, Besinnung* (Frankfurt am Main: Vittorio Klostermann, 1997), 56-7.

25 Late Lacan argued that philosophy had been definitely exhausted and replaced by history of thinking. Where Heidegger introduces *Denken*, Lacan sees a chance for psychoanalysis: "une chance de repartir." Lacan, *Mon enseignement, sa nature et ses fins* in *Mon enseignement* (Paris: Seuil, 2005), 97.

26 See in this line Žižek, *The Indivisible Remainder: On Schelling and Related Matters* (London and New York: Verso, 2007 [1996]), 74; and ibid., *Event: Philosophy in Transit* (London: Penguin Books, 2014), 49.

27 Lacan, *Le Séminaire. Livre XIX*, 147.

28 In *Les Mots et les choses*, *episteme* is famously described as what "defines the conditions of possibility of all knowledge, whether expressed in a theory or silently invested in a practice." Michel Foucault, *The Order of Things: An Archaeology of the Human Sciences* (New York: Pantheon Books, 1970), 168.

29 Or rather, as the literal translation of the Hebrew original would suggest, it hovered over "the face" of the waters(רוח אלהים מרחפת על-פני המים) .

30 Derrida, *Of Grammatology*, trans. G. Chakravorty Spivak, Baltimore, MD: John Hopkins University Press, 1997 [1976]), 155.

31 Cf. Bernhard Lakebrink, *Kommentar zu Hegels "Logik" in seiner "Enzyklopädie" von 1830*, Band 2 (Freiburg/München: Karl Alber, 1985), 329-36; Rebecca Comay and Frank Ruda, *The Dash—The Other Side of Absolute Knowing* (Cambridge, MA, and London: MIT Press, 2018), 28. On the relation between Hegel and Aristotle, see Alfredo Ferrarin, *Hegel and Aristotle* (Cambridge: Cambridge University Press, 2001).

32 Aristotle, *Metaphysics*, XII, 7, 1072b.

33 Ibid., XII, 9, 1074b. See also Hannah Arendt, "Thinking," in *The Life of the Mind* (San Diego, CA: A Harvest Book, 1981), 123-4.

34 This difference demonstrates that Marcuse's claim about the relation between Hegel and Aristotle is far too summary: "Hegel's philosophy is in a large sense a re-interpretation of Aristotle's ontology, rescued from the distortion of metaphysical dogma and linked to the pervasive demand of modern rationalism that the world be transformed into a medium for the freely developing subject, that the world become, in short, the reality of reason." Herbert Marcuse, *Reason and Revolution: Hegel and the Rise of Social Theory* (London: Routledge & Kegan Paul, 1955), 42.

35 Cf. Lakebrink, *Kommentar zu Hegels "Logik,"* Band 2, 335.

36 As Heidegger put it succinctly, "Die Sache des Denkens ist für Hegel das Sein als das sich selbst denkende Denken, welches Denken erst im Prozeß seiner spekulativen Entwicklung zu sich selbst kommt und somit Stufen der je verschieden entwickelten und daher zuvor notwendig unentwickelten Gestalten durchläuft." Heidegger, *Die onto-theo-logische Verfassung der Metaphysik (1956/57)* in *Gesamtausgabe, Band 11, Identität und Differenz* (Frankfurt am Main: Vittorio Klostermann, 2006), 55.

37 In *Die Phänomenologie des Geistes*, Hegel underlines the indeed illusory and obsessively repetitive movement of understanding:

> In this tautological process understanding, as the above shows, holds fast to the changeless unity of its object, and the process takes effect solely within understanding itself, not in the object. It is an explanation that not only explains nothing, but is so plain that, while it makes as if it would say something different from what is already said, it really says nothing at all, but merely repeats the same thing over again. So far as the fact itself goes, this process gives rise to nothing new; the process is only of account as a process of understanding.

Hegel, *The Phenomenology of Mind*, trans. J. B. Baillie (New York: Humanities Press, 1977 [1910]), 201.

38 In the *Lectures on the History of Philosophy*, Hegel describes Descartes in terms that, besides the obvious appropriation of the forefather, depict his own thought astonishingly well:

> Descartes expresses the fact that we must begin from thought as such alone, by saying that we must doubt everything …; and that is an absolute beginning. He thus makes the abolition of all determination the first condition of Philosophy. This first proposition has not, however, the same signification as Scepticism, which sets before it no other aim than doubt itself, and requires that we should remain in this indecision of mind, an indecision wherein mind finds its freedom. It rather signifies that we should renounce all prepossessions—that is, all hypotheses which are accepted as true in their immediacy—and commence from thought, so that from it we should in the first place attain to some fixed and settled basis, and make a true beginning.

Hegel, *Lectures on the History of Philosophy*, trans. E. S. Haldane and F. H. Simson, Vol. 3 (London: Kegan Paul, Trench, Trübner & Co., 1892–6), 224–5.

39 From all this it is easy to understand why faith has such great power, and why no good works, nor even all good works put together, can compare with it; since no work can cleave to the word of God, or be in the soul. Faith alone and the word reign in it; and such as is the word, such is the soul made by it; just as iron exposed to fire glows like fire, on account of its union with the fire. It is clear then that to a

Christian man his faith suffices for everything, and that he has no need of works for justification.

Martin Luther, *Concerning Christian Liberty*, trans. B. Wolfmueller (Aurora: Hope Lutheran Church, 2017), 19. See also Lev Shestov, *Athens and Jerusalem*, trans. B. Martin (Athens, OH: Ohio University Press, 1966), 163–6.

40 On the detailed relationship of Hegel to Protestantism, see Merold Westphal, *Hegel, Freedom, and Modernity* (Albany, NY: State University of Nerw York Press, 1992), 149–81. The direct link between the self-assertion of spirit in the Polar Star and Protestantism is acknowledged in the *Philosophy of Right*, where Hegel writes:

> The conscious identity of form and content is the philosophical idea. It is a self-assertion, which does honour to man, to recognize nothing in sentiment which is not justified by thought. This self-will is a feature of modern times, being indeed the peculiar principle of Protestantism. What was initiated by Luther as faith in feeling and the witness of the spirit, the more mature mind strives to apprehend in conception. In that way it seeks to free itself in the present, and so find there itself.

Hegel, *The Philosophy of Right*, trans. S. W. Dyde (Kitchener, Ontario: Batoche Books, 2001), 20.

41 See Žižek, *Sex and the Failed Absolute*, 17.
42 Kant's dualism between human entanglement in the causal chain and radical freedom is the matrix of modern split. From our perspective, the discovery of the split itself is much more original than its exact positioning. Kant and Hegel are two extremities of the continuum, along which the split is placed differently between the subject and reality.
43 See Heiko A. Oberman, *The Reformation: Roots and Ramifications*, trans. A. C. Gow (London and New York: T&T Clark, 2004), 66–73.
44 Hegel, *Phänomenologie des Geistes* (Stuttgart: Reclam, 2009 [1807]), 310.
45 Ibid., *The Phenomenology of Mind*, 457–8 [modified translation].
46 Friedrich Nietzsche, *The Gay Science*, trans. J. Nauckhoff and A. Del Caro (Cambridge: Cambridge University Press, 2001), 194–5.
47 Johann Gottlieb Fichte, *The Science of Knowledge*, trans. A. E. Kroeger (London: Trübner & Co., 1889), 21–2.
48 Lacan, *Le Séminaire. Livre XI—Les Quatre concepts fondamentaux de la psychanalyse* (Paris: Seuil, 1973), 12.
49 This structure repeats itself in Schelling's pra-choice which determines the character of an individual. See Žižek, *The Indivisible Remainder*, 13–22; and ibid., *The Parallax View* (Cambridge, MA, and London: MIT Press, 2009), 118.
50 Comay and Ruda, *The Dash . . .*, 112.
51 This interpretation of the non-Whole and its remainder is obviously informed by Lacanian and post-Lacanian thinking. Cf. Žižek, *On Belief* (London and New York: Routledge, 2004), 101–2; ibid., *Incontinence of the Void: Economico-Political Spandrels* (Cambridge, MA: MIT Press, 2017), 33–40; ibid., *Disparities*, 10–16; ibid., *Less than Nothing*, 52–8, 847; and ibid., *Absolute Recoil: Towards a New Foundation of Dialectical Materialism* (London and New York: Verso, 2014), 244–56.
52 In Badiou's theory, the event straddles between belonging and not belonging to a situation. In each of these intertwined aspects, it triggers paradoxes. See Alain Badiou, *Being and Event*, trans. O. Feltham (London and New York: Continuum, 2005), 182–3.

53 Cf. Žižek, *Less than Nothing*, 359–62, 500, 666.
54 In this light, Heidegger's call for "Wege, nicht Werke" ("paths, not works")—the motto of his *Gesamtausgabe*—embodies the modern errancy of philosophy drifting through the bleak ocean. Modernity warps all "works" long before their "authors" had the chance to read Barthes, Foucault, or Eco. We are left with "paths" because sovereignty excludes stable frameworks of reference and makes it possible only to collect traces marked while traversing its realms. We can hardly preserve anything in time: no work could be properly written down, read, and adequately understood. Our interpretations keep starting anew and each time lead to another path.
55 Max Horkheimer and Theodor W. Adorno, *Dialectic of Enlightenment: Philosophical Fragments*, trans. E. Jephcott, (Bloomington, IL: Stanford University Press, 2002 [1947]), 18.
56 Sloterdijk rightly interprets Nazism as one of the most powerful, if not the most powerful, movements of simplification, in itself a perverse heir to modern avant-guarde:

> Fascism and its side currents were after all—viewed philosophically—in large part *movements of simplification*. But that precisely the town criers of the new simplicity (good—evil, friend-foe, "front," "identity," "bond") for their part had gone through the modern nihilist school of artfulness, bluff, and deception—that was to become clear to the masses much too late.

Sloterdijk, *Critique of Cynical Reason*, 483.
57 See also Derrida, *La Bête et le souverain*, Vol. 1, 134–5.
58 Franz Kafka, "Before the Law," in *The Complete Stories*, ed. N. N. Glatzer (New York: Schocken Books, 1976), 3–4.
59 Michel Foucault, "The Subject and Power," in *Essential Works of Foucault: Power*, trans. R. Hurley and others (New York: New Press, 2000), 340, 342.
60 Modern political sovereignty was forged as a force of resistance against the empty place previously occupied by God, the pope, or the emperor. See Jean Bethke Elshtain, *Sovereignty: God, State, and Self* (New York: Basic Books, 2008), 77–158.
61 Aristotle, *Metaphysics*, IX, 8, 1050a.
62 In this sense, the process of radical purification described by Badiou—embodied in such different phenomena as Heidegger's thinking, the first avangarde in art or political passion for the Real, responsible for triggering terror—is not essentially specific to the twentieth century. It is only radicalization of the mechanism established with the onset of modernity. See Badiou, *Le Siècle* (Paris: Seuil, 2005), 82–91.
63 See also Žižek, *Sex and the Failed Absolute*, 67–70.
64 Heidegger's "ontotheology" is a concept that attempts to cut through the distinction between premodernity and modernity. The outside of ontotheology is, according to him, possible only now—or in the future—that is after "metaphysics" was completed. But such demarcation is in itself marked by Heidegger's position within modernity and a spectral projection of his own division onto history. And, in this regard, it requires deeper reconsidering.
65 Heidegger, *Die onto-theo-logische Verfassung der Metaphysik*..., 63–78.
66 Quentin Meillassoux, *Après la finitude: Essai sur la nécessité de la contingence* (Paris: Seuil, 2006).
67 Ibid., 21.
68 It is for this reason that the modern universe has no external border and cannot present itself to itself, at least not without a paradox. The impossibility of presentation of the world, understood as an all-encompassing totality, within its own boundaries,

was recently explored by Markus Gabriel in *Warum es die Welt nicht gibt?* (Berlin: Ullstein, 2016). In a Wittgensteinian line, Gabriel argues that the world does not appear in itself (ibid., 98). Nonetheless, his reflection is surprisingly ahistorical and even the musings on modernity in the later part of the book (177–256) seem to be very loosely linked to his ontology.

69 The closure of the modern universe was, perhaps, first grasped by Schelling in *Weltalter*, a stunning, internally broken and chaotic piece, whose incoherence and inner failure correspond to the elusiveness of modernity. Schelling writes:

> It already simply follows from the containment, the external finitude, not only of visible nature, but of the cosmos, that there is a force contracting the cosmos from the outside toward the inside and by which the cosmos first became spatial. Hence, this force, since it encompasses and includes the whole, is the force that really posits objectives and boundaries ... But the Eternal can only be finite to Itself. Only the Eternal Itself can comprehend and circumscribe its own Being. Hence, the finitude of the world on the outside contains a consummate infinity on the inside.

Schelling, *The Ages of the World*, 93–4. Schelling conceives of the world as *circumscribed*, kept in its finite external form by a force which is turned not outwards, but inwards. However, Schelling's quasi-Lurianic imagery, enriched in metaphysical speculations, cannot grasp the entanglement between secularity and history in modernity. His picture is still universal, not historically embedded.

70 Vladimir Lenin, *Collected Works*, trans. Y. Sdobnikov and G. Hanna, Vol. 26 (Moscow: Progress Publishers, 1972), 236.

71 Badiou, *L'Hypothèse communiste* (Paris: Nouvelles Editions Lignes, 2009), 33.

72 In this sense, Adorno's dismissive claim about Heidegger's transcendence as a blind absolutized immanence refers not only specifically to Heidegger, but to the whole construction in which modern sovereignty takes place of premodern transcendence. Heidegger would be a special case in modern philosophy, because he most clearly epitomized the triangle of immanence, transcendence, and sovereignty. Theodor W. Adorno, *Negative Dialectics*, trans. E. B. Ashton (New York and London: Continuum, 2007 [1973]), 106–7.

73 This initial gesture of the philosophical sovereign, who conserves, unites and explains, echoes in the *Lectures on the History of Philosophy*, where Hegel remarks: "To this point the World-spirit has come, and each stage has its own form in the true system of Philosophy; nothing is lost, all principles are preserved, since Philosophy in its final aspect is the totality of forms" (Hegel, *Lectures on the History of Philosophy*, Vol. 3, 546). The certainty that nothing can be truly lost accompanies the position of sovereignty. It is as if this place were immune to the power of time and could subordinate time to itself, turning it into a kind of a film roll which contains all events and might be looked through at will and out of time.

74 Cf. Jacques D'Hondt, *Hegel: Biographie* (Paris: Calmann-Lévy, 1998), 227–30; Pinkard, *Hegel*, 225.

75 Cf. Pinkard, *Hegel*, 611–12.

76 See Hotho cited in Walter Kaufmann, *Hegel: A Reinterpretation* (Notre Dame, ID: University of Notre Dame Press, 1978), 357–62.

77 Hegel, *Konzept der Rede*, 417.

78 In his *Encyclopedia*, Hegel clearly links imagination (in all its visual connotations) with religion and thinking (reason, notion) with philosophy. Hegel, *Enzyklopädie der*

philosophischen Wissenschaften im Grundrisse in *Werke*, Band 10, 378. Cf. also Hegel, *The Phenomenology of Mind*, 681–808.
79 Hegel, *Konzept der Rede*, 417.
80 Luther's faith splits the world in two. There is the unredeemable realm of unfaithfulness and sin, above which the realm of faith towers unshakeably. Martin Luther, *De Servo Arbitrio "On the Enslaved Will" or The Bondage of Will*, trans. H. Cole (Grand Rapids, MI: Christian Classics Ethereal Library, 2005), 156. In this regard, Luther anticipates Hegel: faith comes into the world as a (at least partially) external factor that cuts from the fallen universe a space of salvation.
81 Also, in Luther's view, there is no neutral space between faith and sin, as evidenced in his commentary on a fragment from the Epistle to the Romans. Ibid., 167. Apparently, neutral space evaporates just like the premodern world in Hegel.
82 Friedrich Hölderlin, *Patmos* in *Gesammelte Werke*, hrsg. von H. J. Balmes (Frankfurt am Main: Fischer, 2014), 197. Žižek calls "Hölderlinian paradigm" the belief that the present is the time of greatest fall that will take a sudden turn and open a new epoch. See Žižek, *Absolute Recoil*, 344.
83 Heidegger notoriously conflates the greatest misery with the highest possibility of salvation, demonstrating staged humility which is meant to attract redemption. This is another version of the old political saying, "The worse, the better," but pushed to extreme passivity. At the end of his brief post-war text entitled *Logos*, he wrote:

> Um das Denken freilich ist es eine eigene Sache. Das Wort der Denker hat keine Autorität. Das Wort der Denker kennt keine Autoren im Sinne der Schriftsteller. Das Wort des Denkens ist bildarm und ohne Reiz. Das Wort des Denkens ruht in der Ernüchterung zu dem, was es sagt. Gleichwohl verändert das Den-ken die Welt. Es verändert sie in die jedesmal dunklere Brunnentiefe eines Rätsels, die als dunklere das Versprechen auf eine höhere Helle ist.

Heidegger, *Logos* in *Gesamtausgabe, Band 7, Vorträge und Aufsätze*, Frankfurt am Main: Vittorio Klostermann, 2000, 234. "The dark well depth of the riddle" overlaps here with "the promise of higher brightness," just as if renouncing all action in the silence of thinking were to attract the silent god.
84 Carl Schmitt, *The Problem of Sovereignty* in *Political Theology: Four Chapters on the Concept of Sovereignty*, trans. G. Schwab (Cambridge, MA, and London: MIT Press, 1985), 2–35.
85 On the stabilizing and naturalizing function of law, see Louis Althusser, *Sur la reproduction* (Paris: PUF, 1995), 88–99.
86 Žižek, *The Sublime Object of Ideology* (London and New York: Verso, 2008 [1989]), 15–16, 24–33; ibid., *For They Know not What They Do: Enjoyment as a Political Factor* (London and New York: Verso, 2008 [1993]), xxii; ibid., *Like a Thief in Broad Daylight: Power in the Era of Post-Humanity* (London: Allen Lane, 2018), 201; and ibid., *The Year of Dreaming Dangerously* (London and New York: Verso, 2012), 1–31, 47–52.
87 A similar confession opens Hegel's *Lectures on the History of Philosophy*. See Hegel, *Lectures on the History of Philosophy*, Vol. 1, xiii.
88 Kafka, *Before the Law*.
89 In his essay, *D'un ton apocalyptique adopté naguère en philosophie*, in itself stretching the eschatological line, Derrida refers to a specific tone of philosophy, which proclaims the end (of history, philosophy, class struggle, etc.), speaking in the name of truth which is revealed. Derrida, *D'un ton apocalyptique adopté naguère en philosophie* (Paris: Galilée, 1983), 59–60, 69. By the use of this tone, the truth itself becomes the

end, "the structure of the truth would be here apocalyptic." Ibid., 69. Then Derrida proceeds to venturing a braver thought—that the apocalyptical is the transcendental condition of all discourse and experience. Ibid., 77–8. This claim, however, abstracts from the context of modernity, whereas Kant's text which Derrida comments in his essay—*Von einem neuerdings erhobenen vornehmen Ton in der Philosophie*—is already located on our side of the tectonic rift that inaugurated modern times. Therefore, should the traces of apocalyptic discourse—or even, traces pointing to the transcendental condition of all discourse—be temporally universalized? Or should we rather link them to the arch-trace of modernity, *the short circuit between its (unknown) origin and the curvature of its space*?

90 Alain Badiou rightly called the twentieth century "the age of war": not of any war, but always of "the last war." Badiou, *Le siècle*, 56.
91 As Viktor Klemperer noted, the language of total mobilization, endless "last efforts" and crucial, ultimate decisions flourished in the jargon which the Nazis built up as part and parcel of their machine of power. Viktor Klemperer, *LTI. Lingua Tertii Imperii. Die Sprache des Deutschen Reiches. Notizbuch eines Philologen* (Leipzig: Reclam, 1975), 228–240. If Nazism is a black well that allows us to look into the abyss of modern sovereignty—in its most radicalized form—then we should conclude that each sovereign power produces its own language, dependent on the device of suspension and mobilization.
92 Derrida, *Glas* (Paris: Galilée, 1974).
93 See Comay and Ruda, *The Dash . . .*, 66.
94 Ibid., 2.
95 Cf. D'Hondt, *Hegel*, 208–9.
96 Karl Marx and Friedrich Engels, *Economic and Philosophic Manuscripts of 1844*, trans. M. Milligan (Amherst: Prometheus Books, 1988), 163. This recognition can be heard as late as in Derrida, who notes that: "Le savoir absolu est *présent* au point zéro de l'exposition philosophique." Derrida, *La dissémination* (Paris: Seuil, 1972), 29.
97 In his *Metaphysics of Morals*, Kant asks whether the legal category of "person" is "a *stella mirabilis* . . . or merely a *shooting star*." Kant, *The Metaphysics of Morals*, trans. M. Gregor (Cambridge: Cambridge University Press, 1991), 165.
98 Hegel, *The Phenomenology of Mind*, 800.
99 Alexandre Kojève, *Introduction à la lecture de Hegel* (Paris: Gallimard, 1968 [1947]), 378–95; and ibid., *Le Concept, le Temps et le Discours. Introduction au Système du Savoir* (Paris: Gallimard 1990), 148–69.
100 In this sense, contemporary capitalism is strictly dependent on the structure of sovereignty, because, as Joseph Vogl convincingly demonstrated, it is based on *selling the future in the present*. The future becomes its own spectre traded in the present. In this manner, it is sucked into the current constellation of capital. "The true future" understood as what will really happen becomes thus a dimension of the absolutely unpredictable happening. See Joseph Vogl, *The Specter of Capital*, trans. J. Redner and R. Savage (Stanford, CA: Stanford University Press, 2015), 34–57, 103–30.
101 "[P]our Hegel cette fin de l'histoire est marquée par l'avènement de la Science sous la forme d'un Livre, c'est-à-dire par l'apparition dans le Monde du Sage ou du Savoir *absolu*," Kojève, *Introduction*, 380.
102 "Tout au monde, existe pour aboutir à un livre," Stéphane Mallarmé, *Œuvres complètes* (Paris: Pléiade, 1945), 378.
103 This Book, as Derrida notes, is "une totalité ordonnée, le volume d'un livre lourd de sens, se donnant à lire," Derrida, *La dissémination*, 59.

104 Kojève, *Introduction*, 385.
105 Ibid., 386.
106 Ibid.
107 Jewish mysticism was ominously right in decoding the whiteness of Torah as the dimension of continuity beyond meanings created by letters—the divine space of ultimate inscription. See Moshe Idel, *Old Worlds, New Mirrors: On Jewish Mysticism and Twentieth-Century Thought* (Philadelphia, PA: Pennsylvania University Press, 2010), 241; ibid., *Absorbing Perfections: Kabbalah and Interpretation* (New Haven, CT, and London: Yale University Press, 2002), 51–76; Marc-Alain Ouaknin, *Le Livre brûlé: Lire le Talmud* (Rennes: Lieu Commun, 1986), 172, 391. In modernity, it seems to have turned into an emblem of traumatizing, continuous real time over meaningful histories.
108 On the materiality of the Book, see Derrida, *La dissémination*, 59.
109 Gershom Scholem, himself a messianic thinker, highlighted how Jewish messianism is composed of two inseparable ideas: catastrophe and utopian (re)construction. Sometimes, both ideas were epitomized in two different impersonations of the messiah: Messiah ben Josef was supposed to orchestrate the catastrophe, whereas Messiah ben David was to inaugurate the restored utopian world. Gershom Scholem, *The Messianic Idea in Judaism and Other Essays on Jewish Spirituality* (New York: Schocken, 1995 [1971]), 1–20. Nevertheless, even this split might be read as internalization of the traumatic truth of messianism: *each attempt is a failure which needs to be permanently put off.*
110 Hegel, *Lectures on the Philosophy of Religion*, trans. E. B. Speirs and J. Burdon Sanderson, Vol. 3 (London: K. Paul, Trench, Trübner & Co., 1895), 151.
111 Ibid., 553.
112 Ibid.
113 It is in this sense that we might understand the following claim of Heidegger:

> Das Wesen des Seyns ist der Anfang. Die Anfängnis der Anfangs ist der Abschied. Die Anfängnis ist das Ereignis des Untergangs.... Der Abschied ist Ankunft, nicht in die Anwesung eines Vorhandenen, sondern anfängliche Ankunft, die in sich zurücktritt und ihre fernste Ferne innehält.... Der Untergang in den Abchied scheint voller Negativität zu sein, wenn wir metaphysisch denken. Er ist doch der Anfang, wenn wir seynsgeschichtlich das Seyn erfragen.... Das Ereignis des Anfangs ist der Untergang.... Der Untergang ist der Abschied.

Heidegger, *Gesamtausgabe, Band 70, Über den Anfang* (Frankfurt am Main: Vittorio Klostermann, 2005), 24. What Heidegger grasps is the strict link between beginning(ness) and the generalized process of decline, connoted by terms like "downfall" (*Untergang*) or "farewell" (*Abschied*). Nonetheless, in a proper non-metaphysical sense, the beginning is the farewell; it is only from the point of view of metaphysics that we see their difference. In other words, metaphysics is a stumbling block that makes us perceive the farewell—which, in fact, is just the return of the beginning, shrouded by metaphysics. The beginning is always here, as happening itself ("Das Ereignis ist Anfang," ibid., 47). Now Heidegger's imaginary setting might be put in properly modern terms: modernity is an era organized by a structure of permanent throb. Whatever forms of sovereignty arise within it, are already ravaged by downfall and prone to produce apocalyptic discourses. But these apocalypses are local; they concern particular sovereigns and not modernity itself. Apocalypses will necessarily return as a kind of parallax view on forms of sovereignty. For this reason, they always keep happening and never happen. Feelings of exhaustion and downfall linger, no matter what *actually* happens. They are like renewed glimpses at the bare structure of modernity, while each glimpse is separated from another by yet new constellation of sovereignty. For this reason, Heidegger points to the fact that the beginning is always fissured (*zerklüftet*), distributed into beginnings. Ibid., 61. One and the same beginning, which never ceases to begin anew, is viewed in each particular constellation as both its own downfall and a new, unique beginning.

114 "Der Begriff des Fortschritts ist in der Idee der Katastrophe zu fundieren. Daß es 'so weiter' geht, ist die Katastrophe. Sie ist nicht das jeweils Bevorstehende sondern das jeweils Gegebene." Walter Benjamin, *Das Passagen-Werk. Gesammelte Schriften, Band 5*, Vol. 1 (Frankfurt am Main: Suhrkamp, 1982), 592.

115 It is for this reason that Heidegger's beginning (*Anfang*) is referred to as a star that incessantly guides us into the darkness of beginningness: "[es] ist wie ein Stern, der, uns zugewendet, doch sich für eine unendliche Spanne in das Dunkel das Anfängliches verwendet." Heidegger, *Über den Anfang*, 92.

116 Comay and Ruda develop an argument about the structural break between the *Phenomenology* and the *Logic*, marked by a dash. See also Comay and Ruda, *The Dash . . .*, 43, 54–61.

117 In Lacan's late thought, *jouissance* is linked to the primordial split introduced by *trait unaire*, which both creates and blocks access to the excessive enjoyment. Lacan, *Le Séminaire. Livre XVI—De l'Autre à l'autre* (Paris: Seuil, 2006), 127. *Jouissance* is what returns and finds itself in the same place, just as the Pole Star: "La jouissance est ici [à l'expérience psychanalytique] un absolu, c'est le réel, et tel que je l'ai défini comme ce qui revient toujours à la même place." Ibid., 212. "Ce qui nécessite la répétition, c'est la jouissance, terme désigné en propre. . . . Comme tout nous l'indique dans les faits, l'expérience, la clinique—la répétition est fondée sur un retour de la jouissance." Lacan, *Le Séminaire. Livre XVII—L'Envers de la psychanalyse* (Paris: Seuil, 1991), 51. On the relation between *jouissance* and the split of the subject, see Lacan, *Le Séminaire. Livre XVI*, 113–15. See also Nestor A. Braunstein, *La Jouissance, un concept lacanien* (Ramonville Saint-Agne: Éditions érès, 2005).

118 Lacan, *Le Séminaire. Livre XI*, 164.

119 Against the "stupidity" proclaimed on the Hegelian end of history, Derrida noted: "Pour peu qu'on lise et qu'on en fasse autre chose qu'un—disons ici précisément—un demeuré, il va de soi que la fin de l'histoire et de la philosophie ne signifie pas pour Hegel une limite factuelle après laquelle le mouvement de l'histoire se serait stoppé, arrêté, mais que l'horizon et l'ouverture infinie de l'historicité est enfin apparu *comme tel*, ou enfin été pensé comme tel, c'est-à-dire comme ouverture infinie—l'ouverture absolue infinie étant pensée comme telle." Derrida, *Heidegger: La Question de l'Être et l'Histoire. Cours de l'ENS-Ulm 1964–1965* (Paris: Galilée, 2013), 27–8.

120 Franz Rosenzweig, *The Star of Redemption*, trans. B. E. Galli (Madison, WI: University of Wisconsin Press, 2005).

121 Peter Sloterdijk, *Sphären I–III* (Frankfurt am Main: Suhrkamp, 1998, 1999, 2004).

122 Parenthetically, "stars" return not only in analyses of modernity itself, but in some arch-modern concepts like Emmanuel Levinas' "the face." When Levinas argues in *Totality and Infinity* for the resistance of the face against any power or grasp—the resistance which opens up infinity—he juxtaposes it with two elements: matter and stars: "For the resistance to the grasp is not produced as an insurmountable resistance, like the hardness of the rock against which the effort of the hand comes to naught, like the remoteness of the star in the immensity of space." Emmanuel Levinas, *Totality and Infinity: An Essay on Exteriority*, trans. A. Lingis (The Hague:

Martinus Nijhoff, 1979), 197–8. This apparent opposition between "the star" and "the face" is, in fact, the tension of the same Mirror Star between its utmost remoteness and closeness.

123 Ludwig Wittgenstein, *Philosophical Investigations*, trans. G. E. M. Anscombe (Oxford: Basil Blackwell, 1986 [1958]), 194.

124 The difference between salvation and damnation, so pivotal in Protestantism (especially in the Calvinist branch), is no more—like in the Middle Ages—a purely theological and moral question. In modernity, the religious descends from the heavens and coincides with the secular, creating an unbearable mix which might be called *theological praxis*. Former theological categories are at work at the heart of the most prosaic and secular reality. Thus, the difference between salvation and damnation finds its complete realization in the division between *i sommersi* ("the drowned") and *i salvati* ("the saved") from Primo Levi's treatise on the Shoah. Primo Levi, *I sommersi e i salvati* (Torino: Einaudi, 1986); English edition, *The Drowned and the Saved*, trans. R. Rosenthal (New York: Summit Books, 1988).

125 "Im 'Bucklichen Männlein' hat das Volkslied das Gleiche versinnbildlicht. Dies Männlein ist der Insasse des entstellten Lebens; es wird verschwinden, wenn der Messias kommt, von dem ein großer Rabbi gesagt hat, daß er nicht mit Gewalt die Welt verändern wolle, sondern nur um ein Geringes sie zurechtstellen werde." Benjamin, *Franz Kafka. Zur zehnten Wiederkehr seines Todestages* in *Gesammelte Schriften*, Band 2, Vol. 1, 432.

126 Emil L. Fackenheim, *Encounters between Judaism and Modern Philosophy: A Preface to Future Jewish Thought* (New York: Schocken Books, 1980), 101.

127 See Shestov, *Athens and Jerusalem*.

128 Alenka Zupančič, *The Shortest Shadow: Nietzsche's Philosophy of the Two* (Cambridge, MA, and London: MIT Press, 2003), 134.

129 Cf. Christopher Norris, *The Truth about Postmodernism* (Oxford and Cambridge, MA: Blackwell, 1993), 1–9.

130 It is this tension that Lacan attempted to grasp with his famous formula "Toute vérité a une structure de fiction." Lacan, *Le Séminaire. Livre VII—L'Ethique de la psychanalyse* (Paris: Seuil 1986), 21.

131 Cf. Westphal, *Hegel, Freedom, and Modernity*, 156.

132 "Die Unterschiedlosigkeit der totalen Vernutzung entspringt einem 'positiven' Nichtzulassen einer Rangstufung gemäß der Vormacht der Leere aller Zielsetzungen. Diese Unterschiedlosigkeit bezeugt den bereits gesicherten Bestand der Unwelt der Seinsverlassenheit. Die Erde erscheint als die Unwelt des Irrnis. Sie ist seynsgeschichtlich der Irrstern." Heidegger, *Überwindung der Metaphysik* in *Gesamtausgabe, Band 7, Vorträge und Aufsätze*, 96. See also Sloterdijk, *Im Weltinnenraum des Kapitals. Für eine philosophische Theorie der Globaliesierung* (Frankfurt am Main: Suhrkamp, 2005), 219.

133 Heidegger, *What is Called Thinking?*, 29–30.

134 Jean Hyppolyte once noted that whereas Hegel pushes forward in history, Heidegger goes back in order to overcome metaphysics. Jean Hyppolyte, "Note en manière d'introduction à 'Que signifie penser?,'" in *Figures de la pensée philosophique*, Vol. 2 (Paris: PUF, 1991), 626–7. This statement must be understood at a much deeper level: it is not that Hegel and Heidegger represent totally different visions of history. It is, rather, one and the same history which can be traversed to and fro, like space rather than time. Whether we move on or withdraw towards the origins is just a matter of reconfiguration of the framework that already exists, straddling between the bleak

ocean and the star. Hegel and Heidegger simply choose different positions, but the history they refer to is ravaged by the same paradoxes.
135 When at the end of his *Violences of the Dialectic*, Fredric Jameson claims that utopia now has no place in space or time, cannot be imagined as a goal, or any event on the horizon of the future—and that for this reason, it might only be viewed as an alternate world—it is nothing but withdrawing the idea of the end of modernity into the tiniest corner. Such an end is completely dissociated from the modern universe: it is only the most formal and empty difference that sets them apart. Fredric Jameson, *Valences of the Dialectic* (London: Verso, 2009), 612.
136 Kafka, *Zürau Aphorismen* in *Nachgelassene Schriften und Fragmente, Band 2* (Frankfurt am Main: Fischer, 1992), 116.
137 See Nietzsche, *Beyond Good and Evil*, trans. J. Norman (Cambridge: Cambridge University Press, 2002), 69; Heidegger, *Gesamtausgabe, Band 65, Beiträge zur Philosophie (Vom Ereignis)* (Frankfurt am Main: Vittorio Klostermann, 1989), 29.
138 This paradoxical nature of Being was well grasped by Derrida in his polemics with Levinas. Derrida, *Violence and Metaphysics* in *Writing and Difference*, trans. A. Bass (London and New York: Routledge, 2003 [1978]), 167 f.
139 See Heidegger, *Zur Erörterung der Gelassenheit. Aus einem Feldweggespräch über das Denken (1944/45)* in *Gesamtausgabe, Band 13, Aus der Erfahrung des Denkens* (Frankfurt am Main: Vittorio Klostermann, 1983), 37–74. Derrida in *Sauf le nom* provided a refined definiton of *Gelassenheit* as "à la fois le [l'être] quitter et (mais) le laisser (être au-delà de l'être-quelque chose). Sauf son nom—qu'il faut taire là où il se rend lui-même pour y arriver, à son propre effacement." Derrida, *Sauf le nom* (Paris: Galilée, 1993), 100–1.
140 Heidegger, *Zeit und Sein* in *Gesamtausgabe, Band 14, Zur Sache des Denkens* (Frankfurt am Main: Vittorio Klostermann, 2007), 9.
141 "Auf einen Stern zugehen, nur dieses," as reads the motto of Heidegger's path formulated in *Aus der Erfahrung des Denkens*. See Heidegger, *Aus der Erfahrung des Denkens*, in *Gesamtausgabe, Band 13*, 76.
142 "Die Verdüsterung der Welt erreicht nie das Licht des Seyns." Ibid.
143 "Denken ist die Einschränkung auf einen Gedanken, der einst wie ein Stern am Himmel der Welt stehen bleibt." Ibid.
144 In a photo reprinted in *La Contre-allée*, Derrida visits Heidegger's *Hütte*. Catherine Malabou and Jacques Derrida, *La Contre-allée* (La Quinzaine littéraire/Louis Vuitton, 1999), 261. The philosopher stands in the middle; to his right, there is Hermann Heidegger, holding in his hands the wooden star of his father. Derrida is looking at his face begrudgingly, as if turning his eyes from the star. The almost ridiculous meagreness of this object plays an unexpected variation on Heidegger's *Vorhandenheit*.
145 In his *Negative Dialectics*, Adorno claims that the existential theory is nothing but a dark sky without any star. Adorno, *Negative Dialectics*, 131. *Sacrum* no longer exists and the eternal idea in which existence could participate is now nothing but bare affirmation of power. In this vision, Adorno grasps Heidegger's fall with unprecedented lucidity, yet he neglects the real existence and work of the Mirror Star. It is not that if the star is recognized as a lure it may be claimed that it has disappeared. With a Hegelian intuition, we should rather claim that in this form it exists even more strongly, because its luring work is all the more palpable. The modern sky is therefore dark, but not empty: the Mirror Star holds sway over it. Truly, it is a collapse of transcendence and affirmation of power. Yet, it draws its force precisely from these two characteristics.

146 Heidegger was therefore somewhat right when he wanted to present history of philosophy as history of great solitude (*Vereinsamung*). Heidegger, *Gesamtausgabe, Band 94, Überlegungen II–VI (Schwarze Hefte 1931–1938)*, 218. Yet, once again, solitude is related to the beginning of modernity, not of history as such.

147 In its pre-assumed aporeticness, deconstruction is even more at home than Hegel's self-certainty. It is always capable of setting the aporetic trap. Therefore, no failure, but even no success, can surprise it: at bottom, the greatest success will always have an aporia that one may cling to. Therefore, *deconstruction is one of the best forms of modern self-certainty—precisely in its self-doubt.*

148 Heidegger, *Gesamtausgabe, Band 71, Das Ereignis*, 84–5.

149 Ibid., 85.

150 Ibid.

151 Žižek, *Less than Nothing*, 925–63; *Absolute Recoil*, 391–415.

152 Lacan, *Le Séminaire. Livre XXIII—Sinthome* (Paris: Seuil, 2005), 30–1.

153 In his *Lectures on the Philosophy of History*, Hegel openly acknowledges sovereignty as the constructive rule of modernity. In sovereignty, total freedom overlaps with absolute command over the field and the certainty of its own self-preservation: "in Thought, Self moves within the limits of its own sphere; that with which it is occupied—its objects are as absolutely present to it [as they were distinct and separate in the intellectual grade above mentioned]; for in thinking I must elevate the object to Universality. This is utter and absolute Freedom, for the pure Ego, like pure Light, is with itself alone [is not involved with any alien principle] . . . ," Hegel, *Lectures on the Philosophy of History*, trans. J. Sibree, (London: Bell and Sons, 1902), 457.

154 Hannah Arendt, "Personal Responsibility under Dictatorship," in *Responsibility and Judgment* (New York: Schocken Books, 2003), 45.

155 Ibid.

156 Max Horkheimer, *Dämmerung. Notizen in Deutschland* in *Gesammelte Schriften, Band 2: Philosophische Frühschriften 1922–1932* (Berlin: Fischer, 1987), 422.

157 The painful loneliness coupled with an imposed need of self-reliance echoes in late Sloterdijk's philosophy, particularly when he analyzes the position of modern humanity on "the spaceship Earth." In these circumstances, left bare by the wind of modern progress, we are, as Sloterdijk notices, necessarily autodidacts. See Sloterdijk, *Was geschah im 20. Jahrhundert?* (Berlin: Suhrkamp, 2016), 23–43. The new revolution of ecology, austerity, and self-grip builds upon the axiom: "The humanity has only this one Earth at its disposal." Ibid., 33. See also ibid., *Im Weltinnenraum des Kapitals*, 15–16.

158 Hegel, *Lectures on the Philosophy of History*, 464.

159 Ibid., 464–5.

160 Cf. Jean-Jacques Rousseau, "The Social Contract," in *The Social Contract and Discourses* (London and Toronto: Dent and Dutton, 1920), 5.

161 Hegel, *Lectures on the Philosophy of History*, 468.

162 See also Westphal, *Hegel, Freedom, and Modernity*, 176–81.

163 In this context, one could ask Hegel a perverse question: aren't lapsed Catholics, such as Hitler, Heidegger, and Schmitt, "Catholics gone stale," as Jacob Taubes described them, the most devout supporters of unity between the state and the nation? See Jacob Taubes, *The Political Theology of Paul* (Stanford, CA: Stanford University Press, 2003), 103–5.

164 Hegel, *Lectures on the Philosophy of History*, 469.

165 It is this tension that Agamben recognized in *Stasis* as accountable for Hobbes' theory of the civil contract. Hobbesian people may have two forms: the disunited multitude before the creation of the sovereign and the dissolved multitude after the sovereign emerges. The society under sovereignty is always dissolved and on the brink of civil war. Couched in paraphrased Hegelian terms, sovereignty approaches the people as the Mirror Star, with the throb of conflation and estrangement.
166 Thomas Hobbes, *Leviathan*, trans. J. C. A. Gaskin (Oxford: Oxford University Press, 1996 [1988]), 117–18.
167 Ibid., 86–7.
168 It was probably Foucault who first noticed the dangerous overlap between state sovereignty and construction of the self, based on discipline and coercion. See Michel Foucault, *"Society Must Be Defended": Lectures at the Collège de France 1975–1976*, trans. D. Macey (New York: Picador, 2003), 37.
169 Horkheimer noticed that these notions which guarantee the eagerness for bloodshed—"religion" or "nation", are the greatest capitalist taboos (*Dämmerung. Notizen in Deutschland*, 331–2).
170 Carl Schmitt, *Roman Catholicism and Political Form*, trans. G. L. Ulmen (Westport, CT, and London: Greenwood Press, 1996), 1–59.
171 See Nietzsche, *Human, All too Human: A Book for Free Spirits*, trans. R. J. Hollingdale (Cambridge: Cambridge University Press, 1996), 303. It is not until *Ecce Homo* that Nietzsche draws ultimate consequences from this early intuition. First, he claims that the displacement of the closest and the farthest is an essentially modern phenomenon. Second, he comes up with a whole theory of *sovereign self-defense* of the closest (body, diet, climate, habits) against the farthest (idols, religions, political doctrines), which are dependent on the former. Nietzsche, *Ecce Homo* in *The Antichrist, Ecce Homo, The Twilight of the Idols and Other Writings*, trans. J. Norman, (Cambridge: Cambridge University Press, 2005), 98.
172 As usual, Heidegger oscillates before attributing the fatal displacement either to the post-pre-Socratic Western thinking or to modernity (which, from a certain angle, accomplishes the fate of the West, but from another brings some unique features), thereby obfuscating the importance of the modern cut. In the lecture cycle, *What is Called Thinking?* (*Was heißt Denken?*), he analyzes the displacement with reference to Nietzsche. It appears as something which is due to the nature of modern science; poetry, however, has preserved the closeness of things: "Yet we have placed thinking close to poesy, and at a distance from science. Closeness, however, is something essentially different from the vacuous leveling of differences. The essential closeness of poetry and thinking is so far from excluding their difference that, on the contrary, it establishes that difference in an abysmal manner. This is something we moderns have trouble understanding." Heidegger, *What is Called Thinking?*, 134. Then, recalling Plato, Heidegger attempts to restore the appropriate relations of closeness and remoteness. If we let things be, they should begin to appear in their proper dimensions. "The things let be"—"[t]hese things that lie already before us are not, however, what lies farther back in the sense of being remote. They are supremely close *by*, to everything. They are what has come close by, beforehand. But normally we fail to see them in their presence." Ibid., 201.
173 In the subchapter on the method of political economy in *Grundrisse*, Marx attempted to develop a method that would match capitalist interpenetration of the abstract and the concrete. Marx, *Grundrisse: Foundations of the Critique of Political Economy*, trans. M. Nicolaus (New York: Vintage Books, 1973), 100–8. It cannot start

with the apparent "real and the concrete, with the real precondition," because, in modernity, no category exists on its own. Ibid., 100. The categories which seem the most tangible, eternal and already at hand (such as the population), are, in fact, parts of the whole. Taking them in themselves is not an innocent act of direct cognition, but an act of abstraction which bears on the whole process of reasoning. Each category has its own particular bias, but purports to be abstract. This entanglement works both ways: we have no categories for true particularity, because, under capitalism, they are already marked by universality. Yet, all seemingly universal concepts are, in fact, biased by their rootedness in modern bourgeois society. In our times, "modern bourgeois society—is always what is given, in the head as well as in reality," so general analysis of economy is always tainted by the particularity of its categories developed in the bourgeois society. Ibid., 106.

174 In some of his speeches from the rectorate period, Heidegger theorizes students as "workers." In this respect, he is most hideously immersed in the Nazi imagery. Playing on the distinction between *Arbeiter der Faust*, "workers of the fist" and *Arbeiter der Stern*, "workers of the forehead" (in itself used by the Nazi Party propaganda), Heidegger aims to reach a fantasmatic Fascist unity between physical and intellectual work. Cf. Heidegger, *Der Deutsche Student als Arbeiter* in *Gesamtausgabe, Band 16, Reden und andere Zeugnisse eines Lebenweges* (Frankfurt am Main: Vittorio Klostermann, 2000), 204; *Zur Eröffnung der Schulungskurse für die Notstandsarbeiter der Stadt an der Universität* in ibid., 234.

175 Ibid., *Gesamtausgabe, Band 53, Hölderlins Hymne "Der Ister"* (Frankfurt am Main: Vittorio Klostermann, 1993), 68.

176 Ibid., *Gesamtausgabe, Band 71, Das Ereignis*, 86-7; and ibid., *Überwindung der Metaphysik*, 67-98.

177 In his, "Religion within the Boundaries of Pure Reason," Kant presents a Luther-based doctrine of the redemptive act that *has already happened* ("the Kingdom of God is come into us"), but needs time to transform the whole Earthly dominion. The open horizon of infinity is nothing less than the eternity of *a* history opened by sovereignty. See Kant, "Religion within the Boundaries of Pure Reason," in *Religion within the Boundaries of Pure Reason and Other Writings*, trans. A. Wood and G. di Giovanni (Cambridge: Cambridge University Press, 1998), 128.

178 Gottfried Wilhelm Leibniz, *Discourse on Metaphysics* in *Philosophical Papers and Letters*, trans. L. E. Loemker (Dordrecht: Kluwer, 1989) 308.

179 Christoph Schulte, *Zimzum. Gott und Weltursprung* (Berlin: Jüdisches Verlag, 2014), 46-8; Lawrence Fine, *Physician of the Soul, Dealer of the Cosmos. Isaac Luria and his Kabbalistic Fellowship* (Stanford, CA: Stanford University Press, 2003), 40, 126-44.

180 Gershom Scholem, *Main Trends in Jewish Mysticism* (New York: Schocken Books, 1974 [1941]), lecture VII. See also Moshe Idel's critique of Scholem's vision of *tsimtsum* in, Idel, *Old Worlds, New Mirrors*, 96; and Schulte's account of Scholemian *tsimtsum*-based theology of divine absence within the modern universe in, Schulte, *Zimzum*, 383-9. On the possible relation between Hegel and Luria, see Glenn Alexander Magee, *Hegel and the Hermetic Tradition* (Ithaca, NY, and London: Cornell University Press, 2001), 227-36.

181 The emergence of space—not as a neutral, Newtonian grid, but as a problematic something supported by negativity—was spotted already by Schelling in his *Weltalter* (*nota bene*, Lurianic influences, although mixed with Christian reinterpretations, are clearly traceable in this text). Cf. Schelling, *The Ages of the World*, 214.

182 This motive is particularly popular in the late modern revival of Jewish thought within Western philosophy. According to the common doxa, Greek thinking prefers sight as the primary method of interacting with reality—which opens the way for idolatry Idealism, concentrated on stable beings and stable meanings. Jewish thought, on the contrary, is focused on hearing, hearing the word, in particular. It is portrayed as privileging revelation, which is living speech defying all attempts to close it within the framework of stable meanings. In this opposition, sight borders on the position of the source of all calamities of Western thought. Cf. Susan A. Handelman, *The Slayers of Moses: The Emergence of Rabbinic Interpretation in Modern Literary Theory* (Albany, NY: State University of New York Press, 1982), 3–119; and Maurice Blanchot, *L'Entretien infini* (Paris: Gallimard, 1969), 38–45, 184–9.

183 Althusser borrowed this term from Freud in order to explain the specificity of Marxist (chiefly Marx's and Lenin's) contradiction in contrast to Hegel's dialectics. Cf. Louis Althusser, "Sur Marx et Freud," in *Écrits sur la psychanalyse. Freud et Lacan* (Paris: STOCK/IMEC, 1993), 224–5. Apart from the accuracy of this portrayal of Hegel, the term "overdetermination" captures the excess-in-determination of phenomena, which, through too many cross-entangled particular determinations, acquire a kind of proper inertia and cut across the otherwise one-dimensional relation between cause and effect.

Chapter 2 For a Derridean-Copernican Revolution: Modernity Before History

1 See Hartmut Böhme, *Fetishism and Culture: A Different Theory of Modernity*, trans. A. Galt (Berlin/Boston, MA: De Gruyter, 2014); Lefèbvre, *Introduction to Modernity*; Bruno Latour, *We Have Never Been Modern*, trans. C. Porter (Cambridge, MA: Harvard University Press, 1993), notably, Latour considers modernity a rational-subjectivist illusion rather than actual reality; Pippin, *Modernism as a Philosophical Problem*; Jürgen Habermas, *The Philosophical Discourse of Modernity: Twelve Lectures*, trans. F. Lawrence (Cambridge: Polity Press, 1990), 1–44; Berman, *All that is Solid Melts into Air*; Peter Osborne, *The Politics of Time: Modernity and Avant-Garde* (London and New York: Verso, 1995); Hans Blumenberg, *The Legitimacy of the Modern Age*, trans. R. M. Wallace (Cambridge, MA, and London: MIT Press, 1985); Hartmut Rosa, *Social Acceleration: A New Theory of Modernity*, trans. J. Trejo-Mathys (New York: Columbia University Press, 2013); Foucault, *Le Gouvernement de soi et des autres*; ibid., *Naissance de la biopolitique, Cours au Collège de France, 1978–1979* (Paris: Gallimard, Seuil, 2004); and Jameson, *A Singular Modernity*.

2 Fernand Braudel's work is devoted, among others, to demonstrating how the most basic level of society's functioning—eating habits, agricultural methods, local centers of commerce—are resistant to change. While the surrounding world is profoundly transformed—regimes rise and fall, economy has its ups and downs, science introduces new inventions into the tissue of everyday life—there is a kind of *longue durée* below all tectonic displacements of epochs. Nevertheless, Braudel acknowledges the crucial novelty of modern capitalism. See Braudel, *Civilization and Capitalism*.

3 As Blumenberg famously remarked, "The modern age was the first and only age that understood itself as an epoch and, in so doing, simultaneously created the other epochs." Blumenberg, *The Legitimacy of the Modern Age*, 116.

4 The image of mycelium and its center is obviously indebted to Freud, who, in his *Traumdeutung*, theorized the elusive core of each dream which confuses the paths of interpretation. Freud, *The Interpretation of Dreams*, 564. The mycelium metaphor grasps well the process in which interpretation, heading towards its imagined "center," gets drawn into the ramification of paths that gradually lose their symbolic character and reveal their inexplicable grounding. See also Lacan, *Le Séminaire. Livre II Le moi dans la théorie de Freud et dans la technique de la psychanalyse* (Paris: Seuil 1978), 130, 209; ibid., *Le Séminaire. Livre XI*, 26.
5 History became a major philosophical topic in the next century. As Peter Osborne noticed, "Time imposes itself as a problem within nineteenth- and twentieth-century European philosophy, in a qualitatively different way from that in which it previously appeared as a paradigmatic example of the unchanging character of philosophical questions, in the new twofold form of the problem of *history* and the problem of *death*." Osborne, *The Politics of Time*, x. Nonetheless, identifying history *as a problem* was preceded by the perception of how the notion of time was disturbed, ultimately giving rise to "history."
6 David Hume, *An Enquiry Concerning Human Understanding: My Own Life: An Abstract of a Treatise of Human Nature* (La Salle, IL: Open Court, 1992 [1748]), section 7.
7 Ibid., *A Treatise of Human Nature* (London: Noon, 1939 [1739]), 69–179.
8 See also "rehabilitation" of Hume against Kant by Meillassoux: Meillassoux, *Après la finitude*, 111–53.
9 Hume, *A Treatise of Human Nature*, 84–6.
10 Ibid., 86.
11 Heidegger, *Über den Anfang*, 1.
12 Derrida, *Of Grammatology*, 62.
13 "We cannot not periodize," notices Fredric Jameson, pointing to the radically historical drive to self-understanding of modernity. Jameson, *A Singular Modernity*, 29.
14 See Jules Michelet, *Histoire de la Révolution française*, Vol. 1 (Paris, 1889); François Furet, *The French Revolution 1770–1814*, trans. A. Nevill (Oxford: Blackwell, 1996), 3–100.
15 It is in this spirit that Claude Lefort claimed that the French Revolution was, at the beginning of the nineteenth century, experienced as a break that had just occurred, yet not as a break within time, but the one which "establishes a relationship between human beings and time itself, that makes history a mistery." Claude Lefort, "The Permanence of the Theologico-Political?," in *Democracy and Political Theory*, trans. D. Macey (Minneapolis, MN: University of Minnesota Press, 1988), 214. In this vision, the Revolution is not just an event, and not even a world-shattering event. It is, rather, a knot of a particular event and general epochal transformation, which inaugurates a new era under the guise of a local historical process.
16 Kant, *The Critique of the Pure Reason*, 255–349.
17 This withdrawal is quite similar to Žižek's reinterpretation of Hegelian category of "recoil" (*Gegenstoss*). Cf. Žižek, *Absolute Recoil*, 1–4.
18 Kant, *The Critique of Pure Reason*, 23–44.
19 It is most visible in the Nietzschean–Heideggerian line of thinking, but, in various forms, resounds also in Rosenzweig's and Levinas' philosophies. See Peter Eli Gordon, *Rosenzweig and Heidegger: Between Judaism and German Philosophy* (Berkeley, Los Angeles, CA, and London: University of California Press), 2003, 137–62. The last echo

is hearable even in early Derrida, when he opens his famous *Violence and Metaphysics* with acute, almost apocalyptic vision of historicity. Derrida, *Violence and Metaphysics*, 97-8. Derrida assumes here that some fundamental philosophical "error," working from the very beginning, revealed/caused the prolonged death of philosophy. Not accidentally, it seems to have happened with the advent of modernity. The past is therefore organized into a history, a history of actual death, which runs counter to any vision of philosophical prosperity and progress. History is of the highest importance for philosophy: philosophy dies and looks back on itself in the warped mirror of history, from which it can read the death sentence, but not its reasons and roots.
20 Kant, *The Critique of Pure Reason*, 29-30.
21 See parallels to Derrida's concept of the *khora*, the ultimate receptacle: Derrida, *Khôra* (Paris: Galilée, 1993), 20-9.

22 When the Baal Shem had a difficult task before him, he would go to a certain place in the woods, light a fire and meditate in prayer—and what he had set out to perform was done. When a generation later the "Maggid" of Meseritz was faced with the same task he would go to the same place in the woods and say: We can no longer light the fire, but we can still speak the prayers—and what he wanted done became reality. Again, a generation later, Rabbi Moshe Leib of Sassov had to perform this task. And he, too, went into the woods and said: We can no longer light a fire, nor do we know the secret meditations belonging to the prayer, but we do know the place in the woods to which it all belongs—and that must be sufficient; and sufficient it was. But when another generation had passed and Rabbi Israel of Rishin was called upon to perform the task, he sat down on his golden chair in his castle and said: We cannot light the fire, we cannot speak the prayers, we do not know the place, but we can tell the story of how it was done. And, the story-teller adds, the story which he told had the same effect as the actions of the other three.

   Scholem, *Major Trends in Jewish Mysticism*, 350.
23 Derrida, *Of Grammatology*, 313-14.
24 Rousseau's thinking is pervaded with the vision of the irretrievably lost premodern harmony, whose existence proves how deeeply we have fallen. Nonetheless, any attempt to restore it would result in losing the little we already have. See Rousseau, "Observations [to Stanislas, King of Poland]," in *The Discourses and Other Early Political Writings*, edited by V. Gourevitch (Cambridge: Cambridge University Press, 1997), 50-1. See also Pippin, *Modernism as a Philosophical Problem*, xviii.
25 From this point of view, Ernesto Laclau's and Chantal Mouffe's theory of hegemony might be seen as an attempt to take general control over how particularity and universality are sewn by sovereignty in each given knot. Laclau argues that "universality exists only if it is incarnated in—and subverts—some particularity but, conversely, no particularity can become political without also becoming the locus of universalizing effects." Ernesto Laclau, "Structure, History and the Political," in Judith Butler, Ernesto Laclau, and Slavoj Žižek, *Contingency, Hegemony, Universality: Contemporary Dialogues on the Left* (London and New York: Verso, 2000), 207. Consequently, "[t]here is no universality, as we have seen, except through an equivalence between particularities, and such equivalences are always contingent and context-dependent. Any step beyond this limit would necessarily fall into a historical teleology; with the result that universality, which should be considered as a horizon, would become a ground." Ibid., 211. Laclau accepts that there is no abstract

universality and demands that the knot by which it is linked to particularities be consciously and politically determined. Realist as this approach appears, it does not theorize the very necessity of the knot and the fact that no matter if hegemony is consciously constructed, the knot will function anyway. Even if theory of hegemony arises from the necessity of modern sovereignty, it produces an illusion that it generates a universality-particularity constellation and does not inherit its structural necessity from sovereignty.

26 See Herbert Marcuse, *One-Dimensional Man: Studies in the Ideology of Advanced Industrial Society* (London and New York: Routledge, 2002 [1964]), 186.

Chapter 3   Modernity as a Construct of Sovereignty

1   Cf. Lacan, *Le Séminaire. Livre IV—La Relation d'objet* (Paris: Seuil, 1994), 31–3, 218; ibid., *Le Séminaire. Livre X—L'Angoisse* (Paris: Seuil, 2004), 156; ibid., *Le Séminaire. Livre XVI*, 295; ibid., *Le Séminaire. Livre XVII*, 190; ibid., *Le Séminaire. Livre XVIII—D'Un discours qui ne serait pas du semblant* (Paris: Seuil, 2007), 27–9; ibid., *Le Séminaire. Livre XX—Encore* (Paris: Seuil, 1975), 58, 85, 118; ibid., *Le Séminaire. Livre XXIII*, 19–37, 50–86, 116–24, 129; ibid., *Le Triomphe de la religion, précédé de Discours aux catholiques* (Paris: Seuil 2005), 92–100.
2   See Žižek, *The Puppet and the Dwarf: The Perverse Core of Christianity* (Cambridge, MA, and London: MIT Press, 2003), 69–70; ibid., *Incontinence of the Void*, 30–1.
3   Zupančič, *The Shortest Shadow*, 28.
4   This dimension allows Henri Lefèbvre to ask, somewhat histerically (in the properly Lacanian sense): "So-called modern societies, with their transitional character (towards what?) on the point of breaking up, are pregnant—with what? Where is 'modernity' heading? What will be born? A dream become flesh, or a monster? We simply do not know. We know that the child will be born, that perhaps it has been born already, within us, around us." Lefèbvre, *Introduction to Modernity*, 15.
5   Benjamin, "On the Concept of History," in *Illuminations: Essays and Reflections*, trans. H. Zohn (New York: Schocken Books, 1969), 257–8.
6   Kafka, *In der Strafkolonie* in *Erzählungen* (Stuttgart: Reclam, 2012), 156.
7   In this respect, I find the need to radicalize Agamben's remarks on the origins of the word "modern": "Fin dalla sua prima apparizione in una lettera di Gelasio I, ... il termine *modernus* implica sempre una tensione rispetto al passato, quasi che il presente potesse afferrarsi e definirsi solo in uno scarto rispetto a se stesso. Il moderno è, cioè, intimamente storico e arcaico, perché ha bisogno dell'antico per richiamarsi e, insieme, opporsi ad esso." Agamben, *L'uso dei corpi*, 225.
8   As Hartmut Böhme put it, "modernity is a radically historical era. By which I mean: powerful traditions continue to exist in it, despite having nothing to do with modernity genealogically; they nonetheless belong to its present. Although modernity locates itself in a position that opposes all of history (otherwise it would not be modern), at the same time, more than any other era, it embodies the presence of all previous historical periods (otherwise, it would not exist)." Böhme, *Fetishism and Culture*, 14.
9   See Derrida, *La Dissémination*, 220–2.
10 Derrida, "Différance," in *Margins of Philosophy*, trans. A. Bass (Brighton: Harvester Press, 1982), 1–27.
11 Cf. Pippin, *Modernism as a Philosophical Problem*, 36.

12 The horizon of Being is famously brought in the final sentences of *Being and Time*, as if it were an opening of a vast space which engulfed the second volume of the book and gave rise to the *Kehre*. Heidegger, *Being and Time*, trans. J. Stambaugh (Albany, NY: State University of New York Press, 1996), 398. A critical account of Heidegger's idealistic temporality in his early period might be found I, William D. Blatner, *Heidegger's Temporal Idealism* (Cambridge: Cambridge University Press, 1999).
13 Peter Osborne grasped this dualism: "'Modernity,' we have seen, plays a peculiar dual role as a category of historical periodization: it designates the contemporaneity of an epoch to the time of its classification; yet it registers this contemporaneity in terms of a qualitatively new, self-transcending temporality which has the simultaneous effect of distancing the present from even that most recent past with which it is thus identified." Osborne, *The Politics of Time*, 13–14.
14 Agamben, *Homo sacer*, 166–80; ibid., *Quel che resta di Auschwitz*.
15 Analogically, the notion of trans-epoch might pertain to Heidegger's vision of history as ruled by the history of being. When Heidegger claims that "The history of being is the essence of history" (Die Seinsgeschichte ist das Wesen der Geschichte), his *Seinsgeschichte* should be understood precisely as a trans-epoch, determining history while being embedded in it. Heidegger, *Über den Anfang*, 173. Naturally, the pre-Socratic cut which Heidegger believed (at least in some period of his thinking) to be the determining moment needs to be recognized in its ideological misrepresentation: *the determining moment is nothing else than the onset of modernity.*
16 Therefore, "trans-epoch" should not be confused with Hayden White's "metahistory." The latter term refers to methods of constructing the past in historiographic narratives. Hayden White, *Metahistory: The Historical Imagination in Nineteenth-Century Europe* (Baltimore, MD, and London: Johns Hopkins University Press, 1975), 21. "Trans-epoch," however, refers to the very conditions of emergence of particular histories organized around their sovereign center.
17 Heidegger himself notices the difference between a trans-epoch (conceived of as "the essence of history of Being") and a history of events: "Die Vollendung der Metaphysik ist nur aus dem Wesen der Geschichte des Seyns zu erfahren; nicht historisch nach 'Fakten' zu errechnen am Zeitpunkt eines Niederganges." Heidegger, *Gesamtausgabe, Band 71, Das Ereignis*, 267.
18 It is in this sense that Peter Osborne rightly remarks (with an inspiration from Adorno) that modernity can never be identified with temporal characteristics, but it is always qualitative. Osborne, *The Politics of Time*, 9.
19 It is for the very same reason that, as Agamben remarks, our epoch "no longer wants to be a historical epoch." Agamben, *Idea della prosa* (Macerata: Quodlibet, 2002), 71. In an unconscious way, it recognizes that it does not belong to the array of epochs, hence its perpetual historical crisis. As Peter Osborne argued:

> Narrative is in crisis as a "living" form. It can no longer communicate historical experience. This crisis is the very meaning of modernity as a destruction of tradition. So profound is the crisis, in fact, that Benjamin can, literally, no longer conceive of the possibility of a return to tradition; nor, as we shall see, from the standpoint of his conception of history, is it something that appears desirable.

Osborne, *The Politics of Time*, 133.
20 D. A. F. de Sade, "Français! Encore un effort si vous voulez être Républicains!," in *L'Œuvre du Marquis de Sade* (Paris: Bibliothèque des Curieux, 1909), 197–253.

21 As a result, the paradigmatically modern response to the fiasco of a revolution—or of a political project—almost automatically produces the injunction to push forward, mobilize even more forces and spend more effort. See, in this regard, Žižek's appraisal of Lenin's desperation after the world revolution did not happen: Žižek, *Living in the End Times* (London and New York: Verso, 2011), 477–8. The new formation of sovereignty is, in its own perception, invincible, if only it does not give up itself. Only a total catastrophe might eliminate it, although in its own framework, it still seems to exist.

22 "Von allem, was ist, lag die Bedeutung in dem Lichtfaden, durch den es an den Himmel geknüpft war." Hegel, *Phänomenologie des Geistes*, 14.

23 See Catherine Malabou, *The Future of Hegel: Plasticity, Temporality and Dialectic*, trans. L. During (London and New York: Routledge, 2005), 103–14.

24 In the famous fragment from *La gaya scienza*, entitled, "The Madman," Nietzsche notes that *everything has already happened,* but we are just waiting for the moment when we realize it—and this moment may never come. Nietzsche, *The Gay Science*, 119–20.

25 For this reason, the topos of the death of God should be traced rather to Hegel and his self-assertion of humanity in the post-theological emptiness. See Arendt, *Thinking*, 37.

26 Apart from Alenka Zupančič's brilliant interpretation in *The Shortest Shadow*.

27 In one of the most brilliant interpretations of Hegel ever written, Žižek remarks: "subject is the truth of substance: the truth of every substantial thing is that it is the retroactive effect of its own loss. Subject as S does not pre-exist its loss, it emerges from its loss as a return to itself. In other words, subject is not only always barred, lost, failed, it is a name for such a loss which retroactively creates what is lost." Žižek, *Disparities*, 134. This *existence as and through expropriation* should be, however, related to modernity. It is in this epoch that things exist as retroactive effects of their own loss. If so, the name of this wound inflicted by expropriation is sovereignty. For this reason, in each modern being, there is a gaping lack, opened by sovereignty, and controllable by a particular sovereign.

28 Derrida, *Spectres of Marx: The State of the Debt, the Work of Mourning and the New International*, trans. P. Kamuff (New York and London: Routledge, 1994), 20–37.

29 Nietzsche's intuition about the slowness of the coming message on the death of God/gods pervades *La gaya scienza*. See Nietzsche, *The Gay Science*, 109.

30 See Lacan, *Le Séminaire. Livre VI—Le Désir et son interpretation* (Paris: Éditions de la Martinière, 2013), 18; *Le Séminaire. Livre XI*, 143–54, 167; Žižek, *Tarrying with the Negative: Kant, Hegel, and the Critique of Ideology* (Durham, NC: Duke University Press, 1993), 196–9; ibid., *Incontinence of the Void*, 32; ibid., *Less than Nothing*, 228, 487–8.

31 Heidegger, *Überwindung der Metaphysik*, 67–98.

32 In this sense, Marcuse was right when claiming that: "The critical theory of society possesses no concepts which could bridge the gap between the present and its future; holding no promise and showing no success, it remains negative. Thus it wants to remain loyal to those who, without hope, have given and give their life to the Great Refusal." Marcuse, *One-Dimensional Man*, 261. The Great Refusal is nothing but the ultimate negative form of referring to modernity by dissociating from it: we cannot see the new era, but by condemning the current in most radical terms, *we point to it apophantically*.

33 In *Sauf le nom*, Derrida recognizes traces of negative theology in deconstruction which, in his description, is "l'expérience même de la possibilité (impossible) de l'impossible." Derrida, *Sauf le nom*, 32. In the very same manner, the end of modernity

is an impossible possibility of the impossible: an indelible trace of modality, which will always bait us with paths of negative theology and always remain a point of radical impossibility. See also Derrida, *Comment ne pas parler. Dénégations* in *Psyché. Inventions de l'autre* (Paris: Galilée, 1987), 541–52.
34 On the different conceptions of social time in modernity, see Rosa, *Social Acceleration*, 1–20.
35 Cf. Agamben, *Il regno e la gloria*, 120–30. Agamben claims that the modern state in its dissociation between the legislative (producing laws suspended per se) and the executive (applying laws and thus occupying the suspended emptiness of the law) are deducible from Christian theology. Ibid., 159. His perspicacious description of relations between the legislative and the executive must be, however, supplemented with recognition of the fact that it is the essence of modern sovereignty that produces this rift.
36 Ernst Bloch himself elaborated a category which grasps—at least to a certain extent—this multiplicity of histories: the simultaneity of the non-simultaneous ("die Gleichzeitigkeit der Ungleichzeitigen"). The concept stems from the very beginnings of Bloch's thought. See Bloch, *Geist der Utopie* (Frankfurt am Main: Suhrkamp, 1972), 91. It gained its true importance in the analyses of Nazism developed in the late 1920s and the 1930s, finally published in the volume *Erbschaft dieser Zeit*. Bloch, *Werkausgabe, Band 4, Erbschaft dieser Zeit* (Frankfurt am Main: Suhrkamp, 1985). In this usage, it was applied to describe the simultaneous coexistence, within one and the same society, of many elements (social strata, customs, ideologies, beliefs, imageries, etc.) which had their origins in different moments of history. Extrapolating Marx's suggestions, Bloch believed that progress never eradicates the past once and forever. On the contrary, obsolete elements, once defeated by the force of progress, are pushed aside and subsist at the margins of society. Bloch, *Geist der Utopie*, 91. For this reason, modern society is never properly modern: it may as well to a high extent harbor premodern beliefs or prejudices. Society develops by differentiation in time: there are areas which are most up to date and those which lag behind. The success of Fascists and Nazis can be explained by noticing that in their political propaganda, they addressed the obsolete strata of population via their latent out-of-date content of dreams and phantasies. Bloch, *Werkausgabe, Band 4, Erbschaft dieser Zeit*, 98–116. In Bloch's theory, all these non-simultaneous elements coexist at the same time within one and the same society. In a later crucial move, Bloch assumes that times are multiple: each culture is governed by its own. Bloch, *Werkausgabe, Band 13, Tübinger Einleitung in die Philosophie*, 135. Simultaneity of the non-simultaneous is thus transformed into a universal theory of multidimensional times which interact within cultures, societies, or individual thinkers' works, producing unpredictable clashes and synergies. Bloch, *Gespräche mit Ernst Bloch*, edited by Rainer Trauband Harald Wieser (Frankfurt am Main: Suhrkamp, 1975), 197–8.
37 Freud, *Beyond the Pleasure Principle*, trans. J. Strachey (New York and London: W.W. Norton & Co., 1961), 1–58.
38 See Žižek, *Tarrying with the Negative*, 180–1; ibid., *Incontinence of the Void*, 40–1.
39 Cf. Peter Osborne's exquisite reflection on how history can be built only against the end of history, just as Heidegger's *Dasein* is rooted in its anticipated death. Osborne, *The Politics of Time*, 61.
40 Peter Trawny rightly noted Heidegger's naming of this area as *Adyton*, an unapproachable place of divine cryptic murmur and a resort of the weak and the wounded. Trawny, *Adyton*, 7–13. In fact, this is a place of subsovereign perpetuity, in

which all the weakness becomes immortalized and excused, *as it is only waiting for the miracle.*

41 Adorno noted with perspicacity the uncanny affinity between Heidegger's lingering before the final decision (obfuscated by repetitive calls for making one) and the practice of modern sovereign apparatus of power, embodied in administration. Commenting on Heidegger's pedantic style, he noticed in *The Jargon of Authenticity*, Heidegger's "reciprocity of the personal and apersonal in the jargon; the apparent humanization of the thingly, the actual turning of man into thing." Adorno, *The Jargon of Authenticity*, trans. K. Tarnowski and F. Will (London and New York: Routledge, 2003), 67–8.

42 Emil Fackenheim rightly pointed out that Heidegger lacked the ability to say "no" to both Apollo and Baal—the very same "no" which opens the path for Jewish existence. Fackenheim, *Encounters between Judaism and Modern Philosophy*, 223.

43 Heidegger, *Gesamtausgabe, Band 71, Das Ereignis*; and ibid., *Gesamtausgabe, Band 65, Beiträge zur Philosophie.*

44 Cf. Agamben's reinterpretation of *Ereignis* as *avventura*, in which the living become human inasmuch as being happens to them. Agamben, *L'avventura* (Roma: Nottetempo, 2015), 62–6.

45 In his post-*Kehre* period, Heidegger reaches for this "ground-zero" of destitution in writing. In a remarkable way, the modern drive smashes his previous attachment to abstruse styles of German academic writing. In *Beiträge*, he remarks:

> If a history is still to be granted to us, i.e., a style of Da-sein, then this *can* only be the *sheltered history of deep stillness*, in and as which the mastery of the last god opens and shapes beings. Thus, the deep stillness must first come over the world for the earth. This stillness only springs forth from reticence. And this reticence only grows out of reservedness. As grounding-attunement, reservedness thoroughly tunes the intimacy of the strife between world and earth and thus the strifing of the onset of en-ownment.

Heidegger, *Contributions to Philosophy (From Enowning)*, trans. P. Emad and K. Maly (Bloomington and Indianapolis, IN: Indiana University Press, 1999), 25. This silence, "grounding-attunement" is the sought-for destitution as the most basic matrix of modernity.

46 Heidegger, *Gesamtausgabe, Band 69, Die Geschichte des Seyns* (Frankfurt am Main: Vittorio Klostermann, 1998), 140.

47 Freud, *Beyond the Pleasure Principle*, 58.

48 Benjamin, *Agesilaus Santander (erste und zweite Fassung)* in *Gesammelte Schriften, Band 6* (Frankfurt am Main: Suhrkamp, 1991), 520–3.

49 "... ich unterm Saturn zur Welt kam—dem Planeten der langsamen Umdrehung, dem Gestirn des Zögerns und Verspätens" [first version]. Ibid., 521. Or, as developed in the second version, "dem Planeten der Umwege und der Verspätungen." Ibid., 522.

50 Heidegger, *Contributions to Philosophy*, 3. German version: *Gesamtausgabe, Band 65, Beiträge zur Philosophie*, 4.

51 Cf. Derrida, *D'un ton apocalyptique.*

52 Lenin's famous theory propounded in *State and Revolution* demonstrates to which degree he was outtricked by sovereignty. Lenin proclaims, after Engels, that: "The suppression of the bourgeois state by the proletarian state is impossible without a violent revolution. The abolition of the proletarian state, i.e., of the state in general, is impossible except through the process of 'withering away.'" Lenin, *State and Revolution*, trans. T. Chretien (Chicago, IL: Haymarket Books, 2014), 58. Thus, *he*

already imagines the process of dismantling of the state through the lens of sovereign suspension. The state after the revolution turns into the famous "semistate." Ibid., 54. This "semistate" retains the dualist tension inherent in sovereignty. It is both a state and not a state, a state preparing its own "withering away," namely a state at fight with itself. If we stick to the narrow political definition of sovereignty, it might be imagined that the sovereign state "just" gradually disappears. But, if we understand sovereignty broadly enough, with Hegelian inspirations, it turns out that the whole framework in which this "semistate" is put is a manifest work of modern sovereignty. The actual absurdity of the state under real socialism—the state which intensified control, discipline, and coercion while obliquely referring to its supposed future disappearance—repeats the sovereign suspension between reign and government. The state officially ceases to reign, but it governs until it disappears. Thus, its power is *permanently provisional* and, as such, unaccountable in the light of its own principles. Therefore, all the moments when the state "withdraws from itself" by accentuating its transience, "working" character of its institutions (as in Marx's and Lenin's critiques of parliamentarism, which is supposed to be replaced by "working" bodies) open the way to intensifying control and discipline beyond any symbolic frames. Ibid., 82–4. The destruction of the state, therefore, must be just a prelude to a much more serious task: *the overcoming of sovereignty*.
53 See Eric Hobsbawm, *How to Change the Worl: Reflections on Marx and Marxism* (New Haven, CT, and London: Yale University Press, 2011), 54.
54 Georges Sorel, *Reflections on Violence*, trans. J. Jennings (Cambridge: Cambridge University Press, 1999), 105–11.
55 It is ironic that a more adamant rebuttal of nationalism was given by a post-Christian Platonist, Julien Benda, who denounced the process in which nationalism sneaks its way into ordinary life as something obvious and pragmatic. See Benda, *The Treason of the Intellectuals*, trans. R. Kimball (Abingdon: Routledge, 2006 [1928]). Without the sharpness of vision that Benda had, Marxism easily allowed its internationalism to practically degenerate into a cooperation between nationalisms.
56 See Hobsbawm, *Nations and Nationalism since 1780: Programme, Myth, Reality* (Cambridge: Cambridge University Press, 1990).
57 From this point of view, the element of sovereingty in Marxism must be reconsidered with utmost criticism and, by any means, it cannot be eulogized, even mildly—like Jodi Dean does by acknowledging its inescapability. Dean, *The Communist Horizon* (London and New York: Verso, 2012), 118. Sovereignty of the people over itself is a concept rich in side effects, which require an in-depth analysis.
58 As modernity is the spatio-temporal tissue of capitalism, they both share the aura of inner imperishability. Wolfgang Streeck rightly noted that: "the capitalist order still exists may well appear less impressive than that it existed so often on the brink of collapse and had continuously to change, frequently depending on contingent exogenous supports that it was unable to mobilize endogenously." Streeck, *How Will Capitalism End? Essays on a Failing System* (London and New York: Verso, 2016), 4. As Žižek once noted, "capitalism is the first socio-economic order which *de-totalizes* meaning: it is not global at the level of meaning." Žižek, *Trouble in Paradise: From the End of History to the End of Capitalism* (London: Penguin Books, 2015), 7. Hence the blurriness of its boundaries and its inner perspective of everlasting open-endedness.
59 This is, perhaps, what Heidegger calls *Vollendung der Neuzeit*. See Heidegger, *Gesamtausgabe, Band 66, Besinnung*, 23–9.

Chapter 4 The Unfinished Time of Modernity

1. Historical linearity of perspectives provides a milieu for historiographies to develop. Many of them, as Siegfried Kracauer once noted, "conceive[s] of history as an immanent continuous process in linear or chronological time which on its part is thought of as a flow in an irreversible direction, a homogeneous medium indiscriminately comprising all events imaginable." Siegfried Kracauer, *History: The Last Things before the Last* (Princeton, NJ: Markus Wiener Publishers, 1995), 139.
2. On the French revolutionary myth of a new beginning, ushering in the era of freedom, see: Jean Starobinski, *L'Invention de la liberté* (Paris: Skira, 1964); ibid., *Les Emblèmes de la raison* (Paris: Flammarion, 1973).
3. *Le Calendrier républicain: De sa création à sa disparition suivi d'une concordance avec le calendrier grégorien* (Paris: Bureau des longitudes, 1994).
4. As Derrida observes (commenting on Celan), the re-marks epitomized in each calendar (the repeatability of dates, which associate seemingly non-linked events) demonstrate how temporal existence splits into radical unrepeatable singularity and its endless spectral return. Derrida, *Schibboleth pour Paul Celan* (Paris: Galilée, 1986), 37. Yet, perhaps this split is the effect of the modern collapse of transcendence: *existence has no in-built solid time—it always appears as one-off, in all intensity of its singular appearance, only to continue its life as a spectre.*
5. This feature corresponds to Foucault's observation that the modern state opens a horizon of indefinite time. See Foucault, *Security, Territory, Population: Lectures at the Collège De France 1977–78*, trans. G. Burchell (Basingstoke and New York: Palgrave, 2007), 293.
6. See also Chantal Mouffe and Ernesto Laclau, *Hegemony and Socialist Strategy: Towards a Radical Democratic Politics* (London and New York: Verso, 2001 [1985]), 186–8.
7. Immanuel Kant, "Toward Perpetual Peace: A Philosophical Sketch," in *Toward Perpetual Peace and Other Writings on Politics, Peace, and History*, trans. D. L. Colclasure (New Haven, CT, and London: Yale University Press, 2006), 67.
8. Francis Scott Fitzgerald, *The Great Gatsby* (Oxford: Oxford University Press, 2008 [1925]), 144.
9. See Žižek, *In Defence of Lost Causes* (London and New York: Verso, 2008).
10. Kafka, *Zürau Aphorismen*, 114.
11. Zygmunt Bauman, *Living on Borrowed Time: Conversations with Citlali Rovirosa-Madrazo* (Cambridge: Polity Press, 2010).
12. See George Steiner, *In Bluebeard's Castle: Some Notes towards the Re-definition of Culture* (London: Faber & Faber, 1971), 13–27.
13. Marx, *The Poverty of Philosophy* (Moscow: Foreign Languages Publishing House, 1962), 135.
14. Ibid., *Capital: Critique of Political Economy*, trans. B. Fawkes, Vol. 1 (Harmondsworth and New York: Penguin, 1976), 280.
15. See Søren Kierkegaard, *Concluding Unscientific Postscript*, trans. A. Hannay (Cambridge: Cambridge University Press, 2009), 21–43, 51–106.
16. Foucault, *"Society Must Be Defended,"* 15.
17. Robert B. Pippin provided a comprehensive analysis of Hegel's notion—even if sometimes beating about the bush—in Pippin, *Hegel's Idealism: The Satisfaction of Self-Consciousness* (Cambridge: Cambridge University Press, 1989), 232–57.
18. Fredric Jameson put this succinctly: "The ultimate Notion or *Begriff* is then a fully self-sufficient concept which is a kind of *causa sui* or 'cause of itself': Spinoza's 'God or

Nature' would be an appropriate analogy . . ." Jameson, *Valences of the Dialectic*, 76. Kojève pointed out that *Begriff* might be understood only as "l'Uni-totalité qui integer l'*ensemble* des Choses qui 'correspondent' aux Notions et des Notions qui se 'rapportent' aux Choses." Kojève, *Le Concept, le Temps et le Discours*, 102. Annette Sell noticed *Begriff*'s inherently "self-referential structure" which necessarily produces reality. Sell, *Der lebendige Begriff. Leben und Logik bei G. W. F. Hegel* (Freiburg/ München: Karl Alber, 2013), 213. See also Hong-Bin Lim's remark on *Begriff*'s appearance as "the linguistic articulation of self-referential negativity of the very substance." Lim, *Absoluter Unterschied und Begriff in der Philosophie Hegels* (Frankfurt am Main: Peter Lang, 1989), 234.

19 See also Agamben, *La Potenza del pensiero*, 180–1; Comay and Ruda, *The Dash . . .*, 7; and Žižek, *Sex and the Failed Absolute*, 146.
20 See also Lakebrink, *Kommentar zu Hegels "Logik" in seiner "Enzyklopädie" von 1830*, Band 2, 300–2.
21 Kojève, *Introduction à la lecture de Hegel*, 382–4. In his unfinished *Introduction au Système du Savoir*, Kojève takes this discovery for a cornerstone of his exposition, although it becomes normalized in the process. Nevertheless, he lucidly defines *Begriff* as "*la totalité-intégrée de ce qui est concevable (pris en tant que concevable)*" and, in this form, being time itself. Kojève, *Le Concept, le temps et le discours*, 168. For this very same reason, Arendt is not radical enough while claiming that in Hegel "man is time." Arendt, *The Life of the Mind*, 42. *Time is an inherent constructive element of knowledge and sovereignty in modernity.*
22 See Marx, "'Preface' to *A Contribution to the Critique of Political Economy*," in *Early Writings*, trans. R. Livingstone and G. Benton (London: Penguin Books, 1992), 426. See also Althusser and Balibar, *Reading Capital*, 277–8.
23 In this regard, Herbert Marcuse noted perspicaciously that the key differences between Hegel and Marx in their approach to history consist in treating history either as universal (Hegel) or as circumscribed (Marx). Marcuse, *Reason and* Revolution, 315–16.
24 Benjamin, *On the Concept of History*, 261.
25 Jules Michelet, *Histoire de la Révolution française*, Vol. 1 (Paris, 1889), 31–2.
26 René Descartes, "Meditations on the First Philosophy," in *A Discourse on Method; Meditations on the First Philosophy; Principles of Philosophy*, trans. J. Veitch (London: Dent & Sons, 1912), 107–8.
27 See, for example, Žižek's in-depth analysis of Descartes' premodern blindness in relation to the already modern Kant. Žižek, *Tarrying with the Negative*, 10–18.
28 A contingent footnote is a good place to declare when, according to one's own opinion, modernity began. I am tempted to believe it began on 24 October 1776, when Jean-Jacques Rousseau was hit by a car during his strolls in North-Eastern Paris.
29 It is in this sense that we might understand Henri Lefèbvre's general intuition that modernity introduces "the aleatory on a massive scale in all the areas of consciousness, knowledge and action." Lefèbvre, *Introduction to Modernity*, 204.
30 Agamben, *State of Exception*, 39.
31 In the non-recognition of this phenomenon lies the fundamental mistake of Blumenberg's otherwise meticulous account of the beginning of modernity. He claims that modernity arises as an epoch of self-assertion after the disintegration of the medieval order. Blumenberg, *The Legitimacy of the Modern Age*, 137–43. But, in this, he does not take into account that *history as such must be reinscribed into this self-assertion*. As long as modernity is "defended" through a historical description

which proves that it did not originate as a simple secularization of Christianism, the very framework of "proof" is completely unmodern. When, however, history is recognized as equally "self-asserted," the whole problem of modernity's legitimacy and the need of its "defense" disappear.

32 Žižek, *Sex and the Failed Absolute*, 78.
33 It is the reason why Pippin's otherwise suggestive reading of Hegel is tiringly conservative. Pippin notes that according to Hegel, "Modernity itself is then not a 'revolution', or autochthonous or self-grounding; it is the whole of human history that must be seen as 'absolutely' self-supporting or self-grounding, and modernity is just the beginning of the final realization of this self-consciousness itself, as well as a realization of a telos implicit at the origin of the Western experience." Pippin, *Modernism as a Philosophical Problem*, 70. Yet, precisely the contrary should be acknowledged: modernity is a self-grounding revolution which produces "previous" history as part of its historical machinery.
34 See Karl Löwith, *Meaning in History: The Theological Implications of the Philosophy of History* (Chicago, IL: University of Chicago Press, 1949). See also the critique of Löwith in Blumenberg, *The Legitimacy of the Modern Age*, 27–121.
35 Cf. Agamben, *Pilato e Gesú* (Roma: Nottetempo, 2013), 45.
36 Jacob Taubes, *Occidental Eschatology*, trans. D. Ratmoko (Stanford, CA: Stanford University Press, 2009), 13.
37 Taubes or Löwith's visions of "secularization" are ridiculed by the very process which they label so. George Steiner put it succinctly:

> In our current barbarism an extinct theology is at work, a body of transcendent reference whose slow, incomplete death has produced surrogate, parodistic forms. The epilogue to belief, the passage of religious belief into hollow convention, seems to be a more dangerous process than the *philosophes* anticipated. The structures of decay are toxic. Needing Hell, we have learned how to build and run it on earth. A few miles from Goethe's Weimar or on the isles of Greece."

Steiner, *In Bluebeard's Castle*, 48.

38 In this respect, the ending of Taubes' *Occidental Eschatology* errs when describing the reputed liberation from the boundless Ocean:

> As man makes himself into the measure of all things, the shadows takes center stage, and the correspondence of things with God becomes obscured. This is the darkness and night of the world. If, looking into the beauty of night, man does not mistake it but sees the darkness for what it is; if he recognizes his protective shells as mirages; if he perceives his insistence as dogged resistance and unmasks his self-made measures for the lies and errors they are—then day will dawn on this human world, and the transition from insistence to existence will follow. When day dawns all measures will turn upside down. Man will then be brought home by God and will *ex-ist*, since he will find his center in God. For man is nothing in himself unless he is part of God.

Taubes, *Occidental Eschatology*, 194. Apart from the unbearably metaphysical language, Taubes assumes the very possibility of suspending the modern cut through a comparison with the veiled God. It is God that will make human beings complete, but even if it still has not happened, it might be at least theologically described. But this is

precisely the heart of the problem: the night cannot be described otherwise than by the emptiness of the cut, which absorbs the emptied transcendence and makes the universe boundless. No God stands above it and no salvation *waits* around the corner. Modernity can disappear, but cannot end: this is the precise correlate of the modern cut that inaugurated it.
39 Cf. Agamben's concept of secularization in Agamben, *Profanations*, trans. J. Fort (New York: Zone Books, 2007), 77.
40 As Horkheimer noted, the war that the Enlightenment declared on religion, in which its *truth* was at stake, was in a sense won by religion, because the whole process compromised the very possibility of asking about metaphysical truths with the use of reason. As a result, religion must be tolerated as a social fact and cannot be criticized for its fallacy. Max Horkheimer, *The Eclipse of Reason* (London and New York: Continuum, 2004 [1947]), 12–13.
41 In this sense, sovereignty opens up the hiatus between the event and its consequences, suspending the latter and allowing to see the event in its crystallized, ineffective form. Lacan's vision of the dead God—unconscious of its own death, but effective precisely for this reason—is built upon this hiatus. See Lacan, *Le Séminaire. Livre VII*, 209–17.
42 Hartmut Böhme had a strikingly accurate intuition in claiming that the very construction of modern subjectivity relies on fetishism. Böhme, *Fetishism and Culture*, 2. Much as Böhme is concentrated on the fetishism of material objects, the problem itself is much broader: things may be elevated to the position of fetishes only when at the bottom there is already the structure of rift introduced by sovereignty—with the ruling unassailable principle and concrete realm of government which cannot endanger its position. Fetishism, especially in its material form, would then be a concrete embodiment of modern sovereignty. The "but" ("quand même") on which fetishism is built is precisely the hinge that links sovereign center and the reigned realm.
43 Levinas, *Totality and Infinity*, 194–204; *Liberté et commandement* (Montpellier: Fata Morgana, 1994), 66; *Autrement qu'être ou au-delà de l'essence* (La Haye: Nijhoff, 1978), 56. In the epiphany of the face, Levinas uses Heideggerian powers of negativity ostensibly to an ethical purpose. Yet, the engine of his thinking still relies on it, without leaving the trap of endless *rediverting* negativity. One is never more cunning than negativity: at best, the match is a stalemate and negativity wins by deferral.

Chapter 5 Sovereign Suspension and Provisionality

1 Kafka, "An Imperial Message," in *The Complete Stories*, 4–5.
2 On the emergence of the sublime in the context of eighteenth-century melancholy, see Starobinski, *L'invention de la liberté*.
3 Kant, *The Critique of Judgment*, trans. J. H. Bernard (London: Macmillan, 1914), 125.
4 See Jean-François Lyotard, *Lessons on the Analytic of the Sublime*, trans. E. Rottenberg (Stanford, CA: Stanford University Press, 1994), 77–146; Jean-Luc Nancy, *Une Pensée finie* (Paris: Galilée, 1990), 169–93. Parenthetically, Kant's sublime in mathematics may be read as grasping the extortionate disproportion between life-world comprehensibility and the modern language of mathematics, whose history, as George Steiner noted, "is one of progressive untranslatability." Steiner, "The Retreat from the Word," in *Language and Silence: Essays on Language, Literature, and the Inhuman* (New Haven, CT, and London: Yale University Press, 1998), 14.

5 Kant, *The Critique of Judgment*, 109.
6 Ibid., 110.
7 Ibid., 116.
8 See also Lacan, *Le Séminaire. Livre VII*, 303, 363–7; and Zupančič, *Ethics of the Real: Kant, Lacan* (London and New York: Verso, 2000), 158.
9 Kant, *The Critique of Judgment*, 119–20.
10 In comparison with Lyotard's understanding of the sublime as evoked by the differend, this move might be understood as a kind of chiasm: instead of perceiving the differend as a modern phenomenon related to the sublime, the whole of modernity should be viewed as an opening abyss which makes the sublime a basic experience of the continuously opening rift. Lyotard, *Lessons on the Analytic of the Sublime*, 123–4.
11 See Heidegger, *Being and Time*, 229–46.
12 In this respect, Agamben's work is internally incoherent. In *Stato di eccezione*, Agamben openly admits that the state of exception in his understanding emerged at the outbreak of modernity, namely in the French Revolution. Agamben, *Stato di eccezione*, 21–32. The breakthrough of this discovery is, however, obfuscated with "universal" and pan-historical explanations of the state of exception by: (1) assumption of historical continuity (and ample references to Roman or Christian legal devices and concepts), and (2) associating it with functioning of the language itself. Agamben, *The Open: Man and Animal*, trans. K. Attell (Stanford, CA: Stanford University Press, 2004), 27–30, 80; *Che cos'è la filosofia?* (Macerata: Quodlibet, 2016), 25–9, 40; *The Sacrament of Language: An Archeology of the Oath (Homo sacer II, 3)*, trans. Adam Kotsko (Cambridge: Polity Press, 2010), 10–11, 55–8, 68–9; *L'uso dei corpi*, 334.
13 René Descartes, *Discourse on Method* in *Discourse on Method and Metaphysical Meditations*, trans. G. B. Rawlings (London and Felling-on-Tyne: Walter Scott Publishing, 1901), 26–7, 29–30.
14 Žižek, *The Parallax View*, 274. In *Disparities*, he uses this Cartesian metaphor (after Jean-Claude Milner) in order to describe the action of a revolutionary leader: it is not important in which direction s/he leads the revolution, but that there is *some* uniform direction. Žižek, *Disparities*, 252–262. This close circuit between Descartes' evocative image and Stalinist politics points to the modern rule of provisionality.
15 In obvious contrast to Heidegger's Nazi period, which displays a unique blend of Descartianism, modernism, and National Socialism, embodied in a sentence from *Schwarze Hefte*: "Trotz aller Widerstände, Verkehrungen und Rückschläge nicht abbiegen und nicht nachlassen. Aber *wozu* die *Versuche in einer abgelegenen Ecke?*" Heidegger, *Gesamtausgabe. Band 94*, 119. Here, the Mirror Star ominously joins inner drives and self-declared rigidity with an external Nazi goal.
16 Bloch, *Werkausgabe Band 13*, 335.
17 It is in this respect that parables are eerie cognates to other spectral categories which are suspended between existence and non-existence, hovering over the question of existence through their embedment in possibility. Derrida's infrastructures in Gasché's portrayal function analogously: they neither are nor are not. Gasché, *The Tain of the Mirror*, 148–51. They belong to a *space* which in a sense is preontological, not-yet-entangled in ontological categories. It is because possibility is a term that we use in modernity to refer, from our side, to the spectral realm of neither/nor which is the locus of sovereignty.
18 The difference between reign and governance, implied by Foucault and greatly developed by Agamben, requires further study. Contrary to Agamben's ahistorical

deduction of this difference from Christian economy of salvation, the split between the facade of reigning, but suspended principles and the provisional practice of governing which develops in the abyss of suspension, is purely modern. Agamben himself refers to one of the incarnations of this rift—the difference between the legislative and the executive, giving only modern examples (Agamben, *Il regno e la gloria*, 158–9, 300–13). In itself, this difference appeared as a direct epiphenomenon of modern sovereignty. The emptiness of the suspended, which gives rise to the provisional, yet permanent government, is an organizing principle of modernity as a trans-epoch.

19 Foucault perspicaciously recognized provisionality as the feature of modern administration and police, always dealing with concrete details and leaving great principles aside. See Foucault, *Security, Territory, Population*, 340.

20 Primo Levi, *If This is a Man . . .*, trans. S. Woolf (New York: Orion Press, 1959), 159–63.

21 The Third Reich demonstrates in this regard the truly diabolic nature of Carl Schmitt's *katechon*: the alleged "protector," the withholding power, is a true cause of the apocalypse, although shrouded in the cowardly mask of defender against the imaginary chaos. Schmitt claims that "as long as the empire is there, the world does not fall (geht . . . unter)." Frank Hertwec and Dimitrios Kisoudis (eds), "*Solange das Imperium da is.*" *Carl Schmitt im Gespräch 1971* (Berlin: Duncker & Humblot, 2010), 50. This empire, however, is part and parcel of the chaos it allegedly withholds and, as such, might use its permanent provisional position to execute unbridled and atrocious power. *Perhaps then we should not be afraid of chaos, but rather of those who promise to defend us against it.*

22 Levi, *If This is a Man . . .*, 183.

23 Ibid., 185–7.

24 Kafka, "On parables," in *The Complete Stories*, 457.

25 Agamben, *Il fuoco e il racconto* (Roma: Nottetempo, 2014), 35.

26 Nowhere perhaps is this phenomenon more visible than in deconstruction. In his conversations with Maurizio Ferraris, Derrida once declared: "Pourquoi écrire? J'ai toujours le sentiment, à la fois très modeste et hyperboliquement présomptueux, que je n'ai rien à dire. Je n'ai pas le sentiment que j'ai en moi quelque chose d'intéressant qui devrait m'autoriser à dire: 'voilà le livre que j'ai projeté moi-même, sans que personne me l'ait demandé.'" Benoît Peeters, *Derrida* (Paris: Flammarion, 2010), 527–8. This declaration is much more than an act of self-flattering. In truth, deconstruction begins where *one has nothing (positive) to say*. Then the text is borne out of the initial void and rests upon negativity, always marked by its force.

27 Wittgenstein, *Philosophical Investigations*, 93–4.

28 Hans Jonas, "The Concept of God after Auschwitz: A Jewish Voice," *Journal of Religion*, Vol. 67, No. 1 (1987), 12. See also Steiner's much more sober vision, Steiner, "A Kind of Survivor," in *Language and Silence*, 142, and Žižek's view of the appearance of God as "god of sacred terror": *Sex and the Failed Absolute*, 402–3.

29 Lyotard, while depicting his notion of the differend—a radical discrepancy and untranslatability between discourses—noted that:

> the "perfect crime" does not consist in killing the victim or the witnesses (that adds new crimes to the first one and aggravates the difficulty of effacing everything), but rather in obtaining the silence of the witnesses, the deafness of the judges, and the inconsistency (insanity) of the testimony. . . . If there is nobody to adduce the proof, nobody to admit it, and/or if the argument which

upholds it is judged to be absurd, then the plaintiff is dismissed, the wrong he or she complains of cannot be attested. He or she becomes a victim.

Lyotard, *The Differend: Phrases in Dispute*, trans. G. Van Den Abbeele (Manchester: Manchester University Press, 1988), 8. Is not the death of God a perfect crime in which the victim is simultaneously the plaintiff, silenced to death, buried under the muteness of its incomprehensibility?

30 Kafka, "The New Advocate," in *The Complete Stories*, 414–15.
31 Cf. Agamben, *Idea della prosa*, 44–5.
32 See also its development in ahistorical reference to Paul (with a deceiving apology of power that is officially demised, but governs provisionally) in Agamben, *The Time that Remains: A Commentary on the Letter to the Romans*, trans. P. Dailey (Stanford, CA: Stanford University Press, 2005).
33 The paranoia of Daniel Schreber is a great testimony to the backlash of emptiness at the heart of sovereign power clouded in law. See Eric L. Santner, *My Own Private Germany: Daniel Paul Schreber's Secret History of Modernity* (Princeton, NJ: Princeton University Press, 1996).
34 Alain Badiou at least identified the emptiness of provisionality at the very heart of revolutionary projects. Badiou, *L'Hypothèse communiste*, 28.
35 Cf. Bloch, *Gesamtausgabe, Band 6, Naturrecht und menschliche Würde* (Frankfurt am Main: Suhrkamp, 1977), 254–9.
36 "The waiting for the Messiah marks the very duration of time," remarks Levinas. Levinas, *Difficult Freedom: Essays on Judaism*, trans. S. Hand, (Baltimore, MD: John Hopkins University Press, 1997), 26.

Chapter 6 The Big Bang of Modernity

1 Benjamin, *On the Concept of History*, 257–8.
2 Cf. Derrida, *Force de loi: Le Fondement mystique de l'autorité* (Paris: Galilée, 2005).
3 In his splendid essay, "Le langage à l'infini," Foucault tracked the emergence of the language that we know, the one which produces literature. Instead of posing infinity out of itself and making itself a mirror of it—just as premodern language did—modern language turns to its source. It mirrors the humming which fills its own depth in order to make it melt with its own voice; therefore, it never stops and has infinity within itself. De Sade's work is an early and telling example of how modern language explodes from engulfing infinity that pushes it to the brink of signifying force. Foucault, "Le Langage à l'infini," in *Dits et écrits 1954–1988*, Vol. 1 (Paris: Gallimard, 2001), 278–89.
4 Or, as George Steiner would put it, modern language ceased to encompass "the whole of experience and reality" and "the words themselves seem to have lost some of their precision and validity." Steiner, *The Retreat from the Word*, 24–5.
5 See Roberto Esposito, *Politica e negazione. Per una filozofia affermativa* (Torino: Einaudi, 2018), vii–120.
6 For a different account of modern political fetishism see: Böhme, *Fetishism and Culture*, 200–22.
7 Kafka, *The Castle*, trans. A. Bell (Oxford and New York: Oxford University Press, 2009), 236.
8 Maggie Nelson, *Bluets* (London: Jonathan Cape, 2017), 51.

9   As Peter Trawny rightly pointed out, from a certain moment on Heidegger displays a unique kind of ontologico-historical antisemitism ("seinsgeschichtlicher Antisemitismus"). Peter Trawny, *Heidegger und der Mythos der jüdischen Weltverschwörung* (Frankfurt am Main: Klostermann, 2014), 11. See also Nancy, *Banalité de Heidegger* (Paris: Galilée, 2015), 26–7; Donatella di Cesare, *Heidegger e gli ebrei. I "Quaderni neri"* (Torino: Bollati Boringhieri, 2014).
10 Heidegger, *Aus der Erfahrung des Denkens*, 81. In the *Schwarze Hefte* the maxim goes even further: "Nur wenn wir wirklich irren—in die Irre gehen, können wir auf 'Wahrheit' stoßen. Die tiefe, unheimliche und d.h. zugleich große Stimmung des Irrgängers im Ganzen: *der Philosoph*." Heidegger, *Gesamtausgabe, Band 94*, 13.
11 Heidegger, *Antrag auf die Wiedereinstellung in die Lehrtätigkeit (Reintegrierung)* in *Gesamtausgabe, Band 16*, 398.
12 Heidegger, *Das Rektorat 1933/34. Tatsachen und Gedanken* in *Gesamtausgabe, Band 16*, 389–90.
13 This basic presupposition is obviously not Heideggerian in itself; it gives a foothold to many philosophies, including the thought of a great anti-Heideggerianist, Adorno. Cf. Lyotard, *Heidegger et "les juifs"* (Paris: Galilée, 1988), 76–7.
14 See Victor Farías, *Heidegger and Nazism*, trans. by P. Burrell and G. R. Ricci (Philadelphia, PA: Temple University Press, 1989), 79–187.
15 Arendt, for example, noted that: "It apparently never occurred to Heidegger that by making all men who listen to the 'call of conscience' equally guilty, he was actually proclaiming universal innocence: where everybody is guilty, nobody is." Arendt, *Life of Mind*, 184.
16 It is worth noticing that in this manner, Heidegger performs his usual gesture of depth-reaching overbidding, which he so successfully applied to the previous philosophical tradition. Pierre Bourdieu reconstructed with his unique perspicacity how Heidegger entered and conquered the philosophical field by claiming the profundity of his approach, to which everybody needed to relate. Bourdieu, *L'Ontologie politique de Martin Heidegger* (Paris: Éditions de minuit, 1988), 38–75. Justifying his political stance, he does the same: *even though his actions are comparable to actions of other Nazi adherents, his position is allegedly different due to the ungraspably profound philosophical motives*. This is nothing but blackmail, which attempts to conquer the field in advance by building a sovereign ivory tower.
17 Some of the remarks from *Schwarze Hefte* which describe the political transformation of Germany clearly ring an artificially humble tone in describing the role philosophy has in the change; nevertheless, they concern, in fact, only one person who *accidentally* wrote them down. Heidegger refers to "Die Unvergleichbarkeit der Weltstunde, deren Schlagraum die deutsche Philosophie zum Erklingen bringen soll." Heidegger, *Überlegungen II–VI (Schwarze Hefte 1931–1938)*, 109. In this, against all Hegelianism, he reaches the same position in respect to the crossings between philosophy, history, and politics.
18 In this sense, one can even use the otherwise noble term, *encounter*, to express what happened between Nazism and Heidegger's thought. The encounter is not only political. As Georges-Arthur Goldschmidt demonstrated with a great ear for Heidegger's German, the philosopher entered into a deep linguistic affinity with the Nazi language. Goldschmidt, *Heidegger et la langue allemande* (Paris: CNRS, 2016). The hazy indetermination of Heidegger's German is like a door through which comes not only thinking, but also splinters of political fight in the field of language. The bombastic jargon of his philosophy, so miraculously carving out new horizons, is

simultaneously imbued with most low-down nationalism. It is not even a "tragic mistake," as Goldschmidt suggests. Ibid., 191. It is profound spiritual impoverishment which disguises itself as grandiosity.
19 Heidegger seems to display a mystifying cult of passivity, privately professed also by Carl Schmitt. "*Solange das Imperium da ist*," 54.
20 This trait of Heidegger's thinking is clearly visible in his utterly reactionary support for the NSDAP as a party which opposes communism, the reign of "planetary technique" in Heidegger's view. See Rüdiger Safranski, *Ein Meister aus Deutschland. Heidegger und Zeit* (Frankfurt am Main: Fischer, 1997), 258.
21 Peter Sloterdijk, *Nicht gerettet. Versuche nach Heidegger* (Frankfurt am Main: Suhrkamp, 2001), 54.
22 Lucien Goldmann once noticed that the dialectical legacy of German idealism was obliterated in the second part of the nineteenth century only to be inadvertently rekindled by Husserl and Heidegger, as well as Lukács. Lucien Goldmann, *Lukács et Heidegger* (Paris: Denoël / Gouthier, 1973), 65. If so, then Heidegger takes an unambiguously mistyfing approach to his own rediscovery.
23 Questions are not even re-posed, but we are *held in them*, which is a condition that Heidegger sees as part of true contemporary philosophizing: "die Haltung des weitest und tiefst auslegenden Fragens aus dem Grunde des Daseins—als ginge es um nichts anderes als in erster Einsamkeit dem 'Sein' zum Ausbruch zu verhelfen im wirklichen Werk (Überwindung der Seinsfrage)." Ibid., 12.
24 Adorno, *The Jargon of Authenticity*, 21. Safranski notes that: "Heidegger ist ein Meister darin, die Wege lang zu machen." Safranski, *Ein Meister aus Deutschland*, 168.
25 Derrida, *De l'esprit. Heidegger et la question* (Paris: Galilée, 1987), 109.
26 Mallarmé, *Un coup de dés . . .*, 363.
27 Quentin Meillassoux, *Le Nombre et la sirène. Un déchiffrage du "Coup de dés" de Mallarmé* (Paris: Fayard, 2011).
28 Nietzsche, "The Antichrist," in *The Antichrist, Ecce Homo, The Twilight of the Idols and Other Writings*, 3.
29 *Inter-dits* refer to what is both forbidden and said between the lines of a discourse. See Luce Irigaray, *Speculum. De l'autre femme* (Paris: Les Éditions de Minuit, 1974), 172.
30 "Each thing, as far as it can by its own power, strives to persevere in its being. . . . The striving by which each thing strives to persevere in its being is nothing but the actual essence of the thing." Baruch Spinoza, "The Ethics," in *A Spinoza Reader: The Ethics and Other Works*, trans. E. Curley (Princeton, NJ: Princeton University Press, 1994), 159. Lacan found in this concept the truly pioneering quality of Spinoza's thinking. See Lacan, *Le Séminaire. Livre VI*, 16.
31 Nietzsche, *Beyond Good and Evil*, 153.
32 Spinoza, *The Ethics*, 159.
33 Hobbes, *Leviathan*, 79–88; John Locke, *Second Treatise of Government* (Indianapolis, IN, and Cambridge: Hackett, 1980 [1689]), 9–12; Rousseau, *The Social Contract*, 30–2.
34 Agamben, *Homo sacer*; ibid., *Quel che resta di Auschwitz*.
35 It is in this line—as declaration of a truce-paralysis—that Heidegger's remark from *Schwarze Hefte* might be read: "Das Unwesen des Seins hat alles Sein zerrieben. Geblieben ist: die Flüchtigkeit alles Seienden und entsprechend dies leichteste Habhaft-werden-können des Beliebigsten.—Nichts steht, aber auch nichts entgeht." Heidegger, *Gesamtausgabe, Band 94*, 76.

36 In intellectual terms, however, even the post-war period was ravaged by exhausted pessimism. As the emblematic example, see Judith N. Shklar, *After Utopia: The Decline of Political Faith* (Princeton, NJ: Princeton University Press, 1957).
37 Derrida, *Apprendre à vivre enfin. Entretien avec Jean Birnbaum* (Paris: Galilée/Le Monde, 2005).
38 Cf. Aristotle, *Physics*, book 4, pt 8.
39 See Žižek, *Disparities*, 28.
40 Freud, *Beyond the Pleasure Principle*, 49–50.
41 Cf. Žižek's reformulation of the death drive: "Death drive" means precisely that the most radical tendency of a living organism is to maintain a state of tension, to avoid final "relaxation" in obtaining a state of full homeostasis. "Death drive" as "beyond the pleasure principle" is the very insistence of an organism on endlessly repeating the state of tension." Žižek, *Organs without Bodies* (London: Routledge, 2004), 24. In her excellent book, *What is Sex?*, Alenka Zupančič attempts to reconsider inconsistencies in Freud's understanding of the death drive, presenting it as "a kind of fundamental or *ontological fatigue* of life as such," which is not so much a drive "as a fundamental *affect* of life." Zupančič, *What is Sex?* (Cambridge, MA, and London: MIT Press, 2017), 97–8. Given that the death drive and the pleasure principle both consist in detour—at least in Freud's speculation—they are, as Zupančič lucidly notices, the same phenomenon. Ibid., 98. After linking the death drive with sexuality, she draws the conclusion: the death drive is "*repetition within repetition*: namely, repetition of some (partial, and so to speak, extracurricular) satisfaction accidentally produced within this conservative repetition." Ibid., 102. It draws from an "*inbuilt negativity*" of "the ontological order of being," wanting us not to enjoy for the sake of enjoyment, but for the sake of repeating "the lack of being in the very midst of being." Ibid., 104. Extrapolating Zupančič's interpretation, we might now notice that this repetitive cult of negativity constitutes lasting on which bare life stands. Negativity not only wants to be repeated, re-approached, *shepherded*, but it also requires this more and more often, thus turning life into bare life.
42 Heidegger, *Zur Erörterung der Gelassenheit*.
43 Maurice Blanchot, *La Communauté inavouable* (Paris: Éditions de Minuit, 1984).
44 Jean-Luc Nancy, *La Communauté désœuvrée* (Paris: Christian Bourgois, 1983).
45 Agamben, *The Coming Community*, trans. M. Hardt (Minneapolis, MN: University of Minnesota Press, 1993).
46 Edmond Jabès, *Le Livre de l'Hospitalité* (Paris: Gallimard, 1991).
47 See also Agamben, *La Potenza del pensiero*, 163–4.
48 Rainer Maria Rilke, *The Notebooks of Malte Laurids Brigge*, trans. M. Hulse (London and New York: Penguin Classics, 2009).
49 Kafka, *The Trial*, trans. I. Parry (London and New York: Penguin Classics, 2000).
50 Max Horkheimer, "Egoism and Freedom Movements: On the Anthropology of the Bourgeois Era," in *Between Philosophy and Social Science: Selected Early Writings*, trans. G. F. Hunter, M. S. Kramer, and J. Torpey (Cambridge, MA, and London: MIT Press, 1993), 49–51.
51 Ibid., 51.
52 Cf. Žižek, *The Parallax View*, 118.
53 It is perhaps in this line—restrained only to modernity—that Heidegger's note from *Über den Anfang* should be read: "In der Seinsverlassenheit ist das Seiende weder seiend noch nicht seiend." Heidegger, *Über den Anfang*, 121.
54 Ironically, this face of Marx appears when his writings are not only properly *read*, through its blank spots, but also read philosophically, as Althusser and Balibar

demanded. Althusser and Balibar, *Reading Capital*, 14. Extrapolating their claims, one can even naively ask: why does theoretical practice, that is a "material" as well as a "spiritual" system, whose practice is founded on and articulated to the existing economic, political and ideological practices which directly or indirectly provide it with the essentials of its "raw materials," should be able to leave its universe otherwise than in a powerless unsubstantiated jump? Ibid., 42. Why should it be able to see the truth in a form that would be able to challenge its own conditions of existence? Is it not, paradoxically, more Marxist to believe that theoretical practice is a transcendence in immanence which finds the truth only for the price of deactivating it? If so, then Marxism would not be even allowed to describe the emergence of the non-capitalist (and non-modern) movements, because by referring to them, *producing them theoretically*, it would already drag them into the modern predicament of powerlessness.
55 Instead of criticizing this premise from "purely" economist positions, it is better to see it as an engaged act of refusing the abyssal instability of capitalism in the name of justice. Marx cannot accept the capitalist market as an area that sucks all human beings, commodities, and services into itself and then *destroys their own intrinsic value*, attributing to them only passing commodity value. Within capitalism, all elements are, in effect, deprived of their own meaning; value is always a transient reflection of external relations in which a given element is trapped. Therefore, Marx demands that capitalism should be referred to an accountable, comprehensible, and external measure, i.e., labor time. Much as this approach misrepresents capitalism and, in this way, errs in its conclusions, it contains a powerful *non-modern (and non-premodern) rejection of modernity*.
56 Karl Marx, *Capital: Critique of Political Economy*, trans. by B. Fawkes, Vol. 1 (Harmondsworth and New York: Penguin, 1976), 125–44.
57 Ibid., 142–4, 150.
58 Ibid., 137.
59 Ibid., 266.
60 Ibid., 270.
61 Ibid., 191–4.
62 Lacan, *Le Séminaire. Livre XVII*, 92–3, 123, 203.
63 Marx, *Capital*, Vol. 2, 457–8.
64 Ibid., Vol. 1, 275–7.
65 See Marx, Grundrisse, 90–1.
66 Marx, *Capital*, Vol. 1, 274; ibid., Vol. 3, 1004.
67 Gilles Deleuze, Félix Guattari, *Anti-Oedipus: Capitalism and Schizophrenia*, trans. R. Hutley, M. Seem, and H. R. Lane (Minneapolis, MN: Minnesota University Press, 1983), 1–41.
68 Marx, *Capital*, Vol. 1, 275–6.
69 "Everyday brings a man twenty-four hours nearer to his grave, although no one can tell accurately, merely by looking at a man, how many days he has still to travel on that road." Ibid., 311.
70 Ibid., 324–6.
71 See Jameson, *Valences of the Dialectic*, 262. In his Lacanian–Hegelian approach, Žižek points to the structural irremovability of surplus value as a point of self-referential inscription within capitalism: "the Marxian symptom—labor-power—is a commodity whose use value is to generate value: not a point at which use value is inscribed into value, but a point at which *(generating) value is directly inscribed into use value*, as one

of the species of use value. The false appearance of M-M, of money engendering out of itself more money, obfuscates the fact that the detour through use value is necessary in order to generate the surplus." Žižek, *Incontinence of the Void*, 248.

72 Cf. Marx, *Capital*, Vol. 1, 716–17. Reproduction is a key term in Marx, as it joins the reproduction of capital with biological reproduction of workers:

> Because this, his reproduction, is itself a condition for capital, therefore the worker's consumption also appears as the reproduction not of capital directly, but of the relations under which alone it is capital. Living labor capacity belongs just as much among capital's conditions of existence as do raw material and instrument. Thus, it reproduces itself doubly, in its own form, [and] in the worker's consumption, but only to the extent that it reproduces him as living labour capacity.

Marx, Grundrisse, 676.

73 Marx, *Capital*, Vol. 1, 717–19.

74 Althusser and Balibar had early premonitions of Marx's discovery of capitalist time:

> we cannot be satisfied, as the best historians so often are today, by observing the existence of different times and rhythms, without relating them to the concept of their difference, i.e., to the typical dependence which establishes them in the articulation of the levels of the whole.... [W]e must, of absolute necessity, pose the question of the mode of existence of invisible times, *of the invisible rhythms and punctuations concealed beneath the surface of each visible time* (emphasis added). Merely reading *Capital* shows that Marx was highly sensitive to this requirement. It shows, for example, that the time of economic production is a specific time (differing according to the mode of production), but also that, *as a specific time, it is a complex and non-linear time—a time of times*, [emphasis added] a complex time that cannot be read in the continuity of the time of life or clocks, but has to be constructed out of the peculiar structures of production. The time of the capitalist economic production that Marx analysed must be constructed in its concept ... *It is an invisible time, essentially illegible, as invisible and as opaque as the reality of the total capitalist production process itself* (emphasis added). This time, as a complex "intersection" of the different times, rhythms, turnovers, etc., that we have just discussed, is only accessible in its concept, which, like every concept is never immediately "given", never legible in visible reality: like every concept this concept must be *produced, constructed*.

Althusser and Balibar, *Reading Capital*, 100–1. Althusser and Balibar notice thus the uneasy relationship between the circular time of reproduction and the underlying non-linear capitalist time. What they lack, however, is the vision of lasting in relation to life.

75 Agamben, *Creazione e anarchia. L'opera nell'età della religione capitalista* (Vicenza: Neri Pozza, 2017), 49.

76 Cf. Böhme, *Fetishism and Culture*, 33. On the other hand, bare life produces a network of affinities and compulsive dissociations from the condition of animality. It is much easier for the bare life to experience "thingness" than animality, partly due to capitalism's primordial exclusion of non-human animals from the social realm. See Derrida on Descartes' anti-animal revolution in Derrida, *L'Animal que donc je suis* (Paris: Galilée, 2006), 104–8.

77 Moishe Postone, *Time, Labor, and Social Domination: A Reinterpretation of Marx's Critical Theory* (Cambridge: Cambridge University Press, 1993).
78 Ibid., 124.
79 Ibid., 40.
80 Ibid., 66.
81 In this discrepancy lies the age-old history of disputes between communism and revisionism. Henri Lefèbvre once noticed that: "as soon as it is emptied of its political content (dictatorship by the proletariat, increased democracy, the withering away of the proletarian state), the notion of socialism is considerably diluted and weakened. It ends up just as a series of vague projects for economic planning and democracy." Lefèbvre, *Introduction to Modernity*, 201. What is fascinating, however, is that both poles—communism with its idea of redemptive self-constitution and socialism concentrated on ameliorating living standards—are inseparably entangled. Actual movements combine the two goals, usually to swerve in either direction when let loose (communism escalates in revolutionary fervor, openly disregarding the quality of life and fighting only for self-constitution in absolute equality; socialism tends towards opportunistic and reformist concern about details of economy). In this sense, the struggle with opportunism within the communist movement is the communism's inner fight with the Mirror Star.
82 Postone, *Time, Labor, and Social Domination*, 26.
83 Ibid., 27–30.
84 Cf. ibid., pp. 192–215.
85 Ibid., p. 214.
86 Ibid., p. 283.
87 Ibid., pp. 294–300, 377. Marcuse once noticed the consequence of this process: "The suppression of this dimension in the societal universe of operational rationality is a *suppression of history*, and this is not an academic but a political affair. It is suppression of the society's own past—and of its future, inasmuch as this future invokes the qualitative change, the negation of the present." Marcuse, *One-Dimensional Man*, 101.
88 Cf. Agamben's approach: "everything happens as if, in our culture, life were *what cannot be defined, yet, precisely for this reason, must be ceaselessly articulated and divided*." Agamben, *The Open*, 13.
89 Cf. Postone, *Time, Labor, and Social Domination*, 378. See also Marx, Grundrisse, 708.
90 Long after classic philosophy of life (Bergson, Dilthey, Simmel, etc.), the idea of life's inherent excess is continued, for example, in reappropriation of psychoanalysis concentrated on the vital qualities of the undeadness in life. See Eric L. Santner, *On the Psychotheology of Everyday Life: Reflections on Freud and Rosenzweig* (Chicago, IL, and London: Chicago Unviersity Press, 2001), 18 sq.
91 Adorno was right in claiming that capitalism put an end to life understood philosophically—that is, as something which might be good or bad and which might be actively and reasonably shaped. Adorno, Minima Moralia: *Reflections on a Damaged Life*, trans. E. F. N. Jephcott (London and New York: Verso, 2005), 15. This final conclusion concerns, in fact, the imagined precapitalist "true life": the bare life, built on lasting, takes its place.
92 The perception of life as something which can never be grasped directly, as a stream that overflows all our conceptual forms and can be recognized only in forms it leaves behind returns obsessively in modern thinking. Even in times when philosophy of life is well buried, this compulsive idea returns surprisingly unchanged. In his book, *Philosophie du vivre* (Paris: Gallimard, 2011), 11, François Jullien notices the structural inaccessibility of life.

93 It is in this sense that Weber's thesis on the affinity between Protestantism and early capitalism should be understood. If, as Weber argues, some branches of Protestantism (especially Calvinism and Puritanism) made the world essentially secular and rational, but at the same time dependent on God, it must be noted that this God effectively overlapped with the development of the world. Max Weber, *The Protestant Ethic and the Spirit of Capitalism*, trans. T. Parsons (London and New York: Routledge, 2001 [1930]), 110–12. God's judgments, although existing since time immemorial, were to be assessed only after someone's earthly success. In other words, this God was already an empty point of dynamic transcendence, either dissociating from the world (if viewed as an external judge) or overlapping with it (in the secular dimension of the judgment). Perhaps then we should not speak about the influence of Protestantism on early capitalism, but rather of their simultaneous birth from the emerging structure of (modern sovereignty).

94 Sloterdijk remarked aptly that: "Cynicism is *enlightened false consciousness*. It is that modernized, unhappy consciousness, on which enlightenment has labored both successfully and in vain. It has learned its lessons in enlightenment, but it has not, and probably was not able to, put them into practice." Sloterdijk, *Critique of Cynical Reason*, 5. See also Žižek, *Welcome to the Desert of the Real: Five Essays on September 11 and Related Dates* (London and New York: Verso, 2002), 90.

95 Žižek, *The Courage of Hopelessness: Chronicles of a Year of Acting Dangerously* (London: Allen Lane, 2017), 48.

96 Cf. Agamben, *Il Regno e il Giardino* (Vicenza: Neri Pozza, 2019), 117.

97 Naturally, the fall of the Eastern Bloc only laid bare the crisis of official Marxism which was well noticeable beforehand and was hoped to augur a revival of Marx's thought. See Althusser, "Marx dans ses limites," in *Écrits philosophiques et politiques*, Vol. 1, 359–64.

98 Ronald Aronson, *After Marxism* (New York and London: Guilford Press, 1995), 4.

99 Ibid.

100 Žižek is painfully right in recognizing that Hegel's edge over Marx was the ability to perceive the return of negativity which dissolves the world again. Žižek, *Disparities*, 374. Marx still aimed to curb negativity: first, into a revolutionary act, and then into a rational communist society. In other words, it was only Hegel who understood the Mirror Star's returns and cycles.

Conclusion

1 Raymond Benders and Stephan Oettermann, *Friedrich Nietzsche Chronik in Bildern und Texten* (Munich and Vienna: Carl Hanser Verlag, 2000), 801.

2 Ibid., 797.

3 Adorno opens his *Negative Dialectics* with the famous judgment passed on philosophy: "Philosophy, which once seemed obsolete, lives on because it missed the moment of its realization." Adorno, *Negative Dialectics*, trans. E. B. Ashton (New York: Continuum, 1973), 3. In this statement, Adorno rightly discovers the survival quality in philosophy, its *par excellence* afterlife nature. But the afterlife of philosophy is not the result of missing any moment of realization. Modern philosophy was given great promises, but nothing more: the moment of realization was never real. In fact, it was visible from the very beginning and, in this respect, the disappointment of philosophy continuously accompanied its newly emerged hope for transforming reality.

Nevertheless, philosophy had considerable bearing on reality, first of all insofar as it demonstrated for the first time the short circuits of the modern universe and its sovereignty-based construction. But it awaited its power to appear in a different, somewhat vague framework: and here it failed. It never got any command of reality because it never could get it. The promises had always been sandcastles; therefore, philosophy was in its afterlife from the very beginning, *it just needed to take its time to realize that.*

4   Cf. Agamben, *Gusto* (Macerata: Quodlibet, 2015), 57.
5   Benjamin, "Franz Kafka: On the Tenth Anniversary of His Death," in *Illuminations*, 134.
6   See Vogl, *The Specter of Capital*, 103; and Lefèbvre, *Introduction to Modernity*, 236.
7   Éric Vuillard, in his masterpiece, *L'Ordre du jour*, grasped this mix of powerlessness, inertia, and temptation in the imminent danger of Nazism. His essay ends with a devastatingly up-to-date remark on the relation between inert seduction by evil and the mute stillness of history. See Éric Vuillard, *L'Ordre du jour* (Arles: Actes Sud, 2017), 150.
8   It was none other than middle Lacan who claimed that "Les dieux, c'est un mode de révélation du réel. C'est pour cette raison que tout progrès philosophique tend, de par sa nécessité propre, à les éliminer." Lacan, *Le Séminaire. Livre VIII* (Paris: Seuil 1991), 58.
9   Nietzsche, *Ecce homo*, 74.
10 Georg Lukács noted that when revolutionary times ripen, everything becomes shrouded in great confusion. Hence the need for a revolutionary party which would keep the right course. Each deviation *in the process* warps the future revolution. Georg Lukács, *Lenin: A Study on the Unity of his Thought* (London and New York: Verso, 2009), 29. See also Dean, *The Communist Horizon*, 240.
11 Carl Schmitt, *The Concept of the Political: Expanded Edition*, trans. George Schwab (Chicago, IL, and London: University of Chicago Press, 2007), 26.
12 Ibid.
13 See Žižek, *Sex and the Failed Absolute*, 1.
14 Economically and politically, this means the proper and just distribution of what Peter Sloterdijk called "frugality for all," which we discover after learning that each global expansion and excessive productiveness has its limits. Cf. Sloterdijk, *Was geschah im 20. Jahrhundert?*, 33–4.
15 Derrida, *La Dissémination*, 315; and Gasché, *The Tain of the Mirror*, 218.
16 Benjamin, *The Arcades Project*, trans. H. Eiland and K. McLaughlin (New York: Belknap Press, 2002).
17 Benders and Oettermann, *Friedrich Nietzsche Chronik*, 801.

Bibliography

Adorno, Theodor W. Minima Moralia: *Reflections on a Damaged Life*. Trans. E. F. N. Jephcott. London and New York: Verso, 2005.
Adorno, Theodor W. *Negative Dialectics*. 1973. Trans. E. B. Ashton. New York and London: Continuum, 2007.
Adorno, Theodor W. *The Jargon of Authenticity*. Trans K. Tarnowski and F. Will. London and New York: Routledge, 2003.
Agamben, Giorgio. *Altissima povertà. Regole monastiche e forma di vita. Homo sacer IV, 1*. Vicenza: Neri Pozza, 2011.
Agamben, Giorgio. *Autoritratto nello studio*. Milano: Nottetempo, 2017.
Agamben, Giorgio. *Che cos'è la filosofia?* Macerata: Quodlibet, 2016.
Agamben, Giorgio. *Creazione e anarchia. L'opera nell'età della religione capitalista*. Vicenza: Neri Pozza, 2017.
Agamben, Giorgio. *Gusto*. Macerata: Quodlibet, 2015.
Agamben, Giorgio. *Homo sacer. Il potere sovrano e la nuda vita*. Torino: Einaudi, 1995.
Agamben, Giorgio. Homo sacer: *Sovereign Power and Bare Life*. Trans. Daniel Heller-Roazen. Stanford, CA: Stanford University Press 1998.
Agamben, Giorgio. *Idea della prosa*. Macerata: Quodlibet, 2002.
Agamben, Giorgio. *Il fuoco e il racconto*. Roma: Nottetempo, 2014.
Agamben, Giorgio. *Il mistero del male. Benedetto XVI e la fine dei tempi*. Roma e Bari: Laterza 2013.
Agamben, Giorgio. *Il Regno e il Giardino*. Vicenza: Neri Pozza, 2019.
Agamben, Giorgio. *Il regno e la gloria. Per una genealogia teologica dell'economia e del governo. Homo sacer II, 2*. Torino: Bollati Boringhieri, 2009.
Agamben, Giorgio. *Il sacramento del linguaggio. Archeologia del giuramento. Homo sacer II, 3*. Roma-Bari: Laterza, 2008.
Agamben, Giorgio. *Karman. Breve trattato sull'azione, la colpa e il gesto*. Torino: Bollati Boringhieri 2017.
Agamben, Giorgio. *L'avventura*. Roma: Nottetempo, 2015.
Agamben, Giorgio. *L'uso dei corpi. Homo sacer IV, 2*. Vicenza: Neri Pozza, 2014.
Agamben, Giorgio. *La potenza del pensiero. Saggi e conferenze*. Torino: Neri Pozza, 2012.
Agamben, Giorgio. *Opus Dei. Archeologia dell'ufficio. Homo sacer II, 5*. Torino: Bollati Boringhieri, 2012.
Agamben, Giorgio. *Pilato e Gesú*. Roma: Nottetempo, 2013.
Agamben, Giorgio. *Profanations*. Trans. J. Fort. New York: Zone Books, 2007.
Agamben, Giorgio. *Qu'est-ce que le contemporain ?* Trans. M. Rovere. Paris: Payot & Rivages, 2008.
Agamben, Giorgio. *Quel che resta di Auschwitz. L'archivio e il testimone. Homo sacer III*. Torino: Bollati Boringhieri, 1998.
Agamben, Giorgio. S*tasis. La guerra civile come paradigma politico. Homo sacer II, 2*. Torino: Bollati Boringhieri, 2015.
Agamben, Giorgio. *Stato di Eccezione. Homo sacer II, 1*. Torino: Bollati Boringhieri, 2003.

Agamben, Giorgio. *The Coming Community*. Trans. M. Hardt. Minneapolis, MN: University of Minnesota Press, 1993.
Agamben, Giorgio. *The Open: Man and Animal*. Trans. K. Attell. Stanford, CA: Stanford University Press, 2004.
Agamben, Giorgio. *The Sacrament of Language: An Archeology of the Oath. Homo sacer II, 3*. Trans. Adam Kotsko. Cambridge: Polity Press 2010.
Agamben, Giorgio. *The Time that Remains: A Commentary on the Letter to the Romans*. Trans. P. Dailey. Stanford, CA: Stanford University Press, 2005.
Althusser, Louis. *Écrits philosophiques et politiques*. Paris: STOCK/IMEC, 1994.
Althusser, Louis. *Écrits sur la psychanalyse. Freud et Lacan*. Paris: STOCK/IMEC, 1993.
Althusser, Louis. *Sur la reproduction*. Paris: PUF, 1995.
Althusser, Louis and Étienne Balibar. *Reading Capital*. Trans. B. Brewster. London: NLB, 1970.
Arendt, Hannah. "Personal Responsibility under Dictatorship." In *Responsibility and Judgment*, edited by Jerome Kohn, 49–65. New York: Schocken Books, 2003.
Arendt, Hannah. *The Life of the Mind*. San Diego, CA: A Harvest Book, 1981.
Aristotle. *Metaphysics*. Trans. C. D. C. Reeve. Indianapolis, IN: Hackett Publishing, 2016.
Aristotle. *On the Heavens*. Trans. J. Leofric Stocks. Oxford: Clarendon Press, 1922.
Aristotle. *Physics*. Edited by W. D. Ross. Oxford: Clarendon Press, 1936.
Aronson, Ronald. *After Marxism*. New York and London: Guilford Press, 1995.
Badiou, Alain. *Being and Event*. Trans. O. Feltham. London and New York: Continuum, 2005.
Badiou, Alain. *L'Hypothèse communiste*. Paris: Nouvelles Editions Lignes, 2009.
Badiou, Alain. *Le Siècle*. Paris: Seuil, 2005.
Baudrillard, Jean. *Les Stratégies fatales*. Paris: Grasset, 1983.
Bauman, Zygmunt. *Living on Borrowed Time: Conversations with Citlali Rovirosa-Madrazo*. Cambridge: Polity Press, 2010.
Benda, Julien. *The Treason of the Intellectuals*. 1928. Trans. R. Kimball. Abingdon: Routledge, 2006.
Benders, Raymond and Stephan Oettermann. *Friedrich Nietzsche Chronik in Bildern und Texten*. Munich and Vienna: Carl Hanser Verlag, 2000.
Benjamin, Walter. *Arcades Project*. Trans. H. Eiland and K. McLaughlin. New York: Belknap Press, 2002.
Benjamin, Walter. *Gesammelte Schriften, Band 5*. Frankfurt am Main: Suhrkamp, 1982.
Benjamin, Walter. *Gesammelte Schriften, Band 6*. Frankfurt am Main: Suhrkamp, 1991.
Benjamin, Walter. *Illuminations: Essays and Reflections*. Trans. H. Zohn. New York: Schocken Books, 1969.
Benjamin, Walter. *The Origin of German Tragic Drama*. Trans. J. Osborne. London and New York: Verso, 2003.
Berman, Marshall. *All that is Solid Melts into Air: The Experience of Modernity*. New York: Penguin Books, 1988.
Bielik-Robson, Agata. *Jewish Cryptotheologies of Late Modernity*. Abingdon: Routledge, 2014.
Blanchot, Maurice. *L'Écriture du désastre*. Paris: Gallimard 1980.
Blanchot, Maurice. *L'Entretien infini*. Paris: Gallimard, 1969.
Blanchot, Maurice. *La Communauté inavouable*. Paris: Éditions de Minuit, 1984.
Blanchot, Maurice. *Le Pas au-delà*. Paris: Gallimard, 1973.
Blanqui, Louis Auguste. *L'Éternité par les astres*. Paris: Germer Baillière, 1872.
Blatner, William D. *Heidegger's Temporal Idealism*. Cambridge: Cambridge University Press, 1999.

Bloch, Ernst. *Atheism in Christianity: The Religion of the Exodus and the Kingdom*. 1972. London and New York: Verso, 2009.
Bloch, Ernst. *Experimentum Mundi. Frage, Kategorien des Herausbringens, Praxis*. Frankfurt am Main: Suhrkamp, 1975.
Bloch, Ernst. *Geist der Utopie*. 1918. Frankfurt am Main: Suhrkamp, 1972.
Bloch, Ernst. *Gespräche mit Ernst Bloch*. Edited by Rainer Traub and Harald Wieser. Frankfurt am Main: Suhrkamp, 1975.
Bloch, Ernst. *The Principle of Hope*. 1986. Trans. N. Plaice, S. Plaice, and P. Knight. Cambridge, MA: MIT Press, 1995.
Bloch, Ernst. *Werkausgabe, Band 4, Erbschaft dieser Zeit*. Frankfurt am Main: Suhrkamp, 1985.
Bloch, Ernst. *Werkausgabe, Band 6, Naturrecht und menschliche Würde*. Frankfurt am Main: Suhrkamp, 1977.
Bloch, Ernst. *Werkausgabe, Band 13, Tübinger Einleitung in die Philosophie*. Frankfurt am Main: Suhrkamp, 1985.
Blumenberg, Hans. *The Legitimacy of the Modern Age*. Trans. R. M. Wallace. Cambridge, MA, and London: MIT Press, 1985.
Bodin, Jean. *Les Six livres de la république*. 1576. Paris: Fayard, 1985.
Böhme, Hartmut. *Fetishism and Culture: A Different Theory of Modernity*. Trans. A. Galt. Berlin and Boston, MA: De Gruyter, 2014.
Bourdieu, Pierre. *L'Ontologie politique de Martin Heidegger*. Paris: Éditions de minuit, 1988.
Braudel, Fernand. *Civilization and Capitalism, 15th-18th Centuries. Vol. 1: The Structures of Everyday Life. Vol. 2: The Wheels of Commerce*. 1979. Trans. S. Reynolds. Berkeley, CA: University of California Press, 1992.
Braunstein, Nestor A. *La Jouissance, un concept lacanien*. Ramonville Saint-Agne: Éditions érès, 2005.
Bronner, Stephen Eric. *Reclaiming Enlightenment: Towards a Politic of Radical Engagement*. New York: Columbia University Press, 2004.
Butler, Judith, Ernesto Laclau, and Slavoj Žižek. *Contingency, Hegemony, Universality. Contemporary Dialogues on the Left*. London and New York: Verso, 2000.
Buzzati, Dino. *Il deserto dei Tartari*. Milano-Roma: Rizzoli, 1940.
Celan, Paul. Ansprache anlässlich der Entgegennahme des Literaturpreises der freien Hansestadt Bremen in *Gesammelte Werke*, Band 3. Frankfurt am Main: Suhrkamp, 2000.
Celan, Paul. *Gesammelte Werke. Bände I–VII*. Frankfurt am Main: Suhrkamp, 2000.
Cohen, Hermann. *Kants Theorie der Erfahrung*. Berlin: Harrwitz und Gossmann, 1885.
Comay, Rebecca and Frank Ruda. *The Dash—The Other Side of Absolute Knowing*. Cambridge, MA, and London: MIT Press, 2018.
D'Hondt, Jacques. *Hegel. Biographie*. Paris: Calmann-Lévy, 1998.
de Sade, D. A. F. *L'Œuvre du Marquis de Sade*. Paris: Bibliothèque des Curieux, 1909.
Dean, Jodi. *The Communist Horizon*. London and New York: Verso, 2012.
Deleuze, Gilles and Félix Guattari. *Anti-Oedipus: Capitalism and Schizophrenia*. Trans. R. Hutley, M. Seem, and H. R. Lane. Minneapolis, MN: Minnesota University Press, 1983.
Derrida, Jacques. *Apprendre à vivre enfin. Entretien avec Jean Birnbaum*. Paris: Galilée/Le Monde, 2005.
Derrida, Jacques. *D'un ton apocalyptique adopté naguère en philosophie*. Paris: Galilée, 1983.
Derrida, Jacques. *De l'esprit. Heidegger et la question*. Paris: Galilée, 1987.
Derrida, Jacques. *Foi et savoir*. Paris: Seuil, 2001.
Derrida, Jacques. *Force de loi. Le Fondement mystique de l'autorité*. Paris: Galilée, 2005.
Derrida, Jacques. *Glas*. Paris: Galilée, 1974.

Derrida, Jacques. *Heidegger: La question de l'Être et l'Histoire. Cours de l'ENS-Ulm 1964–1965*. Paris: Galilée, 2013.
Derrida, Jacques. *Khôra*. Paris: Galilée, 1993.
Derrida, Jacques. *L'Animal que donc je suis*. Paris: Galilée, 2006.
Derrida, Jacques. *La Bête et le souverain. Séminaire*. Vols 1–2 *(2001–2002)*. Paris: Galilée, 2008/2010.
Derrida, Jacques. *La Dissémination*. Paris: Seuil, 1972.
Derrida, Jacques. *La Solidarité des vivants et le pardon. Conférence et entretiens*. Paris: Hermann, 2016.
Derrida, Jacques. *Le Monolinguisme de l'autre ou la prothèse d'origine*. Paris: Galilée, 1996.
Derrida, Jacques. *Margins of Philosophy*. Trans. A. Bass. Brighton: Harvester Press, 1982.
Derrida, Jacques. *Marx & Sons*. Paris: PUF/Galilée, 2002.
Derrida, Jacques. *Of Grammatology*. 1976. Trans. G. Chakravorty Spivak. Baltimore, MD: John Hopkins University Press, 1997.
Derrida, Jacques. *Psyché. Inventions de l'autre*. Paris: Galilée, 1987.
Derrida, Jacques. *Sauf le nom*. Paris: Galilée, 1993.
Derrida, Jacques. *Schibboleth pour Paul Celan*. Paris: Galilée, 1986.
Derrida, Jacques. *Spectres of Marx: The State of the Debt, the Work of Mourning and the New International*. Trans. P. Kamuff. New York and London: Routledge, 1994.
Derrida, Jacques. *Voyous. Deux essais sur la raison*. Paris: Galilée, 2003.
Derrida, Jacques. *Writing and Difference*. 1978. Trans. A. Bass. London and New York: Routledge, 2003.
Descartes, René. *A Discourse on Method; Meditations on the First Philosophy; Principles of Philosophy*. Trans. J. Veitch, London: Dent & Sons, 1912.
Descartes, René. *Discourse on Method and Metaphysical Meditations*. Trans. G. B. Rawlings. London and Felling-on-Tyne: Walter Scott Publishing, 1901.
di Cesare, Donatella. *Heidegger e gli ebrei. I "Quaderni neri."* Torino: Bollati Boringhieri, 2014.
Dietschy, Beat, Doris Zeilinger, and Rainer E. Zimmermann (eds.). *Bloch-Wörterbuch. Leitbegriffe der Philosophie Ernst Blochs*. Berlin and Boston, MA: De Gruyter, 2012.
Elshtain, Jean Bethke. *Sovereignty: God, State, and Self*. New York: Basic Books, 2008.
Esposito, Roberto. *Politica e negazione. Per una filosofia affermativa*. Torino: Einaudi, 2018.
Fackenheim, Emil L. *Encounters between Judaism and Modern Philosophy: A Preface to Future Jewish Thought*. New York: Schocken Books, 1980.
Farías, Victor. *Heidegger and Nazism*. Trans. P. Burrell and G. R. Ricci. Philadelphia, PA: Temple University Press, 1989.
Ferrarin, Alfredo. *Hegel and Aristotle*. Cambridge: Cambridge University Press, 2001.
Fichte, Johann Gottlieb. *The Science of Knowledge*. Trans. A. E. Kroeger. London: Trübner & Co., 1889.
Fine, Lawrence. *Physician of the Soul, Dealer of the Cosmos. Isaac Luria and his Kabbalistic Fellowship*. Stanford, CA: Stanford University Press, 2003.
Fitzgerald, Francis Scott. *The Great Gatsby*. 1925. Oxford: Oxford University Press, 2008.
Foucault, Michel. *Dits et écrits 1954–1988*. Paris: Gallimard, 2001.
Foucault, Michel. *Le Gouvernement de soi et des autres. Cours au Collège de France, 1982–1983*. Seuil: Gallimard, 2008.
Foucault, Michel. *Naissance de la biopolitique, Cours au CollèFranceFrance, 1978–1979*. Paris: Gallimard, Seuil, 2004.
Foucault, Michel. *Security, Territory, Population: Lectures at the Collège de France 1977–78*. Trans. G. Burchell. Basingstoke and New York: Palgrave, 2007.

Foucault, Michel. *"Society Must Be Defended": Lectures at the Collège de France 1975-1976*. Trans. D. Macey. New York: Picador, 2003.
Foucault, Michel. *The Order of Things: An Archaeology of the Human Sciences*. New York: Pantheon Books, 1970.
Foucault, Michel. "The Subject and Power." In *Essential Works of Foucault: Power*. Edited by James D. Faubion. Trans. R. Hurley and others. New York: New Press, 2000.
Freud, Sigmund. *Beyond the Pleasure Principle*. Trans. J. Strachey. New York, London: W.W. Norton & Co., 1961.
Freud, Sigmund, *The Interpretation of Dreams*. Trans. J. Strachey. New York: Avon Books, 1965.
Furet, François. *The French Revolution 1770-1814*. Trans. A. Nevill. Oxford: Blackwell, 1996.
Gabriel, Markus. *Warum es die Welt nicht gibt?* Berlin: Ullstein, 2016.
Gasché, Rodolphe. *The Tain of the Mirror: Derrida and the Philosophy of Reflection*. Cambridge, MA: Harvard University Press 1986.
Goldmann, Lucien. *Lukács et Heidegger*. Paris: Denoël / Gouthier, 1973.
Goldschmidt, Georges-Arthur. *Heidegger et la langue allemande*. Paris: CNRS, 2016.
Gordon, Peter Eli. *Rosenzweig and Heidegger: Between Judaism and German Philosophy*. Berkeley, Los Angeles, CA, and London: University of California Press, 2003.
Gramsci, Antonio. *Selection from the Prison Notebooks*. Trans. Q. Hoare and G. Nowell Smith. New York: International Publishers, 1971.
Habermas, Jürgen. *The Philosophical Discourse of Modernity: Twelve Lectures*. Trans. F. Lawrence. Cambridge: Polity Press, 1990.
Handelman, Susan A. *The Slayers of Moses: The Emergence of Rabbinic Interpretation in Modern Literary Theory*. Albany, NY: State University of New York Press, 1982.
Harvey, David. *The Condition of Postmodernity*. Hoboken, NJ: Wiley, 1992.
Hegel, Georg Wilhelm Friedrich. *Lectures on the History of Philosophy*. Trans. E. S. Haldane and F. H. Simson. London: Kegan Paul, Trench, Trübner & Co., 1892-6.
Hegel, Georg Wilhelm Friedrich. *Lectures on the Philosophy of History*. Trans. J. Sibree. London: Bell and Sons, 1902.
Hegel, Georg Wilhelm Friedrich. *Lectures on the Philosophy of Religion*. Trans. E. B. Speirs and J. Burdon Sanderson. London: K. Paul, Trench, Trübner & Co., 1895.
Hegel, Georg Wilhelm Friedrich. *Phänomenologie des Geistes*. 1807. Stuttgart: Reclam, 2009.
Hegel, Georg Wilhelm Friedrich. *Political Writings*. Trans. H. B. Nisbet. Cambridge and New York: Cambridge University Press, 1999.
Hegel, Georg Wilhelm Friedrich. *The Phenomenology of Mind*. 1910. Trans. J.B. Baillie. New York: Humanities Press, 1977.
Hegel, Georg Wilhelm Friedrich. *The Philosophy of Right*. Trans. S. W. Dyde. Kitchener, Ontario: Batoche Books, 2001.
Hegel, Georg Wilhelm Friedrich. *Werke*. Edited by Eva Moldenhauer and Karl Markus Michel. Frankfurt am Main: Suhrkamp, 1969-71.
Heidegger, Martin. *Being and Time*. Trans. J. Stambaugh. Albany, NY: SUNY Press, 1996.
Heidegger, Martin. *Contributions to Philosophy (From Enowning)*. Trans. P. Emad and K. Maly. Bloomington and Indianapolis, IN: Indiana University Press, 1999.
Heidegger, Martin. *Gesamtausgabe, Band 7, Vorträge und Aufsätze*. Frankfurt am Main: Vittorio Klostermann, 2000.
Heidegger, Martin. *Gesamtausgabe, Band 11, Identität und Differenz*. Frankfurt am Main: Vittorio Klostermann, 2006.
Heidegger, Martin. *Gesamtausgabe, Band 13, Aus der Erfahrung des Denkens*. Frankfurt am Main: Vittorio Klostermann, 1983.

Heidegger, Martin. *Gesamtausgabe, Band 14, Zur Sache des Denkens*. Frankfurt am Main: Vittorio Klostermann, 2007.
Heidegger, Martin. *Gesamtausgabe, Band 16, Reden und andere Zeugnisse eines Lebenweges*. Frankfurt am Main: Vittorio Klostermann, 2000.
Heidegger, Martin. *Gesamtausgabe, Band 29-30, Die Grundbegriffe der Metaphysik. Welt—Endlichkeit—Einsamkeit*. Frankfurt am Main: Vittorio Klostermann, 1983.
Heidegger, Martin. *Gesamtausgabe, Band 53, Hölderlins Hymne "Der Ister."* Frankfurt am Main: Vittorio Klostermann, 1993.
Heidegger, Martin. *Gesamtausgabe, Band 65, Beiträge zur Philosophie (Vom Ereignis)*. Frankfurt am Main: Vittorio Klostermann, 1989.
Heidegger, Martin. *Gesamtausgabe, Band 66, Besinnung*. Frankfurt am Main: Vittorio Klostermann, 1997.
Heidegger, Martin. *Gesamtausgabe, Band 69, Die Geschichte des Seyns*. Frankfurt am Main: Vittorio Klostermann, 1998.
Heidegger, Martin. *Gesamtausgabe, Band 70, Über den Anfang*. Frankfurt am Main: Vittorio Klostermann, 2005.
Heidegger, Martin. *Gesamtausgabe, Band 71, Das Ereignis*. Frankfurt am Main: Vittorio Klostermann, 2009.
Heidegger, Martin. *Gesamtausgabe, Band 94, Überlegungen II–VI (Schwarze Hefte 1931-1938)*. Frankfurt am Main: Vittorio Klostermann, 2014.
Heidegger, Martin. *Introduction to Metaphysics*. Trans. G. Fried and R. Polt. New Haven, CT, and London: Yale University Press, 2000.
Heidegger, Martin. *Kant and the Problem of Metaphysics*. 1962. Trans. R. Taft, Bloomington and Indianapolis, IN: Indiana University Press, 1997.
Heidegger, Martin. *What is Called Thinking?* Trans. F. D. Wieck and J. Glenn Gray. New York, Evanston, NJ, and London: Harper & Row, 1968.
Hertweck, Frank and Dimitrios Kisoudis (eds.). *"Solange das Imperium da ist". Carl Schmitt im Gespräch 1971*. Berlin: Duncker & Humblot 2010.
Hobbes, Thomas. *Leviathan*. 1988. Trans. J. C. A. Gaskin. Oxford: Oxford University Press, 1996.
Hobsbawm, Eric. *How to Change the World: Reflections on Marx and Marxism*. New Haven, CT, and London: Yale University Press, 2011.
Hobsbawm, Eric. *Nations and Nationalism since 1780: Programme, Myth, Reality*. Cambridge: Cambridge University Press, 1990.
Hölderlin, Friedrich. *Gesammelte Werke*. Hrsg. von H. J. Balmes. Frankfurt am Main: Fischer, 2014.
Horkheimer, Max. *Between Philosophy and Social Science: Selected Early Writings*. Trans. G. F. Hunter, M. S. Kramer, and J. Torpey. Cambridge, MA, and London: MIT Press, 1993.
Horkheimer, Max. *Gesammelte Schriften, Band 2, Philosophische Frühschriften 1922-1932*. Berlin: Fischer, 1987.
Horkheimer, Max. *The Eclipse of Reason*. 1947. London and New York: Continuum, 2004.
Horkheimer, Max and Theodor W. Adorno. *Dialectic of Enlightenment: Philosophical Fragments*. 1947. Trans. E. Jephcott, Bloomington, IN: Stanford University Press, 2002.
Hudson, Wayne. *The Marxist Philosophy of Ernst Bloch*. London and Basingstoke: Macmillan Press, 1992.
Hume, David. *A Treatise of Human Nature*. 1739. London: Noon, 1939.
Hume, David. *An Enquiry Concerning Human Understanding: My Own Life: An Abstract of a Treatise of Human Nature*. 1748. La Salle, IL: Open Court, 1992.
Hyppolyte, Jean. *Figures de la pensée philosophique*. Paris: PUF, 1991.

Idel, Moshe. *Absorbing Perfections: Kabbalah and Interpretation*. New Haven, CT, and London: Yale University Press, 2002.
Idel, Moshe. *Old Worlds, New Mirrors: On Jewish Mysticism and Twentieth-Century Thought*. Philadelphia, PA: Pennsylvania University Press, 2010.
Irigaray, Luce. *Speculum. De l'autre femme*. Paris: Éditions de minuit, 1974.
Jabès, Edmond. *Ça suit son cours*. Montpellier: Fata Morgana, 1982.
Jabès, Edmond. *Le Livre de l'hospitalité*. Paris: Gallimard, 1991.
Jabès, Edmond. *The Book of Questions, Vol. 2: Yaël; Elya; Aely; El, or the Last Book*. Trans. R. Waldrop. Middletown, CT: Wesleyan University Press, 1991.
Jameson, Fredric. *A Singular Modernity: Essay on the Ontology of the Present*. London and New York: Verso, 2002.
Jameson, Fredric. *Valences of the Dialectic*. London: Verso, 2009.
Jonas, Hans. "The Concept of God after Auschwitz: A Jewish Voice." *Journal of Religion*, Vol. 67, No. 1 (1987), 1–13.
Jullien, François. *Philosophie du vivre*. Paris: Gallimard, 2011.
Kafka, Franz. *Erzählungen*. Stuttgart: Reclam, 2012.
Kafka, Franz. *The Castle*. Trans. A. Bell. Oxford and New York: Oxford University Press, 2009.
Kafka, Franz. *The Complete Stories*. Edited by Nachum N. Glatzer. New York: Schocken Books, 1976.
Kafka, Franz. *The Trial*. Trans. I. Parry. London and New York: Penguin Classics, 2000.
Kafka, Franz. *Zürau Aphorismen*. Trans. *Nachgelassene Schriften und Fragmente, Band 2*. Frankfurt am Main: Fischer, 1992.
Kant, Immanuel. *Religion within the Boundaries of Pure Reason and Other Writings*. Trans. A. Wood and G. di Giovanni. Cambridge: Cambridge University Press, 1998.
Kant, Immanuel. *The Critique of Judgment*. Trans. J. H. Bernard. London: Macmillan, 1914.
Kant, Immanuel. *The Critique of Pure Reason*. Trans. T. K. Abbott. London: Longmans, Green & Co., 1879.
Kant, Immanuel. *The Metaphysics of Morals*. Trans. M. Gregor. Cambridge: Cambridge University Press, 1991.
Kant, Immanuel. *Toward Perpetual Peace and Other Writings on Politics, Peace, and History*. Trans. D. L. Colclasure. New Haven, CT, and London: Yale University Press, 2006.
Kaufmann, Walter. *Hegel: A Reinterpretation*. Notre Dame, ID: University of Notre Dame Press, 1978.
Kierkegaard, Søren. *Concluding Unscientific Postscript*. 1846. Trans. A. Hannay, Cambridge: Cambridge University Press, 2009.
Klemperer, Viktor. *LTI. Lingua Tertii Imperii. Die Sprache des Deutschen Reiches. Notizbuch eines Philologen*. Leipzig: Reclam, 1975.
Kojève, Alexandre. *Introduction à la lecture de Hegel*. 1947. Paris: Gallimard, 1968.
Kojève, Alexandre. *Le Concept, le Temps et le Discours. Introduction au Système du Savoir*. Paris: Gallimard 1990.
Kracauer, Siegfried. *History: The Last Things Before the Last*. Princeton, NJ : Markus Wiener Publishers, 1995.
Lacan, Jacques. *Écrits*. Paris: Seuil, 1990.
Lacan, Jacques. *Le Séminaire. Livre I—Les Écrits techniques de Freud*. Paris: Seuil 1975.
Lacan, Jacques. *Le Séminaire. Livre II—Le Moi dans la théorie de Freud et dans la technique de la psychanalyse*. Paris: Seuil 1978.

Lacan, Jacques. *Le Séminaire. Livre III—Les Psychoses*. Paris: Seuil 1981.
Lacan, Jacques. *Le Séminaire. Livre IV—La Relation d'objet*. Paris: Seuil 1994.
Lacan, Jacques. *Le Séminaire. Livre VI—Le Désir et son interpretation*. Paris: Éditions de la Martinière, 2013.
Lacan, Jacques. *Le Séminaire. Livre VII—L'Ethique de la psychanalyse*. Paris: Seuil, 1986.
Lacan, Jacques. *Le Séminaire. Livre VIII—Le Transfert*. Paris: Seuil, 1991.
Lacan, Jacques. *Le Séminaire. Livre X—L'Angoisse*. Paris: Seuil, 2004.
Lacan, Jacques. *Le Séminaire. Livre XI—Les Quatre concepts fondamentaux de la psychanalyse*. Paris: Seuil, 1973.
Lacan, Jacques. *Le Séminaire. Livre XVI—De l'Autre à l'autre*. Paris: Seuil, 2006.
Lacan, Jacques. *Le Séminaire. Livre XVII—L'Envers de la psychanalyse*. Paris: Seuil, 1991.
Lacan, Jacques. *Le Séminaire. Livre XVIII—D'Un discours qui ne serait pas du semblant*. Paris: Seuil, 2007.
Lacan, Jacques. *Le Séminaire. Livre XIX—. . . ou pire*. Paris: Seuil, 2011.
Lacan, Jacques. *Le Séminaire. Livre XX—Encore*. Paris: Seuil, 1975.
Lacan, Jacques. *Le Séminaire. Livre XXIII—Sinthome*. Paris: Seuil, 2005.
Lacan, Jacques. *Le Triomphe de la religion, précédé de Discours aux catholiques*. Paris: Seuil, 2005.
Lacan, Jacques. *Mon enseignement*. Paris: Seuil, 2005.
Lakebrink, Bernhard. *Kommentar zu Hegels "Logik" in seiner "Enzyklopädie" von 1830*. Freiburg/München: Karl Alber, 1985.
Latour, Bruno. *We Have Never Been Modern*. Trans. C. Porter. Cambridge, MA: Harvard University Press, 1993.
Le Calendrier républicain: De sa création à sa disparition suivi d'une concordance avec le calendrier grégorien. Paris: Bureau des longitudes, 1994.
Lefèbvre, Henri. *Introduction to Modernity : Twelve Preludes*. Trans. J. Moore. London and New York: Verso, 1995.
Lefort, Claude. *Democracy and Political Theory*. Trans. D. Macey. Minneapolis, MN: University of Minnesota Press, 1988.
Leibniz, Gottfried Wilhelm. *Philosophical Papers and Letters*. Trans. L. E. Loemker. Dordrecht: Kluwer, 1989.
Lenin, Vladimir. *Collected Works*. Trans. Y. Sdobnikov and G. Hanna. Moscow: Progress Publishers, 1972.
Lenin, Vladimir. *State and Revolution*. Trans. T. Chretien. Chicago, IL: Haymarket Books, 2014.
Levi, Primo. *I sommersi e i salvati*. Torino: Einaudi, 1986.
Levi, Primo. *If This is a Man. . .* Trans. S. Woolf. New York: Orion Press, 1959.
Levinas, Emmanuel. *Autrement qu'être ou au-delà de l'essence*. La Haye: Nijhoff, 1978.
Levinas, Emmanuel. *Difficult Freedom: Essays on Judaism*. Trans. S. Hand. Baltimore, MD: John Hopkins University Press, 1997.
Levinas, Emmanuel. *Liberté et commandement*. Montpellier: Fata Morgana, 1994.
Levinas, Emmanuel. *Totality and Infinity: An Essay on Exteriority*. Trans. A. Lingis. The Hague: Martinus Nijhoff, 1979.
Lim, Hong-Bin. *Absoluter Unterschied und Begriff in der Philosophie Hegels*. Frankfurt am Main: Peter Lang, 1989.
Locke, John. *Second Treatise of Government*. 1689. Indianapolis, IN, and Cambridge: Hackett, 1980.
Löwith, Karl. *Meaning in History: The Theological Implications of the Philosophy of History*. Chicago, IL: University of Chicago Press, 1949.

Lukács, Georg. *Lenin: A Study on the Unity of his Thought*. 1970. London and New York: Verso, 2009.
Luther, Martin. *Concerning Christian Liberty*. Trans. B. Wolfmueller. Aurora, CO: Hope Lutheran Church, 2017.
Luther, Martin. *De Servo Arbitrio "On the Enslaved Will" or The Bondage of Will*. 1904. Trans. H. Cole. Grand Rapids, MI: Christian Classics Ethereal Library, 2005.
Lyotard, Jean-François. *Heidegger et "les juifs."* Paris: Galilée, 1988.
Lyotard, Jean-François. *Lessons on the Analytic of the Sublime*. Trans. E. Rottenberg. Stanford, CA: Stanford University Press, 1994.
Lyotard, Jean-François. *The Differend: Phrases in Dispute*. Trans. G. Van Den Abbeele. Manchester: Manchester University Press, 1988.
Magee, Glenn Alexander. *Hegel and the Hermetic Tradition*. Ithaca, NY, and London: Cornell University Press, 2001.
Malabou, Catherine. *Changer de différance. Le Féminin et la question philosophique*. Paris: Galilée, 2009.
Malabou, Catherine. *The Future of Hegel: Plasticity, Temporality and Dialectic*. Trans. L. During. London and New York: Routledge, 2005.
Malabou, Catherine. *The Heidegger Change: On the Fantastic in Philosophy*. Trans. P. Skafish. Albany: State University of New York Press, 2011.
Malabou, Catherine and Jacques Derrida. *La Contre-allée*. La Quinzaine littéraire/Louis Vuitton, 1999.
Mallarmé, Stéphane. *Œuvres completes*. Paris: Plèiade, 1945.
Marcuse, Herbert. *One-Dimensional Man: Studies in the Ideology of Advanced Industrial Society*. 1964. London and New York: Routledge, 2002.
Marcuse, Herbert. *Reason and Revolution: Hegel and the Rise of Social Theory*. London: Routledge & Kegan Paul, 1955.
Marx Karl. *Capital: Critique of Political Economy*. Trans. B. Fawkes. Harmondsworth and New York: Penguin, 1976 (Vol. 1), 1978 (Vol. 2), 1981 (Vol. 3).
Marx Karl. *Grundrisse: Foundations of the Critique of Political Economy*. Trans. M. Nicolaus. New York: Vintage Books, 1973.
Marx Karl. " 'Preface' to *A Contribution to the Critique of Political Economy*." In *Early Writings*. Trans. R. Livingstone and G. Benton. London: Penguin Books, 1992.
Marx Karl. *The Poverty of Philosophy*. Moscow: Foreign Languages Publishing House, 1962.
Marx, Karl and Friedrich Engels. *Economic and Philosophic Manuscripts of 1844*. Trans. M. Milligan. Amherst: Prometheus Books, 1988.
Marx, Karl and Friedrich Engels. *The German Ideology*. Amherst: Prometheus Books, 1998.
Meillassoux, Quentin. *Après la finitude. Essai sur la nécessité de la contingence*. Paris: Seuil, 2006.
Meillassoux, Quentin. *Le Nombre et la sirène. Un déchiffrage du "Coup de dés" de Mallarmé*. Paris: Fayard, 2011.
Michelet, Jules. *Histoire de la Révolution française*. Paris, 1889.
Miller Jones, John. *Assembling (Post)modernism: The Utopian Philosophy of Ernst Bloch*. New York: Peter Lang, 1995.
Mouffe, Chantal and Ernesto Laclau. *Hegemony and Socialist Strategy: Towards a Radical Democratic Politics*. 1985. London and New York: Verso, 2001.
Nancy, Jean-Luc. *Banalité de Heidegger*. Paris: Galilée, 2015.
Nancy, Jean-Luc. *La Communauté désœuvrée*. Paris: Christian Bourgois, 1983.

Nancy, Jean-Luc. *Une Pensée finie*. Paris: Galilée, 1990.
Nelson, Maggie. *Bluets*. London: Jonathan Cape, 2017.
Nietzsche, Friedrich. *Beyond Good and Evil*. Trans. J. Norman. Cambridge: Cambridge University Press, 2002.
Nietzsche, Friedrich. *Ecce homo. Wie man wird–was man ist*. 1908. Frankfurt am Main: Insel, 1977.
Nietzsche, Friedrich. *The Antichrist, Ecce Homo, The Twilight of the Idols and Other Writings*. Trans. J. Norman, Cambridge: Cambridge University Press, 2005.
Nietzsche, Friedrich. *The Gay Science*. Edited by Bernard Williams. Trans. J. Nauckhoff and A. Del Caro. Cambridge: Cambridge University Press, 2001.
Norris, Christopher. *The Truth about Postmodernism*. Oxford and Cambridge, MA: Blackwell, 1993.
Oberman, Heiko A. *The Reformation. Roots and Ramifications*. Trans. A. C. Gow. London and New York: T&T Clark, 2004.
Osborne, Peter. *The Politics of Time: Modernity and Avant-Garde*. London and New York: Verso, 1995.
Ouaknin, Marc-Alain. *Le Livre brûlé. Lire le Talmud*. Rennes: Lieu Commun, 1986.
Pascal, Blaise. *Pensées*. 1670. Paris: Gallimard, 1969.
Peeters, Benoît. *Derrida*. Paris: Flammarion, 2010.
Pinkard, Terry. *Hegel: A Biography*. Cambridge: Cambridge University Press, 2000.
Pippin, Robert B. *Hegel's Idealism: The Satisfaction of Self-Consciousness*. Cambridge: Cambridge University Press, 1989.
Pippin, Robert B. *Modernism as a Philosophical Problem: On the Dissatisfactions of European High Culture*. Malden, MA, and Oxford: Blackwell, 1999.
Postone, Moishe. *Time, Labor, and Social Domination: A Reinterpretation of Marx's Critical Theory*. Cambridge: Cambridge University Press, 1993.
Rilke Rainer, Maria. *The Notebooks of Malte Laurids Brigge*. Trans. M. Hulse. London and New York: Penguin Classics, 2009.
Rosa, Hartmut. *Social Acceleration: A New Theory of Modernity*. Trans. J. Trejo-Mathys. New York: Columbia University Press, 2013.
Rosenkranz, Karl. *Georg Friedrich Wilhelm Hegels Leben*. 1844. Darmstadt: Wissenschaftliche Buchgesellschaft, 1977.
Rosenzweig, Franz. *The Star of Redemption*. Trans. B. E. Galli. Madison, WI: University of Wisconsin Press, 2005.
Rousseau, Jean-Jacques. "Les Rêveries du promeneur solitaire." In *Œuvres completes*. Edited by Frédéric S. Eigeldinger, Vol. 3. Genève and Paris: Slatkine & Champion, 2002.
Rousseau, Jean-Jacques. *The Discourses and Other Early Political Writings*. Edited by Victor Gourevitch. Cambridge: Cambridge University Press, 1997.
Rousseau, Jean-Jacques. *The Social Contract and Discourses*. London and Toronto: Dent and Dutton, 1920.
Safranski, Rüdiger. *Ein Meister aus Deutschland. Heidegger und Zeit*. Frankfurt am Main: Fischer, 1997.
Santner, Eric L. *My Own Private Germany: Daniel Paul Schreber's Secret History of Modernity*. Princeton, NJ: Princeton University Press, 1996.
Santner, Eric L. *On the Psychotheology of Everyday Life: Reflections on Freud and Rosenzweig*. Chicago, IL, and London: Chicago Unviersity Press, 2001.
Schmitt, Carl. *Der Begriff des Politischen*. 1932. Berlin: Duncker & Humblot, 1979.
Schmitt, Carl. *Political Theology: Four Chapters on the Concept of Sovereignty*. Trans. G. Schwab. Cambridge, MA, and London: MIT Press, 1985.

Schmitt, Carl. *Roman Catholicism and Political Form*. Trans. G. L. Ulmen. Westport, CT, and London: Greenwood Press, 1996.
Schmitt, Carl. *The Concept of the Political: Expanded Edition*. Trans. George Schwab. Chicago, IL, and London: University of Chicago Press, 2007.
Scholem, Gershom. *Main Trends in Jewish Mysticism*. 1941. New York: Schocken Books, 1974.
Scholem, Gershom. *The Messianic Idea in Judaism and Other Essays on Jewish Spirituality*. 1971. New York: Schocken, 1995.
Schulte, Christoph. *Zimzum. Gott und Weltursprung*. Berlin: Jüdisches Verlag, 2014.
Sell, Annette. *Der lebendige Begriff. Leben und Logik bei G. W. F. Hegel*. Freiburg/München: Karl Alber, 2013.
Shallcross, Bożena. *The Holocaust Object in Polish and Polish–Jewish Culture*. Bloomington, IN: Indiana University Press, 2011.
Shestov, Lev. *Athens and Jerusalem*. Trans. B. Martin. Athens, OH: Ohio University Press, 1996.
Shklar, Judith N. *After Utopia: The Decline of Political Faith*. Princeton, NJ: Princeton University Press, 1957.
Sloterdijk, Peter. *Critique of Cynical Reason*. Trans. M. Eldred. Minneapolis, MN, and London: University of Minnesota Press, 1987.
Sloterdijk, Peter. *Im Weltinnenraum des Kapitals. Für eine philosophische Theorie der Globaliesierung*. Frankfurt am Main: Suhrkamp, 2005.
Sloterdijk, Peter. *Nicht gerettet. Versuche nach Heidegger*. Frankfurt am Main: Suhrkamp, 2001.
Sloterdijk, Peter. *Sphären I-III*. Frankfurt am Main: Suhrkamp, 1998, 1999, 2004.
Sloterdijk, Peter. *Was geschah im 20. Jahrhundert?* Suhrkamp, Berlin 2016.
Sorel, Georges. *Reflections on Violence*. Trans. J. Jennings. Cambridge: Cambridge University Press, 1999.
Spinoza, Baruch. *A Spinoza Reader: The Ethics and Other Works*. Trans. E. Curley. Princeton, NJ: Princeton University Press, 1994.
Starobinski, Jean. *L'Invention de la liberté*. Paris: Skira, 1964.
Starobinski, Jean. *Les Emblèmes de la raison*. Paris: Flammarion, 1973.
Steiner, George. *In Bluebeard's Castle: Some Notes towards the Re-definition of Culture*. London: Faber & Faber, 1971.
Steiner, George. *Language and Silence: Essays on Language, Literature, and the Inhuman*. New Haven, CT, and London: Yale University Press, 1998.
Streeck, Wolfgang. *How Will Capitalism End? Essays on a Failing System*. London and New York: Verso, 2016.
Tacik, Przemysław. *The Freedom of Lights: Edmond Jabès and Jewish Philosophy of Modernity*. Trans. P. Poniatowska. Frankfurt am Main: Peter Lang, 2019.
Taubes, Jacob. *Occidental Eschatology*. Trans. D. Ratmoko. Stanford, CA: Stanford University Press, 2009.
Taubes, Jacob. *The Political Theology of Paul*. Stanford, CA: Stanford University Press, 2003.
Trawny, Peter. *Adyton. Heideggers esoterische Philosophie*. Berlin: Matthes & Seitz, 2010.
Trawny, Peter. *Heidegger und der Mythos der jüdischen Weltverschwörung*. Frankfurt am Main: Klostermann, 2014.
Vogl, Joseph. *The Specter of Capital*. Trans. J. Redner and R. Savage. Stanford, CA: Stanford University Press, 2015.
von Schelling, Friedrich Wilhelm Joseph. *The Ages of the World*. Trans. J. M. Wirth. Albany: State University of New York Press, 2000.

Vuillard, Éric. *L'ordre du jour*. Arles: Actes Sud, 2017.
Weber, Max. *The Protestant Ethic and the Spirit of Capitalism*. 1930. Trans. T. Parsons, London and New York: Routledge, 2001.
Westphal, Merold. *Hegel, Freedom, and Modernity*. Albany, NY: State University of New York Press, 1992.
White, Hayden. *Metahistory: The Historical Imagination in Nineteenth-Century Europe*. Baltimore, MD, and London: Johns Hopkins University Press, 1975.
Wittgenstein, Ludwig. *Philosophical Investigations*. 1958. Trans. G. E. M. Anscombe. Oxford: Basil Blackwell, 1986.
Wittgenstein, Ludwig. *Tractatus Logico-Philosophicus*. Trans. C. K. Ogden. London: Kegan Paul, 1922.
Yerushalmi, Yosef Haim. *Zakhor: Jewish History and Jewish Memory*. Seattle, WA, and London: University of Washington Press, 1982.
Zarader, Marlène. *The Unthought Debt: Heidegger and the Hebraic Heritage*. Trans. B. Bergo. Stanford, CA: Stanford University Press, 2006.
Zupančič, Alenka. *Ethics of the Real: Kant, Lacan*. London and New York: Verso, 2000.
Zupančič, Alenka. *The Shortest Shadow: Nietzsche's Philosophy of the Two*. Cambridge, MA, and London: MIT Press, 2003.
Zupančič, Alenka. *What is Sex?* Cambridge, MA, and London: MIT Press, 2017.
Žižek, Slavoj. *Absolute Recoil: Towards a New Foundation of Dialectical Materialism*. London and New York: Verso, 2014.
Žižek, Slavoj. *Did Somebody Say Totalitarianism? Five Interventions in the (Mis)Use of a Notion*. London and New York: Verso, 2001.
Žižek, Slavoj. *Disparities*. London and New York: Bloomsbury, 2016.
Žižek, Slavoj. *Event: Philosophy in Transit*. London: Penguin Books, 2014.
Žižek, Slavoj. *For They Know not What They Do: Enjoyment as a Political Factor*. 1991. London and New York: Verso, 2008.
Žižek, Slavoj. *In Defence of Lost Causes*. London and New York: Verso, 2008.
Žižek, Slavoj. *Incontinence of the Void: Economico-Political Spandrels*. Cambridge, MA: MIT Press, 2017.
Žižek, Slavoj. *Lenin: The Day after the Revolution*. London and New York: Verso, 2017.
Žižek, Slavoj. *Less Than Nothing: Hegel and the Shadow of Dialectical Materialism*. London and New York: Verso, 2012.
Žižek, Slavoj. *Like a Thief in Broad Daylight: Power in the Era of Post-Humanity*. London: Allen Lane, 2018.
Žižek, Slavoj. *Living in the End Times*. London and New York: Verso, 2011.
Žižek, Slavoj. *On Belief*. London and New York: Routledge, 2004.
Žižek, Slavoj. *Organs without Bodies*. London: Routledge, 2004.
Žižek, Slavoj. *Sex and the Failed Absolute*. London and New York: Bloomsbury, 2020.
Žižek, Slavoj. *Tarrying with the Negative: Kant, Hegel, and the Critique of Ideology*. Durham, NC: Duke University Press, 1993.
Žižek, Slavoj. *The Courage of Hopelessness: Chronicles of a Year of Acting Dangerously*. London: Allen Lane, 2017.
Žižek, Slavoj. *The Indivisible Remainder: On Schelling and Related Matters*. 1996. Verso: London and New York, 2007.
Žižek, Slavoj. *The Parallax View*. Cambridge, MA, and London: MIT Press, 2009.
Žižek, Slavoj. *The Puppet and the Dwarf: The Perverse Core of Christianity*. Cambridge, MA, and London: MIT Press, 2003.
Žižek, Slavoj. *The Sublime Object of Ideology*. 1989. London and New York: Verso, 2008.

Žižek, Slavoj. *The Year of Dreaming Dangerously*. London and New York: Verso, 2012.
Žižek, Slavoj. *Trouble in Paradise: From the End of History to the End of Capitalism*. London: Penguin Books, 2015.
Žižek, Slavoj. *Welcome to the Desert of the Real: Five Essays on September 11 and Related Dates*. London and New York: Verso, 2002.

Index

Absolute Knowledge (Hegel's term) 42–5, 48, 96, 104
Adorno, T. W.
   Capitalism 200 n.91
   the Enlightenment 28
   Heidegger 135, 169 n.72, 186 n.41
   modernity 69
   philosophy 201–2 n.3
   and stars 175 n.145
Agamben, G.
   community 140
   contemporaneity 3
   historicity 4, 9, 162 n.17, 183 n.19
   in *Homo sacer* 6, 145
   law 108, 128
   modernity 69, 87, 109, 182 n.7
   sovereignty 148, 177 n.165, 185 n.35, 192–3 n.18
   state of exception 119–20, 192 n.12
Agnon, S. Y. 77
Althusser, L. 68
   and Balibar, É. 197–8 n.54, 199 n.74
antagonism 75
apocalypse 40–1, 50, 61, 97, 170–1 n.89
Arendt, H. 59, 69, 195 n.15
Aristotle
   concept of God 21, 26, 41, 45, 51
   entelechia 30
   ontology 24, 104, 140
   and stars 13, 64
Aronson, R. 148
Auschwitz 123–5, 127

Badiou, A.
   event 27, 34, 74
   history 34, 101
   modernity 2, 168 n.62, 194 n.34
Bar Kochba 47
bare life 125, 138–47, 200 n.88
Bauman, Z. 102
beginnings of modernity

   as barred 76, 82, 107–8, 153
   date 189 n.28
   as a paradox 4, 9, 163 n.2
   in relation to history 69, 73, 85, 102
Begriff (Hegel's term) 42, 104, 106
Being (Heidegger's term) 54–5, 85, 88, 135, 183 n.12
Benda, J. 187 n.55
Benjamin, W. 50, 53, 82, 96
   and messianism 153
   in *Passagenwerk* 159, 173 n.114
   in *Theses on the Concept of History* 100–1, 106, 132
Berlin 14
Berman, M. 163 n.2
Big Bang 32, 131–59
Big Other (*Grand Autre*) 15
biopolitics 138–47
Blanchot, M. 140
Blanqui, A. 10
Bloch, E. 113, 122, 185 n.36
Blumenberg, H. 69, 189–90 n.31
Böhme, H. 182 n.8, 191 n.42, 199 n.76
Book, the 46–7, 51
Bourdieu, P. 195 n.16
Braudel, F. 69
Butler, J. 2

capitalism 26, 63, 142–5, 153, 171 n.100, 187 n.58
Celan, P. vii, 2, 188 n.4
Christianity 48, 139
Comay, R. and Ruda, F. 173 n.116
communism 1, 33, 129, 143–8, 156
concentration camps 87, 123–5
Copernicus 2, 69

death of God 31, 89–90, 98, 127, 134
decision 14–18, 164 n.21–2
deconstruction
   and historicity 4, 73–6

and modernity 3, 132, 161 n.6,
    176 n.147
  writing 5–6, 193 n.26
deferral
  and deconstruction 4
  in law 39
  and modernity 50, 64–8, 90, 93–4, 98,
    122, 128, 131
delay 122, 127
Deleuze, G. and Guattari, F. 144
democracy 99–100
Derrida, J. 5
  in *Glas* 41
  and Heidegger 175 n.144
  historicity 4, 77, 90, 173 n.119, 188 n.4
  life 139
  messianicity 6
  modernity 69, 180–1 n.19
  sovereignty 3
  spectrality 42
  supplement 21, 77
  writing 193 n.26
Descartes, R.
  consciousness 105, 145
  malin génie 11, 106–11
  and nominalism 17
  skepticism 23, 106–7, 120–1, 131, 136,
    158, 166 n.38
dialectics 45, 85, 135, 143, 147
difference
  basic difference 19, 24, 66–7, 75–6
  inoperative differences 44
  modern difference 90
  pure difference 30, 56–7
  temporal difference 72, 85
  tiny difference 53, 58, 66–7
différance (Derrida's term) 73, 77, 85
differentiation 67, 70–9, 90–1
disposition (Hegel's term) 61–3

Einstein, A. 21, 93
Enlightenment, the 9, 28
epoch 73–4
Ereignis (Heidegger's term) 57, 95, 135
ethical, the 157–60
ethics 112–13, 120–2, 149, 156–9
event 5–6, 18, 25–7, 51, 72–6, 89–93
exception 26, 39, 88, 101, 105, 129
exchange and use value 143–5

Fackenheim, E. 186 n.42
fetishism 126, 129, 132–4, 139, 147, 155
Fichte, G. 26, 151
Fitzgerald, F. S. 100–1
Foucault, M.
  on Clausewitz 103
  episteme 19
  modernity 69, 132, 163 n.8, 188 n.5,
    194 n.3
  resistance 30
  sovereignty 177 n.168
Franz Josef I 115
freedom 11, 24, 122, 128
French Revolution, the 9, 13, 74, 76, 99,
    106, 141
Freud, S. 6, 68, 93, 96, 140, 180 n.4

Gabriel, M. 169 n.68
Galileo, G. 140
Gasché, R. 192 n.17
Gelassenheit (Heidegger's term) 55, 64, 140
German Idealism 2, 12–13, 36, 135
Goldmann, L. 196 n.22
Goldschmidt, G.-A. 195–6 n.18

happening 70, 103–5
Hegel, G. W. F.
  Absolute 21–2, 25–6, 51, 136
  Inaugural Address (1818) 1–2, 6,
    13–29, 35–43, 51–7, 68, 119, 140,
    150
  history 7, 52, 75, 104–5, 155
  modernity 9, 40–1, 69, 91, 95–6, 102,
    135, 137, 151–2
  religion 15–16, 47–9, 59–61, 88–9, 105
  resistance 30
  sovereignty 31–5, 38, 59–63, 112, 142,
    156, 176 n.153
  Verstand and *Vernunft* 22–4, 28,
    166 n.37
Heidegger, M. 5
  Geworfenheit 11
  historicity 4, 72, 75, 85, 88, 109,
    183 n.15
  and modernity 69, 91–2, 94–7, 112,
    120, 127–8, 142, 164 n.18, 168 n.54,
    170 n.83, 172 n.113, 177 n.172
  political involvement 95, 133–6,
    192 n.15, 195 n.16–18

in *Sein und Zeit* 119
sovereignty 94–7, 142, 157, 186 n.45,
  196 n.35
and stars 2, 52, 54–5, 57–8, 64–5, 135,
  173 n.115
Heidelberg 14
historical discontinuity 69–79, 83, 108, 160
history
  as a construct of sovereignty 27, 45,
  149
  and identity 90–1
  and modernity 69–79, 81–113, 160
historicity
  and difference 69–79
  modernity and sovereignty 4, 12, 105
Hobbes, T. 62, 138, 148
Hobsbawm, E. 97
Hölderlin, J. C. F. 39
Horkheimer, M. 28, 59, 142, 177 n.169,
  191 n.40
Hume, D. 70, 107, 151
Hyppolyte, J. 174 n.134

identity 62–3, 65–6, 90–1, 98, 148–50,
  153–8
impoverishment
  of the modern universe 15–19, 23–6,
  34, 53–5, 86, 95, 97, 142, 158
  and sovereignty 27, 141
infinity
  law and freedom 10–12
  modern sovereignty 27, 81, 90
inoperativeness 15, 108
inscription 77, 91
Irigaray, L. 138

Jabès, E. 140
Jameson, F. 175 n.135
Jonas, H. 127
Jouīssance (Lacan's term) 51–2, 64, 118,
  140, 142, 173 n.117
Jullien, F. 200 n.92

Kabbalah 6, 96, 108–9, 172 n.107
Kafka, F.
  in *An Imperial Message* 115–17, 121–2,
  129, 131
  and guilt 18
  in *On parables* 125–6

in *The Castle* 133
in *The New Advocate* 127–8
in *The Penal Colony* 83
in *The Trial* 29, 40, 97, 141, 146
in *Zürauer Aphorismen* 54, 101–2
Kant, I.
  Copernican Revolution 9
  critical breakthrough 22, 32, 68
  metaphysics 65
  modernity 95, 102, 108, 132, 151
  perpetual peace 100
  and stars 2, 20, 43, 52, 63
  in *The Critique of Judgment* 117–19
  in *The Critique of Practical Reason*
    9–13, 68, 142
  in *The Critique of Pure Reason* 31, 74–6
Kierkegaard, S. 103
Klemperer, V. 171 n.91
Kojève, A. 44, 46–7, 104, 189 n.21
Kracauer, S. 188 n.1

Lacan, J. 2, 5
  l'enseignement 18, 165 n.25
  God 191 n.41, 202 n.8
  psychoanalysis 26
  surplus value 143
  Yadl'un 19
Laclau, E. and Mouffe, Ch. 181 n.25
lasting 50, 55–6, 59, 93–8, 138–47
lateness 137
law
  as deferral of sovereignty 39–40
  and freedom 11–12
  and modernity 122, 128
Lefèbvre, H. 182 n.4, 189 n.29, 200 n.81
Lefort, C. 180 n.15
Leibniz, G. W. 66
Lenin, V. I.
  politics 133
  proclamation 33–4
  revolution 33–4, 129, 158, 184 n.21
  sovereignty 97, 186–7 n.52
Levi, P. 123–5, 174 n.124
Levinas, E. 112, 157, 173 n.122, 191 n.43,
  194 n.36
life 121, 138–51, 200 n.90
Locke, J. 138
Löwith, K. 109, 154
Lukács, G. 202 n.10

Luria, I. 6, 67, 108–9, 127
Luther, M. 23, 25, 38, 53–5, 156
Lyotard, J.-F. 192, n.10, 193–4 n.29

Malabou, C. 2
Mallarmé, S. 2, 46, 136–8
Marcuse, H. 166 n.34, 184 n.32, 189 n.23, 200 n.87
Marx, K.
  biopolitics 143–9
  concrete abstraction 64, 177–8 n.173
  emancipation 98
  and Hegel 43
  history 11, 75, 103, 105–6, 151, 156–8
  modernity 7, 69, 151, 198 n.55
Marxism
  end of 148–9
  Marxism-Lurianism 7
  and provisionality 128–9
  and sovereignty 3, 97–8, 147, 187 n.57
materiality
  appearance of 46–7
  and history 77, 85
  law and freedom 11–12
  and modernity 15–16, 24–5
  and the symbolic 116
Meillassoux, Q. 32, 136
melancholy
  of the modern universe 19–20, 54, 96
message 116–17, 121–9, 131, 148, 150
messianicism
  Jewish messianism 47–8, 172 n.109, 194 n.36
  and philosophy 45–8, 51, 141
messianicism and modernity
  and history 79, 102, 128–9
  overcoming of modernity 2, 91, 150, 153
  revolution 94, 106
  as structural part of modernity 6–7, 21, 27, 36, 136–42
metaphysics 36, 50, 65, 87–9, 94–5, 111, 122, 148
Michelet, J. 106
Mirror Star, the
  concept 1–2, 6
  and history 87–90, 103, 105
  and modernity 58–9, 62–8, 98, 135–6, 152–9, 175 n.145

and salvation 95–6, 136, 141
and sovereignty 103, 110–11, 129, 147–9, 152–9
Möbius band 68, 144
modern catastrophe
  in Hegel 12–28
  ongoing 70, 119, 122, 134–5, 139
  as the past 89–90
  and philosophy 5, 56
  replay 50
modern cut
  Descartes 107
  and history 28, 69, 72–5, 83, 89–90
  in Kant 12–15, 24
  metaphysics 36
  possibility 110
  ubiquity 3
modernity
  beginnings of *see* beginnings of modernity
  beyond 148
  end of 76, 82–3, 85–6, 91–4, 98
  and historicity 4, 6, 12, 69–79, 81–113, 160
  and *jouissance* 52
  and parable 126
  paradoxality 1–2, 9
  as a precondition 72
  as the provisional turned permanent 122–9, 135, 139, 147, 148–9, 158–9
  and sovereignty 27–30, 50, 55, 67–8, 81–113, 159
  specificity of 69, 72–5, 112, 119
  and theology 23, 32, 127
  and transcendence 31–2, 67–8
  and writing 6, 138
modern universe
  and history 76–8, 103
  nature of 12, 14–20, 56–9, 119, 129, 136–9, 142–60
  and sovereignty 27, 30–2, 43, 63–8, 81–98
  and stars 2
  and tsimtsum 6–7
monotheism 52

Nancy, J.-L. 140
negativity
  creation of the universe 14, 18

and modernity 6, 132
and sovereignty 30, 157, 191 n.43
Nelson, M. 133
Newton, I. 140
Nietzsche, F.
   eternal recurrence 26, 34
   identity 66
   illness 151-2, 160
   modernity 69, 109, 135, 151, 154-5
   nihilism 53
   perspectivism 41
   religion 89-90
   and stars 2, 55, 64, 137
   will to power 138
non-Whole 12, 19, 27, 55, 86, 90
nothingness 10

ocean narrative
   exposition and interpretation 14-21, 23-9, 32, 34, 41-3, 51-7, 141, 150
   and Heidegger 135, 168 n.54
   and Mallarmé 137
   and the sublime 119
Ockham, W. 17
October Revolution, the 33
ontology 12, 87-8
ontotheology (Heidegger's concept) 31, 168 n.64
Osborne, P. 180 n.5, 183 n.13, n.18
overdetermination 68, 76

parable 121-9, 131, 148, 159
Pascal, B. 10
perspectivism 12, 41
   of histories 92-3
   of modernity 49, 66, 78, 81-98, 105-6
philosophy
   afterlife of 4, 46, 151-60, 162 n.10, 201-2 n.3
   modern philosophy 68, 76
   and sovereignty 27, 31, 35-6, 41-5, 50-2, 141
   and writing 5-6
Pippin, B. R. 190 n.33
Plato 151
Polar Star (of sovereignty), the 14, 20-30, 34-5, 38, 42-3, 51-60, 137
political, the 12, 99-100, 132-3, 140, 157-9

"positive material" (Hegel's term) 16, 36-7, 41-5, 53, 58, 75-6, 105, 108
possibility
   and history 86, 93-4, 108-13
   and parable 117
   and sovereignty 65-6, 81, 135, 149
postmodernity 2, 53, 149
Postone, M. 145-51
poststructuralism 3
premodernity 83, 108-10, 122, 126, 140, 142
presence 56
Protestantism 53, 60-3, 201 n.93
proto-history 75-8, 83, 85-6
provisionality 119-29, 131-49, 158-9
psychoanalysis 26, 91, 146

Real, the 75, 81-2
real
   history 103
   time 81-4, 89-92, 146
Reformation 16
remainder
   and faith 38-9
   law and freedom 11-12
   of the modern universe 19, 27, 32, 55, 58, 90, 147
re-mark (Derrida's term) 159-60
representation 19
revolution 1-5, 40, 74, 105-6, 109, 154-6
Rilke, R. M. 141
Rosenzweig, F. 2, 52
Rousseau, J. J.
   beginning of modernity vii, 9, 135, 151, 189
   historical narratives 78
   lost premodern harmony 89, 181
   modern messianicity 91
   social contract 60
   state power 138, 148

Sade, D. A. F. de 9, 88, 91, 94, 118, 141
salvation
   in Hegel 104
   by Marxism 145-50
   as a mirage of sovereignty 34-9, 53
   from modernity 109, 129

Schelling, F. W. J. 17, 164 n.22, 165 n.23, 169 n.69
Schmitt, C. 39, 109, 148, 157–8, 193 n.21
Scholem, G. 53, 67, 77, 153, 172 n.109, 181 n.22
self-preservation 35
Septentrion 137–8
shevirat ha-kelim 6
Shklar, J. N. 197 n.36
skepticism 29, 70–1
Sloterdijk, P.
   in *Critique of Cynical Reason* 162 n.10, 168 n.56, 201 n.94
   on Heidegger 135
   impoverishment 176 n.157, 202 n.14
   in *Spheres* 52
solitude 56–7, 62–3, 68, 148, 155
Sorel, G. 97
sovereign power 58–9, 123–5, 149
sovereignty
   and apocalypse 40–1
   and capitalism 145
   and difference 30, 58
   as displaced transcendence 31–3, 53, 56–7, 65, 88–90, 98, 122, 152
   end of 149
   and historicity 4, 6, 27, 49–51, 69–79, 81–113
   and histories 94–113
   and law 39–40
   and life 138–47
   as possibility 29–30, 108–11
   and postponement 58–9
   and proclamation 33–4
   and revolution 154–6
   and self-certainty 35, 38–43, 60–2, 169 n.73
   and understanding 37, 133
sovereignty and modernity
   affinity 3–6, 50, 63–6, 81–98, 133, 151–9
   faith 53–4
   in Hegel 21
   specificity of modern sovereignty 26–31
space 67, 81, 85–7, 125, 192 n.17
spectrality 11, 15, 19, 46, 99, 119
Spinoza, B. 138
spirit 15, 25, 34, 38, 44–5, 48–9, 61

Starobinski, J. 188 n.2
stars 2, 10, 13, 57–8, 95, 137–8, 154
state 14, 60–3
   of exception 105, 108, 119–20
Steiner, G. 190 n.37, 191 n.4, 194 n.4
Streeck, W. 187 n.58
subjectivity 9
   and modern catastrophe 15
   and sovereignty 11
   split subject 24
sublime, the 117–19
surplus value 143–7
survival 139
suspension
   and history 77, 93, 103, 129
   and identity 66
   and metaphysics 111
   and sovereignty 123, 134, 146, 149
   and the state 61
symbolic, the 72, 81–2, 116

Taubes, J. 109, 154, 190–1 n.38
temporality
   and modernity 122
   and sovereignty 45, 90, 111
   and spatiality 85–7, 89–90
tikkun 7, 21
thinking
   and catastrophe 14–18
   in Hegel 37
   in Heidegger 5, 18, 55, 95, 165 n.24
   loneliness of 14–18, 36
   modernity 131
time
   and Absolute Knowledge 44, 48–9
   and difference 69–79
   and labor 143–7
   and modernity 70–9, 92, 120
   and sovereignty 45–6, 49–51, 92–8, 106
Torah 20
totalitarianism 28, 59, 100, 123
totality 11, 44, 55, 64
transcendence
   and capitalism 147
   collapse of 88–9
   displaced in modernity 31–2, 53, 56–7, 64–5, 68, 88–90, 98, 122, 152
   as the feature of pre-modernity 16, 26, 58

trans-epoch 76-9, 86-7, 94, 107-8, 143, 151-4
Trawny, P. 185-6 n.40, 195 n.9
tsimtsum (Luria's concept) 67, 127

undecidability (Derrida's term) 85
universality 26
   and particularity 78, 159
universe
   and collapse 14-21
   and solitude 56-7
us
   in Hegel 12-13, 62-7
   in Heidegger 55, 135
   and the Mirror Star 129, 140
   and sovereignty 58-9, 147-50, 153-8

Vuillard, É 202 n.7

Weber, M. 201 n.93
White, H. 183 n.16
Wittgenstein, L. 53, 127
writing
   in modernity 131, 138, 193 n.26
   as a philosophical practice 5-6

Žižek, S.
   capitalism 147, 198-9 n.71
   German idealism 2, 184 n.27
   history 101
   ideology 40
   modernity 69, 201 n.100
   ontology 58, 93, 120
   psychoanalysis 197 n.41
   revolution 184 n.21, 192 n.14
Zupančič, A. 2, 53, 82, 197 n.41
Zvi, S. 47

www.ingramcontent.com/pod-product-compliance
Lightning Source LLC
Chambersburg PA
CBHW062220300426
44115CB00012BA/2142